Ozid Guerra
6047885426

Crises in Canadian Work

Crises in Canadian Work

A Critical Sociological Perspective

Norene Pupo
Ann Duffy
Daniel Glenday

OXFORD
UNIVERSITY PRESS

OXFORD
UNIVERSITY PRESS

Oxford University Press is a department of the University of Oxford. It furthers the University's objective of excellence in research, scholarship, and education by publishing worldwide. Oxford is a registered trade mark of Oxford University Press in the UK and in certain other countries.

Published in Canada by
Oxford University Press
8 Sampson Mews, Suite 204,
Don Mills, Ontario M3C 0H5 Canada

www.oupcanada.com

Library and Archives Canada Cataloguing in Publication
Pupo, Norene, 1952–, author
Crises in Canadian work : a critical sociological perspective / Norene Pupo, Ann Duffy, and Daniel Glenday.

(Themes in Canadian sociology)
Includes bibliographical references and index.
ISBN 978-0-19-900834-6 (paperback)

1. Work—Social aspects—Canada. 2. Labor—Canada. 3. Globalization—Canada. 4. Canada–Economic conditions—21st century. I. Duffy, Ann, author II. Glenday, Daniel, 1948-, author III. Title. IV. Series: Themes in Canadian sociology

HD6957.C3P86 2016 306.3'60971 C2016-904357-6

Cover image: © iStock/-strizh-

Oxford University Press is committed to our environment. Wherever possible, our books are printed on paper which comes from responsible sources.

Printed and bound in Canada

1 2 3 4 — 20 19 18 17

Contents

Preface

While growing up, many of us were reminded of the difficult conditions endured by previous generations as they prepared to enter the labour market. As "baby boomers," we heard stories about how our parents and grandparents were awakened early and expected to complete their chores before trekking (uphill) several miles or enduring long bus rides to get to school. Once they left school, they found work easily in their local communities, but often they faced long hours of work and endured physically exhausting and difficult working conditions. At the risk of termination or even "blacklisting," some struggled for union representation or individually appealed to their bosses to lighten up on them. In contrast, "boomers," as children of the "Golden Age of Capitalism," were thought to have it all. Young Canadians of the 50s, 60s, and 70s, especially those who identified as white, Canadian-born, and middle class, had access to higher education, job opportunities that promised a lifetime of security, and a decent standard of living. The vibrant economy, with its booming steel, auto, and primary industries guaranteed a comfortable future. In particular, it was common for young males to follow their fathers' footsteps into the thriving industries straight out of high school. Young women stepped into the growing clerical fields or undertook training as elementary school teachers or nurses—careers they would remain in full-time until marriage or the birth of their first child, often returning part-time when their children were grown. Well-kept single-family homes characterized the urban landscape while evidence of urban sprawl and Canadians' love affair with the automobile and consumer culture flourished. Most Canadians experienced a sense of stability in their work, their neighbourhoods, and their lives in general. With job opportunities readily available in most communities across the country, the failure to achieve was chalked up to character flaws—lack of initiative, laziness, shiftlessness, or immaturity. Individuals were expected to sow their own seeds and set down roots, and failure to do so was harshly judged.

Today, neither our students nor their parents have experienced conditions reminiscent of the golden-age ideal. Instead, most young Canadians today are facing the challenges of unrelenting economic conditions, implacable bosses, crumbling sources of state support and employment standards, harsh working environments, and poor prospects for their futures. Today, many of our undergraduates struggle through school while holding one or more part-time jobs. Upon graduation they are met with enormous debt loads and find themselves holding on to the same jobs they held throughout their years at school. Earlier generations were able to compartmentalize the year by working full-time during the summer months, quitting at the end of the summer, and returning to school unburdened by workplace demands. In that scenario, students benefitted from a more complete post-secondary experience—attending school events, engaging in political debates, listening to guest lectures, involving themselves in discussion groups, and of course enjoying the social life. Now students hurry through their semesters juggling their jobs with course selections, stressing over their bosses' rules around scheduled hours, and worrying over their futures upon graduation.

In our experience over our decades-long teaching careers, we have witnessed shifts in the culture within our classrooms. Students arrive tired from the previous evening's shifts and pack up their books before the class ends in order to punch in on time at work. For many, staying behind a few minutes to clarify the meaning of the class discussion, ask a question, or check on an upcoming assignment is an opportunity lost.

Amongst the writings on work in the contemporary economy, this book fills a particular niche as it provides context for understanding workplace problems and issues workers are experiencing today as they negotiate their way through a maze of part-time or precarious jobs looking for some degree of security and independence. We do not profess here to offer a systematic, historical look at work in Canada. Rather, we focus on particular problems we refer to broadly as crises. Our options for this book were to write an encyclopedic work with broad coverage on an abundance of topics in the sociology of work or to present an issue-oriented critical analysis of a number of outstanding "crises" of work. We opted for the latter as it reflects the most immediate issues and concerns that our students are wrestling with. The book raises many questions and provides explanations for the victories and disappointments currently experienced by Canadian workers in their search for the ever more elusive "good" job. Our intent is to provide our readers with the understandings, insights, and perspectives to appreciate more fully the current crises in work and to demand the profound changes that are needed to respond to these crises. Ultimately, we remain convinced that the struggle toward more humane, equitable, and fulfilling constructions of working lives is both alive and worthwhile.

Acknowledgements

Over the years we have been involved in a number of studies documenting the experiences of workers in various contexts. We would like to thank all the workers, union leaders, and activists we have interviewed and met with for their thoughts and insights on the state of working in Canada today. We appreciate the work of graduate student Vivian Stamatopoulos, who took time away from writing her dissertation to provide us with several of the tables and figures that appear in this book. We would like to thank Ian Gibson, developmental editor, Oxford University Press, for his feedback, consistent support, and encouragement. It's been great working with you, Ian, and we would welcome opportunities to work with you again in the future. We would also like to acknowledge the work of copy editor Jessie Coffey and those involved in production at Oxford University Press.

As always, we thank our family members who provide encouragement, support, love, and much appreciated distractions from the hours we spend in front of our computer screens.

1 The Contemporary Canadian Labour Market in the Global Context

Learning Objectives

- To expose the grim realities in the Canadian economy today
- To establish the framework of feminist political economy and critical sociology as the orientation of the book
- To question the idea of a "New Economy"
- To examine transformations in the Canadian economy within the context of globalization

Introduction

Fifty years ago social forecasters predicted a leisurely future with work occupying substantially less of individuals' time over their life course. Twenty-five years ago analysts concluded that the so-called leisure revolution was misdirected, but still held on to the notion of "Freedom 55"—the ability for seniors to retire early with adequate savings and resources for their later years. Economists are now declaring that "Freedom 55" is a thing of the past. Rather, with the recent downturns and tough economic times, retirement specialists are declaring that Canadians will look instead to "Freedom 68." What happened to the earlier predictions of rosy futures and leisurely years for seniors? Why are some Canadians working harder and longer, unable to get off the treadmill of precarious, low-wage work? Why are other Canadians, particularly young workers, facing inadequate paid work or no prospects of work at all? Why are thousands of Canadians experiencing a heightened sense of insecurity about their futures?

Today work stands at a crossroads with young Canadians in particular finding themselves at a junction, having to negotiate around numerous barriers before landing a "good," relatively secure job (Foster, 2012). Not only are Canadians today generally working harder and facing intensified working conditions, but they are also working longer—starting as young teens in various **McJobs** for substandard or minimum rates of pay, or working as unpaid volunteers or interns, and continuing to work well beyond their "golden" years. For many, the notion of early retirement, and for some, the notion of ever retiring, seems to be slipping by.

In today's economy, we can easily paint a grim picture of work (Grant, Curry, and Kennedy, 2015), including unrelentingly high rates of unemployment, thousands requiring and searching for more hours of work and better pay, growing numbers holding multiple jobs or moonlighting, many working part-time while looking for the elusive full-time position, falling wage rates relative to inflation, inadequate minimum wages, increasing numbers of unpaid jobs, and declining labour standards. All of these conditions impact families by contributing to soaring child poverty rates and by increasing stress for parents as they juggle their schedules to accommodate family and work time demands, extensive and often intensive caregiving responsibilities, growing households as well as educational debt, and adult children returning home. Under these circumstances, communities become hollowed out, losing vibrancy and appeal, and as their economic health declines, they lose educated young workers and fail to attract new industries and services.

What has happened to the transformation of work? Is this the age of austerity? And is this a transition point from which there is no recovery? Classical economists regard the ebbs and flows within the marketplace as occurring "naturally," owing to the availability of resources and products as well as to relative demand within markets. They subscribe to the notion that products and resources increase in value as they become scarce (Stanford, 2008a). They are not necessarily concerned about how resources and products are distributed or produced, but rather, they focus on the value—demands and exchanges—involved in transactions. Their system involves "winners" and "losers" with little concern over who wins and who loses, but rather over the maintenance of the system of exchange. Movements of goods and services, the jockeying back and forth over prices, commodity exchanges, the flows of the markets, and trade cycles are parts of the elaborate "game" of capitalism.

Crises in Canadian Work: Problems and Perspective

The perspective of this book departs from classical or neo-classical thinking. Rather, the authors adopt a **feminist political economy** approach—a perspective that has its roots in the writings of Karl Marx and other critical thinkers. This approach accounts for the structural conditions that sustain and even promote inequalities and class differences. As sociologists embracing the framework of a **critical sociology** we are concerned with the contexts within which people live and work, and the interplay between behaviours, choices, and decisions, and the economic and political contexts within which they occur. Fundamental to our analysis is the notion of the **sociological imagination**, a term coined by C. Wright Mills (1959). Adopting a sociological imagination in order to understand social phenomena allows us to explain the relationship between problems encountered by individuals by viewing them within a broader context. Rather than concluding that personal troubles, such as the inability to find secure employment, are the result of an individual's failures, a sociological imagination allows us to understand such problems in the context of structures of power and processes that have, for example, shifted production overseas or employed advanced technologies to eliminate many forms of employment. Of major concern in a political economy of work are the structures of capitalism and the state giving rise to or maintaining systems of inequality, unequal class structures, and forces of power—corporate owners, stakeholders, and financiers along with their political affiliates—all of whom benefit in various ways from past and present locations within the structures of power and inequality.

In light of our critical approach to the study of work structures and work relations, we are most interested here in studying workplace issues using a grounded approach. A **grounded approach** allows the researcher to start by observing social phenomena and then developing theories to explain those phenomena, rather than starting with theories and applying them to understand the social world. The grounded approach is aligned with **public sociology** (Burawoy, 2005a, 2005b), which engages communities and publics in identifying issues, processes, and problems that concern them. A reading of any daily or community newspaper would confirm that citizens across the country are not only concerned about but also active around work-related issues, including access to work; fairness and workplace policies; harassment; safety; educational, and training requirements; plant closures; job loss; and retirement.

Labour Markets, Jobs, and Unemployment

For the past 25 years, journalists, analysts, economists, and politicians have been abuzz over the state of economies across the globe. Much of the fervour centres on unemployment, especially amongst youth, declining wages, and eroding labour standards. Headlines report on plant closures, workers' movements, and weakening labour markets, while political pundits confront such issues with promises of job creation, retraining for the displaced, and wage replacement initiatives. Crises of work are global in scope. Youth in Italy, Spain, Portugal, and Greece are facing double-digit rates of unemployment (Viscusi, 2014; Ortiz and Tisera, 2011). Economies of Argentina and Venezuela (Porzecanski, 2014), among others, are defaulting on interest payments, while cities like Detroit have faced the ultimate decline into bankruptcy (Patton, 2013). Japan has been battling deflation (Ito and Mishkin, 2006), a trend also concerning Germany (Evans-Pritchard, 2014). In the **Global South**, workers face abysmal working conditions, lack of safety standards, and poverty-level wages as they assemble cell phones and other high tech gadgets or sew designer outfits intended for consumption in the **Global North** (Mosoetsa and Williams, 2012). Unemployment has serious consequences on multiple levels. A recent study analyzing data from 63 countries between 2000 and 2011 concluded that every year, one in five suicides is associated with unemployment (Nordt et al., 2015).

In Canada, high rates of unemployment now and in the past have contributed to a collective sense of insecurity. This has driven some workers to move from job to job, sometimes across the country, disrupting connections to family and community. Contributing to the falling labour force participation rate, many become frustrated by employers' simultaneous demand for experience and unwillingness to provide opportunities for young workers. Under these circumstances, they may become disengaged from the formal economy (Grant, 2012a, 2012b). Thousands of young Canadians focus on finding the ever-elusive job through education and training, piling up credentials along with thousands of dollars of debt in the process.

Concerns over employment immobilize some workers who remain in jobs where they are undervalued or who eke out a living by holding multiple jobs. Under these conditions costs are high as workers must deal with a variety of managerial styles and workplace cultures and demands while juggling their schedules, meeting expectations for quality performance on the job, and dealing with excessive levels of stress and fatigue. A sizeable number within the labour force work overtime, and some of this work is unpaid. In insecure times workers may be drawn into extra work, even if it is unpaid, by vague promises of future promotions or job security. While extra work is in some cases customary, as is the case for shift captains in the fast-food industry, at other times it is regarded as a requisite to character building and recognition. For all their effort, over the last 30 years, Canadians have found themselves working longer and harder, while watching their incomes and benefits dwindle, the size of their work group reduced, and their jobs transformed by new technologies and workplace practices.

As insurance against a difficult labour market, many Canadians are staying in school longer, hoping that they will succeed in the escalating race for recognition by potential employers. Many graduates travel with their freshly minted undergraduate degrees to colleges where they expect to earn job-related knowledge or job-specific skills. Others supplement their diplomas with the backing of a university degree, and increasing numbers attend graduate programs. As **credentialism** skyrockets, so do student debts. A recent report (Macdonald and Shaker, 2012) on tuition across Canada found that tuition fees have become much less affordable since 1990, as compulsory fees for undergraduates have risen on average by 6.2 per cent, or three times the rate of inflation. The average cost to study at a Canadian university ($6,186 in 2012) does not include the cost of books, food, or accommodation.[1]

As a result, about 60 per cent of graduates carry a substantial debt—on average $27,000—as they start their post-university years in the working world. Completing post-secondary schooling is no guarantee that young Canadians are on a clear career path. Data from the Youth in Transition survey conducted between 2000 and 2010 indicate that the majority of Canadian youth remain unsettled in terms of a career path until well into adulthood (Statistics Canada, 2015c).[2] While some level of uncertainty may relate to lack of parental support and encouragement from friends and significant others, young adults, anxious to pay down their schooling debt, may be swayed by their search for a modicum of security rather than by their long-standing dreams of staying the course on a particular career path.

High costs of higher education dissuade many working-class students from going to university, especially if the university of their choice is not located within their communities or within a reasonable commuting distance. Class differences in university attendance are glaring: more than half of youth from families whose income is in the top 25th percentile enroll by age 19, compared to less than one-third from families in the bottom quartile (Frenette, 2007). While young Canadians are urged to get a good education as their ticket into the good-jobs labour market, they are required to pay a greater percentage of the cost of their education as provincial governments scale back on their financial commitments. For example, the proportion of provincial support as a percentage of total university expenditures has declined from 84 per cent to 58 per cent between 1979 and 2009, while the proportion paid for through tuition has increased from 12 to 35 per cent during the same period (Macdonald and Shaker, 2012: 35). As a result, graduates head to the labour market on shaky financial ground and carrying debt, while parents scramble to support them by delaying retirement, taking out second mortgages, or inviting them to move home.

The New Economy and the Transformation of Work

Upon leaving school, most graduates will eventually find work within service, the primary labour market sector, accounting for over 80 per cent of jobs within the Canadian economy. Over the past 40 years Canadians have witnessed transformations in work and a fundamental shift from a manufacturing and resource-based economy to a knowledge-information-service-based economy, or what some refer to as the "**new economy**" (Pupo and Thomas, 2010). Analysts refer to the "new economy" as the replacement of industrial jobs with service sector jobs and often attribute this shift to the widespread application of micro-technologies to a wide variety of production processes and the computerization of work processes. New applications of micro technologies have contributed to the creation of new occupational categories and to the re-tooling of traditional forms of work. Analysts continue to raise questions about the impact of technologies on work and about the shifts within the economy that simultaneously produced new or different forms of work and eliminated a large number and variety of jobs. The underlying question for many is whether or not we do indeed have a "new" economy.

The 30 years following the end of the Second World War (1945–1975) was a period of unprecedented economic growth and expansion of the Canadian economy. During these years, the Gross Domestic Product (GDP) surged, Canada's mining sector and oil and natural gas fields were highly prosperous, and manufacturing industries not only achieved a steady growth in exports but also underwent greater diversification than ever before (Conrad, Finkel, and Fyson, 2015). In addition, Canada's population doubled between 1951 and 1981. At the same time, there was steady growth in foreign ownership that was primarily US direct investment in Canada's manufacturing and natural resources sectors. In manufacturing, US direct investment essentially meant that US companies established branch plants in Canada, modelling the Canadian operations after their production facilities at home. Most often foreign companies built plants in Canada in order to jump the tariff wall.

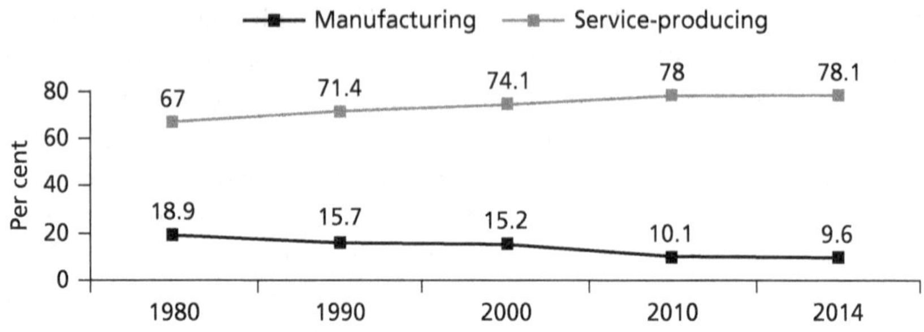

Figure 1.1 Percentage of the Total Labour Force Employed in the Manufacturing and Service-Producing Sectors, 1980–2014 (Canada)

Note: Includes all those employed individuals aged 15 years and older.

Source: Statistics Canada. Table 282-0008

Rather than face the high tariffs Canada had set on a large number of imported goods, companies captured the market of consumer goods by manufacturing their goods on Canadian soil. Foreign direct investment in the Canadian economy was heralded as highly beneficial. Not only was it regarded as a stimulus to the economy, but it also created hundreds of thousands of jobs and opportunities for Canadians.

By the early 1980s, signs of significant economic decline were apparent and a number of changes in political and economic realms began to affect the overall health of the economy. As indicated in Figure 1.1, between 1980 and 2014 the percentage of the labour force involved in manufacturing continued to decline, while the number working in the service sector grew.

The implications of the shift to a service-based economy differed for males and females as indicated in Figure 1.2. While the manufacturing sector remained a male stronghold, women continued to dominate within the service sector.

In 1988 the Canada–US Free Trade Agreement (FTA) and later the North American Free Trade Agreement (NAFTA) dismantled the high tariff walls, thereby significantly slowing down the decisions of US multinational companies to set up

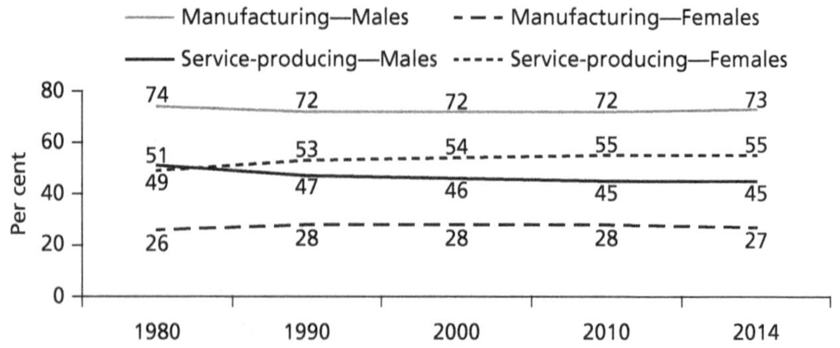

Figure 1.2 Percentage of Females and Males in the Manufacturing and Service-Producing Sectors, 1980–2014 (Canada)

Note: Includes all those employed individuals aged 15 years and older.

Source: Statistics Canada. Table 282-0008

branch plant operations in Canada. Rather, with the tariff walls down, multinationals embraced the option of manufacturing items for the Canadian market more cheaply elsewhere, whether in Mexico, the southern US, or anywhere across the globe. With improvements in transportation and communication, the companies could easily ship goods to Canada and maintain their stronghold on the Canadian consumer market.

Globalization and the New Economy: Connecting Local and Global Spheres

As communication technologies and transportation networks continued to advance, corporations were free to search at will the world over for low-cost production sites with an unlimited supply of low-paid workers. While the process of **globalization** was not new, at this time that there were significant shifts in corporate and national politics as well as in markets and economic developments that affected the Canadian economy in multiple ways, making economic recovery increasingly difficult. Heavy manufacturing sectors, and steel production in particular, experienced tremendous losses, and along with falling rates of production within these sectors, thousands of "good"—relatively secure, high-paying, and unionized—jobs vanished. Many communities have been challenged by the loss of manufacturing jobs—the process of **deindustrialization**—and the de-unionization that accompanies it. As discussed in Box 1.1 below, many workers who experience a plant closure lose hope of finding a replacement within the declining manufacturing sector within their communities and worry about having to adjust their lifestyle as well as their hopes and dreams for an early retirement or even a comfortable life.

Box 1.1 Everyday Work Experiences

When the gates close for good . . .

Across Canada shuttered factories and brownfields now dot the landscape. This is particularly the case in Canada's industrial heartland, Southern Ontario, where overgrown, vacated lands have become familiar sights, especially along the Highway 401 corridor from Windsor to London and Hamilton, and east to Kingston and Belleville. Between 2000 and 2010 manufacturing output in Canada dropped by 16 per cent (in constant dollars) or from 18.4 per cent to 12.8 per cent of the GDP, costing Canadians 505,000 industrial jobs (Jackson, 2012b). Despite expected peaks in production and the development of new high tech industries, thousands of industrial workers have experienced the deep insecurity that accompanies job loss and their move to the more precarious service sector. In some working-class communities, working in

continued

the local factories was a family affair, with generation after generation entering shortly after leaving school and staying until retirement, sometime around their 55th birthdays. Most of the unionized workers lived a relatively comfortable life, with dreams of paying off their mortgages, sending their kids to college, and retiring on a modest pension.

Then one day "out of the blue" an all-too-familiar scene unfolds. Workers on all shifts in all departments are called to a plant-wide meeting. Upon receiving the call, some hold a glimmer of hope that the meeting will bring good news—a new product line, an increasing number of orders, or a restructuring involving dozens of new hires. The majority, however, enter the meeting, often held off-site—sometimes in the ballroom at a downtown hotel—with trepidation. Within "what seemed like 15 seconds," the carefully staged announcement is made, often by a senior executive from head office (in the US or wherever), surrounded by security guards. The executive succinctly announces, "As of . . . whatever date . . . , this plant will be closed." The room falls silent. Heads hang in disbelief and tears flow. And in those few seconds, the lives of hundreds of workers are changed forever. [3]

At the same time as industrial production experienced great losses as corporate power holders fervently sought to trim expenses, particularly by lowering labour costs, increasingly sophisticated microelectronics technologies, advances in digitized information systems, the introduction of complicated sensor and optical equipment, new electronic and digital industrial applications, and sophisticated software gave rise to widespread restructuring of manufacturing enterprises and the re-engineering of an endless range of organizations in both the public and private sectors. Auto manufacturing, mining, petroleum production, natural resources extraction, and other industries and sectors using highly advanced technologies undertook the process of making their organizations lean, by laying off or declaring redundant thousands of workers, starting first with production workers, then moving up to shake the managerial tree, declaring hundreds of mid-level managers, then supervisors and clerks, as superfluous.

Workers at all levels, including mid- and lower-level executives, managers at all ranks, and educated workers with an abundance of skills and years of training, experienced a deeper sense of insecurity than ever before as hundreds of their co-workers, colleagues, and bosses fell victim to corporate downsizing and reorganization of work processes. Not only were thousands of full-time jobs lost across Canada, but also the recovery was painfully slow. Moreover, with the recessions of the early 1980s and 1990s, losses were located in key sectors, particularly steel and auto, and these losses were not easily recovered. The movement of production processes across the globe signalled the end of the "golden years" of capitalism and initiated the long process of Canadian labour market restructuring characterized by the loss of "good" jobs and their replacement with "bad" relatively insecure jobs, the effects of which are felt in the labour market today (Yalnizyan, 2009). Observing the movement of heavy industrial processes across the globe, the tightening of labour markets, the incorporation of new technologies at work, the massive corporate downsizing exercises and most importantly, the growth of service-sector jobs, some analysts concluded that these markers indicated the emergence of a "new economy."

The description of a "new" economy suggests that the trajectory of economic development has taken a turn away from its traditional path. But is this the case? Clearly the condition and structure of work have been transformed in traditional pillars such as manufacturing and resource industries, as well as in the growing service sector in both the public and private sectors. Shifts in the structure of labour markets and the reorganization of workplaces along with the response of workers to the new economic conditions provide us with an understanding of recent changes in social and economic life. Patterns of change within contemporary workplaces and their personal, cultural, and social impact have fuelled the debate over the new economy. A number of government think tanks, policy-makers, and economists (Baily and Lawrence, 2001) studying the workplace and labour markets following the recessions of the 1990s and the downsizing and restructuring aftermath concluded that the upward swing in productivity, output, and innovation is indicative of a new economic profile. Others (Harms and Knapp, 2003; Albo, 2010; Pupo and Thomas, 2010) suggest that rather than contributing to a new economic profile, major changes, including technological advancements, innovations in communications processes and techniques, and escalating sources of knowledge production, have redefined capitalism and the global economy, ultimately affecting the ways in which business is conducted and work is performed. In other words, what may appear to be a *new* economy is simply evidence of new work relations and new practices derived from within the structure of advanced capitalism. The economic transformations, including the movement of work and the inclusion of new technological developments, are products of advanced capitalism. As in the "old" economy that was based on manufacturing and resource extraction rather than on service work, conditions of inequality, hierarchical systems, and power imbalances persist.

Debates regarding the possibility of a new economy together with observations of shifting practices within workplaces, advancements in communication and information technologies, and transformations within economies are complexly interconnected to processes of globalization. Under globalization workers have experienced intensified working conditions as companies shift work overseas to take advantage of lower labour and production costs, while they downsize their operations in high-cost areas. The leaner and meaner workplaces stand as a constant reminder to workers of the portability of their jobs, the threat of unemployment, and the unending insecure times. Yet, technological breakthroughs and the resulting intensified pace of work are accepted by some in exchange for the elimination of the grind of traditional forms of **Fordist** production.

The process of globalization has had profound impacts on social interaction and institutional relationships, and as a result has altered production processes and employment practices, transformed local landscapes, and touched various aspects of social life at local, regional, national, and global levels (Castells, 1996). Analysts argue that this process has been destabilizing as it has reconfigured local communities, affected local cultures and traditions, and introduced new forms of social interaction. Former industrial or mining areas, for example, may be renewed as arts-based communities, as is the case in Cape Breton, Nova Scotia and County Durham in the United Kingdom (Haiven, 2010). "Brands" that are familiar to Canadians and Americans, including Kellogg's, Unilever, McDonald's, and Burger King, to name a few, are transforming tastes and consumer habits worldwide. Shopping, banking, and other everyday transactions are quickly completed through the Internet, impacting one's personal connections to the community.

At the same time, globalization has affected the structure of labour markets, the availability of work, and the structure of opportunity within local communities. In Canada the shift to a service economy resulted in different types of employment possibilities for younger workers as compared to the opportunities available to their parents' generation. New work arrangements have been incorporated in both public and private sector workplaces, and have altered the way people work, the size of work groups, the level of face-to-face interactions, and the permanency of jobs. These shifts, along with the changing nature of labour markets in Canada and the more developed areas of the world have been affected by and, in turn, shape social circumstances abroad.

Key to understanding the impact of globalization on economies and communities are the concepts of restructuring and regulation. **Restructuring** refers to

© Mark Milstein | Dreamstime.com

Globalization transforms local landscapes: Tim Hortons in New York City. The Canadian franchise was founded in Hamilton, Ontario and was acquired by Burger King in 2014. Employment practices both in Canada and abroad are affected as this multinational company continues to compete within the global marketplace.

the reorganization of both the economy and work, including production processes and management practices. Movements of capital abroad and the transition from production and resource-based to service-based economies, particularly in the most developed regions, have given rise to the development of global production and commodity chains, an international and highly mobile labour market, **offshoring** (or the movement of work from more advanced to less advanced economies), and new demands on economic infrastructures and local communities. **Economic restructuring** has meant reorganization of economic and political structures as new partnerships across national boundaries require revisions to trade agreements, foreign policy, and labour standards. It has also affected local and regional development and has contributed to the "hollowing out" of some communities as the industries forming the hub of their economies have been moved offshore (Broad, 2000). These developments, in turn, have pressured states to amend their social contracts and to develop policies that take into account the high levels of unemployment and underemployment, the demands to retrain workers, and the need to respond to the relentless insecurity experienced within the labour force.

Transitions within the global economy and pressures to remain competitive within the global marketplace have produced processes of **work restructuring**. This refers to a broad range of work and employment practices, including **lean production**, telework, flexibility initiatives, and new management and monitoring practices, as well as new contractual arrangements. Together these measures have contributed to work intensification (requiring higher levels of output per shift or specified period of time), precariousness, deskilling (the underutilization of workers' knowledge and abilities), and re-skilling (shifts in skills needed and the requirement of new knowledge). These changes are impacting communities and families as they search for new arrangements to balance work and family responsibilities with their increasingly variable work schedules, and with their jobs that may be located within insecure and vulnerable industries. The impact of economic and work restructuring on communities and families is a major concern for governments, unions, policy analysts, and educators.

Economic and work restructuring in the global economy are inextricably linked to transformations in forms of regulation. Analysts, including Peck and Tickell (2002), Smith (1996), Stanford and Vosko (2004), Marston and Knox (2006), Vosko (2011), and Thomas (2009; 2011), suggest that labour regulation occurs not only on a national scale, but on a number of levels, including through the workplace and structure of the labour process, through the state and labour standards, and through policies of labour market adjustment, immigration, and training. It is also affected by transnational institutions promoting standards, such as the International Labour Organization (ILO), as well as by various forms of governance and self-regulation. Other elements, such as global networks and new social structures of the information society (Castells, 2000), complex interconnections of organizations and their individual modes of operation (Gordon and Turner, 2000), new managerial structures and administrative arrangements, as well as the introduction of new social relations (Law and Hassard, 1999) also impact on regulation.

Literature on regulation within the global economy is concerned primarily with forms of governance and the reformation of the state within a globally competitive context, as it seeks to understand the conditions under which the state provides infrastructural support to enhance or maintain competitiveness and national presence within the global economy. This notion of regulation, however, is narrowly focused and loses sight of various levels of regulation, particularly at the local level. It is important to broaden the notion of regulatory networks and the interconnectedness of spheres of regulation both nationally and globally, allowing us to link forms of regulation within a national context upwards to the global as well as downwards to the local. In other words, to understand our personal troubles within the labour force and economy, we need to engage our sociological imaginations that will allow us to examine the ways in which forms of regulation impact upon nations as well as communities, workplaces, households, and personal lives. Further, discussion of regulation relates to ongoing concerns regarding human rights and social justice. Human rights and social justice movements have drawn attention to the need to balance perspectives of the Global South with those of the North in promoting social citizenship and to account for local practices within a global context. Changing work relations, administrative structures, labour regulation, and labour standards profoundly affect work-time patterns and the corporate and workplace strategies proposed to balance work and family, and their implications for individuals, households, and communities. Shifts in work schedules and practices alter the pace of community life.

Mobility is an outstanding feature of economic globalization. The goal of transnational corporations is to search the globe over for ideal locations for production facilities. Their chief concern is a stable, cheap, docile, and easily trainable labour force. Along with the local labour supply, decisions regarding relocation also assess local state structures and their willingness to accommodate corporations' ways of operating and their requirements and preferences with regard to regulatory practices, rights, and protections. Lax environmental guidelines and lenient health and safety policies operate as enticements for corporate relocations because of the savings involved. Such critical decisions profoundly impact workers, their families, their communities, and the environment. Political leaders work to attract the interest of transnational corporations in order to bolster local economies, provide citizens with a means of livelihood, and contribute to state coffers through taxation. In some circumstances, however, the trade-off in the form of land, resources, and labour power is clearly tipped in favour of the transnationals holding the reins of economic and political power.

Within a globalized economy, the output of individual production facilities may be part of a vast commodity chain, involving workers in various capacities and skill levels contributing to the multitude of parts and processes within any one commodity. Automobile production is the prime example of an end product consisting of numerous parts with origins from various locations around the globe. From the consumer's vantage point, sourcing parts around the globe ultimately means lower priced commodities and cost savings. From a worker's view, however, the commodity chain may represent vast differences in forms and levels of remuneration, social benefits, and security and legal protections embedded within any one commodity.

Within a commodity chain, any one product may involve contributions from workers residing in a number of countries and connected to the process only through their subcontractors. In auto production, for example, parts may come from the world over with final assembly occurring in Canada. These workers are supervised by managers who engage in practices designed to maintain a smooth flow along the chain's network, and the entire process is governed through the transnational's headquarters.

Along with the transnational corporations, within the global economy, out of necessity workers are compelled to become mobile, leaving their homes, communities, cultural contexts, and families in search of work. With the development of a **transnational labour force** increasing numbers of migrant workers search worldwide for a means of livelihood and survival. In some cases they leave their homelands to escape treacherous and politically unstable conditions, only to endure what are often poor working conditions, low rates of pay, hostile environments, and instability within their new worlds and workplaces. Migrant workers settle on such a path in order to ease the lives of family members back home by remitting whatever they can save from their meager earnings.

Considering the transformations of work processes in Canada and around the globe, the shift to a service-based economy, and the movements of work and workers, economies today are in flux, and the circumstances we observe in Canada and refer to as the "new economy," are characterized by multiple flexibilities. **Flexibilization** is a strategy employed by managements to increase productivity and profits while keeping employees in a state of insecurity and dependency on their employers. Flexibility initiatives allow employers to "cut the fat" by staffing each shift with only the optimally determined number of workers on site. For workers this means a decreasing availability of work and an increasing need to multi-task and adapt while on the job. For some, flexible employment practices, such as flextime and teleworking, may leave workers with more personal time to engage in family, recreational, educational, or other activities, thereby reducing work–life conflicts. At the same time, fewer hours of work translate into less pay, greater stress, and escalating levels of employment insecurity.

Globalization, Neoliberalism, and Shifting Landscapes

The pattern of replacing industrial jobs with service jobs, or good jobs with bad jobs, is not unique to Canada. This pattern of shifting landscapes is widespread throughout the rich nations of the world, along with declining investments by governments in social programs and support for the working classes. Globalization extends and intensifies the reach of capitalism across the globe, affecting economies, ways of work, communities, cultures, ideas, and ways of life. Globalization is not a new phenomenon. Consider Paris in the years leading to the First World War. The rapid rate of industrialization, growing trade, new scientific discoveries, and changes in culture, ideas, and ways of life led scholars to describe the period as an era of globalization. At the time there were 600 car manufactories in France, turning out 150 different models (Schofield, 2014). Machines and "new" technologies became the order of the day and were reflected in France's rich artistic culture as artists of all kinds viewed the world from new vantage points and fondly referred to the period as "la belle epoque." But the rapid rate of change was simultaneously welcomed and feared as technology triumphed over craftsmanship (Schofield, 2014) and new ways of life replaced old customs and traditions.

The primary agent of globalization today is the transnational corporation. Globalization involves the interaction and integration of growing numbers of people in the world through international trade and investment, travel and tourism, information technologies, media and communications, and work. It is now widely accepted that the transition to a global economy has given rise to a new era of international relationships variously defined and asserted in economic, political, cultural, and social terms. The global economy is defined by new economic relationships, including international market competition and corporate decentralization of production processes. These global trends and practices have consequences for existing political, cultural, and social relationships, and institutions at local, national, and transnational levels. Globalization affects ways of life. The processes of globalization have removed some of the distinctions and differences among national cultures, harmonized political systems, created interdependencies amongst economies, impacted levels of prosperity including gaps between extreme wealth and extreme poverty, and affected families, relationships, human health, and wellness.

The advantages and disadvantages of globalization processes for particular communities and national domains are relative and subject to debate. Some argue that the global economy has resulted in an upward swing in output levels and productivity and that this movement has the potential to improve the quality and conditions of life in even the poorest economies. Others suggest that the movement of capital and major technological shifts have redefined the ways in which work is deployed, but that these new economic arrangements have not sufficiently changed the nature of global inequality or the conditions of life at local levels. While the overall pattern of growing gaps between poverty and wealth has not changed significantly, day-to-day life in communities has been affected. Consider, for example, the deeper levels of insecurity brought by the closure of plants in the developed world and the correspondingly new-found affordability of beans, rice, and other staples within the communities receiving the relocated industries. Shifting work overseas has redefined local labour markets, transformed communities, and, as a result, reorganized households. The dimensions of globalization test both government strategies for labour market development and strategic responses from workers, their organizations, and their communities. All are challenged by the tumultuous processes of internationalization, new measures of accountability afforded global corporations, consequent regionalized economic development, new forms of work regulation, and work restructuring. Relocations of work, shifts in workplace practices, new practices in labour regulation, and labour organizing have had positive and negative impacts upon workers and their communities.

Globalization has brought a dramatic decentralization in the locus of value generation; less value is now created in factories by large groups of workers in standardized conditions, and more production occurs outside the traditional factory and in less standardized work arrangements. For example, a large part of value creation now takes place by selling or renting products and services in industries such as information services, tourism, entertainment, and the new media. With new work arrangements, the average size of workplaces is shrinking and workers more frequently find themselves working nonstandard hours (part-time, temporary, casual), self-employed, employed sporadically, multiple job holding, or not employed at all within the formal labour market. Stone (2004) refers to the new "boundaryless workplace" and suggests that workers have "boundaryless careers"—unbounded by specific job activities, attachments to particular workplaces, and opportunities to advance within an organization. Within these settings, workers face the recurring possibility of displacement in (virtual or real) location, in job function, or within an industry.

Considering working conditions across the globe and the number of atrocities reported in the news, including the collapse of hastily and shoddily constructed factories and buildings, evidence suggests that in order to coordinate amongst global labour markets and production processes, transnational production chains or networks generally reproduce existing institutional, political, and cultural traditions and inequalities rather than facilitate the development of new practices. On April 24, 2013 an eight-story building collapsed in Savar on the outskirts of Dhaka, Bangladesh, killing more than 1,100 garment workers and injuring over 2,500 others. The Rana Plaza disaster is considered to be both the deadliest garment factory accident as well as one of the most serious structural failures in modern history. The building housed shops, apartments, a bank, and clothing factories. The day prior to the collapse, the tenants were warned about the cracks in the building's foundation that might eventually lead to structural failure. But the garment workers were expected to return to work (Burke, 2014; Yardley, 2013). The Rana Plaza disaster could have been prevented had there been strict regulations with enforceable penalties for building materials, building code, safety precautions, and structural soundness. However, regulating code and other procedures would ultimately add to the costs of production, and with transnational corporations seeking the lowest costs possible, rather than risking loss of business, those in positions of power in nations intent on attracting business may not be as vigilant as possible, or may turn away altogether from reinforcing safety standards and other precautionary measures. Within the global economy, questions over regulation and power dynamics persist. These dynamics play upon state structures and government policy, employment conditions, labour-management relations, and labour movements. In particular, global production raises many concerns regarding the regulation of work, the condition of social citizenship, and the overall level of security experienced by workers and households and guaranteed by the social and political infrastructure of the state.

Along with the transformation to a globalized economy, during the 1970s, as periods of recession loomed and it appeared to many that the "Golden Age" of capitalism was over, Margaret Thatcher and other rightist conservatives promoted monetarist policies as the only way to get Western economies back on track to economic health. Canada, along with other Western states, has adopted a neoliberal worldview. **Neoliberalism** is not simply an economic position; it is a philosophic approach that embraces the principles of the freedom of the market and the primacy of private property. Neoliberal thinking calls for less state interference in political, social, and economic affairs and greater involvement of private enterprise in managing, coordinating, and directing the marketplace and the economy. This means lower state expenditures and cutbacks on health, welfare, and social programs with an aim to promoting independence and self-sufficiency.

Neoliberal thinking replaced **Keynesianism**, a set of ideas that revolved around stimulating the economy by propping up purchasing power and strengthening the welfare state. After the Second World War, in an attempt to avoid another Great Depression as experienced in the 1930s, the state sought to balance the economy by adjusting tax rates, promoting industry through incentive programs, and engaging in initiatives that sought to redistribute income while lowering rates of unemployment. Under this arrangement, business maintained the upper hand over investment and production while workers met more stable levels of employment, enjoyed a measure of wage and income security, and welcomed collective bargaining rights. During this period, often referred to as the "Golden Age" of capitalism, the labour-business "welfare bargain" coincided with the state's adoption of Keynesian fiscal policy. Under Keynesianism, during periods of cyclical downturns and high unemployment, the state would increase its social expenditures and sustain budget deficits to boost aggregate and consumer demand with the goal of generating economic growth and prosperity. Keynesianism was counter-cyclical, and, as such, was a radical departure from traditional Canadian budgetary policies that tended to reinforce rather than offset swings in the economy (Stanford, 2008a: 57–8).

The Keynesian approach promoted the "good life" and provided justification for innovative and improved social welfare programs. Under this system, new and improved social security schemes were legitimated in terms of their stabilizing effects on the process of accumulation and the benefit to capitalism, rather than on their effects in enhancing the quality of people's lives. The "good will" state did not abandon its primary interest in strengthening and promoting private enterprise and ultimately, profit making. Rather, under this system the state acknowledged the role of a contented working class in maintaining balance and harmony within the economy.

Successive recessions beginning in the 1970s, and in the 1980s and 1990s signalled the end of the welfare state. The Canadian political arena, particularly under the Conservative government of Prime Minister Brian Mulroney, shifted to embrace Thatcher's notion of "There Is No Alternative" (TINA)—that the economic, political, and social policies developed under neoliberal thinking constituted the only paths to create wealth and employment, to reduce poverty, and to increase the standard of living across the globe in both more developed and less developed countries. To remain competitive within the world economy by reducing social spending and practicing fiscal restraint, Canadian politicians aligned themselves with world powers similarly latching onto neoliberal agendas by substituting principles of individual responsibility, entrepreneurial capitalism, and fiscal restraint, while abandoning attitudes about the public and community good, popular under the welfare state. Canadians' concerns over work, unemployment, and other measures of insecurity were fuelled by governments' declaration of fiscal crises and their unrelenting attention to deficit reduction. Meanwhile, buffered by corporate-friendly trade agreements, tax breaks, import-export policies, and relaxed labour laws and regulations, corporations sought cheaper and more favourable locations within the Global South, and permanently moved their operations overseas. In this process, key industries, including auto, steel, and other heavy manufacturing enterprises—industries that traditionally offered relatively good, well-paying jobs with benefits and security—were lost to the Canadian landscape, leaving thousands of Canadian workers with limited access to secure employment conditions.

Conclusion

Over the course of the past 30 years, the Canadian economy has lost vibrancy as the manufacturing sector has been hollowed out, as "good" jobs have been replaced by "bad" jobs, and rates of unionization have plummeted. Workers are seriously concerned about their financial futures and young workers, in particular, worry about ever realizing their lifelong dreams of home ownership, a family, and a rewarding career. Indeed, many today are focused on finding some semblance of security in a difficult labour market while paying off their educational debts.

In the chapters that follow, we examine key issues facing Canadian workers within the context of global capitalism where a major concern for all is access to decent work and a measure of security once enjoyed more broadly amongst both working and managerial classes. The "new" world of service sector employment still requires commitment and discipline as in the past without the measure of promise offered under earlier conditions.

Questions for Critical Thought

1. What are some of the difficulties facing young workers today as they enter the labour market in search of full-time jobs?
2. Over the past few decades there have been a number of shifts within the Canadian economy. What are some of these transformations? Do these changes indicate that there is a *new* economy in Canada?
3. What is the relationship between the state's adoption of a neoliberal agenda and the need to remain competitive within a global economy?

Suggested Further Resources

Pugh, Allison J. 2015. *The Tumbleweed Society: Working and Caring in an Age of Insecurity.* New York: Oxford University Press. Based on qualitative research, this book examines the importance of interpersonal, social, and community ties as workers are caught in an endless cycle of precarious jobs and insecure futures.

Rudacille, Deborah. 2010. *Roots of Steel: Boom and Bust in an American Mill Town.* New York: Pantheon Books. This book examines the social and political context of work in the steel industry. Rudacille considers the ways in which the steel company and its politics were woven into the lives of working-class families.

Suggested Websites

Dear John

http://jackielang.com/launch/dear-john/trailer.html

Dear John is a documentary film (produced in a style similar to that of Michael Moore's films) on the closure of the John Deere plant in Welland, Ontario.

International Labour Rights Forum

www.laborrights.org/issues/precarious-work

The ILRF brings together voices from academia, labour, human rights, religious, and other communities to fight the injustices workers face within the international sphere.

Notes

1. According to a report by the Canadian Centre for Policy Alternatives in 2014 (CCPA and Fraser, 2014), there is a wide range of tuitions costs across Canada, with Ontario as the most expensive province in which to earn an undergraduate degree ($7,259 in 2013) and Newfoundland and Labrador ($2,644 in 2013) the least expensive.
2. In the Youth in Transition survey, researchers tracked youth between the ages of 15 and 25 to compare participants' career choices at age 15 compared to their career paths at age 25.
3. The comments here are based on the research and interview data gathered by Ann Duffy, Norene Pupo, and June Corman for their projects, "Displaced Workers and Their Communities" (Ann Duffy, Principal Investigator) and "Women, Deindustrialization and Community" (Norene Pupo, Principal Investigator). These projects were funded by the Social Sciences and Humanities Research Council of Canada in 2010 and 2013 respectively.

2 From Craftwork to Modern Production: Efficiency and Control at Work

Learning Objectives

- To examine control over labour and the process of deskilling work
- To discuss Fordism and the labour process
- To introduce scientific management and to question its relevance today
- To study efficiency engineering and modern approaches to the rationalization of labour processes

Introduction

Maintaining control over the structure and processes of work has always been a major preoccupation for capitalist owners and managers. During the latter years of the nineteenth century and the early years of the twentieth century, economists, social scientists, politicians, and social reformers pointed to labour unrest and the persistent adversarial relationship between workers and their employers as targets for reform. In these years, industrial capitalists and their managers were obsessed with the smooth functioning of their production processes. The goal of managers was to create efficiency in the workplace, and to accomplish this they embraced the thinking of social pragmatists and reformers of the time who were deeply enmeshed in an "efficiency" movement, attempting to study and solve social problems plaguing the developing urban landscapes. For business and industry, the critical question centred on how to generate efficiency at work—an efficiency that would increase productivity and maximize profits, while rendering work forces docile and obedient. This chapter starts with a broad brush of history, focusing on the ways in which social and work relationships were transformed with changes in the economy and the movement from simple forms of production involving basic methods of management and supervision to systematic management involving more detailed and hierarchical forms of control. We will consider the introduction of scientific management and its relevance within past and present-day labour processes. Here we examine the deskilling and degradation of work over the past century and raise questions about re-skilling and decent work. Finally we consider the requirement for flexibility and the lean workplace, indispensable for competitiveness within the global economy.

From Craftwork to the Factory: Simple Supervision to Systematic Management

By the middle of the nineteenth century, features of industrial capitalism were beginning to emerge as larger groups of workers were employed in the growing number of small manufacturing establishments dotting the Canadian landscape. Due to changes in land grant policies decades earlier and the increasing numbers of immigrants settling in Canada, significant pools of workers were amassing within the cities as they looked for work. In earlier times when the majority of people worked the land as independent small landowners and employees were scarce, employers established a close, often paternalistic, relationship with their workers (Palmer, 1983). The scarcity of labour and the threat that the employees might leave to set up independent farms meant that employers were dependent on their employees. At the same time, employees—sometimes referred to as homeless drifters—faced difficulty in finding work and were dependent on employers for a livelihood. At this time the employer–employee relationship was one of mutual dependence, and impersonal forces of the market did not govern this relationship. The employer offered the worker some measure of security by providing tools, clothing, and shelter during tough times to ensure a good supply of labour during peak periods. In turn, workers were somewhat reluctant to leave an employer to search, often in vain, for a more lucrative position. Often, a close, personal relationship developed between the employer and employee due to the balance of bargaining advantage.[1]

In pre-industrial Canada, employers were concerned about preserving their labour supply but after mid-century, with labour's abundance, employers no longer worried about maintaining their labour supply and adjusted their work forces according to their needs, hiring during peak periods and laying off or firing during slack periods. Work relationships were marked by the impersonality of the capitalist labour market (Palmer, 1983). For workers, this change in the nature of work relationships was a very real and subjectively experienced adjustment that not only affected work experiences but also penetrated workers' communities and ways of life. This was not a smooth or easy transition for workers and their communities, as indicated by the tumultuous times in the latter part of the nineteenth century, with numerous walkouts, strikes, and struggles over unionization (Heron, 2012). Prior to this, there was little evidence of strikes, walkouts, or open conflict of any kind between employers and employees on a wide scale. But after mid-century there was a general rising trend in struggles at the workplace. All of these reactions of workers represent their attempts to regulate the new insecurity and regain control over the impersonality of the new capitalist labour market. This included workers' attempts to regulate wages and job tenure.

Despite the changing conditions and atmosphere within workplaces, by the end of the nineteenth century, manufacturing was scattered and relatively small scale. Most production units consisted of several craftsmen, their apprentices, and a few helpers who were required for heavy lifting, fetching materials and tools, and other tasks. Most worked by hand with little mechanization and little specialization. Under these conditions, master craftsmen maintained control over all aspects of their work. They had complete knowledge of the work process and the ability to carry out all of the components embedded within any one product. With their knowledge and skills, master craftsmen were positioned to command high wages, set the pace, and determine the conditions of work. It was important to capitalists—factory owners and their managers—to gain control from the master craftsmen over the conditions of work. By the century's end, the most essential concern of the factory system centred around new techniques of human coordination, supervision, management, and discipline.

With the recognition that master craftsmen "ruled" the day with their intimate knowledge of all aspects of production, factory owners fought back, struggling to gain control and assume the seat of power within their operations—a position they felt was rightly theirs. As the factory system developed, codes of rules, rights, obligations, and penalties ensued. According to the *Report of the Royal Commission on the Relations of Capital and Labour* (Government of Canada, 1889), conditions at work were harsh; employees faced fines or were discharged for minor infractions, including lateness, leaving their workstations, and talking or socializing with co-workers. Grasping the reins of power within their establishments and enforcing the new work discipline, especially on skilled workers, was difficult for employers. Skilled workers were able to impose craft control over the work process and successfully resist arbitrary factory rules.

One of the responses of employers to workers' resistance was to hire women and children, workers they viewed as more manageable. Even then, there was ample evidence of brutality toward these vulnerable workers. Children were sometimes locked in basements overnight, left in the coal boxes with no ventilation, heating, or lighting (Government of Canada, 1889). Such tactics, along with the threat of discharge, were ineffective with skilled craftsmen because it was too difficult for employers to replace them. With their intimate knowledge of the production process, workers' control was the order of the day for skilled craftsmen. Factory owners, intent on wresting control from these workers, soon developed an elaborate system of supervision and management.

The Labour Process and the Locus of Control

Prior to industrial capitalism, factories employed supervisors, but they usually worked in the production process alongside of the workers they supervised. Eventually the role of the supervisor became more specialized. Their primary job was similar to that of a constable; they wore uniforms, sometimes with badges, and they patrolled the factory to enforce the rules. Henry Ford was the mastermind behind developing a solid system of control, and this was especially important at his Highland Park Plant in Michigan that employed 15,000 workers.

Here wresting control from the workers was Ford's primary goal. He openly declared that he was not interested in hiring experienced workers, but instead preferred to employ machine operators who had nothing to "unlearn"; he had a preference for workers "who have no theories of correct surface speeds for metal finishing, [but] will simply do what they are told over and over again, from bell-time to bell-time" (Baritz, 1960). To ensure that workers toed the line and followed orders, Ford developed an enormous supervisory staff—500 overseers, a ratio of 1 to 30, with authority to fire any operative if necessary, to maintain control over 15,000 employees. A detailed study of the plant conducted in 1914 found that there was, on average, a firing a day (Baritz, 1960).

In the transition to industrial capitalism, the challenge for the "captains of industry" was to find a way to get their workers to acquire factory discipline and ethics. To do this, employers like Henry Ford devised and administered a successful code of conduct and system of supervision. This was a difficult process; workers, especially skilled workers, did not readily embrace the new factory codes, nor did they easily accept the new work relationships that came with a cost—the loss of their positions at the helm of the production process and the control over their labours. Workers had to be enticed to accept the new work relationships. It was at this time that management sought to subordinate labour to its rules, decisions, and systems of control.

To understand the driving force behind the development of a system of management and control, we will consider the nature of labour and labour power under industrial capitalism. With no other options to earn a livelihood, workers enter an employment agreement with an employer. The employer's goal is to expand the capital s/he owns, and to do this, the employer converts some of the capital into wages. This sets in motion the labour process, the employer's way of creating **use values**, and the process for expanding capital and creating profit. It is through the labour process that employers accumulate capital. The labour process is shaped by the desire to accumulate capital and increase profits. How does this work? With human labour there is a unity between conception—thinking and planning—and execution—carrying out tasks. Human labour is not only capable of a vast range of activities but it is also adaptable with vast potential. It is this characteristic of human labour that allows capitalists to expand their capital and get the most out of the labour they employ. To this end, capitalists realized that it was essential for them to take control over the labour process away from workers in order to expand their surplus. Simply, to the capitalist, capturing control over the labour process presented itself as the central problem of management.

During the early stages of industrial capitalism, the skilled craftsperson was regarded as an autonomous worker, exerting workers' control over the labour process. Along with the presence of workers' control was the craft person's sense of pride in their work. They were proud of putting out the best quality work possible, and they demanded a say in how the work was done, who would help them, what tools were indispensable to quality output, sub-contracting, and other aspects of work. Individually or collectively through their craft unions, these workers set fair prices for their labour, based on their experience and the quality of their work, and walked away from offers that in their view were substandard and did not respect their standards. Craft pride rather than workers' greed dictated reasonable rates for wages as well as for the amount of work a craft worker could produce in a day (Palmer, 1983). In today's terms, it may seem that in the pre-industrial system workers and their unions had too much control. But the issue is not that workers assumed control, but that owners were not yet managing or controlling the labour process. While we take for granted today that employers, rather than workers, should exercise control over the details of the work process and we accept the notion of managerial rights, what history teaches us is that employers had to find the means whereby they could wrest control over the labour process from the workers.

The driving force behind employers' quest to develop an effective system of supervision was their interest in increasing their capital. To increase their capital, employers aimed to boost the productivity, or the use value, of the labour they hired. The employers' problem was that in their attempts to squeeze more out of their workers, employers confronted constraints imposed by craft production and the sub-contracting system. Because skilled crafts workers were "masters" of their own domain, their work and their time were deeply entrenched cultural values that were very difficult to disperse. As social scientists of the time had forewarned, attitudes and values do not change quickly or easily.

The first step for employers was to force workers to adhere to strict regular hours of work and to obey company rules and regulations. Employers and skilled workers engaged in a "tug of war" that proved to be difficult for both sides, with employers resorting to force, coercion, and brutality and employees determined to maintain the upper hand in decisions over their work. As long as workers maintained control over the knowledge embedded in their crafts, it was impossible for employers to regulate the labour process. Eventually employers understood that they had to break down production, separating craft knowledge from the performance and completion of the process.

The first step in breaking down production was to develop a **detailed division of labour**. As sociologists, we distinguish between the **social division of labour** and a detailed division of labour. The social division of labour is the simple notion that all industrial societies are subdivided by occupations and by types of work. Under a detailed division of labour, occupations and crafts are destroyed as different workers are each assigned a couple of minor tasks within the production of a commodity. In this arrangement, individual workers become specialists in one particular aspect of the entire process, but are unable to carry through any complete production process. Breaking down the labour process and then assigning different elements to different workers destroys craft as a process under the control of workers (Braverman, 1975/2000). With craftwork, there was a unity between knowledge and experience or the execution of the work, and this meant that the craft workers had knowledge, experience, and abilities that their employers did not necessarily have. This craft knowledge allowed the workers to maintain control, but under a detailed division of labour and the separation of conception from execution, control passes on to employers who then organize the production process under their direction. As craft is broken down, individual workers only have the knowledge of one small part of the production process. This process destroys craft.

Deskilling, Management, and the Labour Process

Not only did the development of the detailed division of labour break down and subdivide work, and in the process, destroy craft, allowing employers to gain control over the production process, but it also cheapened the cost of labour. With individual workers assigned to minor tasks within production processes, their skill was lost and they were no longer able to command wages reflecting the skills and knowledge they brought to the workplace. To the employer's advantage, the cost of labour is cheapened because all of the individual elements or tasks involved in production are broken down in such a way that each task may be performed by an "unskilled" or less skilled worker rather than by a craftsperson. This notion is known as the **Babbage principle**, named after Charles Babbage who developed this theory. According to the Babbage principle, by dividing work into different processes, each of which could be priced according to the precise quantity of skill involved, costs are lowered. This scheme is cheaper for the employer than hiring someone who will carry out both the laborious tasks involving mainly brute force as well as the difficult tasks requiring knowledge and experience. This is known as the process of **deskilling** and it is rooted in capitalists' interest in expanding their capital.

The process of deskilling involves separating conception (knowledge, planning, conceptualizing) and execution (carrying out the work). Frederick Winslow Taylor pushed forward the process of deskilling labour and cheapening the production process with his work, *The Principles of Scientific Management*, published in 1910. In a seminal book published in 1975, *Labor and Monopoly Capital: The Degradation of Work in the Twentieth Century*, Harry Braverman argued that the principles of scientific management, or Taylorism, continues to survive as the bases of the organization of production.

Scientific management was a feat of capital; it established firm control for owners while reining in craft workers who held sway over the labour process. Before examining Taylorism and scientific management more closely, let us consider how workers were managed in early industrial establishments. The nature of the twentieth-century work relationship is best understood with regard to the issue of power and control. Examining this relationship allows for a more complete understanding of the roles of management, the purpose and function of managerial technique, and the locus of organizational control. First, let us distinguish between pre-industrial and industrial work relationships (Braverman, 1975/2000; Clawson, 1979; Rinehart, 2006; Edwards, 1979). In the pre-industrial period, the worker was involved in the entire production process as there was unity between conception and execution in the labour process. With factory production, machine power gradually replaced hand power, larger numbers of workers were concentrated under one roof, and a process began whereby skilled labour was gradually replaced by semi-skilled and unskilled labour with the separation of work into distinct job categories. The essence of the factory system was neither the widespread use of machinery nor the amassing of workers under one roof. Rather, its essence was the entailment of a new discipline and new work relationships. Under these conditions, the management process was born.

In early years, relationships between masters and apprentices were based on skill differences between the parties and revolved around the transfer of knowledge to the apprentice. The power differential between the master and apprentice was primarily related to inequalities in knowledge and skill levels and secondarily to the pattern of ownership and difference in status. With the separation of conception and execution and as foremen, supervisors, and other levels of management were employed, the work relationship was based on power differences and the element of control. Here the control was arbitrary, formal, and impersonal as compared to the close, personal relationship of earlier times. Table 2.1 indicates a decrease in the number of manufacturing establishments between 1880 and 1910, and therefore, the growing concentration of workers under one roof. This, in turn, necessitated the development of offices of supervision and management.

The growth of management and its control over the work process evolved through several stages. Here we will focus on two distinct phases,[2] summarized in Tables 2.2 and 2.3,[3] Simple and Systematic Management.[4] During the first phase, Simple Management (roughly 1880–1910), neither the parameters of the occupation of management nor a set of distinct managerial techniques were clearly defined. Managers were simply expected to provide direction to workers and maintain control by employing rudimentary disciplinary techniques. The mere existence of the foreman or supervisor on the shop floor as a representative

Table 2.1 Summary Statistics of Manufacturing Industries, Canada, 1880-1910

Year	No. of Ests.	No. of Employees	Mean No. of Employees Per Est.	Supervisory and Office Employees As % of All Employees
1880	47,079	284,042	5.3	—
1895	69,716	351,139	5.0	—
1900	—	422,824	—	—
1905	15,197	382,702	25.2	9.2
1910	—	509,977	—	8.4

Source: M.C. Urquhart and K.A.H. Buckley, *Historical Statistics of Canada*. Toronto: Macmillan, 1956.

Table 2.2 Simple Management

Period	Source of Direction	Division of Labour	Purpose of Management	Basis of Power
Before 1870	Master craftsman	Simple	Simple direction, teaching, guidance	Knowledge, skill, ownership
1870–1890	Working owners & partners	Growing D of L; separation of conception & execution	Direction, efficiency, clarity of orders	Ownership
1880–1910	Shop supervisor	Developed D of L; separate managerial category; separation of skilled and un-skilled labour	Discipline issue of orders	Ownership or assignment by owner

of the employer's authority was expected to ensure obedience and adequate production levels while providing a "**hidden curriculum**" in teaching workers about the social context underlying the work relationships and the inherent power structure involved.

During the second phase, Systematic Management, specific management principles and techniques began to emerge in order to guarantee efficient production levels and harmonious relations within the workplace. Beginning with Scientific Management, a more precise definition of the role and function of management materialized. By relying on a scientific framework, social and behavioural scientists, business owners, and social reformers anticipated higher levels of productivity along with quieter, well-disciplined work forces. Both the sphere and functions of management grew, as middle management and sub-categories of administration were developed using staff and line criteria. The key function of modern management was coordination for efficiency, marked by elaborate reporting and communication systems.

The practice of both simple and systematic management is concerned with obedience and conformity to a code of rules and discipline. During the early phase, this concern was overt—supervisors and foremen patrolled the shop floor,

Table 2.3 Systematic Management: The Development of Managerial Techniques

Starting From	Source of Direction	Division of Labour	Purpose of Management	Justification of Relationship
1910	Shop supervisor; engineer technologist	Detailed	Efficiency control	Managerial prerogative
1930	Personnel director; dept. manager	Detailed	Efficiency, eliminate source of contention, control	Defined by occupation of management
1950	Dept. of personnel & staff & line managers	Detailed	Coordination efficiency control	Proven necessity of management & leadership

carrying stop watches, whistles, factory codes or rule books, and other tools for disciplining workers and meting out what they felt were suitable punishments for any infractions. During the later phase, behavioural scientists and human relations experts worked to "soften" management's approach by substituting subtle techniques and the use of "anonymous" authority for earlier overt methods. This process required scientific precision and the assurance of managers, business owners, industrialists, and behaviourists of its efficacy. Training in the use of such methods was elaborate and eventually justified its place in colleges and the hallowed halls of higher learning as part of the business curriculum. The professionalization of the occupation of management represents the gradual integration of science into the managerial process

Engineering Efficiency: Scientific Management, Fordism, and the Transformation of Production

Frederick Taylor developed the principles of scientific management at a time when behavioural psychologists, sociologists, and advertisers were beginning to employ scientific methods in order to discover truths about human nature and behaviour. Behavioural scientists were using experimental approaches to investigate problems in areas such as merchandising, advertising, vocational guidance and career planning, educational programming, urban development, and work-related conflict. These scientists embraced a positivistic framework, believing that it was possible to solve social problems if they were properly, that is, scientifically, studied and researched (Baritz, 1960). Social reformers of the time saw promise in the scientific method as the means to deal with growing problems related to industrialization and urban growth, including rising crime rates, immigration and associated housing problems, juvenile delinquency, poverty, and labour strife. People were adjusting their lives, their day-to-day realities, and their priorities to the codes and practices of an industrial economy.

Psychology, and in particular, industrial psychology, developed as part of a general move toward social efficiency and scientific analysis. Industrial psychology was based on the premise that human behaviour profoundly affected management's goals and, as such, it was imperative to business owners and factory managers that psychologists establish, through experimental procedure, some truths about human behaviour. During the first decades of the twentieth century, the social scientist consultant to industry became commonplace, indicative of the professionalization of the social sciences and the recognition of this field of inquiry for purposes of enhancing the bottom line—profits.

It was within this climate that Frederick Taylor focused on the "labour" question with the assumption that eliminating conflicts and unrest at work, and improving productivity were possible if scientific method was applied to these problems. Taylor was not the first to undertake the labour question as a number of psychologists and sociologists had previously done so. But Taylor's work appealed to a broad range of reformers, capitalists, and social scientists because it was both systematic and concretely based.

Taylor and Scientific Management

Frederick W. Taylor was born into a wealthy and prominent Philadelphian family.[5] His father, a lawyer, expected him to follow in his own career path, but while Taylor was at Exeter in preparation for Harvard Law School, he rebelled, dropped out, and took a job at Midvale Steel Works, a company owned by friends of the family. Taylor advanced quickly to the role of gang-foreman of the lathe department and within six years was promoted to the position of chief engineer where he became involved in struggles with the workers over what was to constitute a "fair day's work." He systematically documented his analysis and published a paper on the piece-rate wage system in 1895 and another entitled "Shop Management" in 1903. The publication of these papers, together with his reputation as a top-rated engineer, sparked discussion, interest, and experimentation in the field.

Taylor's main concern was the elimination of "soldiering," or restriction of output, among workers. He argued that to eliminate soldiering, foremen must subject every job to rigorous scientific analysis to determine all the steps involved and the necessary time required for each step. With this knowledge, Taylor said that the manager could then assign the worker his/her duties with the assurance that the time provided would be adequate to complete the tasks. With the scientific evidence amassed by the foremen, workers' concerns regarding the unfairness of employers or their inability to complete tasks in the time frame provided could easily be dismissed. Taylor's methods effectively invested all knowledge regarding the structure, organization, mechanics, limitations, and outcome in the higher levels of the corporation with management, rather than on the shop floor with the workers.

In 1889, Taylor left Midvale Steel Works to assume a position at the Bethlehem Steel Company. Upon joining Bethlehem Steel, Taylor reorganized the machine shop. It was at Bethlehem that he developed the Principles of Scientific Management. In developing these principles, Taylor's main objective was to establish scientific ways of organizing and managing work to replace what he referred to as the existing "rule of thumb" methods. The ideas underlying Taylor's methods were not new, but his systematic documentation regarding the practice of management was clearly of major significance.

The most important feature of Scientific Management was the concept of control over the labour process. Taylor understood the importance of transferring control over decisions, plans, and processes of work to management, leaving workers to engage simply and solely in carrying out their assigned tasks. In transferring control from workers to management, Taylor's primary objective was to increase efficiency on the shop floor. Taylor (1967: 38) explained the process: ". . . all of the planning which under the old system was done by the workman, as a result of his personal experience, must of necessity under the new system be done by management in accordance with the laws of science; because even if the workman was well suited to the development and use of scientific data, it would be physically impossible for him to work at his machine and at a desk at the same time."

As an engineer, Taylor focused on the production process as a whole and the worker's place in it. He considered the labour process as a unified technological sphere and worked to achieve efficiency by looking for means to maximize output and harmony by orienting workers toward management's goals. His fundamental concern was to reorganize and gain control over the labour process, rather than to simply modify workers' roles within the ongoing production process.

Taylor's principles represented a logical extension of the rationality inherent in Max Weber's bureaucratic ideal. They also embraced the notion of a division of labour bounded by specific rules regarding supervision and reporting within a hierarchical structure. Taylor's work appealed to many; not only was it precise and efficient, but it was also backed by scientific principles. Moreover, the rules were clear, the impact was measurable, and the tools required were simple, involving the use of time and motion studies and the stopwatch.

Under Taylorism nothing was left to chance or to the whim of the individual manager. Taylor insisted that for maximum effectiveness it was absolutely necessary that management dictate the *precise* manner in which work was to be carried out. His system went well beyond a simple division of labour; rather his plan called for subdividing and directing every minute detail of work. Braverman (1975/2000) argued that Taylor's principles of scientific management became the basis of all advanced work design and industrial engineering. Within a few years of the publication of *The Principles of Scientific Management*, it was translated into several languages, followed by international dignitaries including Vladimir Lenin and Leon Trotsky, and scores of articles appeared in popular journals of the time with suggestions on how the principles may be applied to various facets of life, including education and teachers' "management" of classrooms (Callahan, 1962). By the 1930s, references to scientific management or Taylor's system were uncommon. However, Braverman (1975/2000: 60) suggests, "that is because, apart from the bad odor of the name, it is no longer the property of a faction, since its fundamental teachings have become the bedrock of all work design."

Taylor's method of extracting productive efficiency from workers was based on three main principles. The first was to establish clear rules on how work was to be done and thereby eliminate reliance on the "rules of thumb." Following this directive effectively sets management's primary position in the labour process. The second principle dissociates the labour process from the skills of the workers by calling for the separation of conception from execution, or what we refer to as the process of deskilling. Thirdly, Taylor's system gave managers a monopoly over the knowledge and techniques necessary to control each step of the labour process. This involved selecting and training as well as providing supervisors with stop watches in order to gather detailed data on every motion and every action of workers. Finally, the work and responsibility is almost equally divided between management and workers. As Taylor writes (1967: 37), "[t]he management take over all work for which they are better fitted than the workmen, while in the past almost all of the work and the greater part of the responsibility were thrown upon the men." As Braverman (1975/2000) points out, Taylor championed the process of deskilling by arguing that it enabled workers to "rise to a higher plane of efficiency" so that instead of "digging ditches," a worker could work on a production line making shoes or any number of consumer commodities.

Today, Taylor's principles may be observed in action in the fast food industry where bells, whistles, and flashing lights signal workers when to flip burgers, raise deep fried foods from the hot oil, and even discard stale coffee or other products. Further, foods are assembled to very specific formulations, including amounts of condiments plopped onto sandwiches, cooking and frying times down to the second, and wrapping and serving procedures. Finally, cashiers or front-line servers are expected to follow rehearsed scripts with each customer and to "calculate" the customer's tab using pre-programmed cash registers, many of which automatically dispense change and receipts. As a result, most food-service workers today know very little about the foods they serve, including the ingredients and the preparation techniques. They are not skilled cooks, having been reduced to an appendage of the kitchen mixing and cooking machines, and the pre-packaged menu items they are expected to put together.

One of Taylor's objectives was to maximize each worker's daily output. He set out to determine "a fair day's work," which he defined as the amount a worker could

© Richard Levine / Alamy Stock Photo

Today Taylor's principles may be observed in action in the fast food industry, where bells and whistles guide food preparation and foods are assembled to very specific formulations.

accomplish in a specific period of time without damaging his/her physical health. He demonstrated that "natural laziness" hampers productivity but that this flaw in character may be minimized or eliminated when workers are directed in each step of the labour process by management. By selecting a pig-iron handler named Schmidt, whom Taylor referred to as "stupid" and requiring complete direction, Taylor demonstrated (1967: 136) that Schmidt's output rose by 3.5 times his usual amount, and this, he said, would justify a 60 per cent increase in his wages. By this thinking, the higher wages and possibility of promotion would prove to be the special incentives required to keep workers committed to their jobs and subservient to management's directives.

In his description, Taylor characterizes the process as agreeable, arguing that it alleviates the worker of the responsibility of planning and that the elevated levels of productivity benefit workers by boosting their wages and management by increasing productivity and profits. Earlier, under simple management, employers' power was justified in terms of "natural rights." The "new science of administration" provided an alternative justification for management's power. Under this new system, workers were studied as "cogs in the machine," as part of the technology to be placed, directed, and manipulated at the whim of management.

Besides its main promise to manage work processes and problem employees, Taylor's system also proposed to resolve many other problems, including the high cost of increased production, low wages, waste of manpower and materials, unemployment, poverty, and disharmony between employers and employees. To address the labour problem, Taylor encouraged workers' identification with the employer and stressed the mutual benefits of worker–management cooperation. To this end, he began the first chapter of *The Principles of Scientific Management* by stating: "The principal object of management should be to secure the maximum prosperity for the employer, coupled with the maximum prosperity for each employee" (1967: 9). He dismissed the notion of an inherent conflict of interest between employers and employees, advocating that scientific management, "has for its very foundation the firm conviction that the true interests of the two are one and the same; . . . and that it is possible to give the workman what he most wants—high wages—and the employer what he wants—a low labour cost—for his manufactures" (1967: 10). Under scientific management, workers were allowed to present complaints to their employers, and grievances were to be settled by scientific method, rather than "*ideologically*" by unions. In part due to the widespread popularity of Taylorism and the assembly line, union membership declined during the 1920s.

Was scientific management a panacea? Taylor made no claims to this effect, declaring that there was no "single panacea" for "all of the troubles of the working-people or of employers." He explained that "as long as some people are born greedy and brutal, as long as vice and crime are with us, just so long will a certain amount of poverty, misery, and unhappiness be with us also. No system of management . . . can insure continuous prosperity to either workmen or employers" (1967: 29). What Taylor did claim is that any community, town, or region "substituting the principles of scientific management for the rule of thumb" will generally be "far more prosperous, far happier, and more free from discord and dissension" as compared to those relying on less organized ways of old forms of management. The overriding claim of Taylorism, then, was in increasing social efficiency.

Despite Taylor's insistence that his system of scientific management benefitted both workers and managers, many decried the mention of Taylorism for its disparaging references to workers. For example, in *The Principles of Scientific Management*, Taylor referred to the "natural laziness of men" (1967: 20) and attempts by workers to "mislead" and "deceive" their employers. He also wrote of the "insufficient mental capacity" of workers and, in reference to Schmidt, the pig-iron handler he selected to demonstrate the benefits of scientific management, he said that, "the man suited to handling pig iron is too stupid to properly train himself." As a result, by the 1920s, Taylorism was viewed as harsh and uncompromising, especially amongst those welcoming an age of humanitarian reform.

Yet, in spite of the growing objections to Scientific Management and Taylor's approach, Braverman (1975/2000) and others who study modern labour processes (Thompson, 1989) argue that the fundamental principles and practices of Taylorism dominate many forms of work today. While we can easily observe the rudiments of scientific management in the service sector, particularly in the fast food industry (Schlosser, 2002), it is important to consider the mechanisms of control and loss of skill within professional and administrative jobs as well (see Shalla, 1997; Ritzer, 2011).

Writing his seminal book, *Labor and Monopoly Capital*, in 1974 and drawing on a Marxist framework, Braverman developed a critical analysis of the ways in which capitalism and technology shaped production processes in the twentieth century. Braverman challenged the notion that modern work processes would require increasing levels of education and skill within workforces. He argued, instead, that managerial processes aimed to break down skilled work into smaller and more simplified parts, and in this process, fewer skills would be required. While workers may enter the labour force with well-developed skills within their fields, they would not necessarily be called upon to deploy these skills in their jobs, nor would their pay rates necessarily reflect their actual skill levels. According to Braverman, there were two reasons for this trend. The first was economic: replacing skilled work with labour requiring little knowledge or training would save employers costs because wages would be adjusted to reflect the skill level necessary for the job. Placing control in the hands of management would contribute to elevated levels of productivity. Secondly, with managers in control, workers were made to be fully dependent upon management for all decisions and would be unable to exercise judgment over the methods and pace of work. The long-term result, Braverman warned, was the **degradation of labour** in which more and more jobs were cheapened, deskilled, and increasingly controlled by management.

Despite Braverman's contributions to labour process theory and the sociology of work, his work was challenged on a number of issues. Following Braverman's rationale that workers will be stripped of their skills and ability to understand or take control of the work process, it is difficult to explain circumstances in which workers challenge or resist management's control. In some respects, if Braverman's analysis is taken to its logical extension, further and further stripping workers of their skills, their knowledge, and the tools with which to challenge management, then they are trapped in an "iron cage" similar to Max Weber's notion of the bureaucratic "ideal." In an often-cited study published well before Braverman's work, Roy (1959) demonstrated the ways in which workers in a garment factory broke up the monotony of their day by engaging together in a number of different games and pranks. One of their daily escapades was referred to as "banana time" whereby a banana would be stolen from one of the workers' lunch boxes at a particular time, and the discovery of the missing banana would result in a few (staged) minutes of mayhem and fun. Years later Michael Burawoy (1979) argued that the games workers engage in are a product of historical struggles between workers and management, but that these games are played within the rules of the workplace and do not necessarily challenge management's control or their profit-making targets. Nevertheless, the games do demonstrate a degree of agency, and although they are played within a context and set of rules defined by management, the worker decides whether or not to opt in, and the game becomes "an end in itself, overshadowing, masking and even inverting the conditions out of which it emerges" (1979: 82).

Richard Edwards (1979) addressed some of the shortcomings of Braverman's work by providing a more sophisticated version of **labour process theory**. He suggested that management systems were more nuanced than the notion of the strict one-way, top-down direction Braverman had put forth. Edwards argued that three types of managerial control had developed over time: simple, technical, and bureaucratic. The first control system, simple management, referred to the straightforward direction foremen, supervisors, or bosses used to direct and discipline workers. Under this form of control, workers sometimes complained of managerial abuses of power and, feeling personally maligned, they would direct their hostility and resentment toward the supervisor most responsible for overseeing them.

Under technical control, management was depersonalized to a degree. The method and pace of work was built into the machinery, as for example, in the speed of the assembly line. With technical control, workers maintained a modicum of control in that there was an opportunity for them to "throw a wrench into the works" by staging work stoppages. Finally, bureaucratic control extracted obedience to the rules and regulations of the workplace at the level of the firm. This form of control drew upon Weber's notion of bureaucracy whereby elaborate sets of rules and procedures were in place, driving production forward, with little access to those standing at the helm. Bureaucratic forms of control are subtle, leaving workers with few answers to questions about "who's in charge" as all employees—line workers, office staff, professionals, administrators—adopt an upward gaze, as they search for understanding about the corporate machine. Bureaucratic systems are self-disciplining; workers acquire an understanding of the normative rules and expectations within a corporate structure along with the behaviours required of them, and then carry this understanding from one corporate setting to another. The key here is to offer workers decent pay, job security, and the possibility of promotions, thereby creating conditions whereby workers identify with the firm and its interests, rather than with the interests of their own social class.

Compartmentalization, Fragmentation, and Robotization

Henry Ford, a contemporary of Frederick Taylor, fully understood the importance of managerial control in increasing efficiency within the production process in order to maximize profits. Ford preferred to hire inexperienced machine operators who would be closely supervised by his enormous staff of overseers who were authorized to fire at will any operative who did not follow orders. Ford's emphasis on supervision, control, and discipline provides evidence that workers did not willingly accept the pace of the machine nor were they agreeable to undertaking work as deskilled machine tenders. Rather, they had to be managed—coerced, disciplined, and supervised—to surrender to the pace of production and the new work relationships that the assembly line entailed.

The development of the assembly line together with an elaborate system of supervision and control, and workers dependent on an employment agreement for their livelihood, set the stage for capitalists to expand their capital and realize enormous profits. The capitalists' interest in expanding their capital sets the labour process in motion. By employing workers who are required to work under managements' rules and conditions, and at a pace determined through the machinery, workers produce **surplus value** for their employers. When capitalists require that workers are strictly supervised and that they continue to work at a pre-determined pace, they profit by ensuring that the time workers take to reproduce the costs of their wages is minimized while the time their work contributes to profit maximization expands. Ford and other capitalists of the day understood the adaptability of human labour and sought ways in which to realize this potential most efficiently.

At his Highland Park Plant in Michigan, Ford set production in motion with the development of the moving assembly line for the infamous "Model T," causing production to soar and the size of the labour force to mushroom. Auto assembly by means of a moving line whereby each worker stood at an assigned point to carry out one specialized task was first introduced for the flywheel, then the engine, and finally in the fall of 1913, the chassis and entire car were assembled on the line. With this process, output soared (Meyer, 1981: 2). In 1903, 125 workers at Highland Park produced 1,700 cars. Five years later, in 1908, a work force of 450 assembled 10,607 Model T's, representing a 9.4 per cent market share. With a fully operational assembly line, in 1914, 12,880 workers produced 248,307 cars, representing a 48 per cent share of the market. Production continued to skyrocket with 32,679 workers making 933,720 cars in 1921. According to historian Alfred Chandler (1977: 280), the labour time involved in making a Model T fell from 12 hours, 8 minutes to 2 hours,

35 minutes. By the spring of 1914, 1,000 cars a day rolled off the lines and the labour time per car plummeted further to 1 hour, 33 minutes. Meanwhile, Ford's net income grew from $3 million in 1909 to $25 million in 1914 and $78 million in 1921 (Meyer, 1981: 2).

Training workers to commit to the relentless pace of the assembly line and to the seemingly endless repetitive movements in robot-like fashion was a challenge.[6] The turnover rate was very high. In 1913, to maintain a target workforce of 14,000, Ford hired 52,000 workers (Worstall, 2012). With the high turnover rate, there were costs related to hiring and training, to adjusting new workers to the pace of the line, to lower levels of production, and to delays as a result of workers vacating their posts. Recognizing that the costs of the turnover were staggering, Ford came up with an irresistible enticement—the $5-a-day wage, more than double the average wage in industry at the time (Cwiek, 2014). Not only did the $5-a-day plan work to reverse the turnover problem as well as curb the absenteeism rate, as Ford workers regarded themselves as privileged compared to operatives at other production facilities, but it also provided them with the means to engage in the burgeoning world of consumerism (Shaiken, 1985). And Ford's profits doubled in less than two years, making it Ford's number one cost-cutting measure (Cwiek, 2014).

Ultimately, the $5-a-day plan, described as "the best investment" Ford ever made (Baritz, 1960: 33), was a measure of control. The five dollars included roughly an equal split between wages and profits (Meyer, 1981). All workers received $2.50 in wages, but the $2.50 derived from profits was "earned" only when workers both on the job and at home met the standards established by the company, including efficiency and obedience on the job and a clean-living home life. Absenteeism dropped from 10 per cent to 0.5 per cent between 1913 and 1915 (Baritz, 1960: 33) According to Ford, the move to adopt a $5-a-day wage was "neither charity nor wages, but profit sharing and efficiency engineering" (cited in Baritz, 1960: 33).

Interestingly, Ford's "Sociology Department" was the body responsible for overseeing the workers' loyalty to the company and ensuring that they did not engage in "objectionable behaviour," such as excessive drinking or extra-marital sexual activities, and that wives kept a clean and tidy home and did not take in boarders. Ford "enforced and recognized" the value of "thrift and good service and sobriety" (*New York Times*, 1914). The demands on immigrant workers went further, with expectations that immigrants attend English and citizenship classes, and adopt "American" standards of living, including customs, morals, values, and work habits. Clearly, Ford's legacy was as much the result of his recognition of the importance of accounting for workers' behaviour as it was for the use of electrical power in an industrial process, the moving assembly line, the routinized and repetitive work, the specialized tasks, and the resultant mass consumption of the Model T. By "investing" in the social aspects of work, Ford improved upon the efficiency ideals embedded within scientific management and contributed to managerial thinking and the importance of maintaining control.

Flexibility and Lean Production: Extending Rationalized Processes

The emphasis on efficiency and control over production processes was firmly established in the early decades of the twentieth century. Corporate leaders understood the importance to their profit lines of keeping their labour forces in check, of robbing workers of the opportunity to engage in shop-floor production-related decisions and to acquire or enhance their skills, and of the need for flexibility and an interchangeable work force. By mid-century, corporations, businesses, workplaces, schools, and public sector institutions had undergone major transformations as they embraced a new **rationality** as the means of social organization. Just after the turn of the century, Max Weber (1968) warned that a modern form of rationality was beginning to dominate social relationships within the industrialized world. The formality of the workplace and the focus on competitiveness, profits, and markets functioned to tie workers to unrelenting processes of production with little regard for humanity and workers' welfare. Weber was concerned that the increasing **rationalization of society** would entrap humanity in an "iron cage" of rules, formality, and external control, leaving them little room for imagination, creative endeavours, and meaningful social relationships. While Weber (1958) wrote about the connection between capitalism and rationality, he was convinced that religion was the key because he observed that capitalism flourished in Protestant countries where hard work, thrift, efficiency, and worldly success were thought to form the path to salvation.

Karl Marx, who developed conflict theory, disagreed with Weber. He argued (1975) that religion was not the pivotal element fusing capitalism and rationality. Rather, for Marx, capitalism itself was the basis of rationalization. The goal of capitalism is profit making, and meeting this goal requires rationality and an emphasis on efficiency. Marx (1975) argued that the ethos of capitalism contributed to feelings of **alienation**, as the needs of workers were cast aside while the interests of capital and the pursuit of profit at any cost were primary. The approaches of both Taylor and Ford, along with others who followed their basic trains of thought, organized the shop floor and the production process by means of deskilling workers, overseeing them closely, determining the rates of production including the speed of the assembly line, and maintaining control over the workforce with help from an army of behavioural scientists, engineers, and specialists in the "new" field of business management. Together their goals extended the logic of capitalism and its quest for profits and growth in such ways that precluded workers' inputs and contributed to the meaninglessness of many forms of modern work. Fast forward to the post-war period and contemporary times; as described in Box 2.1 below, rationality, impersonality, and strict attention to precise rules and procedures guide most forms of work today, including the iconic fast food factories with their fixed set of practices and monotonous approach to serving meals.

Box 2.1 Everyday Work Experiences

Just because she's smiling doesn't mean she's having fun. . . .

Worldwide McDonald's 1.9 million workers serve about 68 million people daily from over 35,000 outlets located in 119 different countries. It is the largest chain of hamburger fast food restaurants globally. Behind Walmart, McDonald's is the world's second largest private employer. Boasting profits in the billions annually, we have to ask how this gargantuan enterprise flourished and grew.

While economists and business savvy experts may point to McDonald's business plan, goals for global expansion, and wide-ranging appeal to children and adults as key to the corporation's bottom line, critical sociologists would highlight the firm's penchant for standardized operations, cost cutting measures, and Taylorized labour process as central to its success. According to sociologist George Ritzer (2011), McDonald's winning formula is so pervasive that McDonaldization—the rationalization of routine tasks and organizational processes—has had a profound impact on work and labour processes across industries and cultures. A few years after Richard and Maurice McDonald opened their hamburger restaurant in 1940, they adopted the "speedy service system" designed by the White Castle restaurant chain, promising fast and affordable meals with efficient service. By the time Ray Kroc, credited as the founder of the modern-day McDonald's, took over in 1955 the template for the modern fast food restaurant was already in place. Kroc, however, took it much further, creating a fast food factory within each store with a line of grillers and servers working with precision and speed as specified in the manual of operation.

Adopting principles developed by Frederick Taylor and Henry Ford, Ray Kroc sped up the "speedy service system" by undertaking time and motion studies and then providing workers with precise instructions on grilling and dressing hamburgers, frying potatoes, pouring drinks, preparing "shakes" and scripting counter service. Workers are conditioned to attend to the bells and whistles of the fryers and other equipment, while putting aside their own preferences and ideas about how to prepare meals and interact with customers. Even the young server's wide smile and final words, "have a nice day" and "come again" are not impromptu remarks, but rather are the mandated response to a completed deal.

With standardized procedures and scripted interactions, the customer's experience of McDonald's and other similarly organized corporations, varies little from culture to culture—a feature appreciated by the less venturous traveller but abhorred by those looking for new and unique cultural experiences. With the exception of a few culturally distinctive alterations in the menu items offered, the "look," the activity, the scripted counter service, and the food preparation routine provide few surprises, including the way work is organized. The proverbial "McJob" became a universal phenomenon. And the age of meaningless work was born.

Lean Production and Efficiency Engineering

Employers, along with their Departments of Human Relations, worked to maintain peaceful work environments despite workers' objections to the deskilled and monotonous work offered on the assembly line. Over the course of the twentieth century, for many, work had become dissatisfying as craftsmanship was lost and workers' input into the labour process was diminished. As we discuss in Chapter 3, advances in technology provided management with new forms of supervision and methods of control as assembly became more refined and the flow of work moved further from the workers' grasp. As Huws (2003; 2013; 2014) argues, advanced technologies have not only affected workers' skills and the division of labour, but they have also had a profound impact on workers' sense of security as processes are easily outsourced or moved off shore.

Together the rationalization of the labour process and the use of advanced technologies are critical to management's need to assert and maintain control over workers' actions and reactions within production processes. Along with the focus on keeping their labour force in line, creating a smooth workflow was also an essential component of efficiency engineering. Techniques developed by the Japanese in the post-war era to improve organizational efficiency are **just-in-time** strategies, **lean production**, and **flexibilization**. Just-in-time strategies eliminate the need for huge parts warehouses or on-site storage spaces and large workstations. Parts are delivered to the line as needed and workers can rotate amongst various jobs, helping to eliminate some of the monotony that comes with traditional **Fordist** structures. Lean production techniques eliminate unnecessary steps and massive supply inventories, but ultimately, these strategies also limit workforces. Under lean production, work is standardized and workers are trained to work as members of flexible teams. Each station within the production process is evaluated regularly in order to eliminate any "fat," a process known as ***kaizen***, or continuous improvement. The auto industry, including General Motors and Toyota, employs lean production to reduce its labour force and minimize inefficiency (Rinehart, 2006). In some operations workers have been called upon to provide advice on lean production strategies for their lines, and this advice eventually resulted in layoffs and intensified working conditions, changes that were challenged by workers through strikes and protests (Rinehart, Huxley, and Robertson, 1997).

Conclusion

A major theme of the literature on work and the labour process relates to questions of efficiency and control. With profits and expansion as capitalists' proverbial "bottom lines," early industrialists searched for more efficient ways to organize work and labour processes. They focused on whittling down expenses in production not only through materials selections and mechanical or technical adjustments within production processes, but more importantly, through supervision and control over workers' movements, skill, and the pace of work. Early in the twentieth century, management was strict and visible, with armies of front-line managers, supervisors, and foremen charged with maintaining a firm grip on workers' output and behaviour on the shop floor. Later, management's presence was less evident but no less effective as forms of control were embedded in product design and workers had become accustomed to deskilled labour processes and management's expectations. While ideas and techniques of Taylor, Ford, and their contemporaries may seem somewhat out-dated today, their views on productivity, efficiency, and organizing and monitoring work are so well integrated into today's operations and systems of control that they are taken for granted and imperceptible. From the fast food industry to modern factory systems to administrative procedures and public services, management systems' bottom line is efficiency—removing excesses. The techniques established during the last century are central to this goal.

In the next chapter we examine the impact of technologies on the organization and management of work and labour processes. We will consider how the introduction and use of technologies extends the quest for production efficiency and corporate profitability. Information technologies have established new standards and a consistent pace of work within industries and across the globe.

Questions for Critical Thought

1. What impact have Taylor's ideas had on today's labour process?
2. Why did Henry Ford institute the $5-a-day plan? Was it an effective strategy for success in Ford's plants?
3. How does the focus on efficiency affect labour processes and expectations of workers in modern factories and services?

Suggested Further Resources

Rinehart, James W. 2006. *The Tyranny of Work: Alienation and the Labour Process*, 5th Edition. Toronto: Nelson. This book examines the roots of alienated labour as developing from the workplace structures and processes.

Ritzer, George F. 2012. *The McDonaldization of Society*, 7th Edition. Thousand Oaks, CA: Sage Publications. In this book, Ritzer develops his theory of rationalization of society, based on the processes of the fast food restaurant.

Suggested Websites

International Labour Process Conference
www.ilpc.org.uk
In response to Harry Braverman's *Labor and Monopoly Capital*, a group of scholars developed an annual conference dedicated to the study of labour processes and labour process theory.

The first conference was held in 1983 and continues to be one of the most popular and important venues for scholarly discussion on work and labour processes.

What Is McDonaldization?
www.mcdonaldization.com/whatisit.shtml
This website provides background and discussion on the process of McDonaldization, as coined by George Ritzer.

Notes

1. The close personal relationship established between employers and employees under pre-capitalism was not necessarily ideal. While some relationships were characterized by mutual respect, others were highly exploitative, mirroring the negative characteristics usually associated with the boss-slave relationships in the southern US under slavery.
2. Due to the uneven development of business and industry across various sectors of the economy and across the country, the phases of development overlap considerably. The presentation here is based on central tendencies within the process as a whole.
3. Tables 2.2 and 2.3 summarize the authors' interpretation of the development of management and the work relationship based on extensive analysis of books, training materials, management guides, and magazine articles of the time. They are also based on an analysis of textbooks and guides adopted in university business programs in Canada (Pupo, 1984).
4. The terms, Simple and Systematic Management are the author's. These terms were adapted from a similar conceptual scheme presented by Edwards (1979).
5. For biographical information on Frederick W. Taylor, see Copley (1923).
6. The difficult task of pacing workers to the speed of the assembly line was captured by Charlie Chaplin in the iconic film, *Modern Times*, released in 1936.

3 Technological Transformations, Conflict, and Control

Learning Objectives

- To trace the significance of the moving assembly line and standardization of work
- To understand the relationship between Fordism, advances in technology, and global production
- To identify the significance of the global commodity chain and work across place, time, and space
- To consider ICTs and the impact on women's work in the office
- To study the impact of robotization and electronic work on work time and the pace of work
- To understand the labour process within call centres
- To consider the disturbing side of technology

Introduction

In the early twentieth century the introduction of the assembly line in the modern factory had tremendous impact on the flow of work and operation of the enterprise. Through the assembly line, management firmly grasped control of the production process. The assembly line allowed management to control the speed and sequence of work as well as to identify shortcomings within the workforce and pitfalls within the system. From their vantage points perched above the moving lines, managers were able to determine optimum line speeds along with the timing for parts to be supplied to work stations. They also observed the assemblers and dispatched an army of supervisors and overseers to discipline workers when necessary in order to keep production flow running smoothly on the shop floor. The assembly line guaranteed an efficiency never known before. By producing 9,000 Model T's a day by 1925, Ford's Highland Park Plant in Michigan significantly altered patterns of consumption and ultimately lifestyles within working-class communities. But beyond the notable contribution to consumer culture and the growing obsession with ownership of automobiles and hundreds of everyday goods, it is the revolution in the organization of production and the consequent impact on the labour process and work relations that deeply transformed workers' lives globally. Today, at the now abandoned site of the Highland Park Plant is a plaque that reads: "Mass production soon moved from here to all phases of American industry, and set a pattern of abundance for 20th century living" (Cwiek, 2014).

Starting with the assembly line and earlier attempts to mechanize production, here we discuss the different ways in which technological innovations transform work processes and work relations. In this chapter we discuss technology as embedded in labour processes from Fordism and the assembly line to the call centre and the fully automated factory. How has the introduction of new technologies contributed to the organization and management of work, and what role has technology played in facilitating production in the global economy? Does technology ease the conditions of work, or have work-related demands escalated with the explosion of new technologies? We also discuss the difficult conditions of work endured by miners and production workers engaged in the industries producing computers and other digital equipment.

Fordism and the Assembly Line

In Chapter 2 we considered Taylorism and the impact of scientific management on production processes and workers' skills. With his moving assembly line, Henry Ford drew from Taylor's principles to create the "modern" factory of the early twentieth century. Prior to the innovation of the moving assembly line, workers would assemble the cars' chassis that were perched atop wooden sawhorses. Each worker was highly skilled and was capable of adding a number of parts to the finished product. The product was increasingly in high demand, and producing cars more quickly and efficiently meant greater returns for the company. Studying the auto assembly process, engineers soon realized that they needed to focus on the methods of production, along with the mechanical aspects of the automobiles, in order to increase productivity and thereby meet the growing demand.

The first step was to ensure that individual parts were interchangeable and that any part would easily fit any car without need for individualized fittings and adjustments. Not only would this save time, but it also meant that the company could hire more unskilled workers[1] at lower rates of pay. The next step was to place the assembly process on a moving conveyor belt. This invention allowed management to better control the pace of the assembly while also keeping workers at a single, fixed station. In turn, this enabled supervisors to keep watch more easily over each assembler. With the parts moving along an assembly line, each assembler was assigned a specific task rather than being responsible for a number of tasks. The work was subdivided among different workers, with each worker assigned to a small number of standardized and repetitious movements. As a result, the length of time to produce items dropped dramatically. The production of a car, for example, fell from hours to minutes, thereby meeting the company's targeted production goals for a mass consumer market.

Over the years, what started as a rudimentary process of moving parts through assembly more quickly led to notable achievements in efficiency engineering.

In the following decades, three interrelated processes—standardization, **compartmentalization**, and **fragmentation**—allowed for smoothly functioning assembly operations that facilitated cost savings and production efficiencies. For workers to attach parts or to put together individual parts ready to be inserted into the main assembly, it was necessary to standardize components. This allowed for any product's individual parts to be manufactured according to specification at various locations, thereby allowing the company to search for the most suitable location to produce parts, taking into account the cost, availability, and skill of the labour force as well as transportation costs to the main assembly plant. Parts requiring advanced skills may be manufactured in locations with an ample supply of highly skilled workers, and those requiring fewer skills may be assembled where the labour force has a lower skill level. This process gives rise to the global assembly line.

For many workers, advances in technology have reduced their work to a series of robotized movements. Spending years on the job often means being physically incapable of switching positions as workers' bodies become accustomed to a particular set of movements and they experience pain and discomfort moving on to a new set of tasks. Over time, advances in technologies have supported the **robotization** of many production processes, reducing the need for large numbers of workers and therefore the number of "good" jobs available in the labour market. Robots also reduce costs while matching or exceeding human productivity[2] (Grant, 2015). In a walk through a contemporary manufacturing operation, whether it is assembling autos or producing auto parts, kitchen appliances, or even processing and packaging foods, one may readily observe how sparsely populated many factories have become. Beyond manufacturing, automated assessment software—artificial intelligence that is designed to grade essays and short written assignments—may replace teaching assistants or free professors' time for research or to carry higher teaching loads (Markoff, 2013). In law offices, artificial intelligence has been designed to conduct legal research, completing assignments in seconds as opposed to the hours a human practitioner would require,[3] while medical applications are programmed to sort through billions of pages of data in seconds for doctors and veterinarians (Gray, 2014a).

In a variety of ways, we can trace technology's role in the globalization of production processes from the simple beginnings of the moving assembly line and the assignment of workers to particular workstations. From complex commodities requiring the assembly of hundreds of pieces, such as a car, to items involving only a few pieces such as a blouse or pair of jeans, to the assembly of simple household gadgets such as a manual can opener, the standardization and fragmentation of the production process gave employers free rein over where a product's assembly may be located, whether it would be in various locations across the country or across the globe. Each part would be sourced at its lowest cost and then shipped to central assembly plants or shipped to secondary plants building components and then on to a central assembly plant that may be closer to the point of consumption. The result of this configuration of production is the compartmentalization experienced by many workers who do not see, or in some cases, even have access to, the final products of their labour.

Looking well beyond the assembly line and features associated with Fordism, advances in technology have continued to play major roles in the globalization of production processes. Improvements in transportation systems, the logistics industry, the spread of new communication media, advances in the complex science of computer and software engineering, and the explosion in information technologies have all combined to facilitate the flow of goods, services, and information. These improvements have also eased the work of coordinating complex global networks and facilitating sales, trades, and exchanges across the globe. In other words, large transnational corporations have developed complex networks allowing them to shift production overseas and to operate simultaneously in several markets. These processes have affected workers and their environments, cultures, ways of life, and communities in myriad ways. It is not uncommon for workers in the Global South to be involved in producing items that they will never afford. With corporations' interest in cost savings and profits, moving production overseas has had a deep impact on what was once a robust manufacturing sector within Canada.

As we discussed in Chapter 1, the manufacturing sector in Canada has decreased in size considerably since its heyday in the post-war period. For Canadian workers this has meant the loss of "good jobs," especially for men who had traditionally occupied the lion's share of jobs in this sector. Together automation, robotization, and the introduction of new technologies alone do not account for the movement of manufacturing processes overseas. Along with the development of more sophisticated transportation and communication networks and the logistics industry, transnational corporations moved many of their operations to low-wage areas, gaining entry through open trade agreements and liberal import-export policies. The heaviest impact of these processes has been on men who had traditionally dominated in the heavy manufacturing sector in the steel, auto, and major appliance industries, all of which boasted relatively good wages, benefits, security, and a high rate of unionization. These processes, in turn, have affected women's labour market positions, household income, security, and family dynamics.

Redefining Capitalism and the Global Economy: Technology and the Development of a Transnational Labour Force

Technological breakthroughs, along with a number of other processes, have facilitated globalization, lean production, and an accelerated pace of work. For many, the growing intensity of work is regarded as a trade-off for the elimination of the drudgery and monotony that characterized many forms of work on the assembly line. At the same time, technological advances have contributed to the homogenizing of work, placing workers on a trajectory of deskilling and degradation. For the consumer, many everyday products include the stamp of many nations as well as the skills and labour of a number of different workforces. Cars purchased in Canada, for example, not only reflect the work of the Canadian autoworker who earns relatively good wages and enjoys benefits including extended health care and dental coverage, pensions, and union protection, but also include parts made by workers labouring under circumstances that are far less appealing and who may lack access to health and safety precautions or must endure forced overtime and poor or no benefits. For consumers it is very difficult, if not impossible, to trace the origins of items in their shopping carts, including groceries, because many items have multiple origins and some may not be labelled clearly.

On the individual level of consumption, advanced communication technologies set in motion the production process through sales desks. When a sales associate is serving a customer at the point of sale, scanning items for the purchase, s/he may be unwittingly connecting with manufacturers abroad, feeding information to their inventory databases to indicate precisely what has been sold. When we order a new car or buy a new sweater, our purchases are tracked. This allows corporate analysts and buyers to follow trends in consumer tastes and maintain accurate inventories while also enabling factories to adjust their manufacturing schedules almost instantaneously.

Global Commodity Chains

Retailers' shelves are stocked with products that represent global **commodity chains** (or global **value chains**), the complex webs of supply, production, and distribution networks that link raw materials and supplies, the assembly of parts, processing and packaging, warehousing, transportation, and distribution networks to the placement on store shelves and the final point of sale (Bonacich and Wilson, 2008). Not only do these intricate webs span the globe, but they also represent various forms of work and labour processes, with dozens of variations in working conditions, labour standards, protections, and labour rights for workers.

Global commodity chains are characterized by three main dimensions (Gereffi, 1994; Gereffi and Fernandez-Stark, 2011): (1) a value dimension in which the structures in the chain add value to the commodity, (2) a territorial dimension indicating the global reach of the chain, and (3) and a governance dimension representing the power relations and direction of authority and decision-making among the links in the chain. Value chains may be driven primarily by producers or by buyers. Fifty years ago under "push" production, manufacturers held sway, deciding on commodities and production levels with the expectation that retailers would sell what they produced. In today's global economy, there is a tendency for the retail sector—headed by mega-corporations like Walmart—to set the process of "pull" production in motion, dictating to the manufacturers what to produce, how much to produce, and at what cost (Bonacich, cited in Pupo, 2011; Appelbaum and Lichenstein, 2007). With retailers in charge, bargaining with producers for the lowest possible prices, the production workers' wages are of primary consideration in keeping prices low. In this process, wages and working conditions in manufacturing industries move closer to those in the service sector. To achieve this price bargain, manufacturers search the world over for low-wage areas in which to produce their goods. This process has contributed to a downward spiralling of manufacturing in Canada as production has been moved offshore to poor countries within the global economy where workers earn a fraction of the wages (cents, rather than dollars, per hour) compared to workers in Canada and other advanced economies.

The nature of work within the now-dominant retail sector is rapidly changing. While formerly work in the retail sector mainly involved face-to-face interactions between sales personnel and customers, "new" retail work also involves work in massive warehouses across the country as well as within the logistics industry. There are two trends fuelling this development and changing the retail landscape: online shopping and the growth of retail giants and big-box stores. In Canada between 2006 and 2011, the number of power centres grew by 8 per cent and the number of big box stores grew by 19.9 per cent (Industry Canada, 2013: 6). Between 2007 and 2010, the number of orders Canadians placed online increased from 70 million to 113.1 million per year, with an average value per person at $1,362 in 2010 (Industry Canada, 2013: 9). Behind our shopping sprees—online or at a nearby big box store—are countless dock and warehouse workers whose duties revolve around the distribution of goods and include loading and unloading trailers, storing and sorting goods, and engaging in logistic services like transporting bulk goods, filling orders, packaging, labelling, and shipping. A massive chain of activity in the transportation and communication sector supports retail giants like Amazon, Walmart, Lowe's, Costco, and Home Depot, among others.

Behind the scenes in the retail sector the character of the work in distribution mirrors work processes in the manufacturing sector more closely than work within the traditional retail outlet. High tech warehouses, such as Amazon, use digital programs and processes that catalogue, sort, and store thousands of items ready for workers to assemble for shipment to consumers. While traditional manufacturing operated with a moving assembly line, bringing parts to workers who assembled them from a stationary workstation, assembling orders in a warehouse requires that workers move through the warehouse pulling carts in which they place the items for the orders they will package and send on. The sheer size of the warehouses, the number of items they store, the size of the orders to be filled, and management's expectations for speed and efficiency create highly stressful, fast-paced working conditions.

The work is difficult, often dangerous, and dirty (McCluskey et al., 2013). The work also carries a degree of insecurity. A survey of warehouse workers in the US indicated that many may be described as "permatemps." Permatemps are workers who are hired as temporary workers but whose status is not converted to permanent despite working in the industry for a number of years (McCluskey et al., 2013: 12). These workers are often members of racial or ethnic minorities and their "permatemp" status leaves them in a very precarious position, unable to request wage hikes, report injuries, or lodge complaints of any kind without fear of reprisal (McCluskey et al., 2013: 12).

Advances in transformation, communications, logistics, and information networks have played a key role in assisting buyers to assume a position of dominance over manufacturers. Information systems that track trends in the marketplace, along with detailed consumption patterns, are central features of this process. In turn, the logistics industry—shipping, trucking, warehousing—assures retail managers of a seamless process with timely movement of products, just-in-time deliveries, and accurate inventories without their having to employ clerks at individual outlets to take stock and forecast sales.

Working across Space, Time, and Place

Within the context of global production, the dimensions of space, time, and place are critical portals through which employers and workers connect with one another and attach themselves to the global economy. The ability to assign material production to a specific physical location or to a number of interconnected spatial locations is a strategic corporate decision, often related to potential cost savings, the supply of labour, the availability of supplies, and transportation routes. Increasingly, employers have organized production to occur across space rather than in a number of specific places. The placelessness of production—achieved through the information and communication technology (ICT) infrastructure, the reorganization of production across numerous locations, and the regulation of economic activities through various nation states—characterizes much of the contemporary global economy. Unlike place, space is elusive, often making it difficult for workers to identify with a fixed "workplace" as it may be in constant flux.

The use of communication and information technologies and related practices has changed the ways work is organized, monitored, and regulated. In 2008, almost one in five employed Canadians worked from home, including just over 11 per cent of employees and about 60 per cent of those who were self-employed (Turcotte, 2010: 3). Advances in technology potentially enable employees to work at home or in distributed work environments and this may increase autonomy to some extent, but it may also invoke corporate control measures and monitoring practices. Workers may have some say over their particular work hours, when they take breaks and for how long, and the physical space they occupy while working. With such arrangements, workers may more easily accommodate childcare and other familial responsibilities by freeing their time to visit their children's schools, taxi children and seniors to appointments and activities, and attend to household chores. Yet those who work from home report that they are dissatisfied with their work–life balance more often than those who never work from home (Turcotte, 2010: 10). Those who work from home may engage in multitasking, starting the evening meal or doing loads of laundry while connected to their virtual office. At the same time, these workers may be under the constant strain of an invisible management monitoring their activity from afar and holding unrealistic expectations for output and productivity.

Virtual workplaces are defined neither by the physical premises that they occupy nor by formal contractual relationships. New forms of distributed work are carried out across company and national boundaries, often over large distances in workspaces that may not resemble the physical location and culture within which the workers are situated or the context surrounding the seat of corporate power. These work forms demand that employees constantly reorient themselves to new situations, colleagues, work cultures, and problems. This reorientation process often takes place outside of familiar national contexts in different types of spaces within the virtual workplace. Although spatial proximity is regarded as crucial for specific types of work due to the need for tacit, social knowledge embedded in local resources, there is a growing spatial dispersion, or at least, a *potential* for dispersion of work. This presents quite a conundrum. As local communities make a plea for locally sourced products and hands-on services, there exists the possibility that work may be moved further afield in both manufacturing and service sectors.

Outsourcing work to developing economies, for example in business process outsourcing, raises issues regarding how workers acquire skills and knowledge in increasingly complex systems requiring more intensive use of information and communication technology (ICT). Advanced technologies require more highly skilled labour forces, yet the training processes and practices, including the knowledge bases, originate in close proximity to the corporate headquarters. Moreover, with increasing polarization between low and highly skilled workers within local labour markets, earnings gaps widen and local identities are affected. There is evidence that while pay gaps between more highly skilled and less skilled jobs have risen, wage dispersion has occurred within as well as across occupational groups. In some localities, the social demand for education and training has outstripped the economic demand for skills and, as a consequence, there are a growing number of over-qualified, under-employed workers particularly within urban areas.

With e-work, new forms of employment in call and contact centres and a burgeoning range of business services are emerging in the service sectors, particularly within South and Southeast Asia, paralleling the established practice of virtual work in Canada, the United States, and the European Union. While it is important to understand the technological innovations and the transformations within localities that these developments require, it is essential to acknowledge the social transformations and the scope of change within communities and between social groups that these changes entail. Transnational workplaces, with multinational and multi-cultural workforces, are shaped by ethnic, linguistic, gender, citizenship, and other axes of identity and give rise to new inequalities, new relations of production and reproduction, new community relations, and new household and family forms and practices.

Work in a Wired World

Over the past several decades there has been considerable interest in the extensive use of computer-based technologies in the office and throughout the service sector. What remains at question is whether these technologies have ultimately improved or deteriorated the lot of white-collar workers. Following the surge in use of computers at work in the 1980s, researchers' concerns focused on the deterioration of work and working conditions, fuelling the "good jobs/bad jobs" debate. Early research on technology at work focused on industrial and manufacturing settings. As a result, it centred mainly on male workers. When attention turned to the office environment and ICTs, the plight of women and racialized workers came into sharper focus. From this perspective, while a few workers through ability, skill, savvy, and luck achieve well-paid permanent core positions, the majority of workers compete with one another for short-term, insecure, or fee-for-service work that is poorly compensated. Braverman (1975/2000) and others associated this "negative paradigm" with deskilling, blocked occupational mobility, polarization of jobs, computer-based monitoring and pacing of work, and an extensive division of labour with its associated graded pay scales and structured work tasks. Within this negative scenario, some suggested that women workers would be particularly vulnerable in the wired workplace as they faced decreased employment opportunities with the elimination of receptionists and other positions, anachronistic job skills, including typing, filing, and secretarial duties, and work that is deskilled (Menzies, 1981; Burris, 1989). Analysts (Scott-Dixon, 2004) also concluded that information technology had little impact on pay or on inequalities with respect to gender, race, ability, and class and that increasingly women would be resigned to deskilled, part-time, casual employment in the service sector. Countering this negative scenario, some analysts adopted a more optimistic interpretation suggesting that the new work order with its prominent pattern of self-employment would allow workers usually relegated to the periphery greater personal autonomy and economic independence because information technology is "neutral." Embedded in this debate is the central concern of whether the wired workplace brought "good" jobs or "bad" jobs.

The relationship of the worker to technologies in the office (both interactive and static) is complex. It evokes old-school notions of the "front office"—the company's "face" to the world, creating either an inviting environment or a cold and unfriendly atmosphere. It is also nuanced, whereby certain aspects of the setting may be highly interactive, whereas others may be set behind a technological front, prompting customers to choose from a seemingly endless list of items in a number of menus in order to "get through" and receive service. Interactive voice response systems or automated attendants have replaced reception and secretarial duties in the front office by directing calls to various departments or to individuals' voice mail. Bell Canada's infamous "Emily," first tested in Ontario in 2002, is the interactive receptionist, a voice recognition system that directs calls by asking customers how "she" can help. "Emily's" soft, calm "voice" and intonation, along with the list of choices offered to callers, mimic real human exchanges. Not only do these systems prove to be cost effective, replacing front office workers who seek pay raises and benefits and require time off, but they also keep callers at bay, away from the executives' phone lines in much the same way that executive secretaries in the past screened visitors and callers for their bosses.

How did workers respond and adapt to the application of technologies in the office? Some analysts adopt a mechanistic model of the relation between workers and technology in which management introduces technological changes and workers' role is reactive as they are forced to confront the consequences, including routinization, deskilling, and ghettoization (Garson, 1989). This perspective paints workers as devoid of agency, with technology dictating certain inevitable and usually negative consequences. In contrast, new work technologies may involve a complex process of formal (or overt) and informal (or covert) negotiation between and amongst workers, employers, managers, and unions as well as worker innovation and resistance. Key here is the question of how the technologies are applied, which in turn, is dependent on the negotiations and relations among the various human elements. Factors such as the nature of the technology, management decisions, and orientations interact with the organizational context, human resource development, and worker ingenuity. Implications of ICT for workers may vary considerably from one work context to another and from one set of economic circumstances to the next.

Over 30 years ago amidst the rapid expansion of technological change in the office and the ICT revolution, Shoshana Zuboff (1988) proposed an interactive, dynamic, and process-focused framework, challenging the negative mechanistic paradigm of technological change. Zuboff argued that the impact of information technology is not fixed and the technology is capable of good jobs that are more consistent with the craft model. Zuboff began her exposition on the "future of work and power" by defining what she meant by technology. For Zuboff (1988: 22), "technology represents intelligence systematically applied to … amplify and surpass the organic limits of the body." She argued that with each progressive stage of technological change (1988: 419) "the amount of physical interaction with the production process is reduced" until workers in modern factories and offices "monitor video terminals that display data reflecting the state of the production process" or textual materials. Clearly, Zuboff acknowledged the possibility that workers may be deskilled if ICTs are used to turn the employee into "just another mechanical variable." However, she claimed that the prognosis was not unequivocally gloomy. She assured us that information technology has the potential to redirect the historical trajectory of automation because micro-processor-based technologies possess the "informating capacity" to lift knowledge entirely out of the body's domain by signalling "the transposition of work activities to the abstract domain of information." All work becomes the manipulation of symbols, and when this occurs, the nature of skills is redefined. According to Zuboff, the application of technology that preserves the body may no longer imply the destruction of knowledge on the factory floor or in the office. Instead it may signal the reconstruction of knowledge of a different sort.

As new technologies remove workers from physically engaging the processes of production, the opportunity for factory and office workers to acquire new knowledge grows. The basis for traditional, craft-like skills was tied to the build-up of knowledge gained from sentient exposure to the varying aspects of paid work. In an office or factory, the worker no longer interacts with the various pieces of equipment. Therefore, the worker does experience deskilling of his/her previous work. However, those "elements" of skill based on long-established sentient experience, whether acquired on the shop floor or in the office, and "most accessible to explication and therefore rationalization," have been "carved out" from these jobs and replaced by new requirements. Until the advent of information technology, "workers lost what was best in their jobs, the body was still in the service of acting-on, while executives lost what was worst in their jobs, retaining full enjoyment of the skilled body as an instrument of acting-with" (Zuboff, 1988: 108). New technology, then, promised to extend the redefinition of skills and the re-animation of work experience to the broad range of office workers.

Zuboff's examination of ICTs in new work environments and her explicit and careful exposition of what she calls "intellective skills" provide a less deterministic, more complex and interactive conception of technological change. Following Zuboff, a number of analysts (Kenney and Florida, 1993; Castells, 1996) also adopted an interactive, naturalistic model that is open to finding elements of both "good" and "bad" jobs in the modern workplace. These authors argue that the impact of information technology is not fixed and that the new technology is capable of generating both good and bad work depending on a variety of factors, including organizational culture, the level and nature of technological application, the process of computer introduction, and the ongoing participation or non-participation of trade unions.

Technology and Work Time

Various technologies may have made workers' jobs less onerous and more flexible, but at the same time certainly have contributed to shifts in the time structure of both paid and unpaid work (Schawbel, 2014). In a recent survey (Angus Reid Institute, 2015), the majority of Canadians polled reported that the Internet, cell phones, and email are "vital" or very important tools for doing their jobs but that having to check them regularly adds to their working day. Long hours at (paid) work-related activities impacts their unpaid work at home as well as their personal time for rest and relaxation. However, most of those polled regarded their use of technology as "overall positive" despite the impact on their working hours, and this sentiment was particularly strong among the "tech intense"—those who use the technologies the most for their jobs.

Canadians who most eagerly embrace the idea of using technological devices, checking and sending email or texts, and answering or making calls on their mobile phones outside of "work" hours report that the "cost" of increased flexibility is an increase in working time. Whether or not this bothers people depends on the type of work they do. Those with positions of greater power and autonomy who are salaried workers do not mind. They like to stay on top of their work and may worry that by avoiding the technologies while on personal time, they may miss important pieces of information or opportunities, or that the work will pile up, making things more difficult in the long run. They have accepted the notion of a fusion between work time and personal time. Those who are employed on an hourly basis have little hope of being reimbursed for their loss of personal time. There is no way to measure how much time is spent on work-related activity, and these workers feel robbed when employers make demands that infringe upon their personal time. These workers may try to avoid answering calls, texts, and emails about work-related matters. But at the same time they might worry about being too inaccessible to their employers and miss out on extra work, favourable reviews, and possible promotions.

Most workers surveyed regarding working time indicated that technology made it difficult to get away from work. Advances in communication technology have facilitated the invasion of the workplace into all facets of workers' lives. Cell phones, laptops, computer networks, BlackBerry devices, electronic organizers, and more to come all ensure that workers are never completely away from work. At the same time workers report feeling stressed, run off their feet, and having to juggle too many balls. Among Canadians reporting feeling highly stressed, 60 per cent identified work as being the most important source of stress (Crompton, 2011: 46). While we cannot conclude that technology contributes to these high levels of stress amongst workers, we should question whether workers are getting enough down time, away from work. We know that technology workers bring various aspects of their work home and have difficulty getting away. With technologies, managers enjoy the comfort of knowing that a replacement worker is only a phone call away. When a manager requires a fill-in for a worker who calls in or goes home sick or to help out during an unexpected rush of business, s/he may call another worker to start earlier or to work on a scheduled day off. This situation presents a dilemma for the worker who may have to choose between enjoying family/personal time and being regarded as a reliable employee. In a labour market characterized by precariousness, most workers have little option but to answer their phones and accept the extra shift.

The technology not only contributes to overwork, or an inability to get away, but it also gives rise to detailed work monitoring, as the technology facilitates both work intensity and work supervision. Many workplaces expect their workers to be available at all times of the day or night. Some analysts suggest that technologies have chained workers to their jobs, generating a white-collar sweatshop. In the midst of growing economic insecurities and intensified global competition, workers realize that questioning their working hours or shifts, or insisting on "real" vacations, may be unwise. There are two factors at play. First, high levels of unemployment and underemployment signal to workers that there may be dozens of job seekers with suitable qualifications for their positions. Second, advances in ICTs and their affordability make it possible for their jobs to be outsourced to lower-waged areas. The publishing industry in Canada, for example, outsources a great deal of its editorial work to editors in India and other areas. On a personal note, over the course of 12 years of co-writing an introductory sociology textbook, the past practice of assigning the authors a local copy editor has been largely eliminated and editors might now live thousands of miles away, often in the Global South. As a result, communication between authors and editors is not as smooth, given some cultural differences in language use and interpretation. Also the 12-to 24-hour difference in time makes it impossible to get an answer quickly, and this can sometimes result in delays of a day or more. Some workers interact through technological and communication processes that may be located in familiar surroundings within their homeland, but these workers find themselves adapting and connecting to "another world" during their work day. Some researchers suggest that in the context of the scarcity of good jobs, downsizing, and layoffs, time-demanding corporate cultures are thriving and are seen as an indicator of employees' commitment and loyalty to the organization.

Call Centres–The McJob of the Knowledge-Based Economy?

Today many jobs, especially in the expanding service sector, are characterized by tedious, highly controlled, highly monitored, and standardized work. These features are epitomized in the burgeoning field of call centre work—the quintessential McJob. Nearly all Canadians have had numerous interactions of different sorts with call centres. Some interactions have been voluntary and include calls to help lines for technical assistance for computers, electronics, or cable TV; to report a lost credit card; or to set up online banking. Some may have been made to federal, provincial, or municipal government offices to ask questions regarding benefits such as employment insurance or old age security, or to report a broken water main on the street. Other interactions may have been annoying unsolicited calls, often during the dinner hour, marketing credit cards, vacation time shares, or products or services for our homes—windows, doors, furnace cleanings, or any number of items.

As a rule, call centres are open workspaces with individual workstations that include a computer and a telephone headset connected to an electronic switching system. Supervisors monitor the employees' output and oversee the workstations. The operation is set up to handle both **inbound** and **outbound** telephone calls. Inbound calls are those from customers who are seeking assistance or ordering something while outbound systems may be used for sales promotions ("telemarketers"), charity fundraising, or for collecting money from individuals with delinquent accounts. Firms may be set up to deal with both types of service or they may exclusively handle inbound or outbound calls. Most telephone orders are handled by call centre workers and not the manufacturers or suppliers of goods or services.

Over the past couple of decades, call centres have experienced phenomenal growth around the world. Fuelled by advances in information technology and the drop in the costs of data transmission, firms have found it cost effective to provide service and sales to customers through "remote technology mediated centres" (Holman, Batt, and Holtgrewe, 2007). In Canada, call centres' revenues grew by 27.7 per cent annually, on average, between 1998 and 2006 (Vincent and McKeown, 2008) but experienced a decline after 2006 as companies sent work offshore, particularly to India and the Philippines, which are both low-cost call centre locations (Silcoff, 2012). Between 2007 and 2011, jobs in Canada's call centres declined by 28 per cent—a loss of over 32,000 jobs (Bracey, 2013: 120). Recently, to offset high unemployment rates in some provinces as well as to address the low customer satisfaction ratings, some companies, including Sears Canada, Primus Telecommunications, and American Express have repatriated hundreds of call centre jobs (Silcoff, 2012).

Call centres operate in both public and private sectors. Those located in the private sector are largely engaged in marketing or in technical support. In Canada, in the public sector, call centres operate at federal, provincial, and municipal levels. Federally, call centres operate as Service Canada (1-800-0-Canada). There are provincial call centres for various ministries and e-health. Municipalities often make use of #311 or other such services. Regardless of whether the call centre handles inbound or outbound calls, or whether it is located in the private or public sector, working conditions for call centre workers are strikingly similar. Call centres in Canada are concentrated in the Maritimes and Ontario. Overall, this is an educated workforce where over half of the employees have completed some postsecondary education (Jaarsveld et al., 2007). Workers report difficulties dealing with customer/client behaviours (rudeness, sexist and racist remarks, nasty and violent comments); scripted materials; stressful, noisy work environments; close supervision; monitored performance; uncomfortable work spaces; repetitive work; and time pressures, including meeting daily quotas, the time allotted per call, and time between calls (Russell, 2009). As a result, there is high turnover within call centres (Bracey, 2013: 123).

Generally, there are two competing characterizations of call centre work that reoccur in the academic literature. The first is that call centres are high-tech, high-skilled work environments in an information economy. This position is fuelled by the tech help lines we call for assistance with computers and other electronics, as well as the public sector call centres that provide information on legislation, including Employment Insurance, Veterans' Affairs, income maintenance programs, pensions, and local services, and medical and health-related matters. While there certainly are differences in conditions and experiences of work within various types of call centres, many researchers' descriptions of call centre work as involving difficult and intense working conditions, physical relocations, and highly monitored client interchanges, tip the balance toward the negative in general conceptualizations of call centre work.[4] To naively suggest that the use of technologies simplifies labour processes, provides solutions to the management of vast amounts of data and resources, and enhances the capacity of work within organizational frameworks overlooks the central features of information and communication technologies and their associated labour processes. These technologically mediated labour processes are dehumanizing because they eliminate face-to-face contact and spontaneity, and they are deskilling when they limit workers from using their accumulated knowledge and experience to do their jobs. Most do not permit deviations from scripts or carefully specified activities. Telework increases the possibility of the relocation of work, thereby escalating workers' insecurity that their job may be offshored, and making the search for meaningful work even more elusive.

A central feature of call centres is standardization of service work. Interactions between clients or customers and service providers are regulated, often by means of scripts, and they are monitored for efficiency, speed, and accuracy. Many call centre workers characterize their work as repetitive, stressful, and tiring in the same way that assembly line workers have described working in a factory on a production line. In their study of public sector call centres, Pupo and Noack (2010) noted that survey respondents described their workplace as a "factory of voices" and as a "production line." This stands in direct contrast to the emotional persona that call centre workers are required to portray, as smiling and helpful service providers with an even-toned voice and manner. Not surprisingly, women tend to be overrepresented among call centre employees, accounting for approximately 69 per cent of customer support services (Jaarsveld et al., 2007). In part, this is because many service provision jobs tend to require feminized skills, such as interpersonal communications. This leads us to ask whether technology has at all enhanced women's position in the structure of inequality within work (Belt, Richardson, and Webster, 2000). Despite the hidden demands on call centre workers to multi task and use their skills, there are few opportunities for promotion due to flat organizational structures. Few employees have access to training that would allow them to be promoted to more senior positions. For the most part, workers are expected to learn on the job. Younger workers hopeful for promotions are forced into an endless cycle of job searches, only to find themselves in similar employment circumstances after several years' experience.

Call centre work—perhaps the form of work most symbolic of the globalized knowledge economy—requires workers to adhere to strict piece rate systems and is tightly controlled by managements. Although we often characterize call centre work as the McJob of the knowledge-based economy, some call centre work is highly skilled, and call centre workers in these jobs worry that the complexity and value of their work is not appreciated. For example, multilingual agents in call centres often use a complex set of skills and abilities to interact in one language and interface with a computer program in another language. Call centre workers in New Delhi or Bangalore, India for example, are expected to transform their own identities while at work by undertaking cultural training, adopting accents and diction to blend with that of their North American or European clients while masking their own real location and identities. These workers often find themselves having to think on their feet and respond quickly, carefully balancing their need to remain "on script" and the evaluation of their heavily monitored performances with the need for a courteous and respectful response to the client.

A key area of concern for call centre workers is the pace of work. Fewer than half of survey respondents in the federal call centres report that their work is manageable, and workers are generally not able to control the speed of incoming calls. Many say that they are unable to prepare adequately for their shifts or for the next call. Calls will often come in only two to three seconds apart, leaving workers not enough time to take a sip of water or take a deep breath. When receiving a call at home, the delayed response from the caller gives us enough time to hang up before the caller greets us. Not only does this contribute to the tension experienced by the workers who are trying to reach their quotas, but it also points to the "sweatshop" conditions and unreasonable pace of the work. For public sector call centre workers, this high-paced environment conflicts with their idea of providing good quality service to the tax-paying public (Pupo and Noack, 2010).

Call centre jobs are often associated with some physical discomfort. Workers are tied to their desks, unable to get up and walk around or to stretch for a few minutes. Workers frequently experience pain, headaches, and stiffness, and often report losing their voice as a result of their work. As in factory work, researchers have documented a series of health issues associated with working in a call centre. Workers experience bodily pain, carpal tunnel syndrome from keyboarding, auditory and vision problems, voice and throat conditions, and musculoskeletal issues related to the sedentary nature of the work. In some workplaces, the office environments are often characterized by poor lighting, cramped spaces, high noise levels, and poor quality air, and this works to exacerbate the stress and discomforts experienced by the workers. As described in Box 3.1, some workers are put off by their dirty work environment as well as by the dirty work they are asked to do.

Time management and statistical record keeping (workers' scores) contribute to an intensified work environment in which the work itself is devalued. Conflicts over quotas, the time allotted per call, and the quality and efficiency are constant sources of tension. Some workers resist the push by managers to shorten calls or to work at a faster pace, but others tend to rate-bust, creating an unhealthy competition amongst workers within a centre. The result of a pace controlled via technology and high levels of time accountability is a high stress work environment. The techniques of supervision and micro-management exacerbate the stresses of time pressures and the physical and mental demands of the job. Workers describe being monitored, timed, and responsible to their managers for every moment of the day.

Box 3.1 Everyday Work Experiences

The Tale of "Dirty" Clean Work

In their study of federal government call centre workers, Pupo and Noack (2010) found that the workers frequently characterized their work environment as dirty and some referred to their work as "dirty work in clean places." For many, one of the most appalling features of their work was that they were not assigned to a particular workstation. Upon arriving for their shifts, they were expected to set up in an available workstation, and for many that meant working in a different station or cubicle each shift. This made it difficult for workers to personalize their workspace with pictures of family members, a pillow for their back or a "touch" of home. Not only did this give employees a sense of impermanence or instability, but it increased the likelihood of germ transmission, as numerous employees would have to share a single headset or keyboard. Some employees compensated by purchasing their own equipment, effectively transferring the burden of maintaining a healthy workplace from the employer to the employees.

For many teleworkers, their workspace has been reduced to accommodate the computer screen with little room left for personal comfort and privacy. With dozens or even hundreds of workers plugged into their headsets within the same room, the noise is often overwhelming. Some compensate by wearing two headsets, but others describe their experience of wearing two headsets as "claustrophobic." One worker described the call centre where she worked as "a jail with sick pay." As workers focus on the caller, they do not realize that their conversations are a source of stress and interruption for others. Many say that in addition to the "constant buzzing" of the headsets, the background noise is "incredible."

Although the physical health problems and undesirable conditions of call centre workers are notable, they may pale in comparison to the effects of the ongoing stress and mental anguish that call centre workers experience. Some of the stress is the result of the conflict between workers' notions of service, whether public or private, marketing or informational, and call centre monitoring and management practices. Speed and efficiency mark the outstanding call centre employee. Employee evaluations are based on statistical performance measures, and this is highly stressful for most. For workers there is often a clash between their personal goals to do a good job providing a service or marketing a product, and maintaining pride in their work, and the organizational demands of meeting efficiency and production quotas. As a result workers under such conditions frequently describe feeling highly conflicted—even dirty—about their jobs.

Some describe management's system of fear and intimidation, the high expectations, and the lack of feedback as very difficult. The "Big Brother" aspect of the call centre, the feeling of being watched as under a microscope, and the zero tolerance for minor infractions, such as the need for a break or for a sip of water, is described by some as more stressful than the work itself.

The Underside of Technology: The Case of Miners and Assemblers in the Technology Industry

Despite the drawbacks of working in a digitized or robotic environment, most Canadians would agree that computers, digital systems, mobile phones, and other devices have made their jobs easier. But for thousands of workers across the globe, the experience of working in and around technologies takes on a very different meaning. There are two outstanding concerns: the dangers faced by the miners involved in extracting the essential raw materials for technological devices, and the working conditions endured by those who assemble computers, laptops, cell phones, and other equipment.

Labour-saving devices or digital devices, such as laptops and cell phones, routinely incorporate raw materials produced by unfree, or even slave, labour. For example, the mining of columbite-tantalite, often referred to as coltan, mainly comes from Rwanda and the Congo. Coltan is crucial in the production of electronics due to its suitability for use in electric capacitors. Central Africa accounts for 80 per cent of the world's coltan, and 64 per cent of the world's reserves are located in the Democratic Republic of the Congo; the very highest concentrations are in the Kahuzi Biega National Park (Smith, 2013; Montegue, 2002; Munn, n.d.). In 2001, 10,000 men, women, and children moved to camps in the park to mine this precious material. These people were in search of decent wages. At the time, the average Congolese worker made $10 per month, but coltan miners could make $10 to $50 per week (Delawala, n.d.). Forces from neighbouring Rwanda, Uganda, and Burundi moved in to cash in on the Congo's coltan and began smuggling the metal out of the Congo, using the revenues they earned from this to sustain their war efforts. This had a devastating impact on biodiversity within the Congo as the miners relied on bushmeat for protein and on wildlife due to the deforestation. It also contributed to thousands of mortalities amongst gorillas and elephants and contributed to exploitation of wood for fuel (Munn, n.d.). Large multinational producers of cell phones, laptops, or video game machines rely on sources of coltan from these countries where armed militias police forced labour and adolescents to work in the mines, under the point of bayonets.

In the factories that make electronics, working conditions are abysmal. In China, Foxconn employs roughly 1.1 million workers to make products for Apple and other tech giants (Greene, 2012). Almost all mobile phones are made in China by Asian contract firms. Here workers' rights are not protected by federal and provincial laws as they are in Canada. After the Taiyuan riots and several suicides, Apple insisted that Foxconn audit workplace conditions. Foxconn complied by addressing several issues such as providing ergonomic breaks, changing the design of workers' equipment to guard against repetitive strain injuries, and updating and enforcing maintenance policies to ensure that equipment is working properly (Greene, 2012). However during peak seasons, like when a new model phone is being released or around Christmas, the work becomes highly intensified. Workers are given, at most,

A laptop computer factory in China. Working conditions in electronics factories continue to reveal the negative effects of technology on the labour force. Workers are subject to long hours performing extremely repetitive and straining tasks, and rights are not protected by federal and provincial laws as they are in Canada.

only one day off after 13 consecutive days and some are allowed no days off in a month. Some workers report working 18 days in a row and others reported working 16-hour shifts. Many employees work excessive overtime but are not compensated for it. Many are inadequately trained and are not protected from the chemicals they are using, while some require an "off-duty permit" for a washroom break (Greene, 2012). Such incredible pressures on workers have led to at least 14 suicides. Under escalating pressures, exhausted workers fall asleep at their desks during their 12-hour shifts (Parsons, 2014). For these workers, the technologies that have opened the world for millions have imprisoned the assemblers in an endless course of tedious production while the products they make have remained out of reach and unaffordable.

Conclusion

A popular image of the "new economy" workplace is that of a highly wired, sparsely populated space where workers are engaged in knowledge-intensive work and use new information and communication technologies to connect to customers and clients around the globe. This positive image does apply to some workers, especially those involved in the creative industries where they may be working on new ways of filming, in telecommunications where workers may be developing new apps or ways of transferring knowledge and contributing to databases, or in the automotive industry where engineers are perfecting the self-driving car or creating sensors and other safety devices. In medical fields, specialists from a variety of fields collaborate to reproduce or "rewire" human limbs or critical organs to regain function following trauma or disease. There are endless creative uses and applications of technologies in the workplace. The critical issue is what side of the power and authority spectrum the worker is on. High tech specialists, engineers, software developers, and a host of others are well situated at the helm using their skills, knowledge bases, and creativity to contribute to quality of health, wellness, and lifestyle while others are chained to headsets or pushed to new levels of speed and efficiency in a number of industries now reliant on information and communication technologies and robotics.

Moving from the macro analysis we have been presenting to the micro, Chapter 4 considers the individual's feelings and experience of work. We will discuss how workers describe their connection to work in light of the transformed labour market, the availability of work, and deterioration in conditions of work within the service economy.

Questions for Critical Thought

1. Do the new technologies contribute to the deskilling process, or do technologies enhance the labour process by reskilling work and providing workers an opportunity to acquire new skills and experiences?
2. With new technologies, are most workers subject to mindless machine tending? Is it possible for this trend to be reversed?
3. How does work in the modern retail sector mirror labour processes within traditional manufacturing facilities?

Suggested Further Resources

Castells, M. 2000. *The Rise of the Network Society: The Information Age, Economy, Society and Culture. Volume 1.* New York: Wiley. This ground-breaking book, the first in a trilogy, examines the impact of the Internet and social transformations within the global economy.

Huws, Ursula. 2014. *Labor in the Global Digital Economy.* New York: Monthly Review Press. Ursula Huws has written extensively on the impact of technology on labour processes. She has analyzed both the significance of work transformations that accompany changes in technology and also the social forces underlying these transformations.

Russell, Bob. 2009. *Smiling Down the Line: Info-Service Work in the Global Economy.* Toronto: University of Toronto Press. Bob Russell employs a cross-national approach to the study of work and labour process within the call centre industry and service work.

Suggested Websites

BBC Panorama, "Amazon.com The Truth Behind the Click"

www.youtube.com/watch?v=F4aRz7NqTOo

Online shopping has grown by leaps and bounds in recent years, and this growth has been met with increasingly robotized environments within warehouses and distribution centres. Amazon has been in the forefront in turning its operations into robotized environments, making workers' jobs highly stressful with the emphasis on efficiency and speed in packaging orders.

Blood Coltan

http://topdocumentaryfilms.com/blood-coltan

The demand for coltan, an essential material in electronics, has fuelled powerful conflicts. Local populations in the Democratic Republic of the Congo, including children, work under the watch of rebel militias to supply European businessmen with this "black gold," despite the UN's sanctions.

Notes

1. We often use the terms "skilled, unskilled, and deskilled workers" in order to describe the type of work in which workers are engaged. But it is important to clarify that the designations of skilled, unskilled, and deskilled refer to the work and labour process, rather than to the individual. Individual workers may bring a host of abilities, talents, and experiences to the workplace; however, they are categorized by the work they are hired to do rather than by the credentials, achievements, and characteristics they actually bring with them.
2. It is expected that the use of robots in Canada will increase as a response to relatively high labour costs within the manufacturing sector. Research from the Boston Consulting Group noted, for example, that a spot welding machine "works" for about $8 per hour whereas a human welder would earn approximately $20 per hour, for the same output (Grant, 2015).
3. "Ross," artificial intelligence designed by University of Toronto law students and developed by IBM using the company's "Watson," an artificially intelligent computer system, is a legal researcher trained on Ontario corporate law decisions and statutes. In 2011, "Watson" made history by winning *Jeopardy!*, drawing on its vast array of general knowledge to edge out its opponents (Gray, 2014a).
4. In Canada, most workers in call centres within the private sector are not unionized, while public sector call centre workers are most often unionized. Service Canada's call centre employees, for example, are members of Public Service Alliance of Canada (PSAC). In contrast, only a small number of private sector employees such as those working for Answernet Telepartners are unionized (UFCW: 2014). In their study of call centres in Canada, Jaarsveld, Frost, and Walker (2007) found that 19.9 per cent of their sample was unionized. Unionization was more common in in-house centres or centres serving the customers of the parent company rather than outsourced centres or those operated by subcontractors to serve customers of one or several companies. Compared with unionized centres, non-union centres have twice the average turnover rate, including employees who quit or were dismissed.

4 Workers' Experience: The Emotional Gamut of Work

Learning Objectives

- To describe the gender and income mix within the Canadian service sector
- To recognize the difference between emotion work and emotional labour
- To understand the importance of emotional labour to service workers and the consequences of surface and deep acting on the health and well-being of service workers
- To recognize who gets paid more and who gets paid less for energetically following the organization's feeling rules
- To reflect on why customers are becoming more aggressive toward service workers

Introduction

For the past 40 years, many Canadians have been under the impression that they are living in a society in which good, secure, and well-paying employment is readily available in the service sector, is based on merit rather than seniority, and where there is more freedom of choice ("consumer sovereignty") and personal responsibility. Is this the reality for the majority of working Canadians? This chapter explores the reality of working in a service-based economy increasingly characterized not only by the exploitation of physical and mental labour but also by the **commodification** of workers' emotional labour whether they are employed on the front line or as trained professionals.

What constitutes emotional labour? There are the corporate messages and the manner by which employees convey the messages to customers and clients. Corporate examples include McDonald's "I'm lovin it," Holiday Inn's "Pleasing people the world over," Marks and Spencer's "The customer is always and completely right," and Disneyland's "The happiest place on earth." When it comes to how employees should behave at work, this chapter takes up Arlie Hochschild's (2003) distinction between emotion work and emotional labour and then proceeds to describe the sociology of emotional labour as a process of the commodification of emotions at work. Employing **labour process theory** (LPT) to the dynamics of the service sector, we address the following questions: What is it about the service sector that potentially lends itself to exploitative and alienating experiences for workers? How do workers strategize about coping within alienating workplaces? How has the shift to a predominantly service-based economy differentially affected men and women workers?

As we have described in Chapter 3, call centre work has become a growing employment node in Canada as well as in most of the developed and developing world. Call centre workers describe the physical and mental toll that their work often requires. Some may argue that the working environment of the contemporary call centre is the exemplar of the modern "electronic sweatshop" foreshadowed by Barbara Garson (1989) almost 30 years ago. However, missing from her description are the additional emotional demands required of service workers in the new economy. By examining emotional labour we will address some of the consequences for individual service workers. We will consider whether those who embrace "deep acting" or those who just "fake it" are more likely to suffer burnout, depression, and other negative health consequences. We will also discuss how workers, as active agents, strategize to cope with changing demands on their physical, mental, and emotional labour. Finally, on the other side of the service workers' interactions with the public, we will question why we hear in the media more and more about customer abuse to service workers.

This chapter begins by describing how the political economy of employment in Canada has witnessed a shift from a largely male, unionized manufacturing landscape to predominantly a service economy characterized by growing numbers of precarious jobs and the continued ghettoization of women within a sub-group of service workers, despite women's influx into the labour market. The chapter begins by establishing the contours of the present political economy of service-based employment with a brief historical backdrop to the rise of the service sector in Canada, a snapshot of the complexity of the service sector, and the gender disparities in terms of employment and the average weekly remuneration paid to workers.

The Service Sector in Canada: Historical Backdrop

The deindustrialization of countries such as Canada, the United States, and the United Kingdom, which took off during the 1970s, has continued into the twenty-first century, as noted in Chapter 1.[1] In Canada, manufacturing employment fell by 22.5 per cent between 2000 and 2010. As a share of total employment, manufacturing fell from 15.6 per cent to 10.35 per cent between 2000 and 2011 (Jackson, 2012b). The accelerated growth of the service industries from the 1970s on may be explained, in part, by the displacement of hundreds of thousands of mostly unionized industrial workers in heavy industries such as steel production, car assembly plants, and paper-making factories resulting from the introduction of information and communications technologies such as industrial robots, flexible manufacturing systems, and computer assisted manufacturing (CADs). Workers who were transitioned to a job outside the factory were often forced to work in non-unionized, low skilled service sector jobs which meant accepting pay cuts, averaging around $10,000 less a year (Alini, 2011).

The speed at which **globalization** has affected the manufacturing sector has increased over the last half-century. Globalization continues to offer cheaper labour and plant facilities abroad, thereby adversely affecting manufacturing employment in Canada. As discussed in Chapter 2, an important development for analyzing recent employment trends in Canada and other advanced countries is the global reach of transnational corporations by, for example, **outsourcing** many once high-paying, unionized manufacturing jobs in Canada, the United States, and elsewhere in the OECD to newly industrializing countries such as India, China, and Vietnam. In addition, improvements in information and communications technologies and transportation links generate increased **interdependence** for goods and services worldwide.

While the general direction of change has been a growing service sector and a declining manufacturing sector, not all "heavy" industries disappeared. Many, including Ford, GM, and Resolute (a newsprint paper company) continue to flourish, but with much reduced workforces as compared to previous decades. Other new smaller manufacturing industries have emerged, producing high-value goods for a global market with relatively small workforces at home. Therefore, although some manufacturing companies in Canada are thriving, they are producing more with far fewer workers.

Other OECD countries witnessed a shift from largely full-time, unionized jobs in heavy industry such as steel and automobile manufacturing to employment in the service, leisure, and consumer industries of the economy. In the United Kingdom, for example, a similar landscape has been drafted with services now contributing more to the UK economy than any other industry. Over time, their contribution to the UK GDP has increased from an estimated 46 per cent in 1948 to 78 per cent in 2012. The percentage of people employed in service industries in the UK is estimated to have increased from 44 per cent in 1948 to 85 per cent in 2012. In contrast, the percentage of people employed in manufacturing industries decreased from 45 per cent in 1948 to 10 per cent in 2012—a figure almost identical to Canada (Jones, 2013).

Married Women in the Canadian Economy

Another profound change in the Canadian economy became unmistakable—the large entry of married women into the labour market. As discussed further in Chapter 7, the shift to a service-based economy and the influx of married women in the labour force can be traced back to the mid-1950s. From 1946 until 1960, employment in all industries rose 28 per cent but employment in service-producing industries grew an astonishing 72 per cent to account for almost 3.2 million workers—or over 53 per cent of the entire workforce.[2]

Working women in the paid labour force is not a new phenomenon in Canada. In 1901, approximately 16 per cent of the women aged 14 years and older were working for pay. The vast majority were single women who usually left the labour market after marriage. During the Second World War, women could be found working in virtually every sector of the Canadian economy. However, in

1941, fewer than four per cent of married women were in the labour force. By 1951, the proportion was over 11 per cent and, by 1961, it had doubled to 22 per cent. By 1980, nearly half the women who were married or living common law in Canada worked for pay. Today, the corresponding proportion hovers around 75 per cent meaning that dual-earner couples are now the norm in most Canadian households (Lu and Morissette, 2010).

The Service Sector of the Canadian Economy

Addressing the deepening exploitation of workers, especially women, requires an understanding of the complexities of the new service economy not only in Canada, but also throughout the developed capitalist economies. Before proceeding with a specific examination of the emotional labour required of service workers, we now provide a brief description of the contours, composition, and the size of the service sector in Canada. By establishing the complex structure of the service economy in Canada, we can proceed to examine the commodification of emotions required of **service workers**.

What constitutes the service sector of the Canadian economy? What is the gender division of labour within each of the service industries? What occupations get paid the most and which the least? Are women concentrated in low-paying sectors of the new service economy? Addressing these questions establishes not only the size of the services sector but the gender and income shares.

Service workers are defined as individuals who work below the professional level where the strategic share of the labour process involves interaction with customers (Korczynski and Evans, 2013). These occupations can be found in the retail trade, arts, entertainment, and hospitality industries. Workers in these industries are generally among the lowest paid and are predominantly women; often, the women are recent immigrants and women of colour. In the United States, United Kingdom, and Canada (see below), roughly 28 per cent of the service sector is comprised of non-professional service workers (Macdonald and Merrill, 2009; Korczynski, 2009).

The Canadian economy may be divided into two statistically relevant components, the goods producing and the services sectors. These two categories replace the previously established nomenclatures of primary or agriculture, fishing, and natural resource extraction; secondary or manufacturing; and tertiary or services sector of the economy. The goods-producing industries contain the following five divisions: agriculture, forestry, and fishing; mining, oil, and gas extraction; utilities; construction; and manufacturing. The services sector is, however, composed of a variety of different occupations ranging from fast food workers to sports broadcasters to brain surgeons. There are 15 industry classifications within the services sector. Common examples include health and welfare; education; information and cultural industries; accommodation and food services, and retail trade; arts, entertainment, and recreation; and tourism, insurance, real estate, banking, and investment (See Figure 4.1).

Goods-Producing	Examples	
	Agriculture, forestry, fishing, and hunting	
	Construction	
	Manufacturing	
	Utilities	
	Mining, quarrying, oil and natural gas extraction	
Service-Producing	Examples	
	Wholesale trade	Merchant wholesalers Farm products Building materials and supplies
	Retail trade	Motor vehicle parts dealers Electronics and appliance stores Gasoline stations Clothing and clothing accessories
	Information and cultural industries	Publishing industries (except Internet) Broadcasting (except Internet) Telecommunications Motion picture and sound recording
	Transportation and warehousing	Air, rail, truck, and water transport Postal service
	Finance and insurance	Central banks
	Real estate, rental and leasing	
	Professional, scientific and technical services	Legal Architectural Accounting Computer systems design
	Management of companies	Holding companies Head offices
	Administrative and support, waste management and remedial services	Travel arrangement and reservation Employment services Office administration
	Educational services	Elementary and secondary Community colleges and CEGEPs Universities Technical and trade schools
	Health care and social assistance	Ambulatory health care Hospitals Nursing and residential care
	Arts, entertainment, and recreation	Performing arts and spectator sports Amusement and gambling
	Accommodation and food services	Traveller including hotels Recreational vehicle parks Rooming and boarding houses Drinking (alcoholic) places Full-service restaurants
	Other services (except public administration)	Repair and maintenance Personal and laundry services
	Public administration	Federal, provincial, and municipal administrations Aboriginal band councils

Figure 4.1 Industry Groupings within the Goods-Producing and Service Producing-Sectors of the Canadian Economy

The discussion here relies heavily on the NAICS[3] classification of service producing industries due to Statistics Canada's reliance on this categorization. However, there are several problems with dividing the Canadian economy into the NAICS classifications. For example, services such as those provided by a lawyer or an accountant working at GM or Ford's head offices in Canada would appear as employment in the goods producing sector. Other industries in the goods-producing sectors may also produce some services such as pest control, plumbing, land subdivision, and house painting.[4] Additionally, goods may be transformed in the process of providing the service, as in the restaurant industry. That is, there may be overlap because occupational classifications do not always neatly conform to rigid statistical boundaries. Pointing to these issues highlights one of the principal characteristics of advanced economies as the complex **interdependence** between the types of activities found in the goods-producing and services sector of the new economy. The focus of this chapter is on the service sector of the new economy and, as such, on people interacting with people and serving customers rather than on transforming physical goods.

That said, an examination of Figure 4.1 reveals the complexity of the services sector in the Canadian economy. There are 15 categories of service industries and Figure 4.1 includes examples from each of them. There are private services such as insurance, management of companies, real estate, and finance including the central banks and credit unions. Among the public services, education, health care, social assistance, and the federal, provincial, territorial, municipal, and Aboriginal public administrations round out the list.

Table 4.1 provides data on the gender breakdown and average weekly salary for each of the five goods and the 15 service producing industries. Reviewing the 15 service industries, we find that in addition to the private and public services, there are high- and low-paying sectors within the 15 service industries and gender inequities where women predominate in certain services and those where men are in the majority.

The average weekly salary in 2014 for the services sector was $871. Taking $1,000 a week and above ($52,000 and above a year) as a marker for a higher than average salary, seven out of the 15 categories rank as higher salary services. They are wholesale trade; transportation and warehousing; professional, scientific and technical services; finance and insurance; management of companies and enterprises; information and cultural industries; and public administration. Six out of these seven are private sector services. Together they account for over two-fifths of the workforce in the service sector.

At the opposite end, selecting $600 per week and below (or $31,200 and below a year) as an indicator of low-paying services, three groups stand out. They are retail trade; arts, entertainment, and recreation; and accommodation and food services. These three account for over one-quarter of service sector workers—those we defined above as service workers.

Table 4.1 Employment by Industry and Sex, 2014 (number in thousands) Average Weekly Earnings (current dollars)

	Both Sexes	Average Weekly Earnings	Men	Women
All industries	17,802.20	$935.31	9,246.3	8,474.2
Goods-producing sector	**3,897.1 (21.9%)**	**$1,217.78**	**3,076.6 (33%)**	**820.5 (9.8%)**
Agriculture	305.1 (1.8%)	—	215.5 (2.4%)	89.6 (1.1%)
Forestry, fishing, mining, quarrying, oil, and gas[1]	368 (2.1%)	—	301.0 (3.2%)	71.6 (0.8%)
Forestry and logging with support activities	49.1	$1,040.47	39.6	9.5
Fishing, hunting, and trapping	15.9	—	14.0	1.9
Mining, quarrying, and oil and gas extraction	307.5	$1,248.30	247.4	60.2
Utilities	136.9 (0.8%)	$1,777.89	104.1 (1.2%)	32.8 (0.4%)
Construction	1,371.5 (7.5%)	$1,224.44	1,208.1 (13%)	163.4 (1.8%)
Manufacturing	1,711.0 (9.8%)	$1,044.18	1,247.9 (14%)	463.1 (5.6%)
Services-producing sector	**13,905.1 (78.1%)**	**$871.01**	**6,251.4 (67%)**	**7,653.7 (90%)**
Trade	2,729.3 (15.3%)	$704.89	1,413.4 (15%)	1,315.9 (15.6%)
Wholesale trade	622	$1,109.65	440.1	182.1
Retail trade	2,107.1	$542.27	973.3	1133.8
Transportation and warehousing	896.8 (4.9%)	$1,004.82	682.2 (7%)	214.6 (2.5%)
Finance, insurance	779.7	$1,166.92	318.9 (5.1%)	460.8 (6%)
Real estate and leasing	304.2	$932.36	168.5	135.7
Professional, scientific, and technical services	1,333.3 (7.6%)	$1,308.06	758.0 (8.3%)	575.3 (6.9%)
Management of companies and enterprises	734.8	$1,335.28	406.5	328.2
Administrative and support, waste management, and remediation services	—	$751.87	—	—
Educational services	1,236.9 (7.3%)	$982.77	390.2 (4.6%)	846.6 (10.2%)
Health care and social assistance	2,219.7 (12.3%)	$853.82	391.7 (4.2%)	1,828.0 (10.2%)
Arts, entertainment, and recreation	—	$581.54	—	—
Information and cultural industries	757.2 (4.4%)	$1,168.60	406.5 (4.5%)	350.7 (4.3%)
Accommodation and food services	1,207.5 (6.4%)	$371.36	468. 3 (5.1%)	721.2 (7.8%)
Other services	795.1 (4.3%)	$755.53	381.9 (3.9%)	413.2 (4.9%)
Public administration	910.7 (5.3%)	$1,201.07	447.3 (5.1%)	463.4 (5.6%)

[1] Also referred to as natural resources.
Sources: Statistics Canada, CANSIM, Table 282-0008 (2010-2014 Employment totals) and table 281-0027.

Women are out-numbered by men in four major groups. They are wholesale trade; transportation and warehousing; professional, scientific and technical services; and the management of companies. Both men and women are roughly equal in information and cultural industries, public administration and other services.

Taken together, women form the majority in three of the low-paying (below $600/week) private services of retail trade; arts, entertainment, and recreation; and accommodation and food industries. Using the Statistics Canada measure of poverty or Low Income Cut Off (LICO), those employed in the accommodation and food services sector, or almost 10 per cent of the service workers, received wages that placed them below the poverty line. Those working in the other two groups were making incomes slightly above the poverty line. In contrast, men outnumber women in the seven groups marked as high-paying or above average services.

While women's contributions to the Canadian economy continues to rise, where they are located matters. Two-thirds of employed Canadian women continue to work in occupations in which women have traditionally been concentrated such as teaching, nursing and related health, clerical/administrative, sales, and service (Statistics Canada, 2006a). In fact, there has been little change in the proportion of women employed in these traditionally female-dominated occupations since the late 1990s (Colman, 2003). In addition to working in largely precarious jobs requiring little training, limited career advancement, and receiving below average wages, these workers are expected to adopt and follow the scripts of their capitalist employers.

Emotional Labour and Its Consequences

What Is Emotional Labour?

The rapid growth in service work over the past 40 years in the developed economies has become fertile soil for applying Arlie Hochschild's (2003) concept of "emotional labour" defined as the process by which emotions at work become **commodified** as **wage labour**. We will employ a political economy labour process theory to address the question of whether service workers are **alienated** in the new economy. But first, we take up the question of what is **emotional labour**.

First, emotional labour is distinct from physical and mental effort. Above, we described the growth, extent, and complexity of the service sector of the Canadian economy. The defining characteristic of the service sector is the production of services or a set of intangible, perishable, and consumable activities such as cleaning, educating, or delivering mail. Within the service sector we defined **service workers** as those individuals who were mostly women, who held precarious and low-paying jobs, and were engaged in **face-to-face** or **voice-to-voice** interaction with customers. They comprise approximately 28 per cent of the jobs in the services sector of the United States, United Kingdom, and Canadian economies.

What is it about work in the service sector that sets it apart from manufacturing and other goods producing industries? To begin, Arlie Hochschild convincingly demonstrated that the work of flight attendants and bill collectors, as examples of service workers, could not be fully described or understood by solely examining the physical aspects (the confined space in airplanes or in call centres) and the cognitive demands (acting quickly and safely in emergency situations) of their work. Rather, a substantial part of their job was dealing with passengers or customers and their emotions. Therefore, employees working in the service sector are not only required to work on tasks and expend physical and mental effort, but they are now compelled to manage their emotions as part of their job.

Hochschild described the three characteristics of service jobs that involve emotional labour as (1) "face-to-face or voice-to-voice contact with the public," (2) the requirement that workers "produce an emotional state in another person—gratitude or fear, for example," and (3) providing the employer "a degree of control over the emotional activities of employees" (Hochschild, 1983: 147). Emotional labour involves managing our emotions to meet our job expectations whether as a call center agent, a flight attendant, or a university professor. In other words, while physical and mental efforts are necessary components of the job, the focus is on emotions as an essential requirement of the job.

Arlie Hochschild (2003) distinguishes between emotion work and emotional labour. In her framework, emotional labour refers to "the management of feeling, to create a publically observable facial and bodily display" (2003: 7). What is most significant about emotional labour is that it is "sold for a wage" and has **exchange value**. In the context of the personal or private sphere, emotion work or emotional management refer to similar observable bebaviours but are viewed as constituting **use value**. Hochschild's concepts of exchange value and use value are derived from Marx where exchange value refers to the commodification of labour within capitalist organizations. She uses **emotional labour** when analyzing "the management of feeling" in the public commercial capitalist realm but relies on **emotion work** or **emotion management** as use value when referring to the "management of feeling" in private social interactions.[5]

For Hochschild, emotional labour must be learned. It must be taught at work. In Hochschild's study, the emotional labour required of the flight attendants and bill collectors required training. The supervisors trained the recruits to use the "company language" which contained standardized "expressions of empathy" (Hochschild, 2003: 109–113). The company, then, governs the corresponding normative instructions and practices required by service workers which Hochschild calls "**feeling rules.**" These become the blueprint for the management of feelings at work. They are codified as "best practice." Often, employees are encouraged by most employers to reach into their own personal emotion work for displaying appropriate emotional labour at work.

Hochschild divides the level of commitment to the company's "feeling rules" into "**surface acting**" or behavioural compliance and "**deep acting**." "Surface Acting" can be "painting on" affective displays or "faking it" while "deep acting" is "modifying inner feelings to match expressions" (see also, Grandey, 2003: 86). "Deep acting" refers to Konstantin Stanislavsky's "method acting" technique. Method acting requires the performer to get into character to such a degree that they don't act; they react just as the character would (Stanislavsky, 1961).

To be fair, participants employed as service workers are more than simply passive recipients of commodified feelings. Hochschild, (1983/2003) always considered the actors' own creativity in subverting the rigid rules and demands of their employers. For example, she showed how flight attendants managed to develop strategies of either coping with unfriendly customers who had offended or humiliated them or, occasionally, finding covert ways of paying them back for their nasty behaviour (Hochschild, 2003: 114). Workers do emotional labour but many try to maintain "loose time" to resist, comply, or simply be themselves (Glenday, 2011).

In her example of flight attendants, Hochschild (1983/2003) notes that what flight attendants were selling was a presentation of an emotional self, but adaptable enough to fit specific circumstances over time. In general, flight attendants were to act as "perfect hosts," to serve "patience" and "sincere friendliness" to passengers (see also, Gotz, 2013: 186). If passengers became angry or afraid, it was the flight attendants' duty to suppress their own anger or fear and soothe them. Flight attendants were required to manage their feelings in order to create a "homelike" atmosphere of comfort, trust, and security.

In addition to the physical and mental skills required to complete their tasks, service workers are now expected to "sell their souls" to the company. A person's emotions are required in order to achieve the organization's goal of control and accumulation. However, it is important to question whether and how the value added by the emotional labour of the worker is recognized and rewarded. Huppartz asserts that women may "capitalize on their femininity and femaleness in order to gain a steady and reasonable income," but "their feminized fields continue to be undervalued and underpaid" (2009: 55, 61).

The degree of emotional labour required of service workers varies greatly depending on the employing company. An example of the extremes to which a company will go to induce its employees to act friendly toward their customers caught media attention recently. Pret a Manger's corporate image became tarnished for enforcing the company's feeling rules on their employees. Pret a Manger, founded in 1984, is an international London (UK)-based chain of restaurants with 289 stores in the United Kingdom, 58 in the United States, 14 in Hong Kong, and 12 in Paris (as of 2014). Pret workers are required to master what the company calls the "Pret Behaviours," which in addition to the usual requirements of courtesy and

Alongside serving beverages, flight attendants work to maintain an atmosphere of comfort, trust, and security during flight. Many service industry workers are required to perform emotional labour of this kind.

efficiency, include "has presence," "creates a sense of fun," and "is happy to be who they are" (Noah, 2013; Preston, 2012).[6]

Also important for Pret workers is touching. In other workplaces, touching a co-worker may get you fired, but at Pret you have to worry about not touching co-workers enough. According to a newspaper interview with Chief Executive Clive Schlee, "The first thing I look at is whether staff are touching each other—are they smiling, reacting to each other, happy, engaged? Look, she's just touched her colleague—squeezed her arm. If I see hands going up in the air, that's a good sign. I can almost predict sales on body language alone" (Preston, 2012).

How does Pret's management enforce the company's feeling rules on its employees? A "mystery shopper" visits every Pret outlet once a week. If the employee who rings up the sale is appropriately enthusiastic and cheerful, then everyone in the shop gets a bonus. If not, nobody does (Noah, 2013). By penalizing the group and not the individual, the company's corporate strategy ensures collective compliance to its "feeling rules" of control and accumulation.

Are Service Workers Alienated in the New Economy?

Are workers alienated in a service economy and if so, what forms does alienation take? Do workers resist the prerogatives of management and if so, what forms does workers' resistance take? Because there is little Canadian research on emotional labour in the service economy, we rely here primarily on United Kingdom and United States sources. To consider these issues, we will draw on the key arguments and assumptions of a political economy labour process theory. A political economy labour process theory posits that human effort is "essentially indeterminate" so that capitalist organizations are faced with the problem of reducing uncertainties surrounding what workers actually *expend* while at work; that is, for service workers today not only physical and mental effort but also their emotional labour (Vincent, 2011). The imperatives to control and accumulate remain central to this theory and constitute the context for how workers express their agential consequences of resistance, compliance, consent, or accommodation (see also Glenday, 2011).

Second, virtually all emotions at work reside within the broader political economy of wage labour. In these circumstances, the management of emotional labour by service workers takes place in the alienated conditions of labour. As a result, workers lose control over their own emotions because they are "owned" by employers and directed as part of the service offered to customers (Brook, 2009). To put it another way, in addition to the deskilling of physical and mental labour, the prescriptions of emotional labour as alienated labour increases the employers' scope to extend their influence into areas of the labour process not previously regulated. However, the managerial direction to control and accumulate is not ubiquitous and the thorough commoditization of emotion at work is not possible (Bolton, 2005). A political economy labour process theory captures the time for workers to experience and express themselves at work (Glenday, 2011).

Service Workers' Strategies of Coping/Resistance

The **misbehaviour thesis** offers a theoretical bridge between the political economy of the labour process and local experiences (Ackroyd and Thompson, 1999). Workers misbehave whenever managers "perceive activities and practices as poorly aligned with the organizations' 'higher interests' of control and accumulation" (Thompson, 2003). These "counterproductive behaviours," as viewed by managers, are workers misbehaving at work.

Emotional misbehaviour can be divided into at least two broad worker strategies. **Alienated emotional misbehaviour** occurs whenever workers "react to managerial prescriptions by withdrawing their agency or disengaging from the act" (Vincent, 2013: 1376). Here, employee enthusiasm for reproducing the emotional scripts weakens as workers become aware that their emotional labour lacks recognition and reward in the face of the misuse and abuse they are confronted with every day by their employers and some customers (Hurrell, 2010). Withdrawal is not inevitable, though, as workers find other ways to endure their experiences of emotional dissonance such as "feeling phoney" and "emotional deadness," otherwise viewed as "surface acting" (see Hochschild, 2003/1983). Korczynski (2003) has observed the formation of collective "communities of coping" to help frontline customer service representatives overcome their negative experiences. The empirical challenge is to identify individual and collective cases of **alienated emotional disengagement**.

Resistant emotional misbehaviour occurs whenever workers realize their interests are different from managerial prerogatives of control and accumulation. They more actively resist the alienated conditions of their work. In these instances, workers self-consciously engage in behaviours other than those imposed by their employer. Taylor and Taylor (2000) document workers actively refusing to follow their employer's emotional script while Hampson and Junor (2005) point to a customer service representative actively siding with the client, thereby placing herself in tension with management and possibly risking employment itself (2005: 175). A further example is provided by a call centre worker who had to apologize to a client for the misinformation communicated to her by one of the managers (Glenday, 2011). Taylor and Bain (2003) reported how employees collectively ridiculed the consensual normative order that their employer preferred. However, in these instances, active trade union involvement was central to the oppositional identities workers had constructed. In a non-union environment at a Canadian call centre, Glenday (2011) reported how opposition to managerial initiatives for building workplace morale by encouraging workers to participate in events such as "pyjama day" or games such as "call centre Olympics" took on more individualized expressions of opposition (2011: 35).

In general, a political economy labour process theory recognizes that owners and managers of service work in capitalist organizations tend to encourage those emotional displays that are perceived to represent the ultimate organizational goals of control and accumulation while reactively discouraging those emotional behaviours that they observe as acting against those interests. While recognizing the real influence of alienation in the management of emotions at work, a political-economy labour process theory eschews the narrow conception of the self that must be either class conscious or ignorant of their situation resulting in some form of false consciousness. Instead, theoretical space is provided for various individual and collective experiences, expressions and displays of how emotional labour is organized, administered, and reacted to by service workers.

For Whom Does Emotional Labour Pay Well?

One important study examined the relationship between the level of emotional labour required to effectively perform a job and the cognitive skills or level of education required to do the job and their relative compensation (Glomb, Kammeyer-Mueller, and Rotundo, 2004). The authors note that their results suggest "higher levels of emotional labor demands are associated with lower wage rates for jobs low in cognitive demands and with higher wage rates for jobs high in cognitive demands" (2004: 700). In other words, jobs at the low end of the service sector, that is, those held by **service workers**, requiring little training, providing little career advancement, and providing low wages require high emotional labour. Those careers at the top end of the income scale requiring professional training will also demand high emotional labour from their employees. That is, well-educated professional workers in the service sector such as family doctors, lawyers, or university professors are well compensated for enthusiastically following their organization's codified "feeling rules." Service workers in call centres, restaurants, and hotels are called upon to express themselves just as energetically but are paid much less for their emotional labour.

The Global Reach of Call Centres and Emotional Labour

As noted in Chapter 3, call centre work has been a focus of research in the United Kingdom and the United States for the past 20 years, in part because the call centre is an exemplar of the interdependence between globalization, advances in information and communications technology, and their impact on individual workers. In Canada, the call centre industry has become big business—one of Canada's largest employment sectors, with half a million Canadians working in over 14,000 call centres by 2008 (Jackson, 2008: 1). Call centres grew at an annual employment rate of seven per cent since the 1990s, outpacing the economy-wide rate of one per cent (Jackson, 2008: 2). As a service industry, the call centre requires not only the physical and mental capabilities of its workers, but also emotional labour. The specifics—what is required, how it is administered and the consequences for the worker's identity, health, and well-being—vary dramatically.

Are All Call Centres Alike?

In an eight-country quantitative analysis,[7] Holman (2013) sought to address the reasons for the significant differences in the quality of jobs in call centres. He defined job quality, not as a qualitative measure of employees' experiences but as the "objective features of the job such as job discretion and ongoing training that foster beneficial outcomes for the employee" (2013: 23). Overall, his conclusions focused on the role of trade unions and the national industrial relations systems in fostering beneficial outcomes for employees. Not surprisingly, call centres located in Denmark, Sweden, and Germany—countries where trade unions are robust and operate within an inclusive national industrial relations system—generated the highest job quality for their employees. Canada, the United Kingdom, and the United States—countries dominated by neoliberal market regimes—fared less favourably, largely due to the absence of strong trade unions in the service sector and the lack of national employment policies extending employment rights to all workers (2013: 33).

However, within the market regimes of these three countries, call centres that were part of large organizations fared worse in fostering positive employee outcomes than independent call centres. Holman (2013) pointed out one explanation for this surprising difference in job quality is that "independent call centres in market regimes might be seeking to differentiate themselves from other call centres by adopting a high-commitment human resource strategy as a means of gaining competitive advantage" (2013: 34).

Individuals' Experiences of Service Work

Hochschild's approach to service work has been picked up by researchers in the United Kingdom and the United States who have examined many occupations within the service sector, especially non-professional service workers in restaurants, luxury retail shops, nursing homes, hotels, and call centres. Call centre workers remain the single largest group of service workers that researchers have investigated sociologically (Thompson, Callaghan, and Van den Brock, 2004).

Early qualitative studies described call centre work with descriptors such as "electronic panopticon" (Fernie and Metcalf, 1998), "assembly lines in the head" (Taylor and Bain, 1999), "human answering machines" (Wylie, 1997), and "bright, satanic offices" (Baldry et al., 1998). Most of the published works on call centres during this early period relied on Marxist or neo-Marxist theoretical frameworks and little attention paid to how workers reacted to managerial prerogatives of control and accumulation. Since this first wave of studies, more recent research has embraced the more nuanced experiences of call centre workers. Among the questions recent research has addressed include: Do workers identify with their work in call centres and if not, how do they view their work experience? Is there such a person as a happy call centre worker? What can we learn about the consequences for workers about how they manage their feelings while employed at call centres?

Individual Identities at Work

Do service workers gain a sense of purpose while doing their jobs? Do their work experiences contribute to whether they see themselves as contributing members of society? Lloyd's (2012) study of call centre work as an insecure, low-paid, and unsatisfying form of service work in the United Kingdom concluded that for the young men and women he studied, their working hours did not serve to define their individual identity. On the contrary, for most, working at a call centre became something to escape from. Many believed they could shed call centre jobs, that with "hard work they believed they could leave the low-paid service sector and never look back" (2012: 631). In the meantime, working at the call centre became "something to be endured in order to go out on the weekend or indulge in shopping sprees" (2012: 631). For young workers trapped in this type of relatively isolated and precarious employment relationship and, contrary to previous generations, they forge their personal identity outside their work experience.[8]

A recent study by Jenkins and Delbridge (2014) sought out the "happy" call centre worker in their qualitative case study of the all-female receptionists at "VoiceTel" (a pseudonym), a United Kingdom family-owned and managed company with a unique technological interface between client and call centre worker. The combination of management initiatives meant to foster "an organizational culture based on the values of care and trust," employee identification with the organization's goals and the ability of employees to "use their discretion and autonomy at work," resulted in the "happy" call centre worker (2014: 883, 884). In the discussion of their research findings, they disagree with the arguments put forward by most critical sociologists who describe "happy workers" as having "false consciousness." Their examination of the "happy workforce" focuses on worker relationships in their organizational context and avoids the notion of viewing service workers as "either manipulated or hoodwicked dupes" (2014: 884). At the same time, these studies may also address the ways in which "happy" workers see themselves relative to others whose working conditions may appear to be far worse or who may not have work at all.

These two qualitative research studies point out the complex relationships between the demographic compositions of call centre service workers, the organizational and technological context of the emotional labour required of workers, and the outcomes of working in this type of service work. In one situation, young workers became quickly disillusioned with their work experience while, in the second, the employees identified with their organization and work experience. On the one hand, young men and women could not wait to "escape" work while the second group of women workers found a sense of purpose and were "happy" to work for the organization.

Managing Emotional Labour at Work

Which Is Worse: Surface or Deep Acting?

Grandey's (2003) study of university administrative assistants is one of the first studies to examine whether employees who used **surface acting** or those who employed **deep acting** experienced greater stress. This job category has been classified as a "high emotional job" (Hochschild, 2003; Wharton, 1993) and the female workers in her study are "routinely evaluated for their attitude and ability to get along with people" (Grandey, 2003: 90; see also, Eaton, 1996). Her findings show that surface acting, not deep acting, was related to higher levels of stress among employees. Moreover, she found that affective delivery ratings or the extent to which the person is "perceived as friendly and warm" was positively related to deep acting but negatively related to surface acting. Deep acting then pays off with reduced **emotional dissonance** and positive responses from clients (2003: 93). She also concluded that "a happy worker may be less likely to need to put on an act with customers" (2003: 89, 93). Other studies have confirmed the *negative* relationships between surface acting and job satisfaction, emotional exhaustion, higher levels of burnout, and personal well-being (Pugh, Groth, and Hennig-Thurau, 2011; Brotheridge and Grandey, 2002; Cote and Morgan, 2002; Grandey, 2003; Grandey, Fisk, and Steiner, 2005; Heuven and Bakker, 2003; Morris and Feldman, 1997).

Service Workers and (Dis)respect

Customer abuse to service workers, whether they are call centre representatives, flight attendants, or servers at a restaurant is a widespread phenomenon. Korczynski and Evans (2013: 780) situate the "social creation of customer abuse as lying within the organization of the service economy" and not the outcome of "disgruntled deviant" individuals. They convincingly argue that there are a number of contributing factors within the fabric of the service economy that account for the recent rise of customer abuse. According to Korczynski and Ott (2004), an important factor has been the recent promotion of the myth of "customer sovereignty" at the organizational and national levels of the new economy, a phenomenon connected to the neoliberal view of "sovereign customers" (Korczynski and Ott, 2004: 771). Taking this argument further, Korczynski and Evans hypothesized that if the appearance of customer sovereignty is a "crucial underpinning of customer abuse, then customer abuse will be higher in neoliberal national economies than in social market economies" (2013: 771). The evidence from 30 book-length ethnographies showed that in neo-liberal countries many customers felt the "prick of powerlessness" not customer sovereignty whenever they faced lower-end service workers doing their job (2013: 770, 780).

In neoliberal countries where the strength of trade unions has been weakened, the authors point out that "service workers are left bearing the cost of customer abuse" (2013: 781). Service workers are simply expected to "take the crap" (Leidner, 1993: 133). They argue for regulation to protect service workers. However, this is unlikely to happen when the "dark side" of the "sovereign customer" remains one of the key elements of the existing neoliberal political economy (Gabriel and Lang, 2006).

Box 4.1 Everyday Work Experiences

"How call centre workers get back at abusive customers"

In the 6 March 2014 issue of *The Globe and Mail*, Rosanna Tamburri reported on a study of call centre workers and how they deal with very angry customers. The article begins by asking its readers the following: "What could be more annoying than an unsolicited phone call from a telemarketer, usually received during dinner or some other equally inconvenient time? It's tempting to fly off the handle." The study's authors (Professors Kevin Kelloway and Jane Mullen) interviewed 100 call centre workers about their experiences with irate customers and how they deal with them.

Naming call centres a "violence prone" industry, the participants in the study reported incidents of customers being rude, cursing and swearing, yelling, and generally being aggressive. The study's authors note that it is particularly bad for those who work in "outbound" call centres where workers make unsolicited calls to potential customers or to collect outstanding debts from those at the other end of the phone. The situation is only a little better for "inbound" call centres because customers are most often calling to complain about a service. The authors asked about how the call centre representatives dealt with being mistreated. The respondents reported taking retaliatory measures, such as not helping customers even if they knew the answers to their questions, keeping customers on hold for longer than necessary, and purposely hanging up and pretending it was an accident. Their study also found that employees were much more likely to retaliate when they were already under stress at work.

Kevin Kelloway stated, "A lot of companies have this mindset that the customer is always right." He then pointed out that this implies the call centre employee is always wrong and has no recourse but to take the abuse. He suggests companies take a second look at those policies. By paying more attention to the psychological health of their employees, Kelloway advises that businesses would have happier workers who provide better service to all customers.

Source: Tamburri, 2014.

Conclusion

The demise of the post-Second World War general political consensus around the social contract between government, large corporations, and industrial trade unions ushered in the return of a right-wing ideology otherwise known as neoliberalism which inflated the social significance of market forces to create good jobs, weakened the influence of trade unions by emphasizing merit over seniority, privatized state-owned enterprises, replaced the concept of the public good with individual responsibility, and ushered in a regime of the myth of "consumer sovereignty."

In Canada, the powerful shifts in the labour market that continue today signal the decline of goods producing industries as major sources for long-term employment in the late twentieth century in favour of more precarious jobs in the service, leisure, and consumer industries in the first decades of the twenty-first century (Bauman, 2005).

This chapter provided evidence of the complexity of the service sector in Canada. Today, many of the jobs available in the lower tier service industries such as accommodation, food and beverage, retail industries, and call centres are precarious in nature. Women and racialized minorities predominate in these lower tiers as service workers. In addition to working in largely precarious jobs requiring little training, limited career advancement and receiving below average wages, these workers are expected to adopt and follow the scripts of the emotional labour of their capitalist employers. Today's service sector workers are required to supply not only their physical competency and mental acumen but also their emotional souls in the name of corporate control and accumulation. The example of Pret a Manger may be extreme but it provides a window on what can be expected in the new employment cauldron.

Service workers, primarily women, bear the brunt of the intensified exploitation characterized by emotional labour. Service workers sell not only their physical and cognitive abilities but also their emotional souls. As alienated labour, these workers react to their exploitation by either alienated emotional misbehaviour or resistant emotional misbehaviour.

How individuals cope with managing the "feeling rules" imposed by their employers can have serious consequences on workers' health and well-being. Sustained use of "surface acting" or "faking it" with customers results in more serious consequences to an person's health and well-being due to the emotional dissonance between the individual's true feelings and their managed ones.

Call centres stand in the forefront of the interdependence between globalization and the latest applications of information and communications technologies. The individual experiences of call centre workers are complex and dependent on a number of factors. For young workers, call centre work is predominately alienating where identities are forged outside their work experiences while, for a minority, call entre work can provide a sense of purpose. The outsourcing of call centre work to countries like India has meant workers strategize about how their identities should be managed. Unfortunately, these workers are constantly exposed to the racism of Western callers.

Confronting customer disrespect and abuse is something service workers face on a daily basis. This phenomenon is not the product of disgruntled deviant individuals but a hallmark of neoliberal regimes that promote the myth of customer sovereignty. Protecting service workers through regulation may be an option but not one that is likely to take hold in a world that promotes individual responsibility and sanctions the myth of customer sovereignty.

Questions for Critical Thought

1. Can you provide any explanation(s) for why a majority of women are working in low-paying service jobs?
2. Why is the study of emotional labour so important to understanding work in the service economy?
3. What is it really like to work in a call centre?

Suggested Further Resources

Guy, Mary, Meredith A. Newman, and Sharon Mastracci. 2015. *Emotional Labor: Putting the Service in Public Service*. New York: Routledge. This book examines the significance of emotional labour in the delivery of public services and the toll it takes on public servants.

Harris, Scott. 2015. *An Invitation to the Sociology of Emotions*. New York: Routledge. Unlike Arlie Hochschild's *The Managed Heart*, which was written for scholars, this book takes beginners as its primary audience. It explains as clearly and engagingly as possible the theoretical concepts that are contained in *The Managed Heart* and the critical research it inspired.

Suggested Websites

"Wearable Eyes Turn You Into Emotional Cyborg"

http://spectrum.ieee.org/automaton/robotics/artificial-intelligence/wearable-eyes-agency glass-emotional-cyborgs

www.youtube.com/watch?v=GhvHxz1NePQ

IEEE Spectrum is the flagship publication of the Institute for Electrical and Electronics Engineers, an organization with more than 360,000 members in industry and academia. This link provides the viewer with a video highlighting Dr. Osawa's invention that adopts cyborg technology to increase the emotional comfort of those around the person wearing the glasses. In this case, the device is a crazy pair of glasses that display eyeballs on their lenses.

"Friend Bars": A Parody on Apple's Genius Bars

www.theonion.com/video/new-apple-friend-bar-gives-customers-someone-to-ta,17693

This URL takes you to *The Onion's* parody of Apple's Genius Bars referred to as "Friend Bars" where Apple employees are taught to be empathetic and use words like "feel" as much as possible. The caption below the video reads: "Tech Trends' Jeff Tate explains the new service that pairs insufferable Apple customers with 'friends' that will listen to them rattle on for hours."

Notes

1. For Canada see Stanford, 2008b; the United Kingdom, see Bauman, 2005; for the United States, see Bluestone and Harrison, 1984 and High and Lewis: 2007.
2. The service sector officially accounted for 51 per cent of total employment in 1958.
3. The North American Industry Classification System (NAICS) is a classification system developed by the statistical agencies of Canada, Mexico and the United States governments. Adopted by all three countries in 1997 and created against the background of the North American Free Trade Agreement (NAFTA), "it is designed to provide common definitions of the industrial structure of the three countries and a common statistical framework to facilitate the analysis of the three economies" (Statistics Canada, 2012h).
4. For an early discussion, see Coffey and McRae (1989) who estimated that between 25 and 35 per cent of all employment in Canada's goods-producing sectors consists of service functions. See Acharya (2006) for more recent data and analysis.

5. Hochschild situates the *same acts* but in different contexts in order to showcase how men and women are encouraged by their employer to dig into their personal emotional experiences when searching for the appropriate emotional responses required to accomplish their task(s).
6. The Pret manual of "Pret Behaviours" tells staff to "use personal phrases that you are comfortable with and treat customers as if they are guests in your own home."
7. The eight countries are Germany, Denmark, Sweden, Austria, France, the United Kingdom, Canada, and the United States.
8. Eli Chinoy's 1955 study of United States automobile workers came to similar conclusions about the nature of work identity in the factory. Instead of identifying with the company, most workers transferred their idea of the American Dream to consumption while many workers stated they were working to help their children strive for the "American Dream."

5 The State and Regulation of Work: Policies, Problems, and Protections

Learning Objectives

- To examine the transformation from the Keynesian welfare state to the neoliberal state
- To consider the impact of neoliberalism and austerity measures on inequalities and opportunities in the labour market
- To examine labour market policies, namely employment standards and employment insurance, and problems associated with them
- To analyze the state's management of the labour market through immigration and the Temporary Foreign Workers' Program
- To discuss the public sector workplace and the impact of neoliberalism on public sector workers

Introduction

Over the past 30 years, globalization has affected political systems, economic prosperity, ways of life, the nature and activities of the state, and inequalities. To maintain competitiveness within the global economy, the Canadian state abandoned its earlier **Keynesian** framework and adopted a neoliberal agenda, removing impediments to capital mobility and capital accumulation. As the "Golden Age" of capitalism waned after the Second World War, an emerging neoliberal program slowly transformed and eventually replaced the liberal welfare state that had been based on a Keynesian approach. The liberal Keynesian state was free spending, engaged in supporting the Canadian population with social services and programs. Conservative economists and politicians raised objections to the liberal state's spending and convinced Canadians that a program of free spending would eventually contribute to a level of debt that would be difficult, if not impossible, to pay down. Embracing neoliberalism has affected labour market policies, standards, and attitudes about the public good. This chapter will discuss the path taken by the Canadian state and the ways in which the neoliberal framework is impacting labour market policies; changing employment standards, regulations, and the rights of trade unions; and transforming public service work, even within the once secure fields of education and health care.

Neoliberal Agendas and the Re-shaping of the State

Since the Second World War, in many advanced industrialized countries neoliberal states espousing austerity and engaging in retrenchment of social programs replaced liberal welfare states that had offered a variety of programs and services to support the working class. The modern welfare state was the result of a series of compromises between capital and labour during a period of unprecedented economic expansion. After the war the government engaged in massive spending programs in order to stimulate the economy. The government's plan was to support the labour force necessary for industrial expansion and manufacturing by developing programs and services as a safety net against illness, retirement, and unemployment. The government financed the program by borrowing and, as a result, amassed considerable debt.

By the mid-1970s the winds of change began to shift on a global scale. Concerns over growing debt and economic volatility prompted right wing think tanks and conservative pundits to promote a program of neoliberalism. Conservative thinkers, including Margaret Thatcher, Ronald Regan, and Brian Mulroney, dominated discussions of economic and social policy, advocating an end to the free spending of Keynesian economists and the "welfare state." In their arguments, they targeted spending on social programs as the primary obstacle to the advancement of Western economies, arguing that individuals must assume responsibility for their own well-being, and no longer rely on the state to the extent guaranteed under the welfare state agenda. Their analysis placed blame for economic difficulties squarely on the shoulders of the poor and working class for draining the public coffers (Wacquant, 2009). With these sweeping changes, including the adoption of a neoliberal framework, free trade, and free rein for transnational corporations, the number of manufacturing jobs, unionization rates, dependable employment, and lifetime security began to wane as social programs were dismantled and as "good" manufacturing jobs were outsourced to low-wage areas where health, safety, and environmental regulations were lax and where labour rights were absent.

Proponents of the welfare state started with the assumption that the state has a duty to assist citizens who have no other resources or means of support. This was a policy of entitlement by citizenship, but many felt that it did nothing to stimulate employment or economic health. In fact, some conservative thinkers worried that the welfare state encouraged idleness and dependency while discouraging self-sufficiency and responsibility. The neoliberal perspective upheld by the **Organization for Economic Cooperation and Development (OECD)** advocated independence and to this end promoted a wide range of reforms including workfare or work for welfare programs. Under neoliberalism the responsibility rested on the individual to find work, to become self-sufficient, and to lead a productive life. Substituting individual responsibility for the practice of individual entitlement that characterized the welfare state was regarded as a necessary adjustment to the global economy (Gilbert, 2004).

Neoliberal public policies and programs were marked by austerity whereby the "kinder, gentler" state of the post-war era was replaced by a program of rigorous cost-cutting and fiscal responsibility. In the years following this transition, gaps between income groups widened and growing numbers of Canadians fell into despair. Evidence suggests, for example, that between 1991 and 2011 income inequality in Canada worsened; incomes amongst middle and low-income groups declined while those of the top income group rose (Mackenzie and Shillington, 2015: 6). While some critics have suggested that the welfare state's level of spending was wasteful and extravagant and its provision of services was too expensive, others disapprove of the current regime of social disengagement.

The Role of the State and the Structure of Power

While governments and the state may appear to be socially disengaged under neoliberalism, this does not mean that the state is not involved in maintaining the structure of power and its role in ensuring that the economy remains on a trajectory of success within the global economy. Under capitalism the state is involved in creating or maintaining optimum economic conditions that satisfy the needs of capital to accumulate profits and to maintain position within the economy. Within the global economic arena, the state operates to ensure that the economy remains competitive and continues to facilitate the accumulation of capital as well as to maintain existing business and attract new ventures. How does the state operate to keep the economy on track within the global sphere? And how do we understand the shift from the welfare state to the neoliberal state?

While the state's actions greatly benefit the capitalist class, the accumulation function is also critical to the state's well-being because the state is dependent upon the prosperity of the capitalist class for its own survival. The state's revenues are derived through taxation from the economy's surplus production capacity. The state promotes profit-making by maintaining an opportune economic climate, by underwriting risks and assuming costs of production and by providing education, health, and welfare services to maintain the labour force. Simply put, the state cannot risk drying up the sources of its own revenue so it draws from the public purse to provide support services and to maintain an economic environment attractive to private profit-makers (O'Connor, 1973).

At the same time that the state is engaged in maintaining a healthy economic climate for capital accumulation and investment, it must preserve harmonious social conditions. The state presents an air of neutrality, to be regarded by the average citizen as balancing a variety of interests and as aiming toward the common good. The state adopts and administers policies, such as social welfare, employment insurance, workers' compensation, pay equity, and health and safety policies, all of which function to foster or restore social harmony, and thereby contribute to economic well-being. With the economy dominated by a small, but powerful, capitalist class (Porter, 1965; Clement, 1975;

Allahar, 1998), by maintaining harmony amongst classes the state is generally operating in the best interests of capital.

Competing interests and needs amongst social classes also act upon and condition state policy. Class contradictions and class struggle are potentially volatile. In order to maintain harmonious relations under capitalism, the state must attempt to smooth over, or quiet down, the most blatant contradictions or clashing interests within society. For example, class contradictions result from the capitalist class' interest in expanding profits by reducing labour costs, by introducing less labour-intensive work processes or machinery, or by laying off or firing employees during recessions or depressions. The result of such actions is a rising unemployment rate. But if unemployment levels become too high, large numbers of people will be unable to participate in the economy by consuming houses, cars, and other high-priced goods. In addition, if the number of unemployed workers is too high, they may begin to organize, to press for change, and to pose a threat to the system. Under such conditions, the state may introduce legislation to try to control this unrest and thereby lessen the contradictions. In fact, it was in response to the constraints and contradictions of capitalism that we understand the introduction of unemployment insurance in Canada (Cuneo, 1979; 1980), as well as the revision of the program under the neoliberal agenda. The important point here is that structural factors—class contradictions and the level of class struggle—determine state policy.

State policy, such as unemployment insurance, is not abstractly determined or the result of humanitarian efforts of free-thinking politicians. Rather, it is the outcome of real events, concrete actions, and the need to establish a balance among various class interests. Social policy is the result of what are often difficult processes including political campaigns, community action, and class struggles. For example, labour organizations had consistently supported the development of unemployment insurance since at least 1919, during the time of the Winnipeg General Strike and what was a peaceful uprising of workers over escalating unemployment. The push for unemployment insurance legislation, however, was really not a major threat until the Great Depression when unemployed workers in vast numbers began to organize and present their demands in a more militant fashion. It was at this point that the state realized the importance of meeting some of the demands of the working class, and moved forward with the passage of the *Unemployment Insurance Act* (Cuneo, 1979). State policy—in this case, Unemployment Insurance— functioned to maintain balance within a society rift with inequalities and on the brink of serious class conflict.

The argument does not suggest that the capitalist class simply orders the state on what to do, nor does it imply that the state marches to the orders of the powerful. Rather, the argument is that the state has a relative degree of autonomy from the capitalist class. For example, the capitalist class as a whole generally opposed Unemployment Insurance. Many felt that the short-term interest of immediate

CP PHOTO

A crowd gathers outside the Union Bank of Canada during the 1919 Winnipeg General Strike. The peaceful protest over rising unemployment may be seen as an early stage in the development of unemployment insurance.

profitability might suffer because of the requirement to contribute to an unemployment insurance fund. However, as the working class became more organized over the issue and began to threaten the long-term, overall interests of capital, the state moved to pass the legislation to ensure the long-term interests of capital were secure at the expense of some immediate short-term interests. Without some autonomy, this would be difficult for the state to accomplish.

Neoliberalism, Austerity, and Employment Insecurities

To understand the impact of recent austerity measures on jobs, we will start by considering labour markets. The definition of what constitutes a labour market is somewhat arbitrary. A **labour market** generally involves a contractual arrangement in which workers exchange labour for wages. There are means to enforce the terms of these arrangements. Labour markets are formal, involving government record-keeping and employment records. Labour exchanges that do not involve government records are informal and they may range from activities in the "**underground economy**" to unpaid household work and caregiving to voluntary labour within the community.

In the decades following the Second World War, and particularly for the last few decades and the coming of the so-called "new economy," Canadian researchers have been diligently tracking changes in the labour market. An important aspect of tracking changes in the labour market is the effect of sectoral shifts. As noted in Chapter 4, productivity in the agricultural or **primary sector** increased through the use of technology and sophisticated farming techniques, workers moved into the growing manufacturing sector, the **secondary sector**. Later, surplus labour moved from the goods-producing sector to the service sector, the **tertiary sector**. This latter shift, often referred to as the post-industrial society, underlies the questions regarding the emergence of a "new economy."

Dual and Segmented Labour Markets

Feminist researchers have identified important links between gender inequality and the structure of work organizations, concluding that these linkages have often operated to the disadvantage of women or racialized workers. To explain this, researchers have advanced the dual-systems theory of inequality at work. Their argument is that capitalists systematically develop conditions that pit groups of workers against each other, creating conflict and division within the labour force. When united, a workforce may demand better working conditions and higher wages. To reduce workers' solidarity, weaken bargaining power, drive down costs, and increase profits, employers exploit racial, ethnic, and gender differences to produce a split or **dual labour market**. In this scenario, one group, usually consisting primarily of white males, holds down the majority of "good" jobs while women or members of racial and ethnic groups are over-represented in low-paying and usually non-unionized jobs that are marked by poor working conditions. According to this theory, under industrial capitalism, two systems of inequality, one based on class and a second based on sex/gender and/or race/ethnic divisions have historically developed. As a result, male workers form common cause with managers, pressing for demands that reinforce their own position as men, and in some cases even exclude women from their labour organizations. This theory draws attention to the ways in which class and gender empirically combine, often limiting women's and racialized workers' access to managerial and professional positions, reinforcing women's place within traditionally sex-typed occupations, and racialized workers' position in precarious, low-wage jobs, in turn reducing the rewards that these workers can expect to receive.

Another group of theorists put forward labour market segmentation theory. Segmentation theorists reject the concept of a single labour market, arguing instead that within any labour market there are multiple sub-markets, characterized by significant differences in working conditions, employment rights, and regulatory processes. At the core of this theory is the idea of labour market dualism, the division of labour markets into primary or core and secondary sectors. Primary sectors are characterized by high levels of employment security and remuneration, occupational mobility through internal labour markets, and control over work. Jobs within the primary market require high levels of formal skills and rely on high levels of technological investment and development. Secondary labour markets are characterized by low wages, job insecurity, few formal skill requirements, little technological investment, and little worker autonomy and mobility. Labour market segmentation is shaped by multiple factors and conditions, including labour demand as required by production and the position of the firm within the market, and labour supply. Segmentation theorists analyze patterns of segmentation in relation to ascribed characteristics of workers, most notably gender and race.

Feminist analysts have identified gendered dimensions to the social organization of labour markets and have developed the concept of feminization to explain several interrelated patterns in the labour markets of industrialized capitalist economies. In the post-war period, the feminization of the workforce—that is, growing levels of participation of women in certain segments of paid work—occurred along with the designation of specific forms of work or work tasks as "women's work." While women's participation in the labour force increased dramatically in the post-war period, increases in participation were not accompanied by increases in the diversity of employment opportunities. Women's pattern of employment reflected highly gendered divisions of labour. In the public sector, women came to dominate early childhood education, childcare, elementary school teaching, social work, and nursing, all of which relate in some measure to women's traditional caring and mothering roles. With the current attack on the public sector under neoliberalism, women are facing an eroding sense of security and growing precariousness. Both the conditions and availability of work, particularly in the education and health care sectors, are diminishing.

During the post-war period, as women's participation in the labour market was beginning to rise, the **Standard Employment Relationship** emerged as the dominant model of male employment. The standard employment relationship is characterized by lifelong, continuous, full-time employment where the worker has one employer and normally works on the employer's premises or under his/her direct supervision. The standard employment relationship—an ideal type and a set of norms around which the expectations of employment during the post-war period could be measured—included job security, predictable and reasonable hours, and a "**family wage**," a wage rate calculated to provide a male breadwinner with an income sufficient to support his family. Many workers, particularly those who were not male and not white, or who were Aboriginals or immigrants, fell outside the bounds of the standard employment relationship, as employment outside the core industrial sectors was characterized by a variety of nonstandard employment relationships.

Coinciding with the massive entry of women into paid employment, beginning in the 1970s there was a marked shift away from the standard employment relationship, and nonstandard employment, including part-time work, temporary or contingent work, own-account self-employment, and multiple job holding, increased. Although women's participation in the labour force rose in the post-war years, women continue to be overrepresented in nonstandard employment. For example, by the end of the 1990s, adult women comprised over 70 per cent of the adult part-time workforce and through the 1990s the growth in women's self-employment was about three times that of men's. Increased flexibility within employment relationships was becoming a necessity for economic competitiveness, saving employers hundreds of hours in wages during slower times on daily, weekly, or seasonal bases. Nonstandard employment relationships served to provide employers with a flexible workforce. The rise of nonstandard employment and temporary jobs that offer little or no security and few, if any, benefits reflects managerial efforts to reduce companies' legal, financial and administrative obligations to employees. For example, by using temporary employees, managers may employ them on-demand and easily terminate them by simply notifying the temp agency that sent them and reporting that the temps will no longer be needed. The growth of nonstandard employment is troubling because it opens up sharp disparities in the positions held by distinct groups of employees. It also undermines the employment stability that workers have traditionally come to expect.

Along with gender, patterns of labour market segmentation are also shaped by **racialization**—the process by which racial categories are constructed as different and unequal in ways that lead to negative social, economic, and political consequences. Racialization also includes the ways in which immigrant and migrant workers are incorporated into the labour market, the association of specific forms of work with racialized groups, the overrepresentation of members of racialized groups in nonstandard and precarious employment, and the marginalization experienced by migrant and immigrant workers.

According to Vic Satzewich (1991) there are four primary ways foreign-born workers are incorporated into the labour market: free immigrant labour, unfree immigrant labour, free migrant labour, and unfree migrant labour. Each form of incorporation is defined by two conditions: the ability of the workers to circulate in the labour market, and the nature of their citizenship status. Limited access to citizenship may be tied to legislative mechanisms that prevent free movement of workers. This has been the case for agricultural workers and domestic workers, those entering Canada under temporary foreign worker programs. Citizenship defines entitlement to rights and protections in the labour market since it legitimizes processes premised on the principle that "foreigners" should not have the same rights (economic, social, and political) as citizens. In this way, citizenship is connected to the creation of groups of highly exploitable and socially excluded workers by shaping the way in which they are incorporated into the labour market in clearly racialized and gendered forms. Patterns of racialization result in labour market divisions whereby racialized workers occupy the most physically demanding and the lowest status jobs. The state supports policy that extends patterns of racialization and discrimination, satisfying employers' needs for marginalized and expendable labour. Such programs are deeply rooted in the overall system of social inequality

In the next two sections, three key labour market policies—Employment Standards, Employment Insurance, and the Temporary Foreign Workers' Program—will be examined to demonstrate the state's involvement in maintaining employer-friendly labour markets despite the costs to workers, and to identify the contradictions and constraints within which the state operates.

Labour Market Policies: Protections, Problems, and Pitfalls

Employment Standards

In the face of powerful and sometimes unscrupulous employers, powerful transnational corporations, and burgeoning numbers of precarious workers, there has been a growing need for state-sanctioned rights and protections for workers. On an international level, the **International Labour Organization** (ILO), located in Geneva, was established in 1919 at the end of the First World War with a mission of providing protection for workers against exploitation within industrializing countries. By 1920 the ILO committee established six important labour conventions covering hours of work in industry, unemployment, maternity protection, night work for women, minimum age, and night work for young people in industry (ILO, 1996–2015). At present, the ILO has numerous campaigns for the rights of workers, including child labour, forced labour, human trafficking and slavery, equality and discrimination, disability and work, and a number of others. The ILO started with the notion that work is central life activity and that people have a right to decent, fair, and safe work that is free from social injustices and discrimination. From its beginnings, the ILO has adopted a social justice agenda, especially designed to protect the most vulnerable, to bring decent work to the forefront, guaranteeing rights at work.

Following the lead of ILO Conventions and operating on national and local levels, employment or labour standards developed to provide employees with basic rights and protections tied to the specifics of labour laws and conventions at home. The vast majority of employees in Canada are covered by employment or labour standards regulated through the provinces.[1] Provincial employment standards legislation is similar from province to province. It sets out *minimum* standards that employers and employees must follow to ensure fairness in the workplace. In order to quality for protection under Employment Standards legislation, a worker must be defined as an employee. Those who are retained as independent contractors or are self-employed are not considered employees, and therefore have no protection under the act. Box 5.1 considers why this distinction is important and the dilemmas faced by workers who are not defined as employees.

Box 5.1 Everyday Work Experiences

Independent Contractors: Are they left out in the cold?

To avoid Employment Standards regulations, employers sometimes prefer to categorize workers as independent contractors, rather than as employees. Independent contractors often find themselves on shakier ground compared to those defined as employees whenever issues covered by Employment Standards arise. Under the legislation, it is up to individual workers to file complaints against their employers. While this is a daunting task for any worker, without the backing of the legislation, independent contractors are alone. Given that *ex-employees* file most complaints, this is an indication that the model does not work (Doorey, cited in Mojtehedzadeh, 2015e). Overall the legislation is weak because the fines issued to employers for infractions are minimal, leaving little incentive against violating again. But some independent contractors may be left even more vulnerable as they are shut out from even minimal forms of protection.

The minimum wage rate is one of the issues covered under Employment Standards. In the face of precarious employment and growing rates of poverty, the adequacy of minimum wage rates is at issue. Across Canada minimum wage rates (2015) range from lows of $10.30 in New Brunswick and $10.45 in British Columbia to $11.25 in Ontario and $12.50 in Northwest Territories[2] (CBC News, 2015; Retail Council of Canada, 2015). Because minimum rates are not calculated on the basis of actual living costs, the difficulties low-wage workers face vary considerably across the country. Costs of living range widely across Canada with very steep costs in Toronto, Vancouver, and Montreal as compared to most of the rest of Canada. From Table 5.1, the share of employees working at the minimum varies by province, giving rise to vast regional differences in quality of life. Provincial governments are reluctant to raise minimum rates as they are concerned that higher labour costs will entice businesses to move out and set up in a lower-wage area within Canada or across the globe.

Debates over minimum wage rates continue. Studies on costs and quality of living suggest that a decent minimum wage is about $15 per hour. Critics argue that this rate would contribute to job loss—that employers simply could not afford the extra costs and they would either shutter their businesses or lay off workers—creating more intensified working conditions—or hire fewer workers. Evidence indicates that there would be some losses, mainly among teenagers, but according to a study in British Columbia, these losses would amount to less than one per cent of the provincial employment rate and a 7.6 per cent reduction in the employment rate among those making between $10.25 and $15.00 (Green, 2015). Interestingly, teens are a minority of minimum wage earners. In British Columbia, only 26 per cent of those earning between $10.25 and $12 and only five per cent of those earning between $12 and $15 are teenagers.

Table 5.1 Share of Employees Working for Minimum Wage or Less by Province, Canada, 2000 to 2012 (percentage)

	2000	2001	2002	2003	2004	2005	2006	2007	2008	2009	2010	2011	2012
Canada	4.7	4.8	4.8	4.1	4.6	4.3	4.4	5.1	5.2	5.8	7.0	6.8	7.0
Newfoundland and Labrador	8.7	5.7	7.3	8.3	6.4	6.0	7.6	7.4	7.8	9.4	11.0	9.7	8.0
Prince Edward Island	3.7	3.2	4.5	4.0	4.3	5.1	4.5	6.7	5.7	4.1	6.0	7.0	11.0
Nova Scotia	4.9	4.1	4.6	5.9	5.5	5.1	5.9	6.3	6.5	6.8	7.4	6.0	8.8
New Brunswick	6.0	4.3	4.2	4.0	2.5	3.1	4.2	5.7	4.8	5.4	6.7	9.7	11.1
Quebec	5.4	7.0	6.1	5.2	4.4	4.6	4.2	5.4	5.9	6.2	6.9	5.7	5.5
Ontario	4.6	4.1	4.0	3.5	5.3	4.4	4.8	6.4	6.7	8.2	10.7	10.3	9.3
Manitoba	5.1	4.5	4.8	4.6	4.9	4.9	4.8	5.5	5.4	3.8	5.3	7.2	8.5
Saskatchewan	5.8	4.4	4.8	5.0	3.3	4.0	5.5	3.2	3.9	3.9	4.3	4.2	2.5
Alberta	2.0	1.5	1.1	1.1	0.9	1.5	1.7	1.2	1.7	1.3	1.3	1.1	1.9
British Columbia	4.6	6.0	7.7	5.6	6.2	5.6	4.7	3.4	2.7	2.3	2.2	3.7	7.2

Source: Special tabulations from Statistics Canada as found in Yalnizan, 2013.

In defense of higher rates, economists argue that benefits for employers include lower turnover rates, lower training costs, and a more experienced workforce because workers are less disposable and more committed (Jackson, 2007). Replacing even low-wage workers is costly. Managers have to review applications, hold interviews, and provide some training. Even when training is minimal, it takes time for the new employee to become accustomed to the ways of the workplace and settle in. Productivity, the primary concern of employers, rises with higher wages, a phenomenon economists refer to as an "efficiency wage" (Baker, 2012). Higher minimum wages reduce labour turnover especially among the least skilled, and provide more stability for both workers and employers. Greater stability boosts workers' confidence about spending. Raising the minimum wage may create incentives for people on assistance to look for work (OECD Employment Outlook, 2007) and would reduce poverty and the related tensions experienced by the working poor, including dependency on partners or other family members (Jackson, 2007).

According to the 2009 OECD Employment Outlook, about 20 per cent of workers in Canada, Germany, the United Kingdom, and Ireland, and about 25 per cent in the US were receiving low wages, defined as earning less than two-thirds of the national median hourly wage (Schmitt, 2012:1). What is significant is the persistence of low-wage work on a global scale. As Figure 5.1 indicates, across Canada the number of minimum wage workers has risen dramatically for more than a decade, with Ontario leading the way with almost 10 per cent of the labour force working for minimum wages (Yalnizyan, 2013). Over one million Canadians were paid at the minimum wage in 2012,[3] and this directly impacted household spending which drives 54 per cent of gross domestic product (Ibid.).

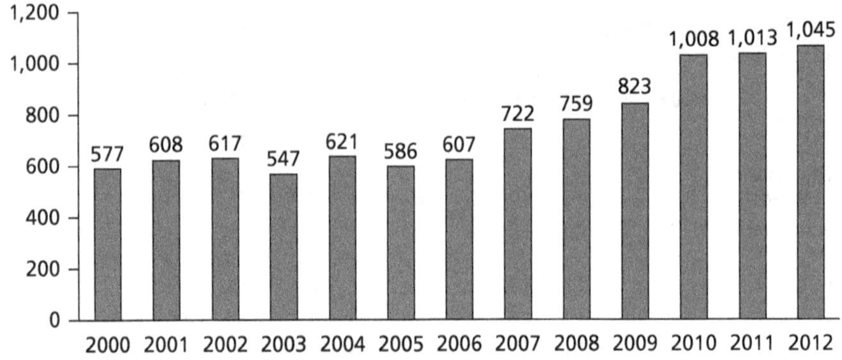

Figure 5.1 Number of Employed Minimum-Wage Workers in Canada, by Annual Averages, (100's), 2000–2012

Source: Special tabulations from Statistics Canada as found in Yalnizan, 2013.

Whenever the question of raising the minimum wage surfaces, there is a public outcry over the plight of small business and the possibility of bankruptcy is raised. A study in the United States analyzed census data between 2009 and 2011 and concluded that most minimum wage earners work for large, profitable companies, that 66 per cent of low-wage workers were employed by firms with more than 100 employees and 92 per cent of the firms were profitable (Zornick, 2012).[4] Low-wage workers are concentrated in service industries and the biggest employers of low-wage labour include Walmart, Yum! Brands (Taco Bell, Pizza Hut, KFC), McDonald's, Target, Sears, Subway, TJMaxx, and Burger King. Walmart, for example, employs 1.4 million Americans, and a vast majority of them at wages under $10 per hour while the highest-paid executive earned over $18.4 million in 2011 (Zonick, 2012). The Canadian pattern mirrors that of the United States. In Canada, between 1998 and 2012, the share of minimum wage workers hired by big business grew from 29.6 per cent of all minimum wage employees to 45.3 per cent (Yalnizyan, 2013). An increasing number of minimum wage workers are over the age of 35. Since 1998, Alberta has doubled its share of adult minimum wage workers, accounting for about 33 per cent of Albertan workers in 2012. Adults account for about 25 per cent of minimum wage workers in Newfoundland and New Brunswick, and in Ontario the number of minimum wage workers grew from 17 to 27 per cent between 2004 and 2012 (Yalnizyan, 2013).

Regardless of the minimum wage rate, it is relatively easy to find "bad bosses" who may pay less than minimum or otherwise break the law by ignoring employment standards, by failing to pay overtime or statutory holiday rates, to given notice of termination, or to maintain adequate employment records, among other infractions.

Employment Insurance

While provincial Employment Standards legislation offers protection for workers in their relationship with a specific employer, Employment Insurance legislation is designed to provide a safeguard for workers who "through no fault of their own" find themselves up against declining economic conditions. The struggle for Unemployment Insurance in Canada was rife with considerable contention, with organized labour pitted against business interests. Labour had campaigned for an unemployment insurance plan since 1919, but faced numerous difficulties in sustaining a nation-wide drive for the legislation. Business interests were united against unemployment insurance, arguing that it would impose a direct tax on employers who would have to contribute to the fund, thereby driving up prices and impeding competition with the United States. Farmers were also opposed, viewing it as a deterrent to the urban unemployed to enter low-paid agricultural work.

By the end of the 1930s, opposition began to wane as many acknowledged that some form of relief was necessary to maintain workers and their families, allowing for the reproduction of the labour force, an essential aspect of economic health. Opposition also broke down among banking and insurance industries, the creditors to municipal governments that were increasingly unable to shoulder the burden of direct relief. The most persuasive factor favouring the adoption of unemployment protection was the desire of Mackenzie King's administration to thwart the unprecedented tide of working-class mobilization and politicization that had begun following the First World War. Mackenzie King was convinced that an important way to appease labour was by introducing social welfare reforms.

Unemployment Insurance of 1941 was a limited victory for labour. Its coverage was restrictive, its terms favoured employers, the level of benefits was low in order to enforce the work ethic, it excluded over half the labour force and most areas of female employment, and it constructed women as homemakers rather than as wage workers. Despite the weakness of the legislation, what became clear is that an economic and political threat by labour is a necessary, though insufficient, condition for welfare state initiatives (Palmer, 2003).

The welfare state in Canada was based on an accord between business and labour, mediated by the state. In this arrangement, business maintained control over investment and production, and with struggle labour gained relatively stable levels of employment, wage and income security, and collective bargaining rights for trade unions. The new labour-business "welfare bargain" coincided with the state's adoption of Keynesian fiscal policy. Under Keynesianism during periods of cyclical downturns and high unemployment, the state would increase its social expenditures and sustain budget deficits to boost aggregate and consumer demand. As a counter-cyclical plan, this was a radical departure from traditional Canadian budgetary policy that tended to reinforce rather than offset swings in the economy. Under this system, new and improved social security schemes were legitimated in terms of their stabilizing effects on the process of accumulation, rather than on their effects in enhancing the quality of people's lives. This provided Canadians with a new perspective on the notion of the "good will" state and emphasized the state's primary interest in enhancing accumulation.

When Unemployment Insurance was first enacted in 1941, the primary goal was to reconcile the consequences of war and the downturned economy for Canadian families. From this time until well into the 1970s, along with the Canada Assistance Plan, Medical Care Act, Workers' Compensation, Canada/Quebec Pension Plans, and Old Age Security, Unemployment Insurance was an essential aspect of Canada's "redistributive welfare system" that enabled citizens to meet their basic needs and maintain a measure of dignity. By the late 1970s, the social safety net began to fray as the state slowly embraced a neoliberal framework. A number of factors, including the emerging economic crisis, the shift to a service economy, increases in part-time and contingent work, and growing internationalization of economic activity, affected the welfare state, placing new constraints on public policy. By the late 1970s new political voices emerged pressuring the state to adopt neoliberal changes. These forces were tied to notions of fiscal restraint, free markets, welfare state cutbacks, and increased international competitiveness. Throughout the 1980s and into the 1990s many questions were raised regarding unemployment, income security and emerging contradictions in the welfare state economy. With the shift to a Conservative government under Prime Minister Brian Mulroney, equity issues were cast aside while the government focused on economic priorities. Economic restructuring became the driving force behind all policy-related decisions and discussions with a central agenda of deregulation, privatization, debt control, and a reliance on market forces. By the mid-1990s funding for social programs, including unemployment insurance plummeted. The government's new agenda led to changes in the Unemployment Insurance program, which was renamed Employment Insurance in 1997.

Under Employment Insurance, the basis for eligibility was changed from weeks to hours worked. Rather than qualifying for Employment Insurance after having worked 12 to 20 weeks, as well as working for at least 15 hours per week for a single employer, workers were required to work a minimum of 12 to 20 weeks based on a 35-hour work week, and this essentially doubled the minimum number of hours required for eligibility. Also, new entrants and re-entrants to the labour market required more hours for eligibility. The rationale for this was to break the cycle of dependency by removing incentives promoting a revolving door of spells of work followed by spells of Employment Insurance. Further changes included increases in clawbacks, reduced premiums, and new requirements for maternity benefits. Overall, the revised program meant that women were disproportionately affected in their ability to qualify for benefits (Porter, 2003). Although the government argued that the changes to an hours-based system were more fair and equitable, women had a harder time acquiring those hours to qualify because of their increased participation in part-time and contingent work (Pupo and Duffy, 2003).

For both men and women, tighter eligibility rules and stricter job search requirements, along with regional differences in eligibility requirements (Busby and Gray, 2011) have resulted in declining recipient rates and declining rates of income replacement (Beland and Myles, 2012; Mendelsohn and Medow, 2010). Evidence suggests that only about 60 per cent of spending on Employment Insurance directly benefits families by replacing a portion of their earnings lost due to unemployment while a significant portion of the fund is used to reduce the deficit or provide retraining programs (Osberg, 2009). Retraining or labour market adjustment programs may help future employability but they do not help meet immediate economic needs. Whether or not jobs will materialize to absorb the newly created job skills depends on future business cycle recovery.

In Canada labour force characteristics are recorded monthly through a survey called the Labour Force Survey. Statistics Canada defines the labour force as "those members of the civilian non-institutionalized population 15 years of age or older, who during the reference week (the week prior to the week of the survey) were employed or unemployed." Employed persons are those who during the reference week "did any work at all" and work is defined as any work for pay or profit in the context of "an employer–employee relationship or self-employment." It also includes unpaid family work if it contributes directly to "the operation of a farm, business, or professional practice owned or operated by a related member of the household." Unemployed persons are those who, during the reference week, were without work but claim that they were actively looking for employment during the past four weeks. It also includes people who were available for work, or who had not been actively looking for work during that time but had been laid off with the expectation that they would return to their past jobs. Unemployed persons include those who had not actively looked for work in the past four weeks but had a new job to start in four weeks or less from the reference week and who were available for work. Together the employed plus the unemployed constitute the labour force.

The definition of the labour force is the critical factor in calculating the rate of unemployment. But the definition of the labour force leaves out large numbers of people who are without work or without adequate work. For example, the official unemployment rate may be reported as seven per cent. But this number would increase to over 10 per cent if discouraged workers (those who have been unemployed for a long time and are no longer actively looking for work) and involuntary part-time workers (those who are working part-time but would prefer to be working full-time) were included. In fact, many Canadians who would describe themselves as unemployed or without work (students, members of the military, women and men engaging exclusively in unpaid household work) are not included in the official unemployment rate.

With the unemployment rate remaining at very high levels, efforts to reform Employment Insurance have failed. There have been significant increases in the number of people working involuntarily in part-time jobs and "marginally attached" to the labour force. The proportion of unemployed Canadians looking for work for over a year nearly doubled between 2007 and 2012. Also, the duration of unemployment has increased, rising from 14.8 weeks on average in 2008 to 20.2 weeks in 2012 (Statistics Canada, 2013a).

Overall, Employment Insurance does little to manage the risk of unemployment and provide a real safety net for unemployed workers.[5] In today's difficult labour market, Canadians need assurance that they will receive unemployment benefits if they are laid off and have access to a reliable safety net for the possibility of long-term unemployment.

Managing the Labour Market

One of the ways in which the state manages the labour market is through immigration and migration. Prior to 1967, Canadian immigration policy was often criticized as discriminatory and racist in that the policy explicitly identified preferences for immigrants in terms of nationality and race. As a result of widespread public discussion and debate, immigration policy was revised and the 1967 *Immigration Act* promised to remove discrimination from the policy. The 1967 *Act* moved to a points system, ostensibly removing overt discrimination. In effect, the *Act* privileged professionals, educated and highly skilled people, justified by the state as a way of recruiting immigrants to meet skill shortages in Canada.

As a result, this policy disadvantaged less skilled and less educated workers from entering Canada. Lower-skilled and less educated applicants simply were unable to accumulate sufficient points to be eligible under the 1967 *Immigration Act*, and as a result their numbers declined, causing employers to clamour about the shortages of workers in lower-skilled occupations. As an answer to employers' concerns, new legislation was introduced to fill the gaps and through this process, Canadian immigration policy began to shift toward a guest worker model, inviting in temporary workers to fill particular shortages, and shifting the policy away from permanent migrant settlement.

Temporary Foreign Workers' Program

As a response to the declining numbers of low-skilled immigrants, legislation, the Non-Immigrant Employment Authorization Program (NIEAP) was introduced in 1973. The timing of this program is significant; it was introduced during a transition phase from a Fordist-Keynesian model to neoliberalism and globalization. The legislation was introduced during a highly racialized debate over the changing character of Canada. The 1967 *Immigration Act* did away with the earlier "preferred nationalities and races" approach to allow racialized individuals to enter Canada as permanent citizens if they had education or skills allowing them to accumulate sufficient points. With this change, Canadians raised concerns that this would detrimentally alter the character of Canadian society. Under NIEAP this "problem" was addressed. NIEAP marks the shift in Canadian immigration policy toward the guest worker by bringing in temporary workers to fill particular labour shortages. This is a shift away from the policy of permanent migrant settlement. By the 1980s the number of workers entering Canada on temporary work permits began outpacing the number of workers entering as permanent residents.

Migrant guest workers are unfree as their non-citizen status is used to justify a number of restrictions on their rights. To enter under the Non-Immigrant Employment Authorization Program, the worker is required to have an identified employer, an identified location of employment, an identified type of employment, and a pre-arranged length of employment. Once the worker enters under NIEAP, he/she is bound to work at a specific job for a specific period of time, for a specific employer. Workers are subject to deportation if they do not comply with these conditions. Once the specified time of employment is over, the worker must leave the country and cannot apply for landed status. In other words, the migrant worker's temporary status is permanent. Their employment relations and permanent temporary status deny them the ability to qualify for and access many social programs and services associated with social citizenship entitlement.

When NIEAP was introduced, it was justified as a program to attract professionals and skilled workers to Canada to fill existing shortages. Professional athletes, entertainers, and visiting professors, for example, were authorized to enter Canada under the program. But consistently, the majority of authorizations have been for non-professional service jobs (caregivers, retail, and clerical), manufacturing (garment industry), and primary sector jobs (agriculture). NIEAP is essentially an employer-driven program allowing employers to request migrant workers to meet their short or long-term needs. The increased use of temporary migrant workers is part of the growing employer preference for a flexible labour force.

In 2002 a new program—the Low Skilled Foreign Worker Program—deepened the shift to temporary migration and transferred primary decision-making around access to permanent residency from the Canadian state to employers. The at most or a maximum of two years job-specific training, was developed primarily to meet employers' claims of shortages. Under this program, Mexican workers began to work outside the agricultural industry in meatpacking plants and hotels, for example, particularly in Alberta and the western provinces. The program requires employers to prove that they are unable to fill their demand for low-skilled workers from within their local labour markets. Employers are expected to advertise extensively through local employment centres and national job banks for a lengthy period of time and prove that they had been unable to fill the positions. Employers require a Labour Market Opinion (LMO) from Human Resources and Skills Development Canada (HRSDC). HRSDC assesses whether a job shortage exists, whether the jobs have been advertised extensively, and whether the wages offered are equivalent to those of Canadian permanent immigrants. If these requirements are satisfied, then the employer gets a positive LMO and Citizenship and Immigration Canada issues a work permit—a visa for up to 12 months. This program resulted in a surge of low skilled workers coming into Canada.

In 2006, after consultations with employers and the provinces, the federal government created the Occupations Under Pressure Lists, expediting Labour Market Opinions and loosening rules. For example, instead of extensive advertising, employers simply had to advertise for seven days for the "occupations under pressure" in Alberta, British Columbia, and Ontario. The maximum time for work permits was extended from one to two years, except for workers under the Seasonal Agricultural Workers Program (SAWP) which remained at eight months. Workers are no longer compelled to leave for four months before reapplying; they are allowed to stay while their employer applies for a new Labour Market Opinion. In Alberta and British Columbia, LMOs have been fast-tracked for 33 occupations—roofers, front desk clerks in hotels, sales clerks, and residential cleaners are among the occupations requiring only five days for employers to advertise openings. For Canada as a whole, this marked an unprecedented wave of temporary workers entering Canada.

Two of the most significant migrant worker programs operating under the umbrella of NIEAP are the Live-in Caregiver Program (LCP), which is often in the news regarding exploitation of nannies brought in through the program, and the Seasonal Agricultural Workers Program (SAWP). SAWP has caught the attention of Canadians for a number of atrocities committed against these workers based solely on their temporary status within the country.

Shortages in agricultural labour in Canada have existed since the beginning of the 1900s. By the 1960s, in the midst of the relative prosperity during the Golden Age of capitalism, with rising productivity levels, an expanding manufacturing sector, increasing numbers of jobs with union wages and benefits, and relatively low unemployment rates, few Canadians were interested in working in the agricultural sector that offered low pay and no benefits. To meet their labour shortages, growers intensified pressure on the state to open the door to migrant labour. As a result, in 1966, the Caribbean Seasonal Agricultural Worker Program (CSAWP) was passed as a pilot project between Canada and Jamaica. The program allowed 264 Jamaican agricultural workers to come to Canada temporarily to harvest tobacco in Southern Ontario. Once the harvest was over, these workers had to leave the country.

Over the years the program has expanded to include workers from more countries and the numbers have skyrocketed to about 104,299 permit holders by 2014. In 2014, Ontario was the main destination, hosting almost 36 per cent of the temporary workers while Alberta hosted just under 20 per cent and British Columbia hosted over 16 per cent (Government of Canada, 2016). Mexico has become the main source of migrants—accounting for more than one-quarter of Canada's temporary workers holding permits in 2014 (Government of Canada, 2016). The number of non-resident workers in Canada has skyrocketed since 1996, and in 2008 for the first time Canada admitted more people on temporary work permits than the number admitted with the right to remain in Canada permanently (Strauss, 2014; Fudge and MacPhail, 2009; Faraday, 2012). Temporary workers are employed in a variety of sectors and, as Table 5.2 indicates, increases between 2005 and 2012 have been escalating.

Table 5.2 Temporary Foreign Workers by Industry Sector, 2005–2012

	2005	2012
Goods-producing sectors	27,195	81,695
Services-producing sectors	55,015	88,875
Canada Total	**82,210**	**202,510**

Source: Government of Canada. Employment and Social Development Canada, 2013. "Number of Temporary Foreign Worker Positions on Positive Labour Market Opinions, by Industry Sector. Updated October 17. http://www.edsc.gc.ca/eng/jobs/foreign_workers/lmo_statistics/annual-industry.shtml

The Seasonal Agricultural Workers Program (SAWP) is the guest worker program that was developed to respond to the labour shortage within the agricultural sector. Despite the decline in the agricultural labour force with mechanized production, migrant labour accounts for an increasing per cent of the agricultural work force (Government of Canada, 2013). The program matches the needs of employers to workers from countries under SAWP and then obtains temporary work permits from Immigration Canada for a maximum of an eight-month stay. Workers are tied to an employer and are not allowed to work for anyone else, and if they are laid off, fired, or terminated, they must leave the country. In the signed contracts with the workers, there is a provision allowing growers to repatriate a worker for "non-compliance, refusal to work, or any other sufficient reason." But there are no guidelines or definitions of what this means, in effect allowing employers to remove workers arbitrarily. For the worker, there is no formal right of appeal if the employer decides to terminate the contract. This provision seriously undermines migrant workers' ability to enforce any rights they might have. This is compounded by the fact that as non-citizens, they have no rights of mobility while in Canada. In other words, they cannot legally get another job.

Agricultural workers, including migrants under SAWP are excluded from the provincial *Labour Relations Acts* in Ontario and Alberta, meaning that they cannot unionize or bargain collectively. Agricultural workers have historically struggled to win rights to unionize, fighting the notions that crops would spoil if unionized workers went on strike and that with the low profit margins in the sector, farmers cannot afford higher wages. These arguments against agricultural workers' rights to unionize are no longer compelling. There has been a significant transformation in agriculture since the 1960s. Farms are more concentrated, larger, and more capitalized, and small family farms have largely been displaced by agribusiness with sizeable greenhouses, winemaking operations, and other specialized capacities.

Without citizenship rights, temporary foreign workers are not eligible for Employment Insurance and other benefits. Despite their ineligibility, it has been estimated that in 2008, temporary foreign workers contributed as much as $126 million in Employment Insurance premiums (EI Task Force, 2011: 15). With regard to qualifying for Employment Insurance, temporary foreign workers are in a catch-22. A requirement for eligibility is that workers must have worked a certain number of hours (depending on the regional rate of employment) within the past 52 weeks to qualify, yet temporary foreign workers are restricted in their employment terms. Further, they must prove that they are available for work and unable to obtain suitable employment. But the employer-specific work permit restricts them from being available for work for other employers. As such, temporary foreign workers with restricted work permits are not available for work and do not qualify for benefits. Their contributions help to swell Canada's Employment Insurance account that has a surplus in the billions of dollars, used by the federal government to pay down the national debt. Canada is profiting by way of a transfer of payments from low-paid migrant workers from developing countries.

Shifting Securities and Opportunities in the Public Sector Labour Market: The State as Employer

Within the public sector in traditional strongholds of health care, social services, and education, work arrangements have been changing. On the one hand, new forms of work and flexibility standards promise to empower workers while promoting organizational efficiency. On the other hand, public sector workers have faced layoffs, downsizing, new management practices, and technological changes that are causing these workers to be concerned about their working conditions as well as about the quality of service delivery (Macdonald, 2011). The new practices produce consequences for individuals, families, and communities as existing social, political, cultural, and legal frameworks connecting them to the various levels of the state and its services are altered.

A complex set of factors, including mounting economic pressures to maintain a Canadian presence in the global economy, rising costs of social reproduction, fiscal crises, technological innovations, new management structures, and flexibility initiatives are transforming the public sector workplace. Transformations have included privatizing some aspects of public sector work, devaluing or deskilling certain categories of work, and eliminating some forms of work altogether. The reorganization of work within the public sector has wide-ranging impacts on workers within that sector and on state policies and programs, the accessibility of governments and state services at local regional and national levels, and the meaning of governance.

Researchers disagree about whether restructuring has had positive impacts on workers, work performance, and communities. Some argue that work reorganization has resulted in increased levels of productivity, greater efficiency, and improvements in service delivery, thereby benefiting the quality and conditions of family and community life. Critics suggest that new work arrangements have transformed the public sector from a bastion of "good jobs" to a harbinger of "bad jobs" and in the process have short-changed the community with regard to the availability of services and service providers and the accessibility of social programs. They argue that the changes have not sufficiently improved the nature and extent of inequalities within and between communities and regions, nor have they enhanced the quality and conditions of life for individuals and families.

Understanding work restructuring within the public sector entails a complex and detailed consideration of the movement of work from the public domain to the realm of private enterprise as well as to the sphere of unpaid work. How is the Canadian state responding to global economic pressures and under what conditions have recent economic transformations within the public sector provided advantages or disadvantages for Canadians? Focusing primarily on the private sector, social analysts have studied global economic transformations and whether they have contributed to greater opportunities or given rise to increased precariousness and insecurity. Many are concerned that there has been a measurable decline in the social condition of work, and that shifts toward insecure, poorly compensated, nonstandard work have overshadowed developments toward quality work. In the context of a general decline in the conditions of work, how does the state as employer rate with regard to equity issues, collective bargaining, security, opportunity, citizenship rights, the employment of social capital, and the commitment to human capital? Transformations within the public sector have redefined the ways in which work is organized and managed, affecting workers' sense of well-being and security, as well as their expectations regarding access to work. The Canadian state's austerity agenda has resulted in a restructuring program that includes cutbacks, undermining unions' victories, privatization of services, contracting out, and changes in labour processes with the shift to call centre formats in some service venues.

Among public sector workers seriously affected by the state's restructuring and austerity agenda are those in health care, including nurses, medical practitioners, personal support workers, and workers within the ancillary services within health care facilities (Armstong and Armstrong, 2010). The changes have affected the quality of care for patients and their families. Shortened hospital stays and short staffing on hospital wards have directly impacted unpaid family caregivers, especially women, who are expected to take over tasks formerly assigned to paid staff, including feeding and personal care of patients while under institutional care. Family members are also obliged to take patients home before they are well enough to care for themselves. Nurses at all levels have seen their caseloads grow along with their responsibilities while their level of compensation does not reflect their increased workload and the accompanying stress and burnout that often accompanies it. Maintenance, housekeeping, and food preparation workers have watched the number of workers in their departments dwindle as their services have been contracted out, often to the lowest bidder, with little regard for the health, safety, and well-being of patients and the staff who care for them.

Conclusion

Once characterized as beneficent under a Keynesian framework, the state's agenda is now defined by austerity. To keep Canada competitive, the state adopted a neoliberal approach in order to align activities, policies, and practices with those of the major players within the global economy. In this process, the state abandoned free spending on public services and costly programs, while satisfying the needs of employers for a flexible yet self-sufficient workforce. In this new regime, work has become less secure and workers can no longer count on a long and stable work life and a strong safety net for those who fall through the cracks.

Questions for Critical Thought

1. What accounts for the shift from the perspective and practice of the welfare state to that of neoliberalism?
2. Under neoliberalism, what are some of the ways in which workers in Canada have lost rights and protections that were previously guaranteed?
3. How have working conditions in the public service changed over the past few decades?

Suggested Further Resources

Armstrong, Pat, and Susan Braedley. 2013. *Troubling Care: Critical Perspectives on Research and Practice.* Toronto: Canadian Scholars' Press. This collection of papers presents a feminist political economy approach to the management of care within Canada's ailing health care system.

Vosko, Leah. 2010. *Managing the Margins: Gender, Citizenship, and the International Regulation of Precarious Employment.* New York: Oxford. This book examines national and international approaches to regulating contemporary labour markets, arguing that the approaches do not account for precarious and low-wage workers, leaving thousands, especially women and migrants, at the margins.

Suggested Websites

Canadian Union of Public Employees (CUPE)
http://cupe.ca/sites/cupe/files/EI-Advisory_Dec_14_2012.pdf
One of the campaigns of the Canadian Union of Public Employees (CUPE) is to raise awareness of the changes to *Employment Insurance Act* and the difficulty that Canadians experience in their attempt to qualify for this benefit.

United Food and Commercial Workers (UFCW)
www.ufcw.ca/Theme/UFCW/images/en/socialjustice/downloadables/trifold_leaflet_EN_online.pdf
For a number of years, the United Food and Commercial Workers (UFCW) has campaigned diligently to bring justice to Canada's foreign temporary workers, raising awareness about the lack of support, benefits, and services that native-born workers enjoy.

Notes

1. About six per cent of employees in Canada are covered under the *Canada Labour Code* (Government of Canada, 2015). Workers in federally regulated sectors, such as banks, federal Crown corporations, radio and television broadcasting, and so on fall under the *Canada Labour Code*. Otherwise, the provincial standards regulate the conditions of work.
2. In some provinces there are alternative rates for a variety of positions, including liquor and food servers, construction workers, homeworkers, live-in caregivers, and students. See http://www.retailcouncil.org/quickfacts/minimum-wage.
3. About half of these minimum wage workers live in Ontario.
4. The 50 largest employers of low-wage workers were all in strong financial positions. Executive compensation in these companies averaged $9.4 million.
5. Both the benefit duration and income replacement levels of EI in Canada are far below the OECD averages as well as the levels of Canadian unemployment insurance in the past.

6 Labour Markets and Work Time

Learning Objectives

- To examine working time and locate the emergence of the standard employment relationship (SER)
- To explore the dramatic growth in nonstandard employment and to consider its implications
- To discuss the specific evolution of *involuntary* nonstandard work times
- To analyze nonstandard work times and intersecting patterns of inequality, notably gender, social class, immigrant status, and age
- To explore persistent concerns about "too much work"
- To consider recent initiatives to address work time inequities

Introduction

Working times may seem natural and inevitable. The 40-hour week, the five-day week, and the eight-hour day have been pretty much taken for granted. However, there is nothing set in stone about working times. The work day and work week we have taken for granted was the result of a prolonged historical struggle. In recent years, notions of standard working times have been steadily eroded, and in their place a wide diversity of nonstandard employment has emerged—including the proliferation of part-time, casual, contract/term, on-call, temporary, and precarious working times. As a result, the labour force experiences of numerous Canadians have been altered. These shifts have had particularly significant implications for women, youth, recent immigrants, and the working class. This ongoing proliferation of nonstandard work times appears key to the entrenchment of economic marginalization for these workers. Not only do women, youth, recent immigrants, and workers who have lost their industrial jobs find themselves forced to accept part-time, short-term, or other irregular working positions, even highly educated recent grads may struggle to land full-time "regular" work. The recent popularization of unpaid internships, in which young workers entering the labour market work for months without pay or for a minimal stipend and without employer commitment, in order to build their resumes and "get a foot in the door," speaks to the scarcity of traditional scheduled work and to the intensification of young workers' time exploitation. Even workers who have secured the five-day, 40-hour week may feel compelled to intensify their work time commitments as they juggle paid and unpaid work, as they face growing employment insecurities, and as they confront the failure of wages to keep up with increased costs of living. Needless to say, workers' organizations and legislators have attempted to push back by, for example, restricting the use of unpaid internships and demanding concessions guaranteeing workers minimum work-pay when they show up for a three hour shift. Nonetheless, the battle over working times is far from resolved.

Locating Working Time in History

To understand working time, we must first locate it in history and identify the momentous changes which set the stage for contemporary constructions of time. If there ever was a "natural" timing of human lives, it was likely located in the context of pre-historic hunting and gathering societies. Here, for the bulk of human history, time was embedded in daily survival needs and seasonal change (Negrey, 2012: 10–14). Days, seasons, and biology framed working lives and, while the struggle for survival was difficult, it appears likely that for the first 30,000 to 50,000 years humans enjoyed greater time flexibility (notably, more time for leisure, sleep, and creative activities) than societies in the past 3,000 years. This relative time fluidity came to a halt as hunting and gathering societies were engulfed by the agricultural revolutions. As humans achieved advances in both agriculture and animal husbandry, more permanent settlements were possible. Now, the productive efforts of men, women, and children were less flexible—crops needed to be planted, tended, and harvested at set times and animals required time-patterned care. In this context, the vast majority of humans toiled from childhood to old age in a daily struggle to produce adequate resources for themselves and their families while the fortunate few were able to live off of their labour. For example, by the early Middle Ages a feudal system was established throughout much of Europe. Peasants provided the daily intense labour in order to produce seasonal crops and then paid a portion of their crops to the local ruler and his soldiers in return for protection. As a result, a significant minority of the population enjoyed relative leisure. The net result was that well before the industrial revolution the time structure of human lives had become both increasingly differentiated and strict: the few enjoyed considerable freedom from time constraints and the majority were constrained to toil daily from earliest childhood to death.

Embedded in the feudal era were the roots for a revolution in working time. Churches, monasteries, and nunneries were often important repositories for cultural and productive life in feudal Europe. Given this role, it is not surprising that they should play a pivotal role in the emergence of new "time" regimes; specifically they first introduced fixed and pre-set times for religious and productive activities and also enshrined the social value of punctuality (Negrey, 2012[1]). Soon, the preoccupation with the accurate measurement of time flooded into the wider society. As merchants rationalized their enterprises, it became increasingly important to keep track of travel times, costs associated with journeys, and the time expended by workers who laboured for them. Needless to say, the introduction of accurate time-keeping played a key role in regularizing working times. By the mid-1300s, mechanical clocks had been developed and clock towers were to be found at the centre of many European cities (Negrey, 2012; Whitrow, 1988). Through the course of the Middle Ages, clockmakers had perfected portability, and pocket watches increasingly diffused time management throughout society. By the end of the 1800s, notably with the introduction of Greenwich Mean Time in 1883, time had been both rationalized and globalized (Negrey 2012, 18; Whitrow 1988).

The stage was set for contemporary life in which the concept of time is at the core of human existence. Through the course of the early 1900s, agricultural production regulated by patterns of day and night and seasons everywhere gave way to the time discipline of craft and industrial production (Hermann, 2015). Increasingly specific time regimens—in education, in paid labour, and in personal life—were highly structured.

These complex developments were, however, far from uncontested. Throughout the past 100-odd years, control over work time was at the centre of various social struggles as well as over the quality of human life. From a straightforward political economy perspective, this specific conflict over working time may be understood in terms of the contradiction between the employers/owners' desire to maximize profit and increase the number of hours worked by his/her employees (to the degree that this increases profitability), and the employees' interest in reducing constraints on their time and maintaining "free" time outside of the workplace (Berg, Bosch, and Charest, 2014). Here, highly skilled, not easily replaced, workers will be in an advantageous negotiating position (Gould, 2010). However, the majority of workers who are (depending on the historical context) easily replaced (such as the **reserve army of labour** including women, the unemployed, seniors, youth, racialized minorities, and immigrants) will usually struggle to exercise control over working time. Generally, they will wrest some "say" if they organize as a collective and use mass withdrawal of labour to challenge the employers' power (for an opposing view, see Edwards, 2010).

In the initial stages of the industrial revolution, workers, generally unorganized, often found themselves faced with onerous work–time expectations and little power. In the absence of alternatives, early factories might engage men, women, and children as workers for 16 hours a day and 70-hour weeks (Golden, 2009: 217). In response to a backlash against the exploitation of child workers in textile mills, the British government introduced in 1819 a 12-hour limit on children's work days. Ultimately, failure to enforce this legislation and pressure by workers' shorter hours committees resulted in the *Factory Acts* (1847) which dictated a 10-hour day for women and children (Hermann, 2015: 110; Federation of International Employers, n.d.). This legislation not only established the notion of a "normal working day" but, importantly, triggered the expansion of the Trade

Union movement in Britain. Control over working time became a core feature of workers' resistance.

Once trade unions were well established, collective agreements became an important site for struggles over work hours. By the early 1890s, an international progressive campaign was launched in Europe, Britain, and North America to introduce the eight-hour day (and a 48-hour work week). Mass rallies and strikes underscored the significance of this initiative. In Canada, the historic six-week general strike in Winnipeg prioritized shorter work hours amongst its demands. However, despite considerable turmoil and struggle, the campaign for shorter hours and control over working times tended to flounder until after the First World War (Hermann, 2015: 115).

These early struggles over workers' time were also directly linked to the dramatic expansion of public education in the early twentieth century. The Canadian government not only funded education to ensure all Canadians, particularly the masses of immigrant children, were taught about strict time schedules and punctuality but also established truancy laws to punish non-attendance. Nowhere was this socialization of Canadian children into a rigid time-work regime more apparent than in governmental endorsement of the residential schools for Canadian Aboriginals, which sought to both annihilate native cultural traditions about time and funnel Aboriginals into the paid labour force. Along with establishing public education for the masses, the federal government and provinces were also creating a hodgepodge of regulations designed to re-enforce work time regimens. The Great Depression of the 1930s interrupted these trends and turned the labour market on its head; workers faced 30 per cent unemployment rates as factories closed or reduced production. Employers, facing reduced demand for products, cut working hours for their remaining workers and by 1932 in the United States more than 50 per cent of all workers and 63 per cent of manufacturing workers were employed part-time (Hermann, 2015: 117). Abruptly, employers were eager to cut working times, and unions endorsed a shorter work day as a means to ensure greater sharing of available work. In Canada, the legislative struggle over work time was complicated; the federal government legislated a 40-hour work week for workers employed on government contracts in 1930, but the provinces did not uniformly follow suit. Ultimately in the post-Second World War era, a compromise was reached across industrialized countries in which an eight-hour work day was normalized, the work week was set at roughly 40 hours, and overtime beyond 40 hours a week generally resulted in over-time pay. By the early twenty-first century, France set the maximum normal working week at 35 hours, and many European countries legislated workers' **right to request** variable work hours (Berg, Bosch, and Charest, 2014: 806; Federation of International Employers, n.d.).

This move to a 40-hour (more or less) work week was clearly contested and the resolution was, as we shall see, decidedly short lived. Predictably, employers resisted giving up the productivity advantage of longer working hours; for example, even today employers benefit from requiring longer hours from one worker (with benefits) rather than having several on the payroll. Canadian workers, through their unions, continued to struggle for reductions in and more control over working hours. Over time, union pressure and dramatic economic growth during the **Golden Age of Capitalism** resulted in significant changes in average manufacturing work hours, which fell from 48 hours in 1944 to 41 hours in 1960 (Hermann, 2015: 122). By the early 1980s, a standard work time of 40 to 44 hours was established across Canada (Hermann, 2015: 123). In addition, the new working regime generally came with routine entitlements to paid time off, for example, for illness and paid vacations (Fudge, 2011: 171). During this Golden Age, "good jobs" flourished in industrial plants and government offices and permanent full-time work generating a **family wage** became increasingly the norm (PEPSO, 2013: 13).

The 1950s and 1960s marked a period of stabilization in working hours and, despite variations across Canada, a **standard employment relationship (SER)** was established and set the social and policy standard for "normal" work (Vosko, 2007). The boxed insert below provides some specifics about current employment time legislation. Importantly, Quebec legislation has for several decades been significantly more progressive in protecting workers' rights to reduced working time.

A Sketch of Some Current Time Regulations in Canada, Ontario, and Quebec

Below are highlights from the Canadian *Employment Standards Act* (CES) and comparable legislation enacted in Quebec and Ontario. The CES applies to all federally regulated employees. The Ontario and Quebec legislation provide examples of provincial laws which apply to workers not covered by the federal regulations.

Maximum number of hours daily: Currently, [Federally] most employees may be required to work a daily maximum of eight hours in any period of 24 consecutive hours. In Ontario, the work day may be longer if this is "the established regular workday." Further, the daily maximum may be exceeded by written agreement between employee and employer. Finally, as long as other requirements are met, work may be scheduled at night or during the day.

Maximum number of hours weekly: [Federally] The maximum number of hours an employee may be required to work in a week is 48. Again, this maximum may be exceeded if there is a written agreement between the employer and the employee and the employer has the approval of the Director of Employment Standards (Ontario). Federally, the "standard" hours of work are 40 hours a week, with a maximum of 48 hours and with at least one full day of rest, usually Sunday. This maximum for hours per week may be exceeded in emergencies and under an averaging plan or a modified work schedule [Federal].

Time free from work: Employees must receive time free from work. [Ontario] In most cases, employees must have at least 11 consecutive hours off work each day.

This rule does not apply to on-call employees. Shift workers must receive at least eight hours off between shifts unless the total time worked on two shifts is not more than 13 hours. An employer and employee may also agree in writing that the employee will receive less than eight hours off between shifts. Exceptional circumstances (emergencies, natural disasters, major equipment failures, accidents, etc.) may negate these requirements and result in employees being required to work more than eight hours a day, more than 48 hours a week and during "free" time. In Quebec, employees are entitled to a rest period of at least 32 consecutive hours each week.

Also, (Ontario) employers are required to provide "eating" periods—employees must not work for more than five hours without a 30-minute meal break. However, if employer and employee agree (orally or in writing) the meal break may be broken into two 15-minute eating periods within every five consecutive hours. In the absence of an employment contract requiring payment, meal breaks are unpaid. Meal breaks are not considered toward overtime. In Quebec, employees must be paid for their meal break if they are not allowed to leave their work station. Other breaks, including "coffee" breaks are not required from the employer. In Quebec, if a coffee break is granted it must be paid and included in calculation of hours worked.

Sources: Government of Canada, 2015 http://www.labour.gc.ca/egn/standards_equity/st/holiday.shtml; Ontario Ministry of Labour, 2015 http://www.labour.gov.on.ca/english/es/pubs/guide/hours.php; Quebec Ministry of Labour, 2015 http://www.cnt.gouv.qc.ca/fileadmin/publications/C_0149a.pdf

What is most notable here is, first, the myriad of "exceptions" and, secondly, the diversity of employer/employee rights across jurisdictions. As a result, many workers, especially those not represented by a union, might hesitate to resist employer pressures for longer or shorter hours or even to ask for employer compliance with their legislated employment rights (Vosko and Thomas, 2014; see also Drache et al., 2014).

The Explosion of Nonstandard Work and Segmentation and Marginalization in the Labour Market[2]

The stabilization of working hours and establishment of SER did not last long. The Golden Age of Capitalism, in which workers not only worked a steady 40 hours a week but also stayed with one employer for "life" and made use of "job ladders" and "career opportunities," went into decline during the 1970s (Drache et al., 2014). Through the 1980s and 1990s, there was an overall drop in full-time employment and, notably, the numbers of young people with full-time jobs declined. Within this overall reduction in full-time work, there were important exceptions. Women aged 25 to 34 increased their full-time participation from 1997 to 2007, but from 2007 to 2012 it dropped slightly. Until the collapse in oil prices 2015, young people, notably males, in oil producing provinces (Alberta, Saskatchewan, and Newfoundland and Labrador) experienced a boom in full-time work (Galarneau, Morissette, Usalcas, 2013: 4, 5).

Turbulence in full-time work was interwoven with increased **hours diversification and polarization**. On the one hand (as discussed below), average annual working hours started rising—especially amongst managerial, professional, transportation, and sales occupations and among the higher wage-earners (typically better educated men). Meanwhile, the short-time labour force, notably part-time work, had been growing exponentially.[3] From the 1960s, numerous wives and mothers entered the paid labour force as did increasing numbers of young people combining education and paid work. Many accepted some form of shorter hours of work. Increasingly, the labour market was split between those working longer and those working shorter hours. Within this polarization a vast array of diverse **nonstandard work** time arrangements emerged.[4]

By the latter part of the twentieth century, analysts were increasingly aware that the old time regime with its standard employment relationship was fraying (Cordova, 1986; Krahn, 1991, 1995; Duffy and Pupo, 1992). In Canada, by the end of the 1980s, almost 30 per cent of work in Canada was nonstandard (Green, Krahn, and Sung, 1993) and by the twenty-first century 37 per cent of Canadian workers were occupied in nonstandard employment (Hunsley, 2013a; Llena-Nozal, 2015). Apparently, 21 per cent of work currently performed in Ontario is nonstandard (Mojtehedzadeh, 2015a). The story is similar throughout much of the industrialized world (Bosch, Dawkins, and Michon, 1993; Huberman and Minns, 2007). A recent study by the **Organisation for Economic Co-operation and Development (OECD)** reported that since the 1990s nonstandard employment has accounted for more than half of all new job creation and now characterizes more than one-third of all employment in industrialized economies (Stewart, 2015; see also Llena-Nozal, 2015). In the United Kingdom, reports indicate *all* net jobs growth since 1995 has been in nonstandard employment. Figure 6.1 reveals some of this upheaval.

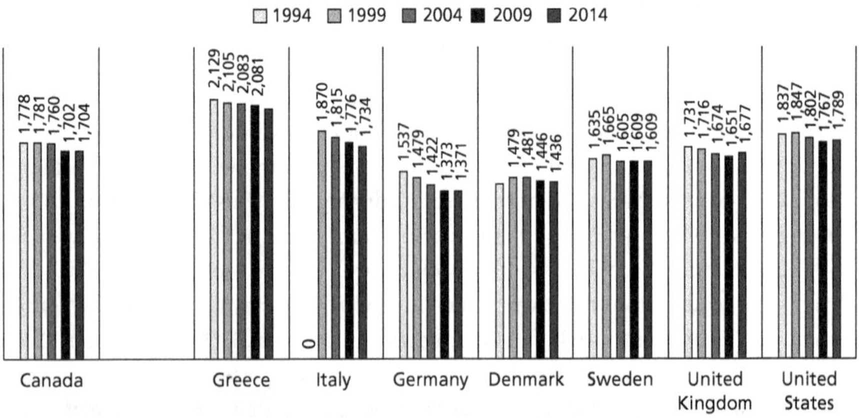

Figure 6.1 Average Annual Hours Worked per Worker, 1994–2014

Source: Dataset - LFS - Average Annual Hours Worked Available at https://stats.oecd.org/.

Average annual hours of work, combining all forms of employment, has tended to decline in many industrialized economies from 1994 to 2014. However, there are notable differences between countries. Imperilled economies, notably Italy and Greece, still record high average hours worked while Germany, Denmark, and, to a lesser degree, Sweden have seen their work hours decline. The United States, followed by Canada, have experienced overall declines but still maintain relatively high average hours when contrasted with countries such as Germany.

The root causes for the shifts in working hours, as discussed in Chapter 1, are complex and diverse (Berg, Bosch, Charest, 2014; Drache et al., 2014; PEPSO, 2013). Certainly the growing size and economic clout of transnational corporations along with the move to financialized capitalism coupled with dramatic advances in technology eased the path to offshoring industrial production to lower-cost countries. In much of North America and Europe the manufacturing jobs built around 40 hours a week plus overtime were rapidly eroded and at the same time, **neoliberalism** supported reductions in public sector standard full-time employment, as many central governments sought efficiencies and economies. Simultaneously, supported by technological innovation, population growth, and suburbanization, there was explosive growth in the consumer economy in the Global North. In particular, service sector employment grew exponentially as fast food restaurants, retail outlets in suburban malls, personal services, and so forth proliferated throughout communities.

In Canada, for example, employment in service producing industries, which had ballooned through the 1980s and 1990s, continued to supplant manufacturing and resource extraction jobs. Between 2000 to 2013 service sector work grew from 73 to 79 per cent of all paid employment. Almost one in five jobs was located in a service-producing industry (Drache et al., 2014). In Toronto alone the number of retail workers grew by 34 per cent to reach 300,000 in the 15 years ending in 2014 (Mojtehedzadeh, 2015a). These service sector positions were seen to necessitate increased nonstandard employment since the need for workers ebbed and flowed during the day and/or seasonally, profit margins were notoriously narrow, and the work required was considered unskilled.

Along with the expanding service sector, technological and population changes also supported nonstandard employment. The information and communication technology (ICT) revolution facilitated working from home or from a satellite office as well as various aspects of self-employment and contract work. Call-centre work was a direct product of advances in communication technologies. Similarly, complex nonstandard work time schedules were made feasible by massive data storage and manipulation. The persistent trend toward urban concentrations also provided a growing market for myriad services, ranging from grocery delivery to home daycare. Finally, the overall aging of the population, common in much of the Global North, dramatically increased the demand for personal and health services. The net effect is a revolution in working time arrangements.

Diversities of Nonstandard Work

While nonstandard work is not a new work phenomenon, its popularization and routinization in many modern labour markets is. Part-time work led the way. In 1953, the first year for which Canadian statistics on part-time workers were collected, data indicated only 3.8 per cent of the labour force were part-timers; by the end of the 1980s, one in seven (15 per cent) Canadian workers was part-time, and growth in part-time work was dramatically out-pacing full-time work (Duffy and Pupo, 1992: 43–5). Today, 18 per cent (almost one in five) of the Canadian workforce is working part-time (Statistics Canada, 2015g).

Other new work time patterns emerged throughout industrialized economies and were further spurred on by the economic downturns in the 1980s, 1990s and, most notably, the 2008 recession. Employers cut their costs and increased their flexibility not only by laying off workers and intensifying the pace of work but also by increasingly turning to various combinations of part-time and full-time schedules embedded in **casual/on-call**, **contract**, **term (short/limited)**, and **temporary** schedules. The casual/on-call worker, for example, has no set hours (although s/he typically is guaranteed a minimum number of work hours per week) but maintains his/her availability to be called in for paid work depending on the employers' needs.

Self-employment has also lent itself to new work time arrangements. Economic uncertainties and restricted employment opportunities have led many Canadians to turn to self-employment; indeed, much recent "job creation" is the result of increases in self-employment. The self-employed are a diverse group, including large, well-capitalized, enterprises with multiple employees as well as **"own account"** self-employed individuals who have no employees. Self-employment has been particularly prominent amongst women, and for a time was popularized by the government as a solution not only to work–family conflict but to workplace gender inequities. In theory, women who started their own business could set their own hours, work from home, and earn a steady wage. With luck, they could achieve economic independence. Between 1996 and 2001 the number of women entrepreneurs grew by 8 per cent compared to 0.6 per cent for men (Karman and Elleithy, 2006). By 2009, 12 per cent of employed women were self-employed. Women (2009) comprised more than one-third of the approximately 3 million self-employed Canadians (Government of Canada, 2016a). Not surprisingly, these self-employed women tend to operate home-based businesses, to be "own account," to work part-time, and to make low average earnings. Their work time flexibility (outside of Quebec) comes at the cost of lack of or restricted access to benefits, pension plans, employment insurance, labour law protections, and maternity leave (*Monthly Labour Review*, 2015; Karman and Elleithy, 2006). Table 6.1 summarizes the major components of nonstandard work in Canada.

Table 6.1 Percentage of Canadians in Nonstandard Employment Forms

Self-employed	30%
Temporary Contract	25%
Permanent Part-time	25%
Temporary Part-time	20%

Source: Llena-Nozal, Ana. 2015. *Non-Standard Work and Inequality*. University of Luxembourg: OECD.

There are also diversities within the various nonstandard forms of employment. Some of the self-employed also engage in another form of nonstandard employment—**multiple job holding**. Working several part-time jobs or combining full-time and part-time work may be seen as a protection against the insecurities of any one working option but likely implies increased work-related stress. Between 2005 and 2014, multiple job holders increased by 22 per cent and today comprise 938,500 Canadian workers. There was a particularly strong growth between 2005 and 2014 amongst those workers who were combining multiple jobs in order to generate 40 hours per week. This population of workers grew by 34 per cent by 2014 (Statistics Canada, 2015i: CANSIM Table 282-0036). Self-employment and multiple job holding may also intersect with another feature of nonstandard work—**contract work**. Unlike the SER, which is premised on some notion of permanency, contract work is structured around a specified finite length of time (also referred to as **short/limited term employment**) or around a specified task. While workers may enjoy the prospect of constant change and challenge implied by "working contract," they must also negotiate its constant economic uncertainties.

Nonstandard employment is also implied in the popularization of various **flexible working arrangements** in the 1980s and 1990s. In response to workers' concerns with family/work conflict and increasing commute times, **flextime** and **flexplace** policies were introduced by various public and private employers (Turcotte, 2010). Working from home (**telecommuting**) allows workers to avoid "the commute" altogether while being more available to family members. Flextime allows employees to start early and leave early or to work longer hours over four days in order to have all or part of the fifth day off. **Job-sharing** allows two (typically) workers to share one full-time job and thereby enjoy part-time hours while maintaining pro-rated benefits, training, and work security. In Canada, these flexible work arrangements (or **family-friendly work**) are not mandated by government policies and are not common outside of public sector workplaces (Sweet, Pitt-Catsouphes, Besen, and Golden, 2014). Given tough economic times, workers with opportunities to exercise control over working time—such as flextime policies offered by employers—have substantially decreased in numbers since 2001 (Duxbury and Higgins, 2014: 13).

While nonstandard work itself is not inherently problematic, analysts are alarmed by dramatic increases in temporary workers. Between 1997 and 2013, growth in temporary jobs, in particular contract jobs, accounted for roughly one-quarter of the overall growth in employment in Canada; by 2012, one in seven jobs in Canada were temporary (Burleton et al., 2013: 2, 15). A significant element in this growth in temporary work has been the dramatic expansion in the numbers and use of **temporary help agencies**. Workers provided by temporary help agencies are often termed **contingent** since their employment at any one location depends on the needs of that client and because they are often paid by their agency (who receives a percentage of their earnings). As a result, their relationship to the workplace is not only temporary but marked by a reduced form of attachment. Increasingly, employers appear to prefer using help agencies since their commitment to the employee is minimized and they save the time and monies necessitated by a search for an appropriate employee. In certain regions and in urban centres, temporary work has been particularly prominent. In British Columbia, between 2009 and 2013, temporary work accounted for 40 per cent of the post-recession job creation and, predictably, grew more quickly than permanent jobs (Longhurst, 2014). The number of temporary workers in Toronto increased by 33 per cent from 2004 to 2014 when it surpassed 340,000 (Mojtehedzadeh, 2015b). This growth of temporary work has also been reflected in reduced length of time spent in specific jobs. The period of time that employees hold their job (**job tenure**) has declined in all OECD countries except France. Short/limited term work has become increasingly normative in several sectors of employment (see Everyday Work Experiences Box 6.1).

Carlos Osorio/Toronto Star via Getty Images

The growth of temporary agencies reveals problems in Canada's labour force. Here workers protesting low wages and *Employment Standards Act* violations demonstrate outside of a temp agency in Toronto. A recent Ministry of Labour enforcement blitz showed that three out of every four temp agencies inspected were violating basic employment standards. The protestors used giant loonies to demonstrate the wage gap for temp agency workers, who are predominantly women and immigrants.

Box 6.1 Everyday Work Experiences

Why Education Is Not a Solution to Nonstandard Work

Dramatic increases in youth unemployment and underemployment have prompted many students to improve their educational qualifications. Indeed, the evidence does suggest that involuntary nonstandard employment, with corresponding low wages and work insecurity, is more common amongst the "low educated."

Ironically, many Canadians find that even with the highest levels of educational accomplishment, they still confront the grim realities of nonstandard and insecure work. Increasingly, Canadian academics seeking employment in both universities and colleges are finding a dearth of full-time, permanent (tenured) positions and, in their place, a variety of insecure, temporary contract positions. Across Canada, academics, despite their doctorates, publications, and strong teaching records, face the prospect of being hired on a course by course basis (sessional appointments) or for short-time contracts (one to two years). Neither type of position provides any guarantee of future employment, although unionized part-time faculty may benefit from seniority clauses. At the end of each term, many contract faculty must compete once again for whatever teaching positions become available.

Although good data on contingent faculty are difficult to find, there are some disturbing fragments of information. In 2012, for example, at the University of British Columbia (2012–2013), approximately 25 per cent of faculty were on limited term contracts and these individuals taught as much as 70 per cent of all undergraduate courses. The overwhelming majority of these instructors hold appointments of less than one year. At the University of Calgary, sessionals comprise almost one-quarter of the faculty and at Wilfrid Laurier University contract academic staff on temporary, per-course contracts taught 52 per cent of all students registered in classes, tutorials, labs, and seminars (up from 38 per cent in 2008). A recent government report noted that one (unnamed) Ontario university's sessional staff accounted for 24 per cent of full-time equivalent staff and taught approximately 40 per cent of courses. These part-time instructors are typically paid about $7,200 per course (three months). On average, sessionals at Laurier teach 2.4 courses per year and earn under $18,000 per year (Charbonneau, 2013; Basen, 2014). A recent CBC report suggests that contract faculty members, teaching four courses, earn $28,000 per year (Basen, 2014). In stark contrast, full-time faculty salaries may start around $90,000.

Evidence suggests that numerous universities are increasingly relying on the economic benefits of hiring non-permanent staff. From 2000 to 2010, the number of full-time equivalent students increased in universities in Ontario by 52 per cent while the number of permanent (tenure-stream) faculty increased by only 30 per cent (Fullick, 2015).

A personal account of these employment realities is provided by an MA graduate employed on a temporary basis at a local community college. She is paid only for her time in the classroom—preparing for classes, speaking with students, and marking assignments are all expected but not included in her hourly contract. As a result, whether she spends two minutes or two hours with students, it is not reflected in her

continued

wages. Her college's collective agreement specifies that as a temporary worker, she is only allowed to teach two consecutive terms in a row and then must stand aside for one term, unless the college hires her as either a permanent part-time or full-time worker. In addition, her wages vary incongruously. If she works 12 hours per week or less she is paid approximately $80/hour but if she works more than 12 hours per week, her wages drop to approximately $40/hour. Finally, her "short" hours may result in disqualification if she applies for Employment Insurance (Personal interview, Summer 2015).

In short, in the new economy's labour market, flexible, and frequently insecure, work time arrangements are multiplying. These changes have led analysts to identify this new class of workers "the **precariat**." Trapped at the margins of the labour market, their hold on employment is unclear and uncertain. Their work may, for example, be not only temporary but also unpredictable if it takes the form of casual or on-call positions. Some researchers include in the precariat the self-employed who do not have employees (for example, contractors, daycare providers, truck drivers) on the grounds that many of these workers often also have a tenuous hold on their employment and financial futures. The precariat, when defined as temporary and own account self-employed workers, now constitutes an estimated 20 per cent of the Canadian labour force and has increased by an estimated 50 per cent or more since 1989 (PEPSO, 2013: 17).

By 2012, slightly more than 10 per cent of all Canadian workers aged 25 to 54 were temporary (Galarneau, Morissette, Usalcas, 2013: 8). And, most of this growth was a result of increased temporary work for men. From 2004 to 2014, the numbers of men (aged 25 and older) working temporarily increased by a surprising 48 per cent while women experienced only a 20 per cent increase (Statistics Canada, 2015b: CANSIM Table 282-0080). These patterns may suggest a generalized weakness in the labour market as employers reduce their commitments by relying on temporary workers.

Finally, nonstandard work times continue to morph into new time constructs. For example, the **zero (hours) contract** has been popularized in Britain and the United States. Zero hours contracts involve workers who are willing to accept a contract for employment with an employer on an on-call basis, with no specified minimum number of hours of work stipulated in the contract. Apparently, desperate for any work, these employees might end up working zero hours on any day, week, or month. Recent reports suggest that 25 per cent of companies in the United Kingdom use these contracts with an estimated 250,000 to 1 million workers involved (as cited in Drache et al., 2014: 14). Currently, Canadian workers are somewhat protected from these arrangements. In Ontario, the "three hours rule" means employees who arrive at work to find their shifts shortened or cancelled must receive three hours, wages for that day (Mojtehedzadeh, 2015a).

Involuntary Nonstandard Work Times

Another significant dimension in the new working time regimes is the growth in involuntary work. These workers, whether working short or long hours and whether working standard or nonstandard schedules, explicitly describe their work times as involuntary. They state, for example, they are working part-time or on call or temporarily because "this is all the work they could find" and/or that "they would prefer other working times, notably full-time work." Swanberg et al. (2014: 427) found that 83 per cent of United States part-time nonstandard hour workers have little to no control over scheduling their hours, 78 per cent are unable to choose their starting and quitting times, and 64 per cent are unable to decide when to take breaks. Predictably, this combination of irregular and unpredictable working hours reduces workers' work-life satisfaction (Hofacker and Konig, 2013). Nonetheless, this facet of the labour force continues to grow and reinforces patterns of social inequality. In the United Kingdom, for example, the post-2008 period was marked not only by unemployment and non-employment but by alarming increases in **involuntary nonstandard employment (INE)** amongst marginalized workers. Increasingly, young people, individuals from non-white ethnic groups and those who were regionally disadvantaged found themselves stuck in INE (Green and Livanos, 2015).

Of course, whether or not individual workers perceive their work time arrangements as involuntary may shift through the life course. During certain periods of life, workers would resist part-time work which is casual or on-call since the number of work hours may be completely unpredictable.[5] With the exception of some employers, such as Costco, part-time work does not necessarily mean a predictable number of hours (and therefore wages) each week or month (see also Charlesworth and Heron, 2011: 171). At some moments in life, this unpredictability is directly linked to increased work–family conflicts (Henly and Lambert, 2014). For example, workers who need to be home at specific times for young children or aging parents would be averse to these kinds of work arrangements and accept them only in the absence of alternatives.

Not only is part-time work involuntary when it is a bad fit to one's life circumstances, it may be experienced as involuntary because of its financial implications. Controlling for hours worked, part-timers, internationally, are often paid less than their full-time counterparts (Preston and Yu, 2015; Government of Canada, 2015). Again, with the exception of employers such as Costco, part-timers are usually exempt from benefits (dental, vision, other medical services) which may become a significant issue for single mothers or for women whose benefitted partner is laid off. The financial drawbacks may be complex. For example, part-timers also run the risk of missing out on government-mandated benefits. Canadian[6] policies on maternity and parental leave stipulate at least 600 hours of paid work over the previous year and, in 2003, one-quarter of new mothers did not quality for leave because they had not accumulated enough hours or they were self-employed

(Hunsley, 2013a). Improvements in pay, through advancement opportunities and training, are also generally less available to part-time workers. Canadian research examining promotions amongst regular and temporary part-timers and temporary full-timers reports that women in these positions are less likely to be promoted than regular full-time workers. Further, even part-timers designated permanent may find that their positions are more precarious that those of full-time workers (Duffy and Pupo, 1992). Significantly, these various drawbacks may not only have immediate implications; they may also incur life-time disadvantages in terms of earnings and retirement income.[7] These long-term negatives are particularly likely amongst the large numbers of women whose marriages or unions end in separation (Hunsley, 2013a). In sum, for a wide variety of intersecting reasons, part-time work may be experienced by workers as involuntary and undesirable.

Despite all these considerations, a wide variety of research points to the numerous workers who embrace part-time or casual work as their preferred work arrangement. Of course, this "choice" must be contextualized in terms of their perceived options. Many wives and mothers, for example, prefer "short" and "unpredictable" and "poorly compensated" hours as a means to manage the onerous competing demands of home and childcare (Iseke, 2014). Mothers face, for example, powerful ideological messages about the importance of "being there" and "spending time" with their children (Vujinovic, 2014; Silver, 2000). As the population ages, aging parents and other relatives will increasingly figure into the demands on women caregivers. Presently, women are more likely to take up these caregiving responsibilities and twice as likely as employed male caregivers to change their work patterns or reduce their working hours in order to respond to these needs (Hunsley, 2013a). These women may be classified as "voluntary" part-timers but their "choices" are clearly constrained by societal pressures.

Within these complex realities of "choosing" part-time work, it is important to recognize that in recent years the numbers of part-timers—male and female—who explicitly indicate they prefer full-time work or cannot find full-time employment has exploded. Today, **involuntary part-time work** accounts for one-third of women part-timers aged 25 to 44; almost half (49 per cent) of comparable male part-timers identify as involuntary (Statistics Canada, 2015j). Youth also comprise a significant portion of the involuntary part-time labour force. Between 2007 and 2012 involuntary part-time work rose to 16 per cent for women workers 15 to 24 and 9.4 per cent for comparable men (essentially returning to earlier 1997 rates) (Galarneau, Morisette, Uscalas, 2013: 8). American analysts suggest that there is "an emerging labor pattern" in which more and more part-time workers are stuck in part-time work while preferring more hours of work (often full-time hours). For example, from 2006 to 2012, the number of **underemployed** (preferring more hours) involuntary part-time workers in the United States increased by 250 per cent (Swanberg et al., 2014: 427).

Research into **underemployment** also speaks to this growth in involuntary forms of worktime. In Australia and many other OECD countries, while unemployment grew post-2008, it was also underemployment which expanded as the economy generated "limited employment growth" and jobs took the form of nonstandard work (Healy, 2015). Predictably, this lack of enough work time (or a mismatch to educational qualifications) is related to a wide variety of adverse effects including financial difficulties, welfare dependence, and problems with subjective well-being. The negative personal effects of *unemployment* have been comprehensively documented. Significantly, recent research suggests that the negative consequences of *underemployment* are, in fact, similar to those of unemployment (Wilkins, 2006).

To sum up, over the course of the past several decades, more and more Canadian workers, regardless of their preferences, are not working eight hours a day, 40 hours a week, with two days (weekends) off (see Cranford, Vosko, and Laxer, 2008). The standard employment relationship, characterized by the standard work day and work week, with corresponding entitlements to training, vacation, sick leave, and so on, has been rapidly disappearing. According to the **dual labour approach**, these 9-to-5 jobs are the "good jobs" or "core jobs" at the centre of the economy. In more and more instances, workers are not "full-time" and are not entitled to benefits even in unionized settings unless they work a specified number of hours. Many are left holding "marginal" or "bad jobs" situated on the periphery of the labour market. While nonstandard work arrangements are not necessarily always a negative experience for individual workers, the precariousness embedded in many nonstandard work regimes is raising growing concerns about threats to the quality of workers' working and personal lives and about the social and economic marginalization of entire segments of the labour force (Craig and Brown, 2015).

Good/core jobs and bad/peripheral jobs are not randomly distributed amongst the labour force. Rather workers' positions in the labour market are directly linked to other forms of inequality, notably gender, race/ethnicity, immigrant status, social class, disability, and age. Predictably, core jobs tend to go to individuals who embody some combination of white, male, upper/middle class (as reflected by high levels of education) and middle-aged. In contrast, nonstandard work is more common amongst women/mothers, recent immigrants, Canadians living with disabilities, youth and seniors, and less well educated Canadians. Significantly, this peripheral location may be difficult to escape. As a result of **labour market marginalization**—economic forces supporting the generation of peripheral types of employment—these workers may find movement into better or core jobs difficult or impossible. For example, jobs on the margins may fail to generate the kinds of income rewards which allow workers to extricate themselves from debt so that they can pursue further education and training or move meaningfully into self-employment. Throughout the OECD, nonstandard work is routinely related to lower wages; hourly wages for nonstandard workers, for example, are 20 to 30 per cent lower (Llena-Nozal, 2015). Similarly, temporary workers generally suffer a wage penalty as reflected not only in lower wages and wage instability but also in slower wage growth. While the boundary between core and marginal work may be permeable—there is growing concern that marginalized jobs are actually trapping many disadvantaged workers in "bad" jobs and intensifying patterns of social inequality and impoverishment (Zeytinoglu and Muteshi, 2000; Hermann, 2015).

Put simply, certain segments of the population are "set up" for nonstandard employment and, once there, may confront pressures towards persistent economic marginalization. While some workers may indeed prefer shorter (or longer) hours, there is considerable evidence that many workers at both ends of the time spectrum are dissatisfied with their work time regimens. While long hours (as discussed below) may contribute to time stress, the inability to locate anything but short hours or temporary work contributes to financial insecurities and, even impoverishment (PEPSO, 2013).

Predictably, as segments of the population find themselves with few options outside nonstandard work and suffer the economic and employment drawbacks of this work, social class polarization along with other patterns of inequity has intensified. After all, in many respects, employers (and shareholders) are the beneficiaries of these new work time arrangements. They may pay nonstandard workers a lower wage; they may decline to pay benefits to such workers; they may draw on their services only when needed and thereby reduce employment costs; they may dramatically increase or decrease hours worked as they prefer; typically, they are able to dismiss nonstandard workers more easily. There is less likelihood of unionization and any resultant increase in wages and benefits. In the current labour market, it is not surprising that those at the top of the income hierarchy are doing better than ever.

In Toronto, in the past 30 years the share of income going to the top 1 per cent of income earners nearly doubled to 12 per cent of all income (PEPSO, 2013: 12). Global evidence suggests this is a widespread phenomenon. In OECD countries, the richest 10 per cent now earns 9.6 times the income of the poorest 10 per cent, up from seven times as much in the 1980s (Stewart, 2015). According to a recent report, the shift has been particularly marked in the United States where wealth inequality now mirrors the Great Depression of the 1930s. The wealthiest 0.1 per cent now own 22 per cent of total household wealth, up from 7 per cent in the late 1970s and they own as much wealth as the poorest 145 million US families. The emerging labour market realities discussed above appear to be crucial ingredients in these patterns of intensifying inequalities (Matthews, 2014).

Too Much Work Time

While many Canadians may be faced with insufficient work time, there are those at the opposite end of the continuum—with too many hours. In 1992, US sociologist

Juliet B. Schor published *The Overworked American,* in which she explored the many ways that time spent at work (in the United States) had skyrocketed in the preceding two decades. As a result of an overall increase in work time of one month per year, Schor argued Americans were losing out on free time and leisure (see also Schaef and Fassel, 1988). These ideas were subsequently followed up by variety of scholars who drew attention to the fact that "harried workers and hurried families" were increasingly the norm in the new economy (Jacobs and Gerson, 2004). Almost 25 years after Schor's book riveted popular attention, Brigid Schulte's new book *Overwhelmed: Work, Love, and Play: When No One Has the Time* (2014) returned to the pressing and complex issue of "too much work."

While Americans have been somewhat stereotyped as overworked and stressed out, Canadians follow close behind. From 1981 to 1992, Canadian workers aged 20 to 64 increased their working hours (defined to include travel to and from work, and meal and coffee breaks at work) by 15 per cent (while also decreasing their "free" time) (Zuzanek and Smale, 2015). In 1998, one-third of Canadians aged 25 to 44 described themselves as "workaholics" and more than half worried they did not have enough time to spend with family and friends (Statistics Canada, 1999). By the beginning of the twenty-first century, high-income employed Canadians (aged 25 to 54) were spending 15 per cent more time at work (averaging 46 hours per week) than low-income workers and were more likely to complain of feeling rushed and time-stressed (Williams, 2002; Hurst, 2008). In 2004, Ipsos surveyed 5,000 people in 11 countries and in all but urban Russia and urban China, respondents agreed to some degree that "there was never enough time in the day to get done what I want to get done" (Ulmer, 2004).

Recent Canadian research suggests that long hours of paid work, once routinely embraced by higher-income families, grew dramatically from 1971 to 2006 and were increasingly common amongst middle and lower-middle income families. Presumably, this is a result of the failure of **real wages** to increase in correspondence to increasing costs of living. These financial pressures have not only reduced the size of the middle class relative to other social classes, they have pushed middle-class families to dramatically increase their paid work commitments. Specifically, more and more couples in middle-class families are devoting longer hours to paid work in an attempt to make up the financial shortfall. The net result is they have less "free" time and more time stress combined with growing financial pressures. This is a perfect formula for a feeling of **time-crunch** (Burton and Phipps, 2010, 2011).

This sense of time pressure and erosion of "personal" time is extensively documented. Researchers found that from 1986 to 2005 the average time workers spent on activities with family members on a work day dropped by 45 minutes (Turcotte, 2007: 9). Personal care time has also been eroded. Canadians, particularly women, spend less time on activities such as sleeping, eating, washing, and dressing (Fast et al., 2001). In 2012, Higgins and Duxbury's national survey of

Canadian workers located in the well-paid and well-educated knowledge sector of the labour force found that time spent in paid employment had increased dramatically with 68 per cent of men and 54 per cent of women surveyed working more than 45 hours per week, up from 55 per cent of men and 39 per cent of women in 2001.

Much of this change may reflect the increased presence of information and communication technology (ICT), which may facilitate productivity but may also dictate a faster-paced work environment, along with more interruptions and multitasking. Computer technology of course, has made the lines between work time, leisure time, and home time highly permeable (Chesley, 2014). A recent survey of Canadian knowledge workers found that these employees worked 50.2 hours a week, and 54 per cent took work home on evenings and weekends, with the average individual spending another seven hours on paid work at home, with work-related e-mail figuring prominently (Duxbury and Higgins, 2012: 4, 5).

Work time pressures appear likely to persist as the Canadian and global economies continue to struggle. A recent survey by recruitment agency Hays Canada reported a pattern of jobless growth with 70 per cent of employers in 2014 expecting to increase their business but only 38 per cent planning new hires. Almost one-third of the surveyed businesses (31 per cent) reported rising stress levels and (34 per cent) declining morale amongst their employees. The survey report suggests that numerous businesses appear to be attempting to increase productivity and profitability by intensifying work demands on current employees (Tencer, 2015).

Prospects for Work Time Improvements

Dramatic increases in nonstandard work along with the expansion of overwork may leave workers with deficits in terms of combinations of income, security, and personal fulfilment. However, despite the numerous serious issues raised in the research literature, there are also positive developments. The very attention being paid to work time issues, the so-far successful public outrage at the proliferation of unpaid internships for new workers, and the ongoing demands for more manageable work–life constellations speak to prospects for positive social change.

Some European countries have instituted government regulations which limit growth in long hours and overtime while encouraging **work-sharing** to keep unemployment rates low (Zuzanek and Smale, 2015). Germany used working time reductions such as temporary reductions in standard working hours, short-time work, and reductions in overtime to achieve a "jobs miracle." Unlike other European economies that struggled with skyrocketing unemployment, Germany was able to maintain stronger employment levels. **Working time accounts** (a practice accessible to about half of German employees in 2009) were used to allow workers to draw on work time (and thereby wages) accumulated in previous more prosperous periods and, conversely, workers were able to, in a sense, borrow time (wages) from their working time accounts when there was insufficient work at hand. They then would work extra hours in the future to make up this deficit. In these ways, Germans avoided in the short term[8] many of the pressures of job loss and nonstandard employment (Herzog-Stein and Zapf, 2014; Berg, Bosch, and Charest, 2014).

In Canada, organized labour has registered some victories in the work time struggle. For example, in 2015, Metro grocery stores in Toronto reached an agreement with the union representing 4,000 employees which addressed inadequate and unpredictable hours. Although previously part-time workers had no right to minimum hours, under the new contract they are guaranteed 15 hours of work after one year of employment and 24 hours after eight years. Furthermore, notice of scheduling increased from three days to five days ahead of time. Finally, wages will now increase each year by 25 cents an hour (Mojtehedzadeh, 2015c).

Conclusion

After lengthy struggles to attain a standard employment relationship, many workers today confront pressures from nonstandard work arrangements as well as unresolved work–life conflicts. Nonstandard work times have grown rapidly as the economy responds to a variety of internal and external pressures. As a result, many workers find themselves with insecure and insufficient work time arrangements. Those who escape many of the problems of nonstandard work may find themselves under pressure to work longer hours, particularly when addressing both paid and unpaid work obligations. While there have been some legislative and labour union accomplishments in addressing work time, it is clear that much remains to be done.

Questions for Critical Thought

1. Why has the 40-hour, five-day week become less common amongst Canadian workers?
2. Why are some workers plagued by "too much work" while others are stuck in involuntary underemployment?
3. What will the average working day look like in 30 years, and why?

Suggested Further Resources

Hermann, Christoph. 2015. *Capitalism and the Political Economy of Work Time*. London: Routledge, Francis and Taylor Group. Rooted in a detailed review of various theoretical positions on working time, the author explores international efforts to reduce working times in the context of neoliberal victories in the erosion of work time regulation.

Negrey, Cynthia L. 2012. *Work Time: Conflict, Control and Change*. Cambridge: Polity. The author provides a comprehensive history of work time from agricultural settlements to contemporary struggles to reduce working time in the interests of environmental sustainability.

Suggested Websites

International Labour Organization (ILO)
www.ilo.org
The statistical wing of the United Nations, the International Labour Organization (ILO) provides a wealth of international information on the growth and national patterns of working times and nonstandard work.

Canadian Centre for Policy Alternatives
www.policyalternatives.ca
The Canadian Centre for Policy Alternatives is an independent, non-profit research organization which focuses on a wide variety of research questions of importance to Canadians. In recent years it has played an important part in examining shifts in labour market experiences, including the rise of the precariat and temporary agency work.

Notes

1. For a less Eurocentric discussion, see Whitrow (1988).
2. Nonstandard work forms are not "new" (Drache, et al., 2014). Throughout the industrialized past, various workers have been employed in a variety of regimens outside of the 40-hour week. What is new is their growing proportion in newly created jobs (Zeytinoglu and Muteshi, 2000).
3. On a personal level, the pressures behind these moves toward more work time for some and less for others are myriad and potentially contradictory. Workers, particularly in periods of economic or industry uncertainty, may feel compelled to work longer hours to satisfy their employers' demands and to secure their work position; they may opt for longer hours in order to ensure adequate wages or to improve their chances for higher wages and advancement (and, thereby, possible advance their families' economic well-being); and they may work longer hours as a reflection of the culture of their occupation (for example, various professions). Conditions in the labour market may mean that many workers are only able to locate short-term, insecure jobs with insufficient hours while others, notably wives and mothers and students, may have a decided preference for shorter hours. Furthermore, within these pressures toward longer and shorter hours, there are significant shifts in the permanent/temporary nature of work and the predictability/flexibility of working time arrangements. Regardless of the personal roots, there has clearly been an explosion in **nonstandard employment** time arrangements, notably amongst those sharing intersecting characteristics by gender, immigrant status, racialized identity, and low income.
4. Amongst employed US women, women at the bottom of the income hierarchy worked sharply fewer hours than those in the middle, and their hours decreased again in the top fifth before they dropped sharply for those women in the top 5 per cent. The pattern is somewhat similar amongst employed US men with men at the bottom working fewer hours, those in the middle working longer hours (20 per cent of US workers are employed for 50 hours or more per week) and those at the top working only slightly fewer hours than those just above average (Clawson and Gerstel, 2014: 33; Golden, 2009: 218).

5. Analysts refer to this constant fluctuation in scheduling as "churning" and point out its negative implications for workers (Clawson and Gerstel, 2014: 36).
6. Quebec is a notable exception here again. In 2006, Quebec introduced parental/maternity leave provisions that covered self-employed individuals and extended the leave periods (Hunsley, 2013a).
7. In Europe, regulations prohibit a distinction between full-time and part-time pay rates; this is not the case in Canada (Fister, 2014).
8. Recent reports indicate that 20 per cent of German workers are employed in "minijobs" suggesting that Germany is increasingly embracing nonstandard work in response to economic pressures (as cited in Drache et al., 2014: 14).

7 Work–Family and Work–Life Conflict

Learning Objectives

- To identify the diverse social, economic, and historic factors which precipitated the mass movement of wives and, especially, mothers into paid employment
- To explore the specific nature of the conflicts between women's unpaid home and paid work responsibilities
- To detail the complex diversities impacting the balance between work and home
- To examine the numerous public and private strategies which individuals employ to manage these conflicts

Introduction

The recognition of a conflict between home and paid work is "taken-for-granted" in contemporary Canada. Almost everyone understands the stressful juggling act that befalls Canadian workers, particularly the mothers and fathers of young children, who are combining paid work with family obligations. While family formation is often a trigger to this conflict, many point out that the intensification of both education and paid work time obligations (see Chapter 6) mean that workers often must sacrifice the quality of their personal lives, as well as family time, in the pursuit of paid employment. Not surprisingly, some pine for the **Golden Age of Capitalism** in which male workers were much more likely to earn a **family wage**. However, this moment in history has passed by and in its place is a tension between the demands of domestic and personal life and the intensifying requirements of paid work.

Despite dramatic advances in the role of women in paid employment and greater popularization of gender equity in domestic roles, much of this burden continues to fall on the shoulders of wives and mothers. Everyday experience as much as academic research documents the struggles experienced by mothers (and fathers) of young children who also engage in paid work. In response, mothers and fathers, social activists, and policy makers have sought to construct remedies—located in the workplace as well as the home—to this conflict. However, such efforts have not tended to address the fundamental issues of gender inequalities and work–life quality.

Mothers' Historic Move into Paid Work

One of the most dramatic social transformations in the twentieth century was the massive movement of women into paid employment. Certainly women worked in the past. Historically, throughout their lives the vast majority of women (peasants) worked side-by-side in the fields with men. Through pregnancy, childbirth, and child-rearing, women expected to contribute to planting and harvesting crops, tending herds, and processing or preparing food products. Of course, today this economic arrangement continues as the norm around the globe. Women's work is typically key to every community's basic survival. While women may now be picking coffee beans for international conglomerates or selling produce in a local market, their foundational work role persists everywhere.

For women living in the **Global North**, the evolution of women's roles in paid and **unpaid work** took a particularly sharp turn with the declaration, in 1939, of the Second World War. While men were mobilized as a military force, women, even wives and mothers, were strongly encouraged to contribute to the war effort by taking on men's paid work (Pierson, 1986: 215). While **Rosie the Riveter** was an American icon, she aptly embodies the ideological shift in society's view of women workers. Not only were women now deemed fully capable of doing "men's work," they had a moral obligation to do so. To facilitate the mobilization of wives and mothers, the government even took audacious steps to provide childcare.

TinaImages / Shutterstock.com

Rosie the Riveter

At the end of the war, as the troops came home, women were openly compelled to give up their paid work positions. As publicized in women's magazines, patriotic duty now entailed giving your job back to deserving soldiers and having children. Women retreated completely from any well-paid industrial positions and those who were young and unmarried were segregated once more in traditionally female jobs as clerks, retail workers, and nurses. Meanwhile, wage gains enjoyed by male industrial workers during the war as well as a dramatic surge in post-war manufacturing meant that working class men were now routinely earning a **family wage**—that was sufficient income to reasonably support a wife and children. The **male breadwinner model of the family**, in which women raised the children while men provided the family income, became increasingly the norm.

Indeed, the 1950s and 1960s, the "Golden Age" of capitalism, the fortunes of working-class men and their unions prospered alongside a dramatic growth in Canada's industrial and trade capacity. Unemployment was at record lows and home ownership along with consumerism became increasingly normative in working-class communities. Life was good[1] unless, of course, you were a divorcée, single mother, or widow, and unless you were a wife/mother/woman who wanted to enjoy some financial autonomy or a meaningful career.

The Struggle for Gender Equality at Work and at Home

By the 1950s, women's **labour force participation** had slowly edged up from about 15 per cent in 1901 to less than 25 per cent in 1951 (Phillips and Phillips, 1993: 33). It was poised to explode. Through the 1960s and 1970s, the increase in women's participation in paid work would equal that of the past 60 years. By 1976, women comprised 37 per cent of the Canadian labour force (Status of Women, 2015). Not only were massive numbers of women entering paid labour, but their segregation into "female" occupations and sectors of the economy along with their wage disadvantage was being challenged, sometimes successfully. Most importantly, the impediments, ideological and economic, to wives and, especially, mothers entering paid work were dramatically eroded. Not only mothers, but mothers of very young children, would soon be commonplace in paid work.

Behind this societal transformation, there are a variety of factors. Some women eagerly embraced paid work while others were pushed and pulled by diverse economic, ideological, and societal forces. Indeed, the so-called decision to work for pay is, at best, a complex and multi-faceted process that may entail little actual "choice." Rather, women often found themselves at the intersection of diverse pressures that ultimately led to the paid labour force.

While the need for many women to have paid work may seem obvious today, in the 1970s and 1980s, new social and economic realities pushed women not only to enter but to stay in paid work. This meant not only holding a paying position but also accepting shorter and shorter "time-outs" for bearing and raising children. Financial pressures were intensifying; families faced the general failure of "real" wages (adjusted for inflation) to grow in any meaningful way. For example, from 1981 and 1988 the real purchasing power of workers declined by 4 per cent and between 1980 and 1984 average real income for Canadian families shrank by 5.7 per cent (Duffy and Pupo, 1992: 26, 27). From 2007 to 2013, Canada saw wage packets grow by only 5 per cent (while each year inflation increased by around 2 per cent) (CBC News, 2014). The inadequate growth in "real" wages meant many families struggled financially. To maintain their standard of living, they needed either significant pay increases and/or the mobilization into paid work of other family members, notably the wife/mother.

This deterioration in family wages was, in turn, a product of profound economic shifts. The previous Golden Age of Capitalism gave way to a series of economic crises. Technological advances in communication and production along with the internationalization of corporations in pursuit of profit meant that numerous industries were facing stiff competition from various emerging economies in the Global South. Industrial jobs stagnated and their unions were slowly eroded. While growth in public sector employment and public sector unionization shored up the middle-classes in the short term, families were facing increasing economic instability (Daguerre 2014: 327). Their precariousness was further underscored during the crisis of the early 1980s when inflation soared and mortgage interest rates skyrocketed to astonishing rates of 18 and 19 per cent. Since this time, families' overall economic well-being has tended, with a few bursts of sunshine, to follow a downward trajectory. The 2008 recession marked a new low point and, eight years later, the uncertainties persist as reflected in a troubled global economy and persistent high rates of un- and under-employment, especially amongst youth.

Today, the persistent financial precariousness of many Canadian families is revealed in the steady and dramatic increments in average household debt. Despite the mobilization of wives, mothers, and youth into the paid labour force, many families have turned to increased indebtedness to maintain their standard of living. By the fourth quarter of 2014, average **household debt ratio** hit a record 163 per cent, up markedly from about 75 to 80 per cent in 1990 (Marr, 2015). In an era of unusually low interest (and, therefore mortgage) rates, many Canadian families appear to be making up the shortfall in income or the mismatch between income and desired lifestyle by taking on more and more debt (McCloud and Dwyer, 2011). This is, of course, far from surprising when escalating housing and food costs and dramatic increases in tuition lead analysts to suggest that it will cost a Canadian family $678,952.99 to raise a child to maturity (McMahon, 2013).

Not only have increased costs of living pushed mothers to intensify their labour market contributions, but shifting marriage norms have underscored the foolhardiness of relying solely on a male breadwinner. Changes in divorce legislation (notably no-fault legislation in 1968) along with shifting social mores have translated into a dramatic increase in the divorce rate (standing today at slightly fewer than one in two marriages ending in divorce) (White, Martin, and Bartolic, 2013: 240). As a result, young women face the social fact that their economic well-being and that of their children cannot be premised on the belief that marriage is forever. Should their marriage end in divorce they (and, to a less degree, their husbands) face devastating financial implications. In 2011, 21 per cent of female lone parent families (and 12 per cent of male lone parent families) lived below the low-income cut-offs (Statistics Canada, 2014a). In this context, women opting to be stay-at-home mothers for any significant length of time clearly run a significant financial risk.

Recent shifts in marriage and family, most notably, postponement of marriage along with the popularization of informal common-law arrangements, postponement or elimination of child-rearing, and increases in living unattached, underscore new realities in women's lives (see Table 7.1 below). Because they are marrying later in life, women who enter into couple relationships often do so as individuals with considerable investments of time and energy in education and/or employment. In 2008, women's average age at first marriage was 30 and men's 31 (Milan, Keown, and Urquijo, 2011: 7, 15). Of course, many men and women now enter marriage after common-law relationships. According to the latest (2011) census, common-law couples continue to increase as a proportion of all couples, growing at four times the rate of married couples. Similarly, the proportion of lone parents also continues to expand so that lone parent families made up 16 per cent of all census families (up 8 per cent from 2006 to 2011) (Statistics Canada, 2012g: 3). All of these trends would, of course, underscore the significance of financial self-sufficiency for young women. And, these realities apply to most Canadian women because the clear majority will live some portion of their lives in a couple relationship, despite increases in the numbers of Canadians living alone.

Finally, as noted above, later marriage, postponed/reduced child-bearing, increased gender equity, and new gender norms mean women are now reaching adulthood with substantially improved educational qualifications (Turcotte, 2011). Indeed, women outnumber men as undergraduate (57 per cent) and master's (54 per cent) students in Canadian universities and, although gender segregation in specific programs persists, women figure prominently in graduate and professional programs (including medicine, law, and pharmacy) (Canadian Association

Table 7.1 Canadian Women's Marital Status*

	1981 (%)	2011 (%)
Part of a couple	60**	56
Married	56	45
Common-law	3	11
Not part of a couple	40	44
Never married	25	25
Divorced/Separated	6	10
Widowed	10	9

*Women aged 15 and older
**All figures rounded up
Source: Derived from Milan, 2015, 17.

of University Teachers [CAUT], 2013–14). Indeed, between 1991 and 2011, the proportion of employed women aged 25 to 34 with a university degree rose from 19 per cent to 40 per cent while for men, the increase was from 17 to 27 per cent (Uppal and LaRochelle-Cote, 2014: 1). Clearly, many Canadian women enter marriage and motherhood with important educational assets, achieved at significant cost and effort, which they may be loath to abandon to become a full-time homemaker or a part-time worker (Galarneau, Morissette, and Usalcas, 2013). Further, these educational credentials position them for improved economic and personal rewards when they participate in paid employment.

Of course, all of these various "pushes" into paid employment would count for very little if many major obstacles to "working" mothers had not been cleared over the past 50 years. For example, the legalization of birth control in the 1960s, the generalized acceptance of abortion, and the popularization of smaller families have translated into a dramatically reduced fertility rate. Fewer children and the ability to "plan" children have reduced some of both the intensity and unpredictability of domestic work. The total fertility rate dropped from approximately 4.0 children per woman in the late 1950s to 1.68 in 2008 (Milan, Keown, and Urquijo, 2011: 13). Also, the pressures of child-related household work have been markedly reduced by the increased provision (despite persistent availability and quality issues) of childcare services. For more well-off families, cleaning services and advances in cleaning technologies have reduced the number of housework hours. Domestic work has also been affected by the proliferation of fast-food/home delivery food services, pre-prepared grocery store meals, and technological advances in food preparation.

Most importantly, women have met a growing demand for women workers. Since the 1950s the industrial and resource extraction economies have steadily given way to a dramatic expansion of service sector employment. Today, approximately three-quarters of Canadian workers are employed in some aspect of the service sector—from retail and restaurant workers to daycare workers and personal support aides. Indeed, over the past several decades, the primary source of employment growth has been in service occupations. Traditionally, following the gender stereotype of women as care providers, service sector work has typically been considered more appropriate for women. The net effect of its dramatic growth was that women were likely to find paid work when they looked. In 2012, women occupied 55 per cent of all jobs in the service sector, in contrast to 22 per cent of jobs in goods-producing (manufacturing) (Status of Women, 2015).

This growth in service sector work has also been coupled with a significant expansion in non-traditional forms of work; that is, part-time, contract, on-call, and precarious employment. While certainly not all mothers are looking for part-time, shift, or on-call work, the proliferation of these working arrangements did provide many with an alternative that was more manageable in light of their domestic/child-rearing responsibilities. By 2013, reflecting a three-decade pattern, women comprised almost 70 per cent of part-time workers, and predictably, women remained much more inclined than their male counterparts to hold part-time positions during mid-life. Almost one in five women aged 25 to 44 are part-timers (30 hours or less) while 6 per cent of men work part-time at this age (Status of Women, 2015; Ferrao, 2010: 14).

Finally, policy shifts, reflecting a growing social acceptance of gender equity in employment, have meant that certain service sector areas in which women tended to be underrepresented in the past have opened up. For example, according to Statistics Canada's 2011 National Household Survey, women aged 25 to 34 went from 13 per cent of police officers in 1991 to 24 per cent in 2011 (Uppal and LaRochelle-Cote, 2014: 1). Not only have occupations accepted women, more valued locations within service sector work, notably managerial and supervisory positions, are increasingly occupied by women.

Today, women comprise almost half of the Canadian labour force (46 per cent), a dramatic increase from 37 per cent in 1976. Women's (aged 15 and older) labour force participation rate is currently 61 per cent, only slightly less than men's (70 per cent). During their prime working years, ages 25 to 54, 82 per cent of women participate in the paid labour force (Status of Women, 2015). Indeed, women's paid work participation is outpacing men's. From 1976 to 2012 the full-time employment rate for women aged 25 to 34 increased from 41 per cent to 65 per cent (in the non-oil producing provinces) while comparable men's rate decreased from 90 to 80 per cent (Galarneau, Morissette, and Usalcas, 2013: 5). By 2008, 29 per cent of wives in dual-earner families were earning higher incomes than their husbands (Williams, 2010: 19). Although it appears today that women's amazing advances in employment are more a result of declines amongst many men, especially middle-aged men, they do indicate a dramatic generational shift (Lewchuk, 2013; Stanfors, 2014). From the late baby boomers (born 1957 to 1966) to generation Y (born 1981 to 1990), there has been a steady narrowing of the gap between men's and women's daily participation rate in paid work. In 1986, late baby boomer men did, on average, 1.4 more hours of paid work per day than women but by 2010, the male–female gap for Generation Y was only 1.1 hours per day.

Mothers' historic shift into the paid labour force has also been facilitated by an uneven but steady erosion of traditional gender roles in the family and a popularization of the belief that women and men should share in domestic responsibilities. Of course, this has not translated into equality. Typically, women continue to shoulder the lion's share of routine care work in the home. They, rather than their husbands/partners, tend to assume primary responsibility for the care, feeding, clothing, and emotional support of children, and this pattern is reflected in their greater hourly commitment to care work in general (Milan, Keown, and Urquijo, 2011: 20–3). If there are dependent older members of the family, women spend more hours than men providing for their care (Milan, Keown, and Urquijo, 2011: 24). Each generation has experienced a shrinking of the gender gap in household work but not its elimination. Baby boomer men (aged 20 to 29) averaged 44 minutes on housework daily while Generation Y men (aged 20 to 29) averaged 1 hour and 1 minute. Baby boomer women (aged 20 to 29) averaged 1 hour and 54 minutes on housework while Generation Y women (aged 20 to 29) averaged a reduced 1 hour and 26 minutes (Marshall, 2011: 17, 20, 21). Generationally, men are doing more housework and women are doing less but women still do more than men.

Similarly, obstacles to gender equity persist in the labour market. Employed women in Canada confront **glass ceilings** (limits on their rise to the top) and **sticky floors** (traps in low level employment) which continue to be reflected in a **wage gap** between men and women (Christofides, Polycarpou, and Vrachimis, 2013). Factoring in industry, occupation, age, job tenure, province, marital, and union status, by 2011 women's *annual* wages amounted to 92 per cent of male wages. Similarly, by 2011, women's (aged 17 to 64) average *hourly* wages amounted to 87 per cent of men's (in contrast to 77 per cent in 1981) (Status of Women, 2015). Significant progress has occurred, but a gap remains, and this inequity is deeply rooted in women's inequitable unpaid work responsibilities (Campbell and Pearlman, 2013). These domestic obligations are reflected in adult women's extensive part-time employment and their withdrawal from paid employment for childbirth and childcare. Predictably, reduced working time along with time-outs from the workplace routinely translate into both restrictions on income and inhibited career development.

In general, the labour market still tends to be characterized by **gender segregation**; that is, certain professions and occupations are defined as "female," and this translates into relatively lower wages and social standing (and vice versa). In 1991, 2006 and again in 2011, more than one in five female university graduates aged 25 to 35 were concentrated in three occupations: elementary and kindergarten teachers, registered nurses, and secondary school teachers. In contrast, male university graduates of the same age were much less likely to be concentrated in a small number of occupations. This gender segregation of occupations was even higher and more stable amongst women without a university degree (Uppal and LaRochelle-Cote, 2014: 10). This segregation is also experienced in terms of power and authority since women continue to be very poorly represented in power positions such as corporate executive positions, memberships on corporate boards, or in high level political positions (Status of Women, 2015). Ironically, the very growth of women's involvement in a traditionally "male" occupation or profession often translates into a **wage penalty**. Women find themselves going "up" the "down" staircase because their growing numbers in high-paid, previously male-dominated occupations leads to reduced pay (and status) levels in those occupations (Mandel, 2013).

In short, the evidence is two-sided. It documents the growing presence of women, notably mothers of young children, in the paid labour force (see Table 7.2). Despite persistent gender inequities, dramatic advances in women's labour force experience have been made. Nonetheless, a conflict zone between home and personal life and paid employment remains. Mothers of young children are particularly likely to find themselves at the focal point of these tensions. As discussed below, efforts to reconcile these conflicts and reduce their impact on workers' lives continue to have limited success.

Table 7.2 Employment Rate of Canadian Women by Age of Youngest Child

	Youngest child less than 3 (%)	Youngest child aged 3 to 5 (%)	Youngest child 6 to 15 (%)	Youngest child less than 16 (%)	Women with no children at home (%)
1976	28*	37	46	39	61
1996	58	61	70	65	72
2009	64	70	79	73	80

*Percentages rounded up.
Source: Derived from Ferrao 2010, 9.

Work–Family and Work–Life Conflict: What Is It?

Brough et al. define work-life balance in common-sense terms as "an individual's subjective appraisal of the accord between his/her work and non-work activities and life in general" (2014: 2728). They operationalize this approach with four statements which respondents answer to on a five point scale of agreement (from strongly agree to strongly disagree). These statements range from "I have difficulty balancing work and non-work" to "I believe that my work and non-work life are balanced" (2014: 2730). Not surprisingly, when there is difficulty balancing work and non-work, individuals commonly describe their lives as "stressful."

Depending upon the specific situation, workers describe their efforts to manage conflicting responsibilities in negative terms. They feel that they have more to do than they can manage or that they do not have enough time for themselves. Stress, of course, is relative and may range from "no stress" to "highly stressed." The problem is that workers who are living with high levels of stress may experience negative outcomes at work, at home, and in their own physical and emotional health (Gordon and Rouse, 2013). In the workplace, stressed workers are less productive, more likely to be absent, reduce their work output, and make increased use of disability claims (Crompton, 2011: 46). Stress may be brought home and radiate to others, increasing, for example, depression in one's social circle, or raise the risk of relationship dissolution (Crompton, 2011: 51; Olah and Gahler, 2014). If stress is long-term, it is associated with sleep deprivation, anxiety, depression, and chronic physical illness (including heart disease, stroke, and high blood pressure) (Crompton, 2011: 41). Predictably, living with stress may contribute to unhealthy behaviours such as smoking, over-consumption of alcohol, and unhealthy eating.

Not surprisingly, many workers experience stress, especially as employment in the twenty-first century becomes increasingly insecure (see Chapter 6). However, it is crucial to realize that the overwhelming majority (two-thirds) of workers experiencing stress because of family issues are women and most of these women have children at home (Crompton, 2011: 52). Further, since 2003, women have been more likely than men to report that most days were "quite a bit" or "extremely stressful." In 2013, one in four women described their lives in these terms and the percentage of women reporting "high levels of stress" peaked between the ages of

35 to 54 (Statistics Canada, 2014b). Most recently, BMO's Annual Women's Day study reported that less than half (47 per cent) of Canadian women feel they have achieved the right work–life balance and most would like to see changes both at home and in the workplace (BMO Financial Group, 2015).

Why are women in the middle of their lives so stressed? Some commentators continue to assert that "women can't have it all." Although, as discussed below, mothers (and fathers) have been striving to create strategies for less stressful lives, the evidence continues to suggest that women who are paid workers and mothers are often "overwhelmed" and feel they have no time for work, love, and play (Schulte, 2014). While there is a wide array of evidence, both anecdotal and scholarly, on this topic it is perhaps interesting to simply note that from 2001 to 2011, it was consistently women in their prime working years (aged 25 to 44) who lost more work days to personal or family responsibilities and to illness or disability than men in the same age range (Statistics Canada, 2012f: 117, 118).

Diversities in Work–Family Conflicts

It is important to point out that work–family conflicts are amazingly diverse. Certainly, personal factors figure prominently. If you are low-income and live in a poor, underserviced, and/or unsafe neighbourhood/reserve or in a strong, supportive community; if you have multiple dependent children, have children who are infants or preschool-aged, or have a child who is disabled (Crettenden, Wright, and Skinner, 2014); if you are a single parent (Bakker and Karsten, 2013); if you have elderly parents in need of care or a disabled, an ill spouse in need of support, or receive strong spousal support then your experience of work–life conflict will vary (Skinner and Ichii, 2015; Lee, Zvonkovic, and Crawford, 2014; Minnotte, 2012). Of course, the **sandwich generation** faces compound issues since they shoulder the multiple care-giving obligations involving not only children but at the same time elderly parents. Predictably, these experiences of work–family conflict generally change over the life course, with the intensity of family (or work) demands maximizing during "acute situations" such as childbirth or sudden illness amongst family members or, at work, periods of plant closures and downsizing (Brough et al., 2014; Young, 2015; Parr, 2012; Wattis, Standing, and Yerkes, 2013; Zuberi, 2011).

This diversity of experiences is also reflected in one's location in the labour market. Top executives—male and female—have similar but also different work–life balance issues reflecting their relative power and affluence (for example, affording them more quality time with their children) as well as their extreme work demands and long work hours (Stock, Bauer, and Bieling, 2014: 1815; Balzan, Domingues, and Gonzalez, 2014). Not only one's location in the employment hierarchy but one's specific job location—social worker, nurse, doctor—may produce a particular relationship to work–family conflict (Kalliath and Kalliath, 2015). Recent Canadian research suggests that socio-economic status (education, income, occupation, and economic well-being) may complexly intersect with work–family stress.

For example, a physician who is on-call may feel his/her family time intruded upon; however, the sense of feeling one's work is important, influential, and productive may mute these negative feelings. Similarly, frequent family contact while at work may be work-disruptive but at the same time produce a positive effect in terms of feeling socially integrated with one's family (Schieman and Narisada, 2014: 367).

Moving beyond these specifics, the economic context also figures prominently. Periods of economic crisis and employment uncertainty tend to intensify the difficulties mothers face. For example, it is problematic to ask for workplace changes when your job lacks occupational status, when your workplace is not organized around a professional association or union, and when there is a large **reserve army of labour** eager to take on your job (Foster and Ren, 2015). Similarly, cultural and societal factors matter. Countries which measure high on gender empowerment measures are more inclined to support and invest in supportive strategies for those struggling with work–family conflict (Stavrou, Casper, and Ierodiakonou, 2015).

Within all this diversity, it is, of course, important to acknowledge that work–family and work–life conflict are not simply gendered phenomena. Men, particularly as fathers, may find that their work or family activities conflict with one another and produce feelings of dissatisfaction in one or both venues (Kingston, 2015). Certainly, the birth of the first child has important implications for both men and women in heterosexual couples with fathers appearing to, over time, intensify their paid work by working longer hours (Weinshenker, 2015; Kaufman and Bernhardt, 2015). Researchers are currently exploring in more depth the ways in which fathers seek to balance adult identities as they combine the emergent ideologies of the ideal father, the "contented man" and the model paid worker. Not surprisingly, many men struggle to achieve a balance between these sometimes contradictory images (Wada, Backman, and Forwell, 2014).

Lastly, it is key to understand that experiences of stress and dissatisfaction are sculpted by historical and societal forces. Our understandings of what it means to be a mother (or a father) are rooted in familial ideologies which are supported and promulgated by the mass media and various societal institutions and which change over time. The stress employed mothers routinely experience balancing home and paid work is, in part, rooted in the persistence of traditional ideologies. The notion that the home is mother's purview and the romanticized image of mothers making cookies and maintaining a sparkling household have certainly not been obliterated. Indeed, when the first child is born, both men's and women's attitudes toward mothering and the gendered division of labour appear to become more traditional, with more acceptance of mothering as women's most important role (Fox, 2009; Baxter et al., 2014). Of course, this conception of motherhood is supported not only by the mass media and advertisers but also by the economy and the state which relies on "the" family as a "haven in a heartless world" where men, the young, the elderly, and the needy can expect comfort and support. While the intensification of paid work time, the movement of paid work into many homes (working from home), and the invasion of work-oriented technology (cell phones and computers) into home life have all challenged the notion of "separate spheres" between home and work, beliefs in the home as a refuge and in mothers as the primary caregivers have not been dismantled, despite their inconsistency with many of our real-life experiences (Davies and Frink, 2014; Liu and Dyer, 2014).

Indeed, contemporary analysts argue that the ideology around "being a mother" has become more intense and constraining. Growing concerns about public safety and crime in the risk society have supported the emergence of an "intensive" model of mothering—the so-called "helicopter mother." Regardless of women's paid labour force participation, they are expected to "invest vast amounts of time, money, energy, and emotional labor in mothering" (Elliott, Powell, and Brenton, 2015: 351). All mothers, regardless of class or race, are supposed to sacrifice their own emotional and physical well-being in the interests of protecting and supporting their children. The resultant ideology of "putting family first" and "being a mother first" means that negotiating personal needs, demands from the workplace, and mothering responsibilities become even more tension-filled (Wall, 2013).

In popular parlance, these contradictions surrounding mothers' paid employment are reflected in the **mommy wars**. For several decades, the popular media have engaged with this debate about whether "good" mothers stay home with their children or combine paid work and mothering. Numerous popular magazines articles and a seemingly unending flurry of books clearly communicate the ongoing societal concerns about mothers' negotiation of familial and paid work roles. The titles reflect the intensity of the unresolved conflict: *Opting Out: Why Women Really Quit Careers and Head Home* (Stone, 2007); *Mommy Wars: Stay-at-Home and Career Moms Face Off on Their Choices, Their Lives, Their Families* (Steiner, 2007), *The Mommy Myth: The Idealization of Motherhood and How It Has Undermined All Women* (Douglas, 2005), *The Truth Behind the Mommy Wars: Who Decides What Makes a Good Mother* (Peskowtiz, 2005). Given the centrality of motherhood to many women's self-esteem along with the absence of any cultural resolution about how motherhood "should" be negotiated, it is not surprising that there is a continuous appetite for this discussion and continued stress at the personal level.

Work-Family Conflict: Efforts to Manage Family Pressures

Grocery shopping, childcare, meal preparation, home cleaning, and so on all still need to be done repetitively and take considerable time to do. Most families cannot afford to completely off-site or off-load these obligations. As noted above, many families, even with two earners, have struggled with incomes that have failed to keep up with rising housing, education, and food costs. Aside from the top 1 per cent of income earners, the financial ability to "solve" domestic needs is often simply not there. In the absence of these solutions, it is mothers who, despite their paid work, are most heavily impacted. For example, when there are dependent children in the home, women contribute less to a couple's total paid work time and more to unpaid household work (Milan, Keown, and Urquijo, 2011: 6, 13, 20, 21, 23). Meanwhile, many unpaid familial work demands are mushrooming. With an aging population, more have responsibilities for elderly and/or ill members in need of caregiving. In 2012, 30 per cent of Canadian women and 26 per cent of men aged 15 and over were providing help or care for a friend or relative with a chronic (long-term) health problem (Turcotte, 2013: 2).

Much of this burden is rooted in inadequate and outmoded childcare policies (as well as inadequate support for aging seniors). With the exclusion of the province of Quebec which has prioritized accessible, high quality, and low-cost childcare as a government responsibility, Canadians often face the prospects of inadequate, unlicensed, inaccessible, and/or expensive childcare. While extremely well-to-do families may be able to employ nannies to provide a reliable, on-site support system, average Canadians can ill afford the salary as well as living arrangements required by this option. Instead, excluding Quebec, average Canadians with children under the age of five must locate reliable, affordable childcare on their own. Yet, especially in urban centres, good quality childcare is typically expensive and difficult to access. For example, a two-earner family with two average incomes and two children can expect to spend 18 per cent of their net income on childcare and a two-earner, two-child family where one earner is average and one is low wage will spend 29 per cent of their net income on childcare (Baker, 2011: 56). Even those families who can afford these expenses may still face long wait lists. Further, the options that are available to many families are often for profit and/or unlicensed (and of questionable reliability), raising questions about the quality of care and, even, the safety of the children. These concerns about unlicensed providers led to new Ontario legislation limiting the numbers of young children an unlicensed day-care provider may care for and dramatically increasing the fines for infractions of the new rules on unlicensed centres. Given that many unlicensed providers have indicated they will withdraw from providing services under the new legislation, it is not surprising that the Wynne government in Ontario has prioritized the provision of new *licensed* childcare spaces, notably within schools. In April 2015, the province announced it was allocating $120 million over the next three years to creating safe, licensed childcare spaces in schools (Ontario Ministry of Education, 2015). However, even when secured, childcare concerns persist because arrangements for drop-off and pick-up also must be negotiated within the constrictions of parental employment schedules, illnesses, out-of-town work obligations, and so forth. Once children attend full-time kindergarten, which is now increasingly available, parents must still determine before and after school care, care for sick children, holiday-care, and transportation.

The stresses attached to all these daily concerns are, of course, socially constructed rather than inevitable. As evident internationally and provincially, some mothers are supported by a much more compassionate and extensive social support system providing an easier path back to paid employment after childbirth (Baker, 2011: 55). For example, Sweden has generous maternal and parental leave provisions along with an option to switch to part-time work until the child is 12 years of age (Stanfors, 2014: 534n). In Denmark, parents get two "nurture days" monthly per child under the age of eight so that they can more easily attend parent–teacher conferences, school events, and so forth. In the United Kingdom, families have the "right to request" flexible working hours and can only be turned down by their employer if their working plan would hurt the business's bottom line. Currently, 1 million British families have requested flexible schedules (Rosen, 2014).

Canada (and the United States) presents a stark contrast to Europe. In Canada (excepting Quebec), many women must rely on personal savings, good will from their employer and family relations, and relatively miserly Employment Insurance (EI) benefits for their childbirth leave arrangements (Albanese, 2011: 137). Guaranteed under employment regulations, only 15 weeks of maternity leave and 35 weeks of parental leave at 55 per cent of their previous salary are provided. As such, it is not surprising that many new mothers return to paid employment quickly after birth and rely on childcare options while others, especially in low-paid jobs, drop out of paid work entirely (see Box 7.1). The continued growth of precarious, non-standard employment, typically lacking parental leave benefits, suggests more and more mothers will have only this EI option. Of course, things might be worse. At the far end of the spectrum of parental leave policies is the United States, which is the only developed country not to offer any paid maternity leave as part of federal policy and in which only 59 per cent of workers are offered any paid maternity/parental leave by their employers (Miller, 2014).

Box 7.1 Everyday Work Experiences

Taking Time for Baby: The Swedish versus the Canadian Option

The maternity and parental benefits for Canadian families will vary depending upon their access to various employment benefits. However, as with many countries, the government provides a basic support plan based in our Employment Insurance plan. Under this legislation, an eligible mother who gives birth can apply for 15 weeks of maternity benefits; these 15 weeks may start up to eight weeks prior to birth or may extend 17 weeks for the woman who postpones benefits until the day of birth. The 17 weeks reflects the 15 weeks of benefits which is preceded by a two week (unpaid) waiting period. Also, parents—biological mothers, fathers, adoptive, and legally recognized—may apply to receive a maximum of 35 weeks of parental benefits. These 35 weeks of benefits may be shared in a variety of fashions by the parents. If you have a multiple birth or adopt more than one child, your benefits remain the same.

continued

Eligibility requires that you have at least 600 hours of insurable (payments made by you and your employer into the employment insurance plan) in the 52-week period prior to your benefit period. Self-employed workers are eligible if they have earned a specified income and opted into the program. Your eligibility is also determined by the fact that your normal weekly earnings have been reduced by more than 40 per cent because of your new caregiving responsibilities. If you satisfy these requirements, you will receive 55 per cent of your average insurable weekly earnings, up to a maximum (as of 1 January 2015) of $524.00 per week. This amount is taxable. Women who work during the maternity benefit period will have the entirety of any income deducted dollar for dollar from their benefits, and women or men on parental benefits may earn no more than $50 per week to top up their income. For low-income families with a net yearly income of $25,921 or less, there are family supplements available (Government of Canada, Service Canada, 2015).

Sweden is a revealing contrast. Swedish legislation allows for a total of 480 calendar days (approximately 69 weeks) of parental leave. During a full 390 of these days, parents receive 80 per cent of their previous income, to a maximum of 3,160 euros a month. The remaining 90 days are paid at 20 euros a day for a total of 1,800 euros. These benefits are targeted to biological and adoptive mothers and to their partners. Of the 480 days, 60 days *must be* "daddy months" or "partner months." This means women have a total of approximately 14 months and their partners two months. Fathers and partners have been encouraged to take up this parenting leave not only by an extensive media campaign but also by the fact that if these days are not used by the father/partner they are lost rather than returning to the mother. To further encourage greater gender equality in early parenting, depending upon the number of leave days that parents share equally, they receive a further bonus of up to 1,500 euros. While only 12 per cent of Swedish couples equally share the parenting leave, the net result has been a dramatic increase in fathers taking parental leaves when their children are infants (Martinez, 2015). In addition, further benefits are available for those having twins or triplets, those struggling with low income, and those who are currently not employed (for example, students) (Swedish Social Insurance Agency, 2014). Given these provisions, it is not surprising that Sweden in 2014 ranked fourth amongst 142 countries in terms of the overall gender gap while Canada ranked nineteenth (World Economic Forum, 2014).

For many Canadian mothers who are in the paid labour force, childcare presents a sizable hurdle. Despite the 1970 recommendation by the Royal Commission on the Status of Women that a national daycare system be provided to ensure Canadians the availability of affordable, high quality childcare, parents, particularly mothers, must turn to a patchwork quilt of solutions. In the current social and political climate, childcare is understood by various layers of government as a personal choice and individual responsibility. Reduced federal government transfers to the provinces along with "deficit" fighting on the provincial level translate into less and less support for childcare. Between 1989 and 1993 the annual growth rate in regulated childcare spots declined from 13 to 3.5 per cent.

Reflecting the assumed personal responsibility for childcare arrangements, governments have tended to respond to concerns about childcare inadequacies by providing tax deductions for childcare expenses, grants to for-profit centres, and business incentives to create workplace childcare. Most recently, however, the federal government has created a much more generous Canada Child Benefit which varies per family depending on family income and age and number of children. For families struggling with very low income, the benefit for a child under age six is $6,400 per year and for a child between 6 and 17 the benefit is $5,400 per year (Smith and Monsebraaten, 2016). This policy marks a significant turning-point in support for low-income families and employed mothers.

Quebec exceptionalism surrounding childcare supports warrants some further clarification because these policies have already demonstrated both what is possible and how it is feasible to facilitate women's paid labour force participation. In 1997, the Quebec government introduced a $5-per-day (later increased to $7) childcare program to be provided through non-profit centres and family childcare homes. This "fixed-fee" childcare was provided to all children up to age four, regardless of mothers' participation in paid labour. Childcare was then followed by full-day kindergarten provided to age five. While critics have raised questions about both the costs and mixed quality of Quebec childcare, Quebec policy underscores the possibilities for encouraging both maternal labour force participation and greater economic equality for women (McKenzie, 2014; Baker, 2011: 57). It remains to be seen if the new federal policy produces similar advances across Canada.

Currently, Quebec childcare compares reasonably with Sweden where public childcare is guaranteed to all parents and operates from 6:30 a.m. to 6:30 p.m.; where free pre-school is available to all children aged three to six for up to 15 hours a week, and additional hours cost parents no more than 3 per cent of family income to a maximum of 146 euros per month (European Platform for Investing in Children [EPIC], 2014). The impact on women's employment patterns is also apparent in both locales. The percentage of Quebec two-parent families with children under age six whose parents were employed grew from 56 in 1996 to 68 in 2005 and employed lone-parents with children under six grew from 46 per cent in 1996 to 64 per cent in 2005 (Albanese, 2011: 140). In Sweden, the employment rate for mothers with children under six reached 77 per cent by 2012 (EPIC, 2014).

Work-Family Conflict: Efforts to Manage Workplace Pressures

While scattered advances in childcare provisions offer some hope, much of that hope remains unfulfilled. Meanwhile, work-family conflict has actually been intensified by the shifting nature of paid work in the **new economy**. The dramatic increases in labour force precarity, un- and underemployment, and the proliferation of nonstandard work forms have all tended to intensify paid work obligations

(Duffy and Pupo, 2011). Underemployment, as well as unemployment, routinely translates into increased time and energy spent looking for work or for alternative work. **Multiple job holding** (combining several part-time positions) translates into increased commuting time. As widely recognized, advances in technology, notably cell phones, laptops, and tablets translate into longer hours engaged in work-related activities. Work insecurity means that many employees feel compelled to accept constant availability (notably, the popularization of on-call scheduling) and "self-sacrificial dedication" as workplace necessities (Correll et al., 2014). These shifts in the labour market amplify the stress and vulnerability experienced by parents struggling to combine paid and unpaid work.

Mothers have sought to reduce the work-based pressures through a wide variety of strategies including **part-time employment, work-sharing, flextime, compressed work week, telecommuting, self-employment, onsite childcare, working from home, multiple job holding, shift work**, and **satellite offices**. Each has its advantages and disadvantages. Part-time employment has been particularly popular. In Canada, the movement of mothers into paid employment in the 1970s and 1980s often meant part-time work. In 1983, more than one in three employed women with preschool children and a husband in the home worked part-time, and by 1989 almost three-quarters of married women with children under five worked part-time (as cited in Duffy and Pupo 1992: 47). This gender pattern persisted in 2014; almost one in three employed Canadian women worked part-time. As a result, women made up 67 per cent of the part-time labour force but only 43 per cent of the full-time labour force (Statistics Canada 2015d, CANSIM, Table 282-0002). Particularly during prime child-bearing and rearing ages (25 to 44) women lean toward working part-time. In 2014, almost one in five of employed women 25 to 44, but only 6 per cent of similarly aged employed men, were part-timers. Finally, as is clear from Table 7.3 women, much more than men, explain their part-time work in terms of child-care and personal preference. However in recent years, women's "choice" of part-time work may be fading. By 2014, three times as many mid-life women as men explained their part-time work as "other"—indicating they are involuntary part-time workers because they are unable to locate the full-time work they would prefer.

Table 7.3 Women and Men Aged 25 to 44 Reasons for Part-Time Work, 2014

	Women (%)	Men (%)
Own illness	3	6
Caring for children	32	4
Other personal/family responsibilities	4	2
Going to school	9	18
Personal preference	16	17
Other voluntary	3	4
Other (business conditions and unable to find full-time work)	19	6

Source: Derived from Statistics Canada, 2014, CANSIM, table 282-0014, 281-001 and catalogue no. 89F-133XIE.

Women have also turned to other forms of nonstandard work in response to work–life conflicts. In 1976, only 9 per cent of employed women were self-employed and they made up only 26 per cent of the self-employed. By 2009, 12 per cent of employed women were self-employed and they made up more than one-third of all self-employed Canadians (Ferrao, 2010: 16). In 1987, women made up 42 per cent of multiple job holders; by 2009 they made up 56 per cent (Ferrao, 2010: 18). Similarly, when available, women (and men) have opted for more flexible hours or for commuting to a satellite office in order to be closer to home. Predictably, single parents and employed parents of young children report that flexible working hours were actually a necessity if they are to hope to reconcile work–family responsibilities (Galea, Houkes, and De Rijk, 2014: 1108).

These work-oriented solutions to the work–family conflict are, sadly, problematic. For example, working part-time may reduce the daily burden of paid work but at considerable costs. Part-timers are routinely marginalized, assumed to be "less serious" about their careers, and at the bottom rung in terms of opportunities for training, advancement, and wage increases, and occupy notoriously insecure positions. By definition, these jobs produce fewer financial and other benefits. While this may "work" in a dual-earner family, in the event of divorce, disability, or death, this lack of benefits, adequate income, and career advancement may trigger an instant financial crisis. Further, from a life-course perspective, women may find that entering full-time paid work once their children are older may be both difficult and frustrating since, for example, their role as the family's primary unpaid worker has been established.

From an international perspective, part-time work may (as in Sweden) give the misleading impression of growing gender equity when in fact an examination of at-work hours reveals that women's domestic responsibilities, as reflected in work absences and part-time employment, interfere with and significantly reduce women's actual labour force participation (Stanfors, 2014). Only in some locales, such as the Netherlands, do part-time workers receive sufficient support and protection from government policies (for example, in terms of wages, holiday entitlements, overtime payments, bonuses, and training) that equity is not jeopardized (Roeters and Craig, 2014: 191).

Job-sharing appears to solve many drawbacks inherent in part-time employment. In job-sharing, typically two employees "share" one full-time employment position, including salary, benefits, opportunities for advancement, work security, and so on. They negotiate (on their own time) on a daily or weekly basis how the work responsibilities and work time will be shared. Unfortunately, job-sharing has won few advocates or practitioners.

Self-employment offers a similarly flawed alternative. While self-employment has grown faster than both private and public sector employment, this is likely the result of high rates of unemployment and an insecure labour market (Grant, 2013). While self-employment does offer more flexibility and creativity as well as the option of working from home, it has a significant downside since it comes with real economic risks in an uncertain economy, does not provide for retirement or health benefits, and often results in both unreliable and diminished financial returns when compared to traditional full-time work. Moreover, it typically allows for an unequal division of household responsibilities, with the bulk falling to the parent—typically the mother—who is "at home" (Craig, Powell, and Cortis, 2012). The problematic nature of the self-employment solution is further underscored by both the high rates of small business bankruptcies and the relatively small number of self-employed women whose business is large enough to include paid employees (Toneguzzi, 2015). In 2013, Industry Canada reported that almost one-third of micro-businesses (with one to four employees) did not survive two years (Industry Canada, 2013a: 13). Nonetheless, women, particularly those over age 45, have flooded into self-employment, accounting for three-quarters of the newly self-employed in 2012, and much of the job growth in 2015 took the form of self-employment. This appears not to be so much an endorsement for starting your own business as a reflection of a very troubled labour market (Grant, 2013).

Outside of self-employment, efforts to improve the "work" element in work–life conflict by changing the location, timing, and scheduling of work depend heavily on the goodwill of the employer and/or the strength of workers' organizations and the state of the economy. As unemployment has increased and the economy remains uncertain, employers have been disinclined to embrace alternative or flexible working arrangements. Research in the United States documents a downward trend in both the availability and promotion of flexible work arrangements since 2008 (Sweet et al., 2014). Typically, only when the government legislates the provision of family-friendly policies are there significant advances. Under neoliberalism, such policy initiatives are extremely rare.

Ironically, even when family-friendly policies are introduced, they may not be endorsed by management or fellow workers, both of whom may stigmatize those who opt for working from home or taking a compressed work week as not truly dedicated employees (Fiksenbaum, 2014; Agarwala et al., 2014). Even high status professionals, such as university faculty, face stigmatization if they opt for flexible work arrangements (Cech and Blair-Loy, 2014). Overall, family-friendly work arrangements have typically failed to challenge the "time-intensive" models of paid work and have tended to be adopted only when they benefit employers (Cady, 2013: 408). Finally, the labour movement, under pressures from all sides, is rarely in a position to pressure for improved working conditions for mothers and fathers.

Conclusion

The solutions to work–family–life conflict are not obscure. The BMO Annual Women's Day Study (2015) reported that women asked for, at home, more help around the house, more understanding of their work schedule, and more sharing of childcare responsibilities and, at work, better benefits, flexible time, and sick/family emergency days. Though not included in this survey, presumably affordable, accessible, quality childcare would be prominent on a wish list of both fathers and mothers. Other analysts have easily identified services and leave that would benefit employed mothers—childcare for under-threes, care for sick children, co-ordination of work and school schedules, and care for children during school holidays (Tobio and Cordon, 2013). Advocates for a solution from the social welfare state point to its past successes in challenging racism, sexism, and ableism and urge government policies (such as a national childcare program) which will ease the strain between work and family and work and life (Fudge, 2011; Chou and Cheung, 2013). However, employers continue to be concerned about the potential costs of such policies, and in the absence of strong interventions from governments or forceful lobbying by employee organizations, they remain inclined to maintain the status quo or actually reduce alternative working arrangements (Pasamar and Valle, 2015).

In the absence of such policy initiatives, employees turn to individual solutions. In response to many women's need to postpone parenting until their career is established, Apple in 2015 promised to pay for the costs of egg freezing for their female employees. Currently, Apple provides $4,000 in "baby cash" to new mothers and pays up to $15,000 for fertility treatments (Alba, 2014). The limitations of such private solutions along with their class bias are clear (Covert, 2014). This is not only because of their inherent shortcomings but primarily because the "solutions" are targeted at adjusting women's lives rather than addressing the fundamental issues of gender inequality in the home and workplace (Craig and Powell, 2012).

Questions for Critical Thought

1. Was the mass movement of mothers into paid employment an inevitable product of economic and historical change?
2. Why have Quebec, Sweden, and other locales been more successful in supporting mothers' paid employment?
3. In what ways is each solution–part-time work, self-employment, job-sharing–a flawed response to work-life conflict?

Suggested Further Resources

Cooper, Marianne. 2014. *Cut Adrift: Families in Insecure Times*. Berkeley: University of California Press. The author explores the ways in which families from different social classes struggle to cope with current economic insecurities and the impact of those insecurities on their daily lives.

Schulte, Ingrid. 2014. *Overwhelmed: Work, Love and Play When No One Has the Time*. New York: Penguin. This is one of the most recent popular examinations of the ways in which women find their lives overwhelmed by work and family demands that leave too little time for a personal life.

Suggested Websites

Canadian Centre for Occupational Health and Safety
www.ccohs.ca/healthyworkplaces/topics/worklifeblance/html
The Canadian Centre for Occupational Health and Safety provides a compendium of useful, practical information on work-life balance, including reports, fact sheets, handbooks, and links to other Canadian resources.

Vanier Institute of the Family
www.vanierinstitute.ca
The Vanier Institute of the Family is a national, independent, charitable organization which publishes research on Canadian families, including a number of topics relevant to mothers' paid employment, changes in family forms, and work-family conflict.

Note

1. Of course, women were not alone in this regard; numerous other segments of the population were also being marginalized. The LGBTQ community was basically in enforced social exile; non-"whites," especially Aboriginals, were kept to the economic margins; immigrants struggled against both Anglophone and Francophone prejudices; the elderly and disabled were, as is often the case today, essentially rendered invisible unless they enjoyed an exalted class position.

8 Unemployment or Opportunities for Youth?

Learning Objectives

- To understand the present economic and social conditions youth encounter in finding "good jobs" in today's economy
- To become familiar with the complexity of statistically mapping young Canadians in and out of work
- To introduce recent theories about youth's employment/unemployment experiences
- To explore whether entrepreneurship is a viable employment option for young graduates of university or community college/CEGEP

Introduction

Many critics of the new economy have pointed to myriad difficulties in locating good jobs and settling into careers. Today's "storm" of young job seekers, labelled as Millennials, confronts new challenges as many face ballooning student debt and struggle to get meaningful job experience. This chapter examines patterns of employment/unemployment amongst young Canadians—men and women between the ages of 15 and 25—and the challenges they face as they enter the labour market careers. Here we consider three distinct categories of young Canadians: those proceeding to post-secondary education (40 per cent), those gainfully employed (45 per cent), and a third group known as **NEETs**—neither employed nor enrolled—who are neither employed nor enrolled in training programs.

In the developed world, recent research confirms that many in the generations born since the 1970s experience the transition from school to work and adulthood with some difficulty, unlike the baby boom generation. The main drivers of this uncertain process are neoliberalism and globalization. Upon graduation, many young Canadians find themselves working in precarious jobs while juggling the re-payment of high student debt loads. Moreover, more young people than before in Canada and elsewhere in mature capitalist countries experience underemployment or what Coté and Allahar (2001) call the "credentialism paradox" or the mismatch between higher level skills held by some young people and their jobs requiring lower level skills. We conclude by examining explanations that have been put forward to make sense of the conditions that have contributed to the difficulties young people face as they search for stable positions within the labour market

Youth and the Labour Market

Employed and Unemployed Youth

Forty years ago, young boomers could easily move from high school to decent paying employment with union coverage and benefits in auto, steel, and other manufacturing industries. Today, this option has been severely curtailed. As David Foot dramatically noted over 20 years ago, the "unskilled entry-level jobs leading to middle-class security no longer exist" (qtd. in Coté and Allahar, 1998: 128). As discussed in previous chapters, the twin processes of globalization and neoliberalism account for the dramatic shift in employment opportunities from manufacturing and natural resource industries to a predominantly service-based economy in Canada and elsewhere in the developed world.

In Canada, the **youth labour force** includes all persons between the ages of 15 and 24 who were employed or unemployed over a specified time period. **unemployed youth** covers all persons between the ages of 15 and 24 who during a reference period had not worked for any economic activity such as paid employment or self-employment; were currently available for work; and were actively seeking work; that is, they had taken active steps to seek work during a specified recent period, usually the past four weeks (ILO, 2011).

After undertaking statistically sophisticated analysis of the labour market in the 1990s, Beaudry, Lemieux, and Parent (2000) warned of the importance of focusing on the participation rate of youth as a highly relevant issue. They expressed concerned over the heavy declines in the labour market attachment of youth at a time when improvements were expected (2000: S65). They wrap up their analysis by concluding that for men 15 to 19 (student and non-student), the main cause of decline in participation rates is a general deterioration in labour market conditions.[1] For women aged 15 to 24 and men aged 20 to 24, in addition to the deterioration of labour market conditions, many became students because of the perceived net gains from education (2000: S81). The analysis pointed out that teenaged males with or without high school diplomas were especially at risk for gaining meaningful employment. However, a significant proportion of young women between 15 to 24 and young men between 20 and 24 began looking to post-secondary education to better their chances for well-paying, meaningful employment.

The perceived benefits of higher education by young Canadians have resulted in dramatic increases in enrolments at both the community college/CEGEP[2] and university levels. Nearly 2 million students were enrolled in post-secondary institutions in 2011–2012. Of these students, approximately 63 per cent and 37 per cent were enrolled in a university or community college/CEGEP respectively (Rajotte, 2014). In 2012, about 53.6 per cent of Canadians aged 15 years and over had trade certificates, college diplomas, and university degrees. This was an increase of 20.9 percentage points since 1990. Among Canada's adult population aged 25 to 64 years, 51 per cent had completed post-secondary education in 2010, the highest percentage among OECD member countries, and well above the OECD average of 31 per cent (Statistics Canada, 2014d).

Among the set of well-established indicators used to assess the labour market performance of youth, including the employment rate and long-term unemployment rate, the level of unemployment is a significant measure to illustrate the structural consequences of globalization and the neoliberal state on young people. The unemployment rate is probably the best known and most used labour market indicator. The unemployment rate reflects the inability of an economy to generate employment for job-seekers who are ready and willing to work (ILO, 2011). Since 1976, Canada's youth unemployment rate[3] has consistently exceeded the rate for the population aged 25 and over. Specifically, over the period from January 1976 to December 2013, the youth unemployment rate was, on average, 2.1 times the rate for people aged 25 and older while in 2013, it was 2.3 times higher. The youth unemployment rate since the 2008 recession has been highest for teenage girls at 18.7 per cent and 25.2 per cent for teenage boys. For men aged 20 to 24 years, the unemployment rate was 15.7 per cent and 23 per cent for those who had not graduated from high school (Rajotte, 2014: 23).

The long-term effect of high levels of unemployment for young Canadians may also contribute to declining real wages in today's labour market. According to Statistics Canada "[i]n 2012, the median hourly wages (in real terms) of men and women aged 17 to 24 were 13 per cent and 8 per cent lower, respectively, than their counterparts in 1981" (Galarneau, Morissette, and Usalcas, 2013: 5). Over the 30-year period from 1981 to 2012, young men and women aged 17 to 24 experienced real declines in their hourly wages: albeit young men suffered the larger losses. However, women aged 25 to 34 experienced an "improvement in full-time employment rates and wages, while for their male counterparts living in non-oil-producing provinces, as well as for those aged 24 and under, it was just the opposite" (2013:8)

The sustained higher unemployment rates between youth and adult populations are not unique to Canada. In 2011, for example, youth in countries making up the Organisation for Economic Co-operation and Development (OECD) recorded higher unemployment rates than did adults (Rajotte, 2014: 27–8). According to André Bernard, "among G7 countries, Italy, the United Kingdom, and France reported the largest gaps between youth and adults, while Germany and Japan reported the smallest" (Bernard, 2013: 1).

For young people, finding a job can be especially difficult when an economic recession occurs. Normally, some employers cease to hire workers and, when downsizing their workforce, lay off younger workers prior to more experienced employees. Statistics Canada data indicate that, on average in 2009, 2.8 per cent of youth who were working in a given month became unemployed in the following month; for those aged 25 and older, this percentage was 1.4 per cent (Bernard, 2013).

Table 8.1 Unemployment Rate by Province, 1st Half of 2008 and 1st Half of 2013, Persons Aged 15-19 years and 20-24 years

	Rate (%) 15–19 yrs			Rate (%) 20–24 yrs		
PROVINCE	**1st Half of 2008**	**1st Half of 2013**	**Variation (%)**	**1st Half of 2008**	**1st Half of 2013**	**Variation (%)**
Newfoundland & Labrador	22.5	20.9	−6.9	19.5	16.0	−17.8
Prince Edward Island	20.4	19.4	−5.0	15.4	19.5	26.9
Nova Scotia	17.2	27.4	59.4	12.5	16.2	29.4
New Brunswick	16.3	23.5	43.6	16.7	17.6	5.9
Québec	16.9	20.5	21.3	10.4	9.8	−6.2
Ontario	18.3	23.1	26.1	11.0	13.1	18.8
Manitoba	14.1	14.7	4.2	6.2	7.8	25.2
Saskatchewan	11.3	11.6	2.9	4.8	7.3	51.7
Alberta	11.0	13.4	21.4	5.2	7.2	37.6
British Columbia	11.1	18.5	66.6	6.2	10.2	63.4
Total	**15.7**	**20.1**	**27.8**	**9.4**	**11.1**	**18.0**

Source: Compiled from Tables 4 and 5, Youth Employment in Canada: Challenges and Potential Solutions, 2014, pp. 25–26. Statistics Canada, Table 282-0001, "Labour Force survey estimates (LFS), by sex and detailed age group, unadjusted for seasonality," CANSIM (database), accessed on 15 January 2014.

Table 8.1 provides data on youth unemployment for two time periods: the first half of 2008 (recession) and the first half of 2013 (post-recession) by province.

Variations in the youth unemployment rate between the first half of 2008 and the first half of 2013 have differed across provinces and between the two groups of youth aged 15 to 19 and youth aged 20 to 24. On a percentage basis, between the first half of 2008 and the first half of 2013, the unemployment rate for persons aged 15 to 19 increased the most in British Columbia, Nova Scotia, and New Brunswick while the rate in Newfoundland and Labrador and in Prince Edward Island fell. For youth aged 20 to 24, between the first half of 2008 and the first half of 2013, the unemployment rate, on a percentage basis, increased the most in British Columbia, Saskatchewan, and Alberta while the rate *declined* in both Newfoundland and Labrador and Québec.

A closer examination of Table 8.1 reveals the wide variation in unemployment for both age cohorts. For the 15–19 cohort, all the provinces east of Saskatchewan recorded unemployment rates above 14 per cent for the first half of 2008. The unemployment rate in Saskatchewan, Alberta, and British Columbia came in at around 11 per cent. For the later period, only the oil producing provinces of Saskatchewan and Alberta recovered most of the ground lost from the recession.

The story is somewhat different for those aged 20 to 24 years. The western provinces recorded unemployment rates *below* the national average at between 5 and 6 per cent for the first half of 2008. Manitoba, Saskatchewan, and Alberta posted unemployment rates at close to the national average of approximately 7 per cent during the second half of 2013. Once more British Columbia falls from grace in Western Canada for the first half of 2013 with an unemployment rate above 10 per cent.

Interestingly, except for Québec with an unemployment rate of 9.8 per cent for 20- to 24-year-olds, the remaining provinces in the country posted youth unemployment rates over twice the national average. However, the employment prospects for young Canadians in Canada's oil producing provinces will disproportionately feel the impact of the dramatic decline in oil prices that began in the fall of 2014, continuing into 2016.

Finally, while we have shown that youth unemployment rates vary across two demographic groups of young Canadians and by provinces, some groups of young people such as Aboriginal Canadians, immigrants, visible minorities, and those with a disability often have relatively greater difficulties in the labour market. It is important to note that the problem of youth unemployment is even more serious in these marginalized communities. People living in poverty, Aboriginal youth, and immigrant youth are being affected to a greater degree by youth unemployment.

As shown in Table 8.2, unemployment rates for young people in the four subgroups were significantly higher than those for other young people. Individuals aged 15 to 19 years of age with Aboriginal status and with a disability ranked the highest with 25.9 per cent unemployment while those between 20 and 24 years old who were Aboriginals, visible minorities, or immigrants posted smaller but significant differences compared with those with non-Aboriginal, non-visible minority, or non-immigrant status.

The statistical evidence marshalled above draws attention to the complex picture of youth unemployment in Canada. Variations by province and by demographic characteristics such as visible minority or Aboriginal status point to significant gaps between the unemployment rates of youths and adults. According to André Bernard (2013), differences in the unemployment rates of youths and adults have not decreased since the early 1990s, and have even increased slightly since 2010. The largest gap since 1977 occurred in 2012 when youth unemployment rate was 2.4 times that of workers aged 25 to 54. The widening of the gap may indicate

Table 8.2 Youth Unemployment Rate by Selected Demographic Group, 2011 or 2012 (%)

Characteristic	15 to 19 Years (2011)	20 to 24 Years (2011)
Aboriginal identity	25.9	22.6
Non-Aboriginal identity	19.5	14.4
Immigrant	24.9	16.9
Non-immigrant	19.3	14.4
Visible minority	26.7	17.7
Not a visible minority	18.6	14.1
With a disability	25.9 (2012)	
Without a disability	15.3 (2012)	

Note: Data for "with a disability" or "without a disability" are not available by five-year age groups 15 to 19 and 20 to 24 years for 2011.

Sources: Aboriginal identity and immigrant status: Statistics Canada, "2011 National Household Survey," Data Tables, Labour Force Status by Aboriginal identity, immigrant status and visible minority status; Presence of disability: Statistics Canada, "2012 Canadian Survey on Disability." Table 8.2 adapted from Table 3 in YOUTH EMPLOYMENT IN CANADA: CHALLENGES AND POTENTIAL SOLUTIONS, Report of the Standing Committee on Finance, June 2014, pp. 24.

that the level of employment among young people had not returned to its pre-recession level (Bloskie and Gellatly, 2012). However, the labour force participation rate of youth may be at an historic low compared to that of adults mainly because a majority of young people now attend school well into their 20s (Bernard, 2013).

Education, Training, and the Labour Market

The segment of the youth population who are confronted with more restricted employment opportunities, with fewer financial supports from their families and limited access to public programs are in a more vulnerable situation than their middle and upper class counterparts. Structurally, young people from the lowest socio-economic sectors are overrepresented among the unemployed and the poor and this unsurprisingly affects their routes to well-paying, full-time employment. In this context, European researchers have labelled some of these young people NEETs, or Not in Education, Employment or Training.[4] The term was coined in Britain after reports that an increasing number of older teenagers were leaving school and remaining jobless for long periods of time. These young people were particularly at risk for labour market and social exclusion (Eurofound, 2013).

Bynner and Parsons (2002) showed that certain at-risk youth were more likely to become NEET and were subsequently prone to experience poor labour market prospects, depression, early parenthood, and poor housing. In reaction to this trend, remedial programs were developed in Britain to reduce the number of NEET youth (Yates and Payne, 2006). However, the phenomenon was not limited to Britain. Quintini and Martin (2006) found that more than 10 per cent of youth between the ages of 15 to 24 in Italy, Greece, France, and Spain were in a continual state of NEET for five years. As a result of the use of NEET in OECD research studies, Statistics Canada began to analyze the occurrence and characteristics of NEET candidates in this country.

In Canada, in 2011, 44 per cent of youth were students, 43 per cent were employed, and 13 per cent were labelled NEET (Marshall, 2012).

Table 8.3 provides Canadian data from 1976 until 2011 on the distribution of youth between the ages of 15 and 29 by schooling including university/community college/CEGEP, their employment status while in school, youth who are employed, and NEET status. Over this time period, the overall NEET rate decreased from 22 per cent in 1976 to 13 per cent in 2011. However, in the years since the economic downturn of 2008, the NEET rate has climbed up by as much as two percentage points.

Table 8.3 describes the steady increase since 1976 of the percentage of youth attending school for all age groups, from 65 to 81 per cent for those aged 15 to 19, 18 to 40 per cent for those 20 to 24, and 7 to 13 per cent for those 25 to 29. Over the past decade, there has also been a steady increase in the proportion of students aged 15 to 24 who hold a job while attending school. This is particularly true for those aged 20 to 24. Since 2001, almost one-half combine school and work (Marshall, 2010; Marshall, 2012). Many graduates who start looking for career employment after their education may benefit from their part-time work experience. However,

Table 8.3 Student Status, Employment Status, and NEET[1] 1976-2011 in Percentages

Age/Year	1976	1981	1991	2001	2008	2011
15–19						
Student	65	66	78	81	80	81
—Employed	17	22	32	28	31	27*
—Not Employed	48	45	46	53	49	54*
Employed	21	21	12	11	13	11*
NEET	14	13	10	7	7	8
20–24						
Student	18	16	30	36	39	40
—Employed	7	7	14	18	20	19
—Not Employed	11	9	16	19	19	21*
Employed	59	63	49	48	48	45*
NEET	23	21	21	16	13	15*
25–29						
Student	7	7	9	12	12	13
—Employed	4	4	5	6	7	7
—Not Employed	3	2	4	5	5	5
Employed	65	69	68	72	73	70*
NEET	28	24	23	16	15	17*

1. Not enrolled in school or employed.
* Denotes statistically significant difference between 2011 and 2008 at the 0.01 level
Source: Adapted from Table 2 in Marshall, Katherine. 2012. "Youth neither enrolled nor employed", Perspectives on Labour and Income, Vol. 24, Number 2, 1–15. pg. 8.

it remains unclear how working in the retail service sector, where most young students find jobs, benefits long-term, full-time employment.

Table 8.3 shows that the percentage of those between the ages of 15 and 24 who were employed has fallen since the recession while their school attendance rate has risen. Conversely, although the school attendance rate has increased for those aged 25 to 29, the percentage employed has also increased from 65 per cent in 1976 to 70 per cent in 2011, probably reflecting the increasing employment rate of women. Following the recent downturn, there have been small but significant decreases in the employment rates of students under age 20 and all non-students under age 30. At the same time, the overall NEET rate increased, as did the percentage of unemployed youth age 20 and over.

According to Katherine Marshall (2012), in 2011, 13 per cent of youth aged 15 to 29 or 904,000 out of 6.8 million young Canadians were neither enrolled in school nor employed. The NEET population was equally divided between men and women and most are older. Seventy-nine per cent of male NEET youth were between the ages of 20 and 29, as were 85 per cent of female NEET youth. While older male NEET youth were unemployed, most female NEET youth were not in the labour force (NILF) (2012: 8–9). NEETs are among those groups of young people who become targets of surveillance and exclusion from public spaces by the use of such devices as the Mosquito (See Everyday Work Experiences Box 8.1). Begun in the UK, this audio-device is now available and in use in several provinces in Canada.

Box 8.1 Everyday Work Experiences
"Youth Fight for Jobs—Youth Fight Austerity"

Who Is Youth Fight for Jobs—Youth Fight Austerity?

Youth Fight for Jobs was launched as a result of a "March for Jobs" on 2 April 2009 during the G20 London Summit. It held its foundation conference in May 2009.

Youth Fight for Jobs (YFFJ) is a campaigning youth organization based across England, Scotland and Wales. Seven national UK trade unions as well as individual trade union branches, student unions, and labour movement figures support the organization.

Excerpt Taken From YFFJ website:

Raise the minimum wage: £10 now with no youth exemptions

Scrap zero-hours contracts!

"We campaign on a range of issues relating to young people. Most importantly, we are fighting for decent jobs with guaranteed hours and full trade union rights for everyone. We say no to the twin scourges of unemployment and underemployment."

"Perfect storm for youth.

No education, no jobs, no homes, no services. This is the bleak future that young people face. We are expected to pay for a crisis caused by the rotten system we live under.

There are currently 1 million 18–24 year olds out of work in the UK Yet the government tries to punish the unemployed by forcing them to work for their dole. This gives their big business mates the opportunity to get some work done on the cheap."

YFFJ Fighting Against the Mosquito: Anti-Youth Audio Device

"Suffering from anxiety is difficult, even something simple like walking through the town can be difficult. But what makes things much worse is having to suffer the piercing sound of a Mosquito audio device (weapon). This self-described "youth deterrent" (its sound is only audible to those under the age of 25) has been on 24/7 and is causing myself, and many others, distress and in some cases ill health. This area of town is also home to the job centre and food bank, meaning users of both are also affected. I've not been well, but when the device meant I couldn't pick up my 'book prescription' or enter the job centre, I decided that we needed to do something about it. It started with a Facebook post and had now become a fully-fledged campaign with researchers, local charity endorsements and now a stand-off with the owners of the buildings. ***Youth Fight for Jobs*** is building a strong case for the removal of this audio-weapon, but, with actions and protests potentially taking place, we will need all the help we can get to get there."

Why do you think there is not an equivalent organization in Canada to the UK-based Youth Fight For Jobs (YFJ)?

Source: perm obtained from Claire Laker-Mansfield Youth Fight for Jobs - youthfightforjobs@gmail.com

Aside from the growing obligations to spend time in educational institutions, youth seeking to enter the labour market may find more and more nonstandard options. Presently, 59 per cent of youth (15 to 24 years old) who hold part-time work are female and 41 per cent are male (all figures derived from Statistics Canada, 2015d). Generally, analysts have not been bothered by the expansion of youth part-time employment when it occurs in the context of ongoing education and does not interfere with academic work. Instead, concerns have arisen when part-time and other nonstandard forms of employment have become increasingly normative post-graduation. Analysts worry that the lost generation of youth will find themselves stuck in nonstandard, low wage, and temporary employment for long periods of time (Kapsalis and Tourigny, 2004) and that this lost ground may have a permanent impact on wages, savings, and career advancement.

The precarity of more and more young workers is also apparent in their growing role in temporary employment. From 1997 to 2012, close to 30 per cent of Canadians aged 15 to 24 (who were not students) were employed on a temporary basis. Between 2007 and 2009 about 23 per cent of non-student workers aged 16 to 29 experienced some employment instability. Of this group, more than half (56 per cent) were in temporary jobs (part- or full-time), 26 per cent were in permanent part-time jobs and almost one in five (19 per cent) were unemployed. Research data indicate that one in eight of Canada's non-student youth is "loosely attached" to the labour market (LaRochelle-Cote, 2013), and as a result, recent generations are struggling as they attempt to access the labour market.

Statistics also suggest youth are not transitioning into standard employment relationships (SERs). From 2010 to 2014, young women aged 15 to 24 experienced more of a decline in permanent jobs than comparably aged men (Statistics Canada,

Rick Eglinton/Toronto Star via Getty Images

Increasingly youth in Canada are turning to the service sector for employment. Teens fill out applications during the first day of the Vaughan Mills Career Fair, a two-day event that was held to fill 3,000 openings at the new 200-store mall in Vaughan, Ontario.

2015b). Within this temporary work category, there has been a small increase in **term or contract** jobs between 2010 and 2014 for young men and women (15 to 24). The most notable net percentage change is an 11 per cent increase from 2010 to 2014 for women and men aged 15 to 24 in **casual** jobs (Statistics Canada, 2015b). However, even full-time work did not mitigate other economic issues for youth as indicated by the drop in real wages for both men and women aged 17 to 24.

Researchers are now exploring the degree to which temporary, insecure employment may function as a long-lasting disadvantage, and such research seems particularly pertinent to youth's experience of the current labour market. Sylvia Fuller and Natasha Stecy-Hildebrandt (2014) report from a nationally representative sample of Canadian temporary workers (and a matched sample of permanent workers), that over the course of five years, temporary workers, who typically start out with lower wages, fail to catch up in terms of income and access to good quality permanent jobs. Women, who are more likely than men to work temporary jobs, experienced a more pronounced persistent disadvantage over that time period (see also Vincent, 2013). Significantly, even when workers move into permanent positions, their prior temporary jobs continue to be associated with long-term disadvantages, although over time workers who work more and move into permanent positions improve their employment situations. However, as with periods of unemployment, there appears to be a "scarring" effect when workers experience a period of temporary work. While not as dire as a period of unemployment, working on a part-time temporary basis is likely to become an "ongoing" disadvantage (Fuller and Stecy-Hildebrandt, 2014). Given the dramatic growth in temporary employment amongst youth, it is important to keep in mind these long-term and gendered disadvantages.

Finally, any discussion of youth and nonstandard work time arrangements would be incomplete without mention of the expansion of compulsory volunteering and unpaid internships (Perlin, 2012a). One of the outstanding recent shifts in working times has been the popularization of unpaid work. In these instances, work time has been disconnected from wages. While volunteering has a long and illustrious past, the very meaning of volunteering has changed remarkably in the new economy. In 2010, Canadian volunteers provided nearly 2.07 million hours to groups and organizations. However, volunteering amongst Canadians 25 to 54 declined over the past 20 years, presumably as a result of paid work intensification as more women moved into full-time employment and men worked longer hours (Turcotte and Gaudet, 2013). In this context, volunteer work has become increasingly required. For example, volunteer work for a specified number of hours is currently mandatory in various locales in Canada and Australia as part of the requirements for completing secondary school education. Similarly, many applicants for service sector education (e.g., applicants to social work and childcare programs) find that they are required to provide evidence of substantial volunteer involvement in order to qualify for education in their chosen field (Pupo and Duffy, 2011).

In the actual education process, individuals may find that as part of their academic program they are expected to provide unpaid labour in their field. While some "co-ops" are remunerated, many academic programs offering "situated learning" and "experiential education," require "work time" but do not come with wages. In one notorious example, thousands of low-paid interns worked at Walt Disney World flipping burgers and parking cars to earn academic credits (Perlin, 2011). Graduate students may similarly be "offered" unpaid research assistantships (Perlin, 2012b). It appears that required volunteering and unpaid work are increasingly embedded in the education process. It is estimated in the United States that 70 to 75 per cent of college students are given the opportunity to take on "unpaid" internships (Clawson and Gerstel, 2014: 34).

Upon graduation, increasing numbers of unemployed and underemployed youth may find they have little recourse other than poorly paid or unpaid internships with time commitments of typically six months and, sometimes, onerous daily work times.[5] Canadian analysts estimate (no statistical data is collected) that there are as many as 300,000 unpaid or poorly paid interns working for some of Canada's wealthiest corporations (Goodman, 2014). Ross Perlin, author of *Intern Nation* (2012a), suggests there are approximately 500,000 unpaid US interns, saving companies $2 billion annually in labour costs (Miller and Horn, 2014). Despite no remuneration for time spent at work, no future commitment of employment, and no access to workplace protections (such as the Employment Standards) interns have become increasingly common. Bell Canada along with the Canadian magazines *Walrus* and *Toronto Life* for example, in 2014 responded to public pressure by ending their controversial unpaid internship programs (McKnight, 2014; Oved, 2014).

Finally, this exploitation of young people's time may have important social class and social mobility implications. By definition these positions require "workers" who are able to afford to "work" for no or little pay. As a result, access to unpaid internships may emerge as another key ingredient in the intensification of social class inequalities.

Credentialism: The Push for Over-Educating and Over-Training?

Over the past 30 to 40 years, ever-increasing numbers of young people between the ages of 15 and 25/29 in the developed world delay making decisions over looking for well-paying, full-time employment by remaining in school longer. Forty-four per cent of young Canadians attend universities or community colleges/CEGEP as their ticket to well-compensated, secure employment (Marshall, 2011). The traditional post-war pathway from education-to-work has become disrupted (Dwyer and Wyn, 2001). Rapid advances in information and communications technology require an ongoing updating of job-related or employment-linked knowledge. Today, media pundits, business organizations, and most politicians are quick to point out that life-long learning is the key to security. That is to say, school is regarded as the place where "learning" occurs while the workplace is where knowledge is "applied." Youth observe that careers may be beyond reach and that work is often short-term and requires few skills (Dwyer and Wyn, 2001: 25). Under these circumstances, an increasing number are staying in school longer, working in temporary jobs before entering the full-time labour market, or remaining in part-time employment after graduation (Dwyer and Wyn, 2001).

According to the 2013 CBC documentary *Generation Jobless*, the real crisis is not youth unemployment but rather, the **underemployment** of increasing numbers of university and college graduates who work in low-paid, part-time jobs that do not require a degree. Unfortunately, there are no official statistics in Canada about the level of underemployment of young Canadians. However, the documentary estimates that after graduating, one in three 25- to 29-year-olds with a college or university degree ends up in a low-skilled job (see also Kolm, 2013). According to CareerBuilder North America, 36 per cent of employers are now hiring college and university graduates for jobs that used to require only a high school diploma (Kolm, 2013). As a result, many graduates are settling for jobs that have not traditionally required the level of training they have attained. Today, nearly half of young Canadians are employed in retail, food service, or clerical work where they earn wages that do not offer long-term financial security.

Coté and Allahar (2001) refer to a disconnection between university level education and workplace skills as the "**credentialism paradox**" (2001: 268), more commonly referred to as **underemployment**. That is to say, formal educational credentials may have little to do with the work that is eventually performed. However, without entry-level credentials, a person's employability and potential earning power are put at risk. Today, young Canadians are learning that the undergraduate degree has lost its lustre and are entering postgraduate and professional programs in greater numbers. As more university graduates have flooded the market, bachelors' degrees have been devalued—what Coté and Allahar (2007; 2011) refer to as the proletarianization of undergraduate programs—and this contributes to underemployment among graduates (2011: 258).

Under the process of "proletarianization," university culture has become more rule-minded, mirroring the practices of monitoring students within high schools (Coté and Allahar, 2011). The forms of autonomy formerly fostered by universities now appear to be less common in undergraduate programs. These changes mean that the undergraduate degree has become devalued as a prerequisite for a good job and, for the working class, this process closes a pathway to social mobility. The portal to good jobs today is the postgraduate degree, an option of greater benefit to students from more affluent backgrounds (Coté, 2014: 536).

Underemployment is a tricky concept to measure. It includes people who are involuntarily working part-time or fewer hours than they wish. It also refers to jobs that do not use workers' complete skill sets. Underemployment occurs when employers raise the formal education required for entry-level positions, thereby underutilizing workers' expertise, giving rise to huge numbers of overqualified employees (Kelly et al., 1997). "Seventy-two per cent of net new jobs created between 2008 and 2013 fall into the precarious or underemployed category" (MacEwen, 2014, cited in Goar, 2014b).

David Livingstone has written extensively on the underemployment of Canadians. Unlike those who maintain the main issue facing those entering the new knowledge economy is the under-qualification of the labour force, Livingstone's research demonstrates that while work experience lessens underemployment, overall, underemployment continues to increase among all service, industrial, and non-white immigrant workers (2010; Livingstone and Raykov, 2008). Over the past 30 years, employers, not only in Canada but also in the United States and Great Britain, are predisposed to estimate their workers' capabilities in terms of additional formal educational qualifications or other credentials. As a result, Livingstone contends that underemployment is an unrelenting issue within advanced market economies (2010: 211).

In Canada underemployment has grown since the last recession. Today, one in four millennials with a university degree is employed full-time in a job that does not require that level of education (Statistics Canada, 2013b). That number climbs to one in three when considering those aged between 25 and 29 years.

This rise in underemployment may be due to a number of factors, including increasing rates of part-time work, corporate policies of cutting hours in order to cut costs, and the corporate shift to flexible labour markets with no fixed contracts or guarantees for working hours. It may also derive from the dramatic increase in higher educational qualifications of workers in the developing world such as China and India who now contend for jobs that were once the preserve of workers in the advanced market economies (International Monetary Fund, 2007: 167–92). Increasing formal educational demands for entry-level jobs in Canada and elsewhere in the OECD may be an expedient measure to ensure certain jobs remain in the developed economies.

Clearly, the evidence suggests that youth today have been dealt a difficult hand when compared to previous generations. In today's world, the transition from school to work for middle class youth is becoming more difficult and taking longer to achieve. For those without sufficient parental resources, the pathway to secure careers is even harder and usually requires a combination of large student loans and part-time employment. Whether it is the credential paradox or underemployment, the devalued undergraduate degree, high student tuition and student debt, above average unemployment, and the growth in precarious employment in the service sector, we must acknowledge the dilemmas facing youth looking for a good career in contemporary society.

Personal Crisis or Social Issue? Emerging Adulthood, Social Generation, or Social Class?

Theorizing Youth Struggles for Full Employment

In recent years, social scientists in Canada and other OECD countries found that the transition from school to work is taking longer to complete. Young people are living with their parents longer, are more highly educated, and attend school for more years than their parents did (Beaupré, Turcotte, and Milan, 2006; Boyd and

Norris, 1999). As noted in Chapter 7, the age at marriage has been rising, fertility rates have been falling, and the age at which women have their first child has been increasing.

Many young Canadians are delaying their entry into the labour market and pursuing higher education, at either university or community college/CEGEP. For example, since 1990, the number of jobs requiring a university degree has doubled, while the number demanding high school education or less has shrunk (AUCC, 2007). Young people are increasingly expected to continue their schooling. For instance, 95 per cent of parents with children under age 19 believe that education after high school is important or very important (Shipley, Ouellette, and Cartwright, 2003). In addition, tuition fees have been increasing more quickly than inflation since the early 1990s, and the amount students owe to government student loan programs has also been escalating (Finnie, 2002; Statistics Canada, 2006b). Currently, students studying in Ontario and the Maritimes have the highest average debt loads, averaging more than $28,000 (CCPA, 2014).

In other jurisdictions, a massive student mobilization in Québec in 2005 forced Jean Charest's Liberal government to reverse $103 million in cuts to a bursary program directed at students most in need. From 13 February to 7 September 2012, Québec experienced the longest student strike in Québec and Canadian history. Almost on a daily basis there were major demonstrations in Montréal and in other cities and towns across the province against increases in tuition fees. The strike began after Jean Charest's Liberal government introduced tuition fee increases in the March 2011 provincial budget. At the beginning of December 2011, more than 60,000 students formed a temporary coalition called CLASSE (Coalition large de l'Association pour une solidarité syndicale étudiante, or Broad Coalition of the Association for Student Union Solidarity) with the aim of triggering a general strike. On 22 March 2012, there were between 100,000–200,000 students demonstrating in Montréal with close to 310,000 out of the 400,000 students in the province on strike. The strike was supported by most of the Québec cultural community. A small red square pinned to people's clothes became the symbol of the fight against the tuition fee increase. Opposition came from a small group of students who formed the Mouvement des étudiants socialement responsables du Québec (MÉSRQ), or "Socially Responsible Students Movement." There was also little support from students in other provinces where tuition fees are much higher than those in Québec.

On 8 May 2012, the National Assembly of Québec passed a special law. Bill 78 included steep fines for individuals, student associations, and trade unions that interfered with class schedules. The Bill also restricted the right to demonstrate. Denounced by the opposition parties and the United Nations, students and other Québecers defied the law and demonstrated their unhappiness in the streets of Montréal by banging on pots. These spontaneous outbursts became known as the "concerts de casseroles" (concerts of pots and pans). On 1 August 2012, Jean Charest called a general election to settle the matter. His government was defeated and a Parti Québecois minority government was elected with the promise not to raise tuition fees. Collective action has afforded Québec both the lowest tuition fees and lowest levels of student debt of any province at just over $13,000 (CCPA, 2014).

Students in Newfoundland and Labrador have been successful in lobbying consecutive governments to freeze and reduce tuition fees since 1999. In 2007, the provincial government implemented an up-front needs-based grant program. As a result, student debt in Newfoundland and Labrador has decreased significantly (CFS, n.d.). However, despite these positive examples, in Canada and elsewhere in mature capitalist countries, the high cost of post-secondary education coupled with massive student debts involves young people's continued reliance on their parents. Unlike the baby boom generation, for example, youth today face different sets of obstacles toward achieving independence through secure well-paying careers while, for some, delaying entry into the labour market by working for advanced degrees and credentials can mean increased opportunities in the workplace and adult life.

One of the more important concerns for youth today is the transition from school to work. Many analysts use the era of the 1960s as a benchmark for evaluating the changes in the transition from school to work and independent adult life. For example, Jeffrey Arnett's (2000; 2004) theory of emerging adulthood uses survey data collected in the United States to support his case for the recognition of a new phase of development past the teenage years and well into the 20s. His theory puts forward an argument for recognizing a new stage of the life-course between adolescence and adulthood where many young people spend their time in post-secondary education (often working in part-time jobs) in order to get the more and more elusive well-paying, secure jobs. Arnett's concept of "emerging adulthood" reflects the extension of youth brought about by globalization and technological change through the increasing premium placed by employers on qualifications and the uncertainty about the future this implies (Arnett, 2006). With many young people having to balance school and part-time, young adulthood experiences—starting careers and a family—often do not begin before their thirtieth birthdays (Bynner, 2005: 368–9).

The main difficulties with "emerging adulthood" centre on its descriptive psychological assumptions of individual choice and how individuals achieve desired normative outcomes. Arnett's theory leaves unanswered the root causes for delaying adulthood by extending the period of time in post-secondary education and in part-time precarious employment over the past 30 years in advanced capitalist countries. Moreover, "emerging adulthood" is said to characterize all youth in the contemporary period. There does not appear to be sufficient recognition of the impact of the structural changes of globalization and neoliberalism on youth's transition from school to meaningful full employment within and between advanced capitalist societies.

In a cross-national study, John Bynner (2005) points out that while there is a strong case for Arnett's theory, its psychological bias overlooks the ways in which individual experiences are affected by their position in the social structure (Bynner, 2005: 378). Moreover, Bynner (2005) contends that structural factors differ across time and by national context, and for this reason, he calls for a broader range of "pathways" in order to chart the ways that those with common biographies (class, gender, race, for example) may face similar circumstances as they move from one "status passage to the next" (2005: 378). Specifically, "emerging adulthood" does not capture the experiences of *all youth* in advanced capitalist societies. It does make sense to those young people who forego entering the labour market hoping to achieve better careers through higher education. However, as we have noted above, these individuals comprise approximately 50 per cent of the population in Canada and other advanced capitalist societies. This means that researchers must acknowledge that the *traditional routes* to gaining meaningful employment, with fewer signs of its emergent status, remain in place for a significant number of youth. In general, young people from middle and upper class backgrounds experience *different routes* on the road between secondary education and the world of careers and meaningful work (Miranda, 2012; Bendit and Miranda, 2015).

For other researchers, the negative impacts of globalization and neoliberalism along with the recent global recession are disproportionately affecting not only disadvantaged youth but also young people as a whole, as a distinct quantitative and qualitative generation, even as a separate social class.

Social generation is a recent concept that tries to capture the totality of experiences affecting youth in their transition from school to meaningful employment. The concept was developed by a group of Australian researchers at the Melbourne Youth Research Centre (Wyn and Woodman, 2006; Wyn and Andres, 2011; Woodman, 2013; Woodman and Wyn, 2013). Their argument derives from the attitudes and experiences collected in a longitudinal research project entitled "Life Patterns," begun in 1991 and 1996 of two groups roughly corresponding to Generation X (born in 1973) and Generation Y (born in 1989). The project owed its inspiration to an earlier Canadian 22-year longitudinal research project examining the transition from post-secondary education, work, and other life activities of a British Columbia secondary school graduating class of 1988 (Andres and Wyn, 2010).

Social generation stands for "specific sets of economic, social, cultural and political conditions," and provides a novel approach to understanding "generations" without relying on age or birth cohorts as the central element (Wyn and Woodman, 2006: 499). That is, social generation is conceived as encompassing a specific collective identity. Those who prefer to conceptualize young people today across the Western developed world as a social generation maintain that their distinctiveness rests with a lengthened transition from school to meaningful employment relative to their predecessors. Social generation then represents a generational shift as opposed to an extension of time from adolescence, to post-secondary education and ending with secure careers, as claimed by other researchers.

While acknowledging that the popular media's labelling of broad generational categories such as "Generation X" or "Baby Boomers" is overly simplistic, they maintain that such labels do at least acknowledge the unique, defining experiences of successive generations. They contend that those who are living at home, going to school, and finding careers—otherwise known as "Generation Y" or "Millennials" (born between 1971 and 1999)—are contending with a different social context than previous and probably subsequent generations (France and Roberts, 2015: 217–18). As such, each social generation shares a script of "their" collective development in the course of "their" historical period. That is, for Wyn and Woodman (2006) in addition to sharing a common set of historical conditions such as their unique transitions from school to long-term engagement with the labour market, each social generation contains an accompanying set of young people's subjectivities and meanings. What makes this possible is that generations are not free floating cohorts in a society. While there may be a place for social generation in the study of young people's move from high school to post-secondary education to meaningful employment in advanced capitalist societies, each social generation is historically constituted and evolves through a life course with other social generations.

Some researchers are quick to envelop the experiences of unemployed and underemployed youth in post-industrial societies as a specific new social class. Standing (2010) points out that youth in Western democratic capitalist societies are becoming a new social class he calls the "**precariat**." Young people now suffer from what he calls precarity, or the moving in and out of temporary and insecure work contracts. As a result, young people are often unable to leave their parents' homes, develop an independent life, or plan their future. Because young people, as a whole, according to Standing (2010), have greater difficulty in finding permanent, well-paying employment, they, as a group, are experiencing a process of downward social mobility.

Finally, James Coté and Anton Allahar (1998; 2001; 2006; 2007; 2011) bring to the table two different concepts: **competition ratio** and **youth as proletariat**. They begin by pointing out that, since the Second World War, the Canadian population is living longer. In 1941, the life expectancy of males was 63 years while for females it was 66.3 years. By 2011, men could expect to live to 79.1 years and women to 83.4 years (Statistics Canada, 2014c). Pointing to the increased longevity draws attention to the possibility that there exists a generational competition over the country's resources, especially those found in the labour market. Coté and Allahar (2006) introduce the term "competition ratio" to refer to "the competition between younger (15 to 29 years) and older (30 to 64 years) cohorts in statistical terms" (2006: 37; see also Betcherman and Morissette, 1994). They go further by pointing out that when comparing the same age groups in 1861 to recent census data, there were more young people (aged 15 to 29 years) than the older cohort at the time of the first census (1861). This meant that "at one time, young people could have been considered a 'majority group' in Canadian society in terms of age-status" (2006: 37). Today, there are now more than twice as many older people (30 to 64 years) than younger people (15 to 29 years) and this is part of a long-term trend. Coté and

Allahar suggest that older Canadians are now "potential competitors" in the new economy, and this negatively affects the relative value of young workers, especially males (2006: 38).

Coté and Allahar (1998; 2001; 2006) and Coté (2014) adopt a neo-Marxist political economy perspective in order to define, situate, and recognize the reasons for intergenerational inequalities, the corporate manipulation of the present young, and possible progressive collective action. Young people constitute a social class in terms of the "material conditions of the entire youth segment of the population relative to the adult segment" (Coté, 2014: 528).

While acknowledging the progress made with regard to workplace rights for women and minority workers, "capital has sought and found in the young a new source of cheap labour—essentially a **youth proletariat**" (Coté and Allahar, 2001: 247). They contend that youth-as-proletariat is both a source of cheap labour and an expanding base for consumption. Structurally, youth in Western democracies experience a greater share of unemployment than their adult counterparts. This makes them more pliable sources of cheap labour. In addition, keeping youth in school longer, making available a variety of precarious jobs in the service sector, and restricting their access to well-paying, full-time employment via the **credentialism paradox** results in their increased dependence on their safety net parents. The researchers are concerned about the consequences of denying young people full partnership in the material benefits of advanced capitalist societies. They suggest that young people's recognition of their difficult and unjust circumstances as they eke out a meagre existence, one paycheque away from poverty, may spur political action and possibly violence (2001: 270).

However, why have young people remained acquiescent in the face of their exploitation? The simple answer is false consciousness. Coté and Allahar (2006) suggest that one of the tasks of political economists is to understand the role of false consciousness in masking youth disenfranchisement so that they submit to practices and ideas that counter their self-interests (2006: 80). False consciousness, then, requires the acceptance of one's own alienation as a normal state of affairs. With few exceptions, such as the year-long struggle of Québec's youth against tuition increases, young people in Western democracies have shied away from political change and taken on the mantle of consumerism as freedom.

Young Entrepreneurs

Can youth in the contemporary period escape their predicament by becoming capitalists? According to Industry Canada (2013), the percentage of Canadian small businesses owned by persons younger than 30 years of age declined from 2.9 per cent in 2004 to 2.8 per cent in 2007 and 1.6 per cent in 2011. During the proceedings of the Standing Committee on Finance on Youth Employment in Canada both the Canadian Federation of Students and the Fédération étudiante universitaire du Québec highlighted that students with high levels of debt are not willing to risk starting their own business. The Fédération étudiante universitaire du Québec reported the results of its 2009 survey that found that 45 per cent of Québec students who wish to start a business are unable to do so because of their student debt (Rajotte, 2014).

Conclusion

Today there are numerous pathways for young people to take on the protracted routes from education to the labour market. Youth are confronted with the increased need for credentials required to gain meaningful employment. More and more students are carrying crushing educational debts and many find it extremely difficult to find jobs other than low entry, precarious employment, even with an undergraduate degree. However, it may be misleading to present the "plight" of contemporary youth as representing a novel set of marching orders heralded by neoliberalism and globalization that require new theorizing. Much of the rationale given for creating a flurry of new and contradictory concepts has been the increased dependence on parents and delayed family relationships for the approximately 50 per cent of young people who attend post-secondary schools in postindustrial societies.

Specifically, how does conceptualizing youth today as a "precariat," or "youth as proletariat" help us understand the close to 50 per cent of the population in mature capitalist countries who follow the more traditional routes from education to the labour market and family life? What *all* young people are encountering today is not unique generational outcomes but a continuation of a process that began with industrial capitalism and involves both social change and the maintenance of the class system and gender relations.

Questions for Critical Thought

1. What is the more important issue facing young people in Canada who have graduated with some post-secondary education: unemployment or underemployment? Why?
2. Why has youth unemployment remained higher than the national average over the past 30 years?
3. Upon graduation with a post-secondary degree or diploma, why is it still difficult for a young Canadian to get meaningful employment?

Suggested Further Resources

Chodos, Bob. 2009. "Education: Who and what?" with articles by Jacques Parizeau, Jean-François Lisée, and John Richards, *Inroads: The Canadian Journal of Opinion*. Issue No. 25 (Summer/Fall): 71–99.

The articles in this issue examine how to change the poor job prospects for teenage boys who drop out of high school not only among Québec Francophones and Anglophones but also across Canada.

Generation Jobless. Directed by Sharon Bartlett and Maria LeRose, CBC, Doc Zone, Dreamfilm Productions. The film includes several experts who weigh in on what many are calling the most important social issue of our time—including Francis Fong, TD Bank economist and author of the report *The Plight of Younger Workers*, which paints a bleak picture of youth employment in Canada; Armine Yalnizyan, senior economist, Canadian Centre for Policy Alternatives, who has been tracking trends in the labour market for two decades; and Dr Paul Cappon, former head of the Canadian Council on Learning, a research and advocacy program focused on learning in Canada.

Sonnet, Anne, and Vincent Vandenberghe. 2008. *Jobs for Youth (Des employs pour les jeunes)*. Canada, Paris: OECD. This publication is the only available, thorough thematic review of policies in Canada which support the transition from school to work and improves the career prospects of Canada's youth.

Suggested Websites

Youth Fight for Jobs and Education (UK)
www.youthfightforjobs.com
Youth Fight for Jobs and Education (UK) is an advocacy group of young people located across the United Kingdom in twelve separate constituencies including London, Yorkshire, East and West Midlands, Scotland, and Wales.

Youth Employment Strategy (YES)
www.servicecanada.gc.ca/eng/epb/yi/yep/newprog/yesprograms.shtml
The Youth Employment Strategy (YES) is a Canadian federal government initiative and is comprised of three program streams: Skills Link, Career Focus, and Summer Work Experience.

Notes

1. Jacques Parizeau (2009) sparked a heated debate about the high dropout rate of francophone teenage boys in Québec's school system in an article published in the September 2008 issue of *Le Journal de Montréal*. Referring to a recent Québec study of all high school graduates, Parizeau stated that "only three out of five young Québecers complete high school without repeating a grade or dropping out" (2009: 75). However, he points out that the results are worse if gender and language are taken into account. Parizeau states that "the proportion of boys in the Anglophone sector graduating after five years is nearly *twice* that of francophone boys. After seven years, more than half the francophone boys still haven't graduated, against just 20 per cent of Anglophone boys . . . The plain fact is that we face a shocking situation, a huge waste of human talent that imperils our future" (2009: 76, emphasis added). A significant proportion of young francophone boys in Québec face dire employment prospects with the likelihood of turning to crime or suicide as viable options.
2. The postsecondary system in Quebec is unique in that the community colleges (CEGEPs or Collège d'Enseignement Général et Professionnel) provide a program that is a requirement for entry to university. Students who graduate from high school, normally after 11 years of schooling, must complete two years of the "general program" of the colleges, as opposed to the "vocational" programs. They then proceed to university for completion of their program, which normally takes three years for a Pass Bachelor's degree in arts or science.

3. $$\text{The youth unemployment rate} = \frac{\text{Number of Unemployed Young Persons} \times 100}{\text{Youth Labour Force}}$$

4. The European Foundation for the Improvement of Living and Working Conditions (Eurofound) draws attention to the multi-dimensional nature of the disadvantaged young. Factors influencing the probability of becoming a NEET include dropping out of school early without any qualifications, status as an immigrant youth, a low household income, parents who experienced unemployment, and parents with a low level of education (Eurofound: 2013).
5. The term 22-22-22 has been popularized to refer to 22-year-olds willing to work 22 hours a day for $22,000 a year.

9 The Movement of Work and Workers

Learning Objectives

- To assess the use of the world-systems global commodity chain (WSGCC) to understand the exploitation of cheap labour in low-wage countries
- To recognize the differences between offshoring and outsourcing and the impact of reshoring on Canadian jobs
- To understand why international organizations and governments view child labour as destructive to children's ability to achieve their full potential
- To examine why transnational corporations set up manufacturing operations, otherwise known as export processing zones, in low-income countries
- To be aware of the cycle of exploitation experienced by "second generation" temporary migrant workers in Canada

Introduction

Coffee is Canadians' number one beverage of choice. But how does our affinity for this aromatic brew connect us to one of the most important global commodity chains? In this chapter we examine the movement of work and workers in the present configuration of the world economy through global commodity chains. The coffee commodity chain is the second most important and lucrative global commodity in the world and provides us with an example of how workers are exploited at the bottom of the chain. Next, we examine child labour in the cocoa commodity chain. By examining agricultural commodity chains, this chapter explores how the deregulation of commodity prices brought about by globalization and neoliberal policies negatively impacts people living in low-income countries. We move from the exploitation of labour within agricultural commodity chains to manufacturing industries located in export processing zones in low-income countries. We bring the movement of work and workers home to Canada by examining the cycle of exploitation of "second generation" migrant workers.

Globalization and the Transnational Corporation

Globalization, facilitated by transnational corporations, information and communications technologies, compliant states, and neoliberalism, has created a new world order where world inequality in good jobs, stable and secure incomes, and diversified development have radically increased (Wallerstein, 2014; Maskin, 2014). While the rich are getting richer within the world economy, so are the poor becoming poorer. According to Wallerstein (2014), the world economy has entered a period of systemic crisis because it is becoming a bifurcated system of high and low-income countries. Bi-polar world-systems are inherently unstable. In order to maintain access to privileges and wealth, those on the top will find new ways to exploit those on the bottom while those on the bottom will more clearly be in a position to struggle for social justice, equality, and democracy.

According to world-systems theory, the exploitation of cheap labour in the world economy will take new forms (e.g., Export Processing Zones) because transnational corporations are experiencing increasing difficulty in finding new geographical areas of cheap unskilled labour. In the past, capitalists could search out new sources of cheap labour from rural economies located in the periphery of the world economy. This solution is proving more difficult simply because there are so few new frontiers to incorporate. As Wallerstein (2014: 17) notes, corporate decisions to flee to ever more remote areas are related to the search for rural labour, a resource that is becoming exhausted due to the "de-ruralization of the world-system today."

The exploitation of cheap labour, whether in high, or low-income countries, remains an integral component in the expansion of capitalism. Today, globalization and neoliberalism through international institutions such as the IMF and the World Bank continue to break down the remaining impediments in national, local, or community labour markets. Therefore, in a neoliberal world of competition where labour markets are deregulated, labour must also compete. This competition is conceptualized and regulated as *individual* workers rather than as the collective power of protected labour markets (Kalleberg and Hewison, 2013: 277).

Global Commodity Chains and the Global Interconnection of Work and Workers

Discussions of the impact of globalization on economic restructuring within high-income or advanced capitalist countries and of the effect of market liberalization and deregulation on developing nations have moved from national or sectoral analysis to commodity-specific dynamics of transformation, exchange, and consumption. Recent scholarship has concentrated on global commodity chains as hierarchical and spatially distinct structures. The work of Immanuel Wallerstein and his colleagues centres on the world-systems global commodity chains (WSGCC) and is distinct from the global commodity chains (GCC) research of Gary Gereffi and Miguel Korzeniewicz (1994). The latter approach to economic development (GCC) studies specific commodities[1] by covering all, or most, processes and transactions from primary processing to consumption. GCC research consists of applied or policy-oriented studies of global chains and occasionally industries that cross two or three international boundaries. Global commodity chain (GCC) analysis has become the accepted analytical framework increasingly used by international financial institutions, including the World Trade Organization and the World Bank (Neilsen, 2014; Gereffi, 2014).[2]

However, the world-systems approach provides the required critical tools to examine commodity chains within the world economic system. The original world-systems-inspired tradition of "commodity chain" research dates from a ground-breaking article where Hopkins and Wallerstein (1977: 128) outline their vision of the research agenda that should orient the world-systems program. A consumable item, they suggest, may be studied by tracing back its roots including "prior transformations, the raw materials, the transportation mechanisms, the labor input into each of the material processes, and the food inputs into the labor." Studying the clothing chain, for example, would map out the beginnings from the cotton fields, to cloth manufacturing, and to the production of other materials (thread, buttons, zippers, synthetics, etc.) and would include the "reproduction of labor involved in these productive activities" (1977: 128).

Hopkins and Wallerstein's concept of commodity chains is embedded within capitalism as a world historical system characterized by the "widespread commodification of processes"—exchange, production, distribution, and investment processes" (Wallerstein, 1983: 15). World-systems theory distinguishes between the core and the periphery. This distinction specifies the unequal allocation of rewards within the activities constituting a commodity chain (Arrighi and Drangel, 1986: 16). Simply, the lower the process is located inside the commodity chain, the cheaper the labour. We will examine coffee and cocoa as two examples of commodity chains and how labour is cheapened as a result of neoliberal policies.

The world-systems approach considers how the *unequal* returns to the creation, development, and transportation of a particular good creates a *stratified* world-system. As well as being explicitly transnational, this school of thought focuses attention on the *spatial* dynamics of uneven development. From a world-systems perspective, the core-periphery relationship emerges from a series of linked "economic activities structured in commodity chains that cut across state boundaries" (Arrighi and Drangel, 1986: 11). The pivotal question asked is, "If one thinks of the entire chain as having a total amount of surplus value that has been appropriated, what is the division of this surplus value among the boxes of the chain?" (Hopkins and Wallerstein, 1986: 49). That is to say, these activities are not distributed randomly across geographic space, but rather tend to cluster. Some activities—those commanding high wages—are positioned in protected labour markets and are normally located in high-income core countries. Other "boxes" or nodes in a commodity chain are more globally dispersed, characterized by higher degrees of competition, and are sources for cheap labour or low income countries.

The Coffee Commodity Chain

Introduction

Let us look at the commodity chain that ends in the consumption of your favourite beverage from the local Starbucks made by a barista, or bought at the Tim Horton's drive-through. Coffee bar chains have spread dramatically, selling ambiance and social positioning along with coffee. In short, the global coffee commodity chain has gone through what Dicum and Luttinger (2006) call a "latte revolution" where consumers can choose from and will pay hugely inflated prices for hundreds of combinations of coffee varieties, origins, brewing and grinding methods, flavouring, packaging and, of course, social "content" or atmosphere.

It is estimated that the number of Americans drinking specialty coffees, which include mochas, lattes, espressos, cappuccinos, and frozen/iced coffee beverages, grew to 30 million daily in 2015, up from only 7 million in 1997. By 2015, specialty coffee sales increased by 20 per cent per year and account for nearly 8 per cent of the $18 billion US coffee market (E-importz.com, 2015). Canadians drink 2.1 billion servings of coffee in specialty coffee chains. The data suggest Canadians aged 18 to 35 consume one of every three servings of hot specialty coffee, and women consume 65 per cent of all servings. Boomers remain the biggest consumers of hot brewed coffee at 37 per cent, while those aged 18 to 35 increased their consumption by 6 per cent in 2014 (Cardwell, 2015). Drinking coffee is a highly profitable global business in Canada and the US.

The "Starbucks Factor"[3]

The evolution of specialty coffee cannot be appreciated without making a reference to the "Starbucks factor." Starbucks was founded in 1971 in Seattle and spent most of the 1980s building a loyal customer base and informing consumers on the qualities of their coffees. What made Starbucks a corporate success was the creation of a café atmosphere where customers could hang out in a place that was neither home nor work. This happened at the same time that other consumer food products were being recast as more authentic, flavourful, and healthy—micro-brewed beer, specialty breads, and organic vegetables, for instance. By combining ambiance with coffee consumption and providing consumers the choice of type, origin, roast, and grind, Starbucks managed to sell coffee "pre-packaged with lifestyle signifiers" (Dicum and Luttinger, 2006: 153).

Starbucks is among the leaders in the creation of a single, global institutional system through which production and trade of coffee is organized. The company's coffee commodity chain controls the production and subsequent transportation of the "green" coffee beans from Latin America, Africa, and Vietnam, to the United States and Europe in ocean containers. Once in the US, Starbucks has six centres where the beans are roasted and packaged in a manner similar to the manufacture of standardized products by fast food chains like McDonalds (Supplychainquarterly.com, 2010).

All products used in each Starbucks store are supplied by a central distribution centre. Starbucks uses 33 distribution centres in the United States, seven in the Asia/Pacific region, five in Canada, and three in Europe. As a result of controlling their coffee commodity chain, Starbucks has become the largest coffeehouse company in the world. Starbucks employs approximately 182,000 people across more than 19,700 company-operated and licensed stores in 62 countries and is a major global transnational corporation with revenues topping $15 billion in 2014 (Supplychainquarterly, 2010).

The Coffee Commodity Chain

Coffee is the world's *second* most valuable traded commodity, behind only petroleum. Globally there are approximately 25 million farmers and coffee workers in over 50 countries involved in producing coffee. An estimated 11 million hectares of the world's farmland are dedicated to coffee cultivation. Worldwide, the annual consumption of coffee has expanded to 12 billion pounds. Coffee is the *largest* food import of the United States and in 2014, Canada placed fifth among the world's top 10 importing countries (Indexmundi.com, 2016). The global commodity chain is a hierarchical structure beginning with farmers/workers, moving up to middlemen, exporters, importers, roasters, and retailers before reaching the consumer (Globalexchange.org, n.d.). Figure 9.1 highlights the substantial inequality between what is paid to the farmers/workers and what the consumer pays. Each box in the coffee commodity chain appropriates part of the surplus but leaves the lion's share to the transnational corporations based in high-income countries.

Today, most of the world's coffee is grown in Colombia, Vietnam, and Brazil. Across the globe, various processes, technologies, and forms of human labour are employed in the coffee chain before reaching the consumer. Coming into force on 1 July 1963, 37 countries representing coffee exporters and coffee consuming nations entered into the International Coffee Agreement, which fixed prices at $4.40 to $5.30 per kilogram. Each coffee-producing country had an agreed-upon "fair" allotment of the market. This had been set up to counter the rise of communism in Asia and South America. In addition, historic colonial trading routes continue to remain important in shaping the coffee commodity chain. A sizeable proportion of East African coffee finds its way to Germany and

Farmer Paid	Exporter Paid	Importer Paid	Roaster Paid	Café Paid	Consumer
.50/kg	$2/kg	$10/kg	$30/kg	$300/kg	
		(100 servings @ $3)			

Figure 9.1 Conventional Coffee Commodity Chain (Approximate Prices Paid per Kilogram)

Source: Adapted from Oxfam and Baskerville, Peter. 2015. 'Reimagining the coffee supply chain'. http://espressocoffee.quora.com/Reimagining-the-coffee-supply-chain

the UK France maintains close relations with Côte d'Ivoire and other Francophone countries. Dutch trading links with Indonesia remain important as well (Dicum and Luttinger, 2006).

But in 1989 the US withdrew from the agreement. The market soon became unregulated. The World Bank encouraged Vietnam to move into coffee production despite the already large supply of coffee on the world market. By 2011, Vietnam accounted for approximately 14 per cent of global coffee production, ranking it as the world's second largest coffee producer (Choudhary et al., 2011). The glut on the market caused prices to plummet below the cost of production.

International prices for the raw product (either Arabica or Robusta) have remained low, hovering around $1.60 per pound for the past decade (International Coffee Organization [ICO], 2014: 23). The low price of coffee is good for the transnational corporations that control the commodity chain since they can realize high profits at other stages in the chain. However, coffee is a vital source of export for many of the developing countries that grow it. Today, small-scale farmers produce over 75 per cent of the world's coffee. Market liberalization and deregulation in producing countries have decreased their capability of controlling exports and building up stocks, therefore weakening their market power. In addition, coffee farmers in low-income countries are facing increased costs for replanting and other high costs for fertilizer and diesel fuel (Fitter and Kaplinksy, 2001).

Coffee price decline and volatility have had negative economic impacts on developing countries. One result has been declining export revenues, reducing the ability of the state to invest in rural development, which, in turn, leads to increased poverty in coffee producing areas, declining labour standards, and unsustainable land use (Jaffee, 2014; Lyon, 2010). The surplus generated by the coffee commodity chain comes largely at the expense of those at the bottom. As a result of globalization, the institutional frameworks have moved away from a formal and relatively stable system where producers had an established voice toward today's more informal and buyer dominated system.

In the coffee producing countries, the farmers through their cooperatives find it difficult to compete with local subsidiaries of international trading firms. As trade liberalization and deregulation force governments to retreat from the regulation of domestic coffee markets, farmers' organizations lose a political forum of negotiation. The weakness and inherent instability of the institutional framework falls straight on the shoulders of coffee farmers in developing countries. In the process, a "substantial proportion of total income generated in the coffee chain has been transferred from farmers to consuming country operators" (Ponte, 2002: 1116). We should ask ourselves, what difference does it make to a smallholder if a consumer can buy a double tall decaf latte for $4, or if specialty beans are sold at $18 per pound in the United States or Canada, if the farmer gets less than 50 cents for the same pound of coffee (Fitter and Kaplinsky, 2001)?

Offshoring: The Movement of Work and Impacts on Community

The terms **outsourcing** and **offshoring** are often used interchangeably in much of the popular literature today. However, there is a difference. When a company outsources, it buys from a *different* company a part or service it uses to produce either within the country or abroad. For instance, General Motors can outsource production of an auto part to a different company in the United States or anywhere in the world. However, if a company offshores, it moves its service provision or production process to a different country. For example, if GM opens a factory in China and shifts production to its factory there from the US, it is offshoring, *not* outsourcing because it is still running the factory from its US headquarters. Offshoring allows a company to make the product or offer the service at a much lower price because it is able to take advantage of cheaper labour costs, lax government regulations on working conditions and the environment, restrictions on trade unions, and attractive tax incentives (Fifarek, 2007). Therefore, many early offshore practices involved the movement of low-skilled, labour-intensive manufacturing positions to other countries, especially in the developing world.

Advances in telecommunications and information technology have led to offshoring service positions such as remote operations of call centres. Another example is the offshoring of knowledge work such as research and development including software maintenance and development (Farrell and Fenwick, 2007). Intel increased its engineering workforce 150 per cent by adding 600 engineers to its research and development operations in Russia (Foremski, 2004; Mangum, 2012). Offshoring services or technological developments allow global corporations to produce around the clock, and this results in lower costs.

Writing in *The Economist*, Tamzin Booth (2013) refers to the phenomenon of "bringing work home" or **reshoring** work that was once done offshore. Among the companies Booth names as engaging in reshoring are Google, General Electric, Caterpillar, and Ford Motor Company. With regard to the loss of manufacturing jobs in Canada, a large portion of employment in Canada's manufacturing base came from foreign, primarily US-based transnational corporations such as GM, Ford, GE, John Deere, Nabisco, Kellogg's, and Kraft. An example of a US-based transnational closing shop and moving jobs to the US is provided by Energizer, a transnational corporation manufacturing batteries and personal care products with headquarters in Town and Country, Missouri. The company is well known for its Energizer and Eveready batteries; Schick, Wilkinson Sword, and Edge shaving products; Playtex feminine hygiene products; and Hawaiian Tropic and Banana Boat sunscreen products. The company announced its feminine care facility in Montreal would close by 2017 with the loss of 450 jobs. As an example of reshoring, the closing of the Montreal factory is part of a restructuring program that will see production consolidated at Energizer's Delaware facility (Business News Network, 2014).

Child Labour: From Apple to Chocolate

What Is Child Labour?

The International Labour Organization (ILO) separates negative child labour that should be eliminated from positive child labour that may contribute to a child's well-being. For example, children or adolescents' participation in work that does not affect their health and personal development or interfere with their schooling is generally regarded as positive. This includes activities such as earning money outside school hours and during school holidays. Often these jobs provide children with skills and experience to prepare them to be productive members of society during their adult life.

The ILO refers to negative **child labour** when children aged five to 17 years work in conditions that are physically or mentally harmful, socially or morally dangerous, interfering with schooling, or requiring children to attempt to combine school attendance with excessively long and heavy work. Although the number of children exposed to negative child labour has declined from 246 million in 2000 to 168 million in 2012, the number of children involved in these destructive practices is alarming (ILO, 2015b).

In 2013, the largest percentage of children exposed to negative child labour practices was in agriculture (58.6 per cent), followed by services other than domestic work (25.4 per cent), industry (7.2 per cent), and domestic work (6.9 per cent). Child labourers who work on farms produce cash crops such as cocoa, coffee, cotton, and rubber. Another 20 million are employed in factories that make garments, carpets, toys, matches, and hand-rolled cigarettes (ILO, 2015b).

While statistics on the wages which children receive for the work they do varies by country and industry, the consensus among international organizations is that children are paid pennies an hour. For example, a young child named Soe Min Lwin brings home $35 a month after working in a factory in Yangon, Myanmar. With this money he can buy a sack of rice for $20 to feed his mother, stepfather, two younger brothers, and grandmother for one month (Saberi, 2015).

Brand Name Companies Exposed

In 2013, an internal audit at Apple uncovered several cases of negative child labour in its commodity supply chain, including one Chinese company that employed 74 children under the age of 16. In total, the audit uncovered 106 cases of underage labour employed at 11 factories involved in making its products in 2012. The Apple report came on the heels of a series of worker suicides over working conditions at Foxconn, the Taiwanese company that assembles the iPad and iPhone and operates a number of offshore plants in China (Garside, 2013).

One Chinese company in the Apple commodity chain called Guangdong Real Faith Pingzhou Electronics makes circuit boards. According to Apple, 74 children under the age of 16 had been knowingly recruited to work on its production lines by one of the region's largest labour agencies, Shenzhen Quanshun Human Resources. Apple's investigators found that the agency conspired with families to forge identification documents. Apple has since cut its relationship with the Chinese circuit board supplier (Garside, 2013).

Cocoa, an important global commodity, is critical to the livelihood of thousands of rural farmers especially in West Africa. Western African countries, mostly Ghana and the Ivory Coast, supply almost 70 per cent of the world's cocoa (World Cocoa Foundation, 2015). The main transnational corporate players in the chocolate trade are Archer Daniels Midlands, Cadbury, Hershey, Kraft Foods, and Nestlé. In well-publicized reports in 2010, over 1.8 million children were found to be working under exploitative conditions in cocoa related activities in Côte d'Ivoire, Cameroon, Ghana, and Nigeria (Payson Center for International Development and Technology Transfer, Tulane University, 2011). The International Labor Rights Forum (ILRF) stated that while almost 70 per cent of the world's supply of cocoa comes from Côte d'Ivoire and Ghana, farmers who produce cocoa and work on the plantations are paid below-poverty wages. Low prices in the cocoa industry have left smallholder farmers with impoverished incomes and with no choice but to pull their children from school and have them help on the plantation.

Low prices and low wages combine to perpetuate child trafficking and the worst forms of child labour that characterize the industry. Children are exposed to chemicals and long working hours, and are denied a decent education. The government of Côte d'Ivoire has hampered the reporting of the worst of child labour practices.

A cocoa farmer uses a machete to open a pod of raw cocoa for inspection on a cocoa plantation in Kumasi, Ghana. Cocoa is an important global commodity, critical to the livelihood of thousands of rural farmers. This raw product becomes the chocolate made in Switzerland and other confection-producing nations before export around the world.

For example, in 2010, Ivorian government authorities detained three newspaper journalists after they published an article exposing government corruption in the cocoa sector (*Voice of America*, 16 July 2010). With low levels of education, families in the cocoa sector are caught in a vicious cycle of poverty. Cocoa producers have little bargaining power against the few large transnational companies that control the supply chain and ultimately determine the livelihoods of farming families (International Labor Rights Forum, n.d.). While the ILRF continues its struggle to eliminate child labour from cocoa plantations by shaming corporate giants such as Hershey, negative child labour remains an integral part of the cocoa commodity chain. In much the same way that coffee prices are kept low to ensure large profits for transnational corporations, low prices for cocoa and other commodities consumed in high-income countries have similar affects at the bottom of the commodity chain—namely fewer resources for the state and impoverished families who grow and cultivate the staple commodity.

Work in Export Processing Zones (EPZs)

Globalization has resulted in the proliferation of re-export platforms located mostly in low-income countries of the world economy. Export processing zones (EPZs) are special manufacturing enclaves that are normally, though not always, isolated from the rest of the national economy. The International Labour Organization (ILO) states that EPZs take many forms, including free trade zones, special economic zones, export processing factories, bonded warehouses, free ports, and maquiladoras or maquilas in Mexico. The ILO has defined EPZs as "industrial zones with special incentives set up to attract foreign investors, in which imported materials undergo some degree of processing before being re-exported" (ILO, 2015a). EPZs have become the largest manufacturing centres of globalization and a prime example of why industrialized countries have shed many of their unionized, high-paying manufacturing jobs and moved them there.

Mexico's early experiments with EPZs, known as **maquiladoras**, or **maquilas**, originated with the Mexico–US Border Industrialization Program in 1966 whereby manufacturing plants were located in the border towns of northern Mexico. The maquiladoras are a group of manufacturing plants that use cheap labour and tax incentives to import and assemble duty-free components for export. They became a means of providing employment and significant foreign-exchange earnings for Mexico's developing economy (Hansen, 2003).

Employment in maquiladoras increased from approximately 200,000 in the mid-1980s to more than 1,000,000 by the turn of the century. NAFTA, globalization, and low-cost offshore assembly in China, Asia, and Latin America dramatically affected Mexico's maquiladoras. For example, approximately 529 maquiladoras shut down and investment in assembly plants decreased by 8.2 per cent in 2002 (Shorris, 2006). Despite the decline, however, over 3,000 maquiladoras still exist along the 2,000-mile long stretch of the United States–Mexico border. They provide employment for slightly more than 2 million workers and exports of more than $196 billion (*The Economist*, 2013; Villalobos, 2004). However, very low wages and treacherous working conditions characterize much of the work. For example, Rosa Moreno is one of many women working from 10 p.m. to 7 a.m. at a factory called HD Electronics. Rosa operates a 200-ton hydraulic stamping press every night, six days a week, for 1,300 pesos or $100 a week. If she misses a shift, she loses 300 pesos from her weekly wage (Bosque, 2013).

The latest data from the ILO estimates that, in 2006, 66 million people were employed in over 3,500 EPZs in 130 countries, the majority of whom were women (Boyenge, 2007). These numbers represent a significant increase from ILO estimates in 1997 when 22.5 million employees were counted in 845 EPZs located in 93 countries (ILO, 1998). The main reason driving the rapid growth in EPZs: transnational companies (TNCs) wishing to gain easy access to large numbers of non-unionized, low-wage workers—especially women (Dunaway, 2014). This functions to keep high-paying, knowledge-intensive manufacturing and service activities in the core countries, while outsourcing or offshoring low-wage, labour-intensive fragments of commodity chains to the EPZs of low-income countries (Fernandez-Kelly, 2007; Gallagher and Zarsky, 2007; Sargent and Matthews, 2009).

Over the past three decades, there has been an expansion of manufacturing enclaves in many South and East Asian countries, including designated areas of China. These zones are industrial areas specially set up by governments to attract foreign direct investment and to create employment. Incentives to transnational companies choosing to operate within such zones include duty-free imports of raw materials. Most zones are exempt from the national labour laws while host governments provide transnational corporations with generous, and in some cases, long term, tax concessions.

When it comes to trade unions, the Bangladeshi government, for example, actively promotes its EPZs by citing the fact that even after the 2014 amendments to the *EPZ Act*, traditional trade union activities continue to be forbidden by law and strikes remain illegal (Mirdha, 2014). While workers are permitted to form worker welfare associations (WWA), reports from Human Rights in Bangladesh's Export Processing Zones indicate that these councils are not in place in most companies. The lack of unions does not mean the absence of industrial conflict. As important for establishing industrial peace, EPZs have their own security forces, or "industrial police," specifically trained to maintain order. In 2010, thousands of workers clashed with police at the South Korean Young One facility in the Chittagon EPZ located in southeastern Bangladesh, where it houses 13 garment factories. Four were killed and hundreds wounded[4] (see more at Human Rights and Business Country Guide, 2014).

Where does Nike make its trainers, or Wrangler its jeans? In the same place Raleigh make its bikes and transnational corporations like Walmart, Mothercare, Tesco (UK), and Reebok make everything from pharmaceuticals to fishing rods and baseball caps. The Chittagong export processing zone (EPZ) in Bangladesh is one of the eight EPZs and the largest in Bangladesh, employing 188,768 workers who were mostly women and teenagers as of April 2015. The 453-acre Chittagong Facility holds 137 factories and in 2014–2015 exported over $21.3 USD billion worth of manufactured goods. It claims to have the cheapest labour in the world. Transnational corporations manufacturing goods in Chittagong only pay workers an average of $48 a month or about $1.50 a day (BEPZA, 2015).

Box 9.1 Everyday Work Experiences

Corporate Responsibility and The Human Cost of Cheap Clothing

In 2013, the Rana Plaza—a building that housed five garment-making factories in Bangladesh's Dhaka EPZ—collapsed, killing 1,134 and severely injuring 2,500. The collapse of the Rana Plaza building was the deadliest disaster in the history of the garment industry worldwide, as noted in Chapter 1. Eighty per cent of the workers killed were young teenage women. Their standard shift was 13 to 14 hours a day with only two days off a month. Wages paid to these workers were set at starvation levels. Young helpers, for example, earned **12 cents** an hour, while junior operators took home **22 cents** and senior sewers received **24 cents** an hour (Institute for Global Labour and Human Rights, n.d.).

More than two years later, the Rana Plaza Donors Trust Fund—which was set up by the International Labour Organization to collect funds for compensation—finally reached the target $30 million needed to compensate all the victims. This came after a global campaign to pressure brands to donate and more than two years of negotiations involving the various stakeholders including the ILO, activists chaining themselves to retail shops, global petitions including 1 million signatures asking Benetton to pay its share, statements by G7 leaders and, the final coup de grace, the arrest for trespass in March 2015 of Mahinur Begum, an 18-year-old survivor of the factory collapse who had travelled to New Jersey from Dhaka to deliver a letter to the chief executive of Children's Place.

Brands associated with the world's largest industrial disaster include the Italian-based Benetton; the Belgian-based C&A; Germany's Adler Modemarkte and NKD; Walmart; Children's Place; Zara, owned by Spain's Amanico Ortega, the third richest person in the world; and Canada's Joe Fresh (Loblaw's), owned by the Weston family. Through its British subsidiary, the Weston family also owns Primark (O'Connor, 2014). According to *Forbes* and the Clean Clothes Campaign, Canada's Joe Fresh (Loblaw's) was one of the first to respond to the disaster by sending company representatives to the site. The company has made contributions totalling $3,370,000 toward the Rana Plaza Donors Trust Fund while its UK brand Primark has contributed $1 million to the Fund and a further $6.3 million directly to the New Wave Bottom (Brand) workers.

According to Sam Maher (Behind the Label representative), "The biggest issue is that everyone's wages were so damn low to start with. It's not compensation in

continued

the true sense; it's purely to replace income that was lost" (Hoskins, 2015). Even more disconcerting, with the exception of Canada's Joe Fresh and Primark, was the slowness of companies to respond financially to the disaster. For example, Walmart, the world's largest retailer with net sales of over $480 billion (2015) donated an estimated $1 million. According to Kalpona Akter, executive director of the Bangladesh Center for Worker Solidarity (BCWS): "We believe it could have been sorted out by these companies in a few minutes with a few phone calls. They have money, but they don't want to take responsibility. Ultimately they are the responsible people, who made these children orphans and put these families in a very bad shape emotionally and financially" (Hoskins, 2015).

It was not until the G7 meeting in Germany in June 2015 and under the leadership of Germany's Dr Anja Trebes, who "called upon the business community to close the funding gap of $2.4 million as soon as possible against the backdrop that responsible supply chains are one of the issues highlighted by the German presidency of the G7" (Hoskins, 2015). The final donation needed to reach $30 million was made anonymously. The Rana Plaza Donors Trust Fund reached its goal of $30 million over two years after the largest industrial disaster in the world. However, the workers at Bhopal are still waiting for their money 30 years later.

For an overview of brands that were linked to the Rana building, as well as brands that have a sourcing relationship with Bangladesh, visit www.cleanclothes.org/resources/rana-plaza-actual-and-potential-donors-listed-by-g7-country/view.

Immigrant Workers, Migrant Workers, and the Quest for Social Justice

As we saw in Chapter 5, Canada's immigration policies have undergone several changes. Today, Canada sets annual targets for total admission and by single categories of immigrants. The targets range from 240,000 to 265,000 and represent roughly 0.8 per cent of the total population of about 35 million. According to the OECD, Canada maintained immigration target levels throughout the recession, and even overshot the target to 281,000 in 2010, the fifth highest in the OECD after the United States, the United Kingdom, Italy, and Spain. Over the past several decades, federal government policy has relied on immigration to swell the ranks of available employees as the size of Canadian-born families resulted in negative population growth. By 2012, foreign-born residents in Canada comprise 6.8 million people (as cited in Drache et al., 2014: 30). Their employment experiences have been decidedly mixed.

The three leading countries providing emigrants to Canada since 2010 are the Philippines, China, and India. Regionally, in 2011, immigrants living in the Prairies and British Columbia accounted for more than half the employment growth for Canada's landed immigrants (Statistics Canada, 2013a). While these immigrants made up 31 per cent of Canada's immigrant workforce, they accounted for 53 per cent of immigrant employment growth between 2010 and 2011. When compared to other OECD countries, Canada ranks sixth in terms of the share of immigrants in its population with the foreign-born accounting for 20 per cent of the total population.

Immigrants are well educated. For example, in 2012, 42 per cent of permanent residents between the ages of 25 and 64 years had completed some post-secondary education (OECD, 2014b: 242). The foreign-born population is on average more educated than across OECD countries with 52 per cent reporting some post-secondary education compared to 31 per cent across OECD countries. Thirty-eight per cent of immigrants to Canada come from an OECD high-income country and 46 per cent come to Canada from a country with the same official languages of either English or French (OECD, 2012).

On average, over a third of immigrants to Canada since 2010 have completed some post-secondary education. Since 2000–2001, immigrants have represented 31 per cent of the increase in the highly educated labour force in Canada, but only 21 per cent in the United States and 14 per cent in Europe (Dumont and Liebig, 2014). In addition, immigrant students are becoming one of the main sources of highly skilled foreign labour in all OECD countries. There is ample evidence that foreign education from non-OECD countries is largely discounted in the host country's labour market. Therefore, after graduation from university, many international students decide to remain in Canada or other OECD countries. Employers easily recognize their domestic credentials so that there is little uncertainty regarding the actual "value" of the degree (Dumont, 2014).

Among skilled immigrants who entered Canada in the 1990s, there was a disproportionately high concentration of occupations in the IT sector, specifically engineering and computer-related occupations. As a result, their average earnings were also disproportionately impacted by the collapse of that sector at the beginning of this decade (Government of Canada, 2012).

As noted above, Canada consistently has one of the highest rates of immigration among OECD countries. Moreover, as Table 9.1 shows, even after the recession of 2008–2009, there is near equality in employment rates between the

Table 9.1 Labour Market Outcomes for Native Born and Foreign-Born Men and Women, 2000 and 2012

Employment/Population Ratio	**2000**	**2012**
Native-born men	77.4	75.0
Foreign-born men	77.0	76.1
Native-born women	66.0	70.6
Foreign-born women	59.6	64.5
Unemployment Rate		
Native-born men	5.7	7.6
Foreign-born men	6.1	8.3
Native-born women	6.2	6.4
Foreign-born women	8.7	8.6

Source: OECD, International Migration Outlook, 2014, Canada, pg. 243. DOI: 10.1787/migr_outlook-2014-11-en.

Canadian-born and immigrant-born populations. In terms of labour force participation, the disparity in rates between Canadian-born and immigrant-born females is the lowest among OECD countries and the difference among males remains negligible. However, the difference between the unemployment rate of immigrant men and native-born men increased from 7 per cent in 2000 to 9.2 per cent in 2012. For immigrant women compared to native-born women, the disparity decreased from 40 per cent in 2000 to 34 per cent 2012.

Recent data show that earnings disparities between recent immigrants and Canadian-born workers continued to increase into the first decade of the 2000s. By contrast, in 1980, recent immigrant men with employment income earned 85 cents for each dollar received by Canadian-born men. By 2000, the ratio had dropped to 67 cents, in 2005 to 63 cents but rebounded to 70 cents in 2008. The corresponding ratios for recent immigrant women were 85 cents in 1980, 65 cents in 2000 and 56 cents in 2005. However, the same report noted that low-income rates for immigrants who have been in Canada for longer periods of time are significantly lower (Government of Canada, 2012).

Table 9.2 provides evidence for the increasing importance of economic immigrants into Canada since 1990. In 1990, 45.7 per cent of permanent immigrants were classified as male and 44.8 per cent as female economic immigrants. That percentage continued to increase until 2010 when 69.3 per cent of men and

Table 9.2 Permanent Residents by Gender and Category, 1990–2013

Category	1990	1995	2000	2005	2009	2010	2011	2012	2013
Males									
Family class	33,634 30.8%	32,256 31.7%	23,290 20.7%	25,049 19.6%	26,979 22.1%	24,946 18.2%	23,762 19.5%	27,541 21.8%	33,738 27%
Economic	49,931 45.7%	53,720 52.7%	72,669 64.7%	80,900 63.3%	78,211 64.1%	94,948 69.3%	80,013 65.7%	82,773 65.4%	75,61 60.6%3
Refugees	24.027 22.0%	15,436 15.1%	16,124 14.4%	18,557 14.5%	11,596 9.5%	12,608 9.25	13,967 11.5%	11,545 9.1%	12,124 9.7%
Others	1,733 1.6%	477 0.5%	260 0.2%	3,256 2.4%	5,145 4.2%	4,497 3.3%	4,037 3.3%	4,605 3.6%	3,401 2.7%
Total	**95,817**	**101,889**	**112,343**	**127,763**	**121,970**	**137,002**	**121,780**	**126,469**	**124,876**
Females									
Family class	41,002 30.8%	45,122 40.7%	37,323 32.4%	38,325 28.5%	38,228 29.4%	35,278 24.6%	32,687 25.7%	37,469 28.5%	45,946 34.3%
Economic	47,993 44.8%	52,903 47.7%	63,613 55.3%	75,413 56.1%	75,280 57.8%	91,967 64%	76,105 59.9%	78,048 59.4%	72,568 54.1%
Refugees	16,191 15.1%	12,656 11.4%	13,967 12.1%	17,217 12.8%	11,254 8.6%	12,089 8.4%	13,906 11%	11,554 8.8%	11,925 8.9%
Others	1,868 1.7%	283 0.3%	200 0.2%	3,523 2.6%	5,440 4.2%	4,348 3%	4,268 3.4%	4,355 3.3%	3,638 2.7%
Total	**107,054**	**110,964**	**115,103**	**134,479**	**130,202**	**143,686**	**126,968**	**131,426**	**134,077**

Source: Citizenship and Immigration Canada, Facts and Figures, 2015. http://www.cic.gc.ca/english/resources/statistics/facts2013/permanent/01.asp

64 per cent of women were classified as economic immigrants. From 2010 until 2013, the percentages for both men and women declined to approximately 60 and 54 per cent for both sexes.

The two major categories within economic immigrants include skilled workers and business immigrants. Business immigrants include investors, entrepreneurs, and self-employed individuals. Entrepreneurs are defined as immigrants who have business experience of at least five years prior to their application, have a legally defined net worth of at least $300,000 and can create at least one full-time job for a Canadian citizen or permanent resident (Canada, 2015). However, while nonstandard employment has been woven around gender and age as we discussed in Chapter 6, it has also intersected with **immigration** and years of residence in Canada.

Hira-Friesen's (2014) examination of Canadian Labour Force Survey data from 2006 to 2012 in terms of precarious employment (involuntary part-time work, temporary contracts, or multiple job holding) amongst recent and established immigrants reveals alarming and growing inequities. Recent male and female immigrants (who arrived in the past five years or less) are *much more* likely (three times for males and 2.5 times for females) in comparison to their Canadian-born contemporaries to hold **involuntary part-time** positions (2014: 108). Not only are they over-represented in involuntary part-time work but the trend is increasing (2014: 48). Similarly, recent female immigrants holding multiple jobs have steeply increased since 2006. Further, recent immigrant women are almost twice as likely as Canadian-born women to be temporary workers. As a result, recent immigrants are often underemployed (relative to their educational credentials) and earning lower wages than more established immigrants and Canadian-born workers. In 2009–10, close to 40 per cent of foreign-born immigrants were overqualified for their jobs and 60 per cent of new immigrants find themselves in low-skilled jobs within six months of their arrival (Burleton et al., 2014: 21). Similarly, a recent survey of 450 Toronto immigrants reported, for example, unemployment rates averaging 23 percent, high rates of very low income and frequent underemployment as only 3 per cent were in the professional occupations they occupied before coming to Canada (Bhaskar, 2013; see also Drache et al., 2014). In short, patterns of nonstandard employment amongst recent immigrants suggest both discrimination against this population and economic exploitation of their vulnerability. Immigrants, denied access to "good jobs," may be expected to question the welcome they are receiving from their adopted country.

At the same time, there is mounting concern among growing numbers of citizens in most high-income countries about how to limit the numbers of immigrants entering the country, or how best to manage their stay. Under the banner of securing the nation's borders from unwanted immigrants, political parties such as UKIP in Great Britain, the National Front in France, PEDIDA in Germany, and Party for Freedom in the Netherlands have been supported by those fearful of job loss and the "erosion of national values" (see also Karnitschnig et al., 2015). It has been widely reported that over the past few elections, a number of US Republican

Party members have expressed support for closing the borders between Mexico and the United States to illegal immigrants. To date, Canada has not experienced the anti-immigration fervour that has plagued politics in the United States, the United Kingdom, and the European Union. However, high-income countries such as Canada address labour shortages not by easing restrictive immigration systems but by adopting the more popular solution of creating or expanding "managed" *temporary* migration programs.

"Second Generation" Temporary Workers

In the post-Cold War era, Kofi Annan, the Secretary General of the United Nations, announced a "new era of mobility" had emerged (Annan, 2006). This new era is characterized not by free and open mobility but rather by heightened regulation of the movement of workers through managed temporary worker programs in high-income countries such as Canada, the United States, and Germany. This new era of temporary workers has become known as the "second generation" of migrant labour (Castles, Haas, and Miller, 2013). Today, the dramatic expansion of "second generation" temporary foreign worker programs in Europe and North America according to the OECD, is "one of the most significant trends in recent years" (OECD, 2004).

Low-income countries have not benefitted from globalization as have high-income nations. Many of the poor in low-income countries are finding it increasingly difficult to support their own households due to forced relocation to urban areas where there is intense competition over jobs. Migration to high-income countries for *temporary* employment can mean the difference between starvation and keeping families intact and sustained. Chapter 5 outlined the shifting government policies beginning with the Non-Immigrant Employment Authorization Program (NIEAP) of 1973 with "guest workers," the name given to temporary workers during what is called the "first generation" of migrant temporary labour in the 1970s, and ending with recent changes to the SAWP programs.

During "first generation" era, Canada learned from the experiences of "guest worker" programs in the US and Germany. The United States was the first country with its Bracero program (1942–1964) to bring into the US temporary low skilled Mexican agricultural workers (Bracero History Archive, 2016). From 1955 until 1973, Germany (FRG) was the second developed nation to implement a "guest worker" ("Gastarbeiter") program through multilateral agreements with Turkey, Spain, and Greece.[5] Like the program in Canada from 1973 on, most of the temporary workers who went to Germany were from less developed, rural regions of their countries of origin and took on lower skilled jobs in construction, mining, and heavy industry. Poverty and unemployment were the driving forces for the move to Germany while the temporary jobs in Germany were meant to help support families back home. Both the US and German programs were considered failures because most of the temporary workers remained in the host country. The "second generation" of temporary foreign workers is more strictly managed.

The Cycle of Exploitation of "Second Generation" Temporary Migrant Workers in Canada

The push for temporary employment in countries such as Canada, the United States, and Germany by workers in low-income countries such as Mexico, Jamaica, or Turkey is often met not with resistance but with the voice of necessity. It is not the lure of working in Canada, but rather the push out of their poor villages in Mexico and their desire to support their families that motivate many temporary workers. For example, a Mexican temporary worker under Canada's seasonal agricultural worker program (SAWP) had this to say. "'My cousin and some of the other men in our town have always gone to Canada. I did not plan to go, but things changed and *now I have to.* We need the money'" (qtd in Hennebry, 2008: 345).

What happens to temporary migrant workers once they arrive in Canada? For that matter, what is the process by which they are recruited in their home countries? To answer these questions, we must realize that a "migrant industry" that includes recruiters, lawyers, agents, smugglers, and other go-betweens (Hennebry, 2008: 345) has developed over the years. First, in Mexico, the government through its appropriate ministries selects workers for the Canadian program. The Canadian government through HRSDC evaluates employer requests for workers. In Ontario and Québec, the day-to-day administration of the program is done by the Foreign Agricultural Resources Management Services (FARMS). Federally incorporated in 1987, FARMS is a non-profit private sector organization governed by a board of directors appointed by the groups participating in the program. Employers pay an administration fee to have their requests for workers processed.

Mexican workers travel to and from Canada exclusively through Canadian Agricultural Travel Limited (CanAg Travel). This is the Canadian government and FARMS approved travel agent that manages the air and ground transportation of temporary foreign workers. All the profits of flight sales go to one travel agency and Air Canada or Mexicana Airlines. There are no other options allowed for travel, according to the farmers, although the price may be considerably lower through other airlines (Hennebry, 2008: 347). One of the workers commented on the travel monopoly held by CanAg: "'One year, one of the worker's mother passed away and we wanted to send him home and have him come back after the funeral. It was kinda frustrating since the price with CanAg travel was *twice* as much as Air Canada online. There was no other option'" (qtd in Hennebry, 2008: 347).

Once in Canada, these workers are under complete control of the four main players: the Mexican and Canadian governments, SAWP management, FARMS, and employers. These powerful groups have final say over the assignments of the workers and their timelines within Canada. As such, anything these workers may require, such as a remittance-sending service, is available but at a handsome profit to the provider. In fact this arrangement makes these migrants a "captive market" for intermediaries and businesses targeting migrants.

With regard to recruitment, often the intermediary is a family member who has already worked in Canada or a private agent who is paid and who "knows the ropes" and can assist others to find work in Canada. As one worker confided: "He (a private agent) asked me if I was interested in joining the program to go to Canada. He told me that for 1000 Pesos ($75–$100 CDN), he could help me get in" (qtd in Hennebry, 2008: 348). Because these workers are temporary, they need special services. The growth of international ICTs and services such as international telephone providers and remittance-sending services take advantage of the isolation of these migrant workers. Communicating with family members back home is important but it costs the worker to use international telephone cards. Because there are no provisions for access to telephones at their workplaces, workers typically cannot receive calls and must find telephones offsite to use during free time in order to communicate with their families. In addition, workers must send money home for their families' basic needs and/or debt repayment. For this, they rely on banks and/or Western Union despite the costs associated with transfers in addition to exchange rate fees. As a Mexican worker explained: "'Yes I come here to work so I can send money home. It is my life, for my family and to pay my debts, and therefore yes, it is difficult, but I have to'" (qtd in Hennebry, 2008: 350).

Clearly, the group of "second generation" migrant labour benefits the Canadian agricultural sector and the growing migration industry associated with it. Yet a succession of private agents profit handsomely throughout the migrant workers' exploitation cycle.

Conclusion

This chapter began with the conceptual framework to understand the movement of work and workers in the global economy. From there we moved to an examination of the exploitation of farm labour and child labour in two of the world's most important agricultural commodities for high-income countries—namely coffee and cocoa. Next, we examined how transnational corporations moved production to export processing zones to take advantage of cheap labour with little protection for workers. The degree of exploitation of workers including children and women in export processing zones became symbolized in the Rana Plaza collapse, the largest industrial disaster in recent history. Finally, we brought the exploitation of labour from low-income countries home to Canada with "second generation" temporary migrant workers.

Questions for Critical Thought

1. Governmental and some international organizational actors claim to be making strides to end "the worst" forms of child labour. What jobs would you categorize as the "worst forms"? Are there examples of the "best forms" of child labour? How do we rank the many positions children take as work?
2. Regardless of the work they do, why are there few, if any, protections for workers in low-income countries?
3. Why has Canada not experienced the anti-immigration fervour that has plagued politics in the United States, the United Kingdom, and the European Union?

Suggested Further Resources

Porta, Donatella Della, Massimiliano Andretta, Lorenzo Mosca, and Herbert Reiter. 2006. *Globalization from Below: Transnational Activists and Protest Networks*. Minneapolis: University of Minnesota Press. When violence broke out at the demonstrations surrounding the 2001 G8 summit in Genoa, Italy the protests proved to be a critical moment in the global justice movement. *Globalization from Below* analyzes this movement from the viewpoints of the activists, organizers, and demonstrators themselves. The authors travelled to Genoa with anti-G8 protesters and collected data from more than 800 participants. A year later, they surveyed 2,400 activists at the European Social Forum in Florence.

Wallerstein, Immanuel. 2013. *Uncertain Worlds: World-Systems Analysis in Changing Times*. New York: Paradigm. This book is the definitive presentation of the evolution of world-systems analysis from the point of view of its founder, Immanuel Wallerstein. The book includes a conversation between Immanuel Wallerstein and Charles Lemert about the history of the field as it has come down to the present time, a long essay by Charles Lemert on the uncertainties of the modern world-system, as well as a concluding essay by Immanuel Wallerstein. No other book lends biographical, historical, and personal nuance to world-systems analysis.

Suggested Websites

Oxfam
www.oxfam.org
Oxfam is an international confederation of 17 organizations working in approximately 94 countries worldwide. Originally founded in Great Britain to help in famine relief, OXFAM today seeks out solutions to end poverty by working with partners to improve the livelihoods of the poor. The first overseas Oxfam was founded in Canada in 1963.

The Age of Migration
www.age-of-migration.com
This is the companion website to *The Age of Migration* by Stephen Castles, Hein de Haas, and Mark J. Miller.

Globalization of Commodity Chains: Where did my T-Shirt come from?
http://sociologytoolbox.com/globalization-of-commodity-chains
Four short video segments that begin with the creation of the GMO cotton seed and the harvesting of cotton in Mississippi using information and communications technologies on

automated pickers to collect the cotton with a handful of workers (the US remains the #1 producer of cotton), then video #2 follows the cotton to Colombia, Indonesia, and Bangladesh where it is made into cotton fabric using automated machines that employ only a small number of workers. The third video allows you to see how women's cotton t-shirts are made in Bangladesh and men's cotton t-shirts in Colombia, and video #4 shows how the t-shirts are shipped via containers to the U.S.

Notes

1. Harold Innis, with his staple theory of economic growth and development, is the acknowledged progenitor of the Canadian political economy tradition. A "staple" refers to any resource intensive export or commodity. According to the staples approach, Canada's status as a capitalist nation was inextricably linked to its colonial past. An examination into Canada's patterns of international trade and capital transfers became a significant theoretical and methodological concern for those working within the political economy tradition until roughly the turn of the twenty-first century. The "new" political economy approach became associated with such terms as "growth through trade, not development" or Watkins (1967) "inhibiting export mentality." For a more detailed examination and critique of the foundational literature of this political economy approach see Glenday (1988; 1989).
2. While the world-systems global commodity chain (WSGCC) and global commodity chain (GCC) supporters agree that the commodity chain concept is a useful construct for thinking about the international division of labour characteristic of capitalist production, there are significant differences between the two schools. World-systems theorists understand commodity chains as consisting not only of the steps involved in the transformation of raw materials into final goods, but also as webs connecting that set of productive activities with an equally critical input: namely, the social reproduction of human labour power. Additionally, world-systems theorists are interested in how commodity chains structure and reproduce a stratified and hierarchical world-system. On the other hand, GCC researchers understand commodity chains as sets of inter-firm networks which connect manufacturers, suppliers, and subcontractors in global industries to each other and to international markets. They are principally concerned with the question of how participation in commodity chains can facilitate industrial upgrading for developing country exporters.
3. While Starbucks is a transnational corporation, the main players remain the big four coffee roasters, Kraft, Nestlé, Procter & Gamble, and Sara Lee.
4. The fact that there are no traditional trade unions in these EPZs does not mean there is industrial peace. In 2010, workers were waiting for the implementation of the first government mandated new wage increase since 2006 which would raise their minimum wage from $25/month to $45/month. After several months, garment workers were demanding the implementation of a new minimum wage in the Chittagong EPZ. There were similar protests around Dhaka (*The Korea Times*, 2010).
5. In 2008, the Turkish population, who were once "guest workers," represented the largest settled migrant population in Germany with 2.5 million people, followed by Italians, Greeks, and Poles.

10 Seniors at Work

Learning Objectives

- To explore the dramatic impact of population aging on Canada's demographic profile
- To examine the ways in which the aging tsunami is impacting various labour forces
- To consider the ways in which ageist stereotypes produce a chilly work environment
- To scrutinize the ways in which retirement is currently being socially and economically constructed
- To consider the societal implications of the possible "end of retirement"

Introduction

The tumultuous changes currently impacting the Canadian labour force cannot be understated. In many ways, workers from the 1950s would not recognize the emerging labour market realities, given its ethnic, racial, and gender diversities; its primary preoccupation with services rather than production and extraction; its pervasive engagement with technology; and its global frame. Another crucial element promising to intensify these transformations in working experiences is the aging demographic in Canada and other industrialized countries. Put simply, the population is growing older; there are more and more seniors and fewer children and youth in Canada. This shift promises to force both employers and employees to rethink presuppositions about the labour market and working lives.

Few Canadians are unaware of what has been termed "the aging tsunami." For several decades newspaper headlines and popular books have blared warnings about the enormous numbers of Canadians entering their **senior**[1] years and the profound implications for everything from pension funding to a shortage of skilled job applicants. According to the latest census (2011), the numbers of seniors increased between 2006 and 2011 by 14.1 per cent while the numbers of prime working-age Canadians (15 to 64) grew by only 5.7 per cent, the numbers of children (aged 14 and younger) by a paltry 0.5 per cent and the overall growth rate in Canada was 5.9 per cent. The fastest growing age group was aged 60 to 64, followed next by the rapid increase in the number of Canadians 100 years of age or older (**centenarians**) (Statistics Canada, 2012a).

In the past, Canadian demographics were more likely to mirror the contemporary reality in India. As of 2011, ranking as the most populous country on the planet, India's population pyramid definitely slants toward youthfulness: almost 30 per cent of its population are zero to 14 years of age; another 65 per cent are 15 to 64 and a mere 6 per cent are 65 or older (Teelucksing, 2014: 323). As late as 1931 Canada had a similar profile. Today, analysts predict that by 2031, as baby boomers complete their transition to seniors, seniors will comprise a staggering one-quarter of the population, or roughly one in every four Canadians[2] will be 65 or older (Statistics Canada, 2012b; Milan and Vezina, 2011; Norland, 1994).

The roots of this momentous demographic shift are complex. In large part, these are the population reverberations of the Second World War. Predictably, during the war, while hundreds of thousands of men were deployed as soldiers, population growth bottomed out. When the soldiers returned, there was a dramatic surge in pregnancies in what was termed the "baby boom." As the **baby boomers** age, they have had a wave-like impact on every age category. At present, those born between 1946 and 1965 comprise 30 per cent of the Canadian population (Statistics Canada, 2012b). In 2011 (the most recent census data available), when the first impact of baby boomers (born in 1946) reached 65, there was a clear "greying" of the population. At this point, there were more people aged 55 to 64 (those traditionally seen as on the cusp of leaving the labour force) than those aged 15 to 24 (those traditionally about to enter the labour force). As baby boomers continue to "age out," the proportion of seniors will continue to surge (Statistics Canada, 2012b).

While the baby boom has played a definitive role in aging populations, other factors have amplified this trend. The availability of birth control ensured that families could reduce the numbers of children they produced. While the average number of children per woman was 3.7 between 1946 and 1965, it has now dropped to 1.7 (Statistics Canada, 2012b). The demands of the consumer economy, the increased availability of paid work for wives and mothers, the failure of wages to keep pace with cost of living or for "real" average wages to increase, ideological shifts (most notably the women's movement), and the growing insecurity of traditionally male employment (such as manufacturing) all have encouraged families to raise fewer children. The net result is that for more than a decade the birth rate amongst Canadian families has not been at **replacement level**; in other words, the size of the population would actually decline if there were not vigorous **pro-immigration federal policies**.

Of course, various other elements have contributed to the aging of the population. Most notably, generalized improvements in nutrition, medical interventions, and advances (notably in circulatory and tumour mortality) and improved access to medical care have all meant that **life expectancy** in Canada has increased significantly. Indeed in the decade between 2000 and 2010, life expectancy improved so much it matched (for men) and surpassed (for women) Sweden, the widely recognized world leader in health and quality of life (Auger, Serbon, and Rostila, 2015).

Not only are there more Canadians heading into their senior years, their health, nutrition, and medical support increase the likelihood that they can reasonably expect to live for several decades past 65. According to the latest Statistics Canada data (2007 to 2009), today, at birth, Canadian women can reasonably expect to live to age 83 and men to age 79. In contrast, in 1950 to 1952, men were expected to live on average to age 66 and women to age 71 (Statistics Canada, 2012c). For those Canadians who arrived at age 65 between 2007 and 2009, men could anticipate, on average, another 18.5 years of life (83.5) and women another 21.6 years (86.6) (Statistics Canada, 2012d). Analysts project that by 2036, life expectancy at birth for women will reach 86.2 years and 82.9 years for men (Government of Canada, 2014: 4). Figure 10.1 highlights the significance of these changes in terms of the growing numbers of Canadians 80 years of age or older in the population from 2000 to 2051.

The implications of increased longevity amongst Canadians are most glaring in terms of the increasing numbers becoming **aged**. In 2011, there was close to one-quarter of a million seniors aged 90 and older. Even centenarians, once an anomaly, have become relatively commonplace. In 2001, there were slightly fewer than 4,000 Canadians 100 years or older; by 2011 there were almost 6,000 (84 per cent of whom were women[3]). It is predicted that by 2031 there will be 17,600 centenarians and by 2061, reflecting the baby boom wave, 78,300 (Statistics Canada, 2012e). Unless there are dramatic improvements in medical interventions, it is reasonable to assume that this growing portion of the population will be dependent on the care of others.[4]

The aging of the Canadian population must be located in its diverse regional contexts. At the provincial and territorial level, there are significant differences in the age profile. Alberta, with its (until recently) booming economy, had a younger demographic than provinces such as Newfoundland and Labrador. Indeed, Alberta had the lowest proportion of seniors (11.1 per cent) amongst all the provinces. Likely this youthfulness in the Western provinces is a reflection of higher numbers of

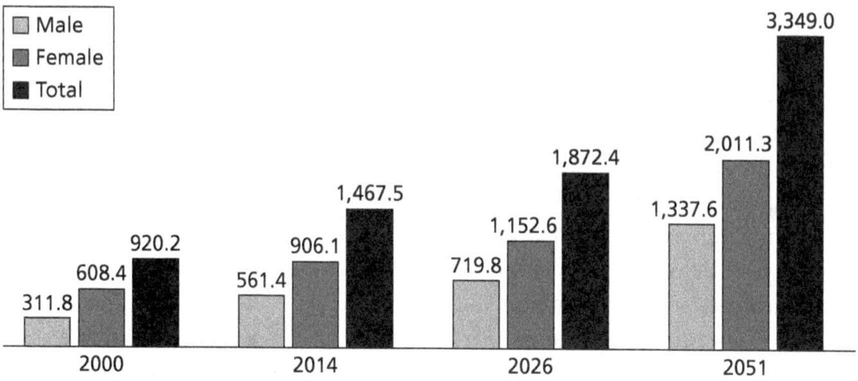

Figure 10.1 Population Aged 80 and Over by Sex, Canada, 2000, 2014, 2026, 2051, Medium-Growth Scenario ('000)

Source: 2000–2051: Statistics Canada, Demography Division, Statistics Canada: Table 051-0001 - Estimate of population, by age group and sex (2014)

immigrants (international as well as inter-provincial), large numbers of Canadian Aboriginals (with their relatively youthful age demographic), and a higher fertility rate amongst immigrants and Aboriginals (Statistics Canada, 2015a). Generally, from 2006 to 2011, the Atlantic provinces and Quebec were distinguished by higher rates of population aging than the rest of Canada (Statistics Canada, 2012a). Needless to say, these regional[5] variations are important in both understanding and responding to the impact of aging on the Canadian labour force.

The larger international context is similarly differentiated. While Canada is definitely greying, it appears absolutely young relative to most other **G8 countries**. Seniors in Japan, for example, in 2011 numbered almost one in four inhabitants; in Germany and Italy, seniors comprise more than 20 per cent of the population. Only the United States and Russia, amongst G8 countries, have a younger age profile than Canada. Similarly, Japan, Italy, France, and the United Kingdom all have a higher rate of centenarians in their populations (Statistics Canada, 2012e). The net result is that Canada has a higher proportion of working-age people than any G8 country other than Russia (Statistics Canada, 2012a). However, as the baby boom generation continues to move into their 60s, this profile is expected to shift dramatically and Canada will more completely mirror other aging industrialized countries. Put simply: there will be, proportionately, more seniors (65+) and fewer working-age (15 to 64) people. Importantly, many of these seniors will be aged 85+.

The Aging of the Labour Force

For Canada and other countries, this shift in population demographics has profound employment and labour force implications. On the one hand, who will take on the employment positions if seniors retire and, conversely, as the labour force shrinks, who will provide the economic foundation (for example, tax support to maintain programs ranging from medical care to national pensions such as the Canadian Pension Plan) for a burgeoning senior population? This emergent problem is evident, for example, in the ratio of those at an age to enter the labour force (15 to 24) and those on the verge of exiting it (55 to 64). In 1931, there were almost three entrants for each individual aged to exit; today (2011), there is one entrant for every exit-aged Canadian and, of course, many of the baby boomers have yet to reach their 60s (Statistics Canada, 2012a). As the **dependency ratio** (the numbers of income-earning individuals relative to the numbers of retired individuals) shifts, concerns have grown about the future economic well-being of various industrialized countries, especially in light of their economic interdependencies. A recent Scottish study, for example, concluded that population aging will likely necessitate either increased taxation or decreased government spending—particularly grim prospects as the international economy continues to struggle (Lisenkova, Merette, and Wright, 2013).

One obvious solution to the decline in working-age Canadians would be a pro-natalist approach. Such policies, which would encourage Canadians to have more children, for example, through tax incentives for larger families, have been tried with some success in Quebec. However, federal policies have tended to look to immigration as the primary solution. As a result over the course of the last decade about 250,000 immigrants a year (260,404 in 2014) have been admitted to Canada, and roughly 150,000 of these immigrants have been economic immigrants (165,088 in 2014) (Government of Canada, 2015). As a result, amongst young Canadians born between 1980 and 1995, almost one in five were born outside Canada (Marshall, 2011: 16). The primary source countries for these new permanent residents, from 2012 to 2014, have been the Philippines, India, and the People's Republic of China, which together account for roughly 100,000 immigrants per year (Government of Canada, 2015). In short, recent immigrants are commonly racialized members of Canadian society, and this reality has implications for the position of senior immigrants in the labour market.

Older immigrants in Canada often face multiple intersecting prejudices: **ageism**, racism, and anti-immigrant sentiments. Currently, visible and ethnic minority seniors who are immigrants comprise 30 per cent of all Canadians 65 and older and reflect a rich diversity of origins: Chinese, African, Korean, Filipino, Iranian, Pakistani, Indian, and so forth (Kembhavi, 2012). Most arrived at a relatively young age (some as children) and others are recent arrivals and, of course, senior immigrants range from political refugees to participants in family reunification programs (Durst and MacLean, 2010).

It is reasonable to believe that older immigrants who are racialized and/or not familiar with Canadian culture or languages will find it particularly difficult to navigate participation in the paid labour force. Research indicates that immigrants, especially men, who arrive after the age of 30 are particularly at risk of poverty. Lacking both experience in the paid labour force and a spouse with higher income, they confront "the greatest economic penalty for arriving in Canada at a relatively late age" (Grant and Townsend, 2010: 139). Suggestive of these problems for senior immigrants is recent research which reports that older immigrants from countries that are dissimilar to Canada in terms of language and culture will be significantly lonelier than their Canadian counterparts. However, even these patterns complexly intersect with family and friendship networks, participation in local activities, and feelings of belonging to Canadian society (Gierveld, Van der Pas, and Keating, 2015).

Given these complexities, it is extremely difficult to generalize about the social locations and workplace experiences of immigrant seniors. There are wealthy Chinese investors and highly skilled retired African doctors who belong to this category along with economically marginalized and socially isolated Indian workers driving taxis and under-employed Filipinos serving as personal support workers in long-term care facilities. The key conclusion here is that discussions about Canadian seniors and their role in the labour force must be couched in terms of the significant (and growing) presence of immigrant seniors within this population.

As a result of this increasing diversification of the Canadian population along with persistent regional variations, any discussion of the aging labour force must be couched in terms of the diverse contexts in which Canadians experience aging. In particular, as discussed in Chapter 7, the labour force has also been increasingly diversified in terms of gender, and the massive movement of wives and mothers into paid work has helped transform paid work. From 2003 to 2012, the ratio of women to men in the job market continued to edge up and reached 0.90—meaning almost one woman for every man in the labour market (Burleton et al., 2013: 12; see also Marshall, 2011: 17). As discussed below, many of these employed women are seniors. In short, any discussion of seniors' employment must take into consideration the ways in which gendered and racialized/immigrant identities intersect with aging and regionalized labour market experience.

Keeping in mind these important diversities and complexities amongst aging workers, it is clear that seniors (65+) and near seniors (55 to 64) are dramatically impacting Canada's labour market. In recent years, more than one in six Canadian workers was a senior (55+) (Carriere and Galarneau, 2011: 6). Between 2000 and 2011, the percentages of persons aged 65 to 69 who were employed or actively looking for employment increased from 16 per cent to 30 per cent, and amongst those 70 and older participation rates increased from 6 to 10 per cent for men and from 2 to 4 per cent for women (Mei, Eales, and Fast, 2013). By 2014, 13 per cent of the over 6 million seniors (65+) in Canada (15.6 per cent of the total population) were participating in the labour force—a dramatic increase from the 6 per cent who were employed in 2000 (Government of Canada, 2014: 4, 9). This impact is also evident in the fact that people 60 or older have accounted for almost one-third of all new job gains in the Canadian economy from mid-2009 to 2012 (Lu, 2012). Between 2002 and 2012 seniors (65+) who made up only 3 to 4 per cent of the national job market, accounted for 11.5 per cent of all net new full-time positions and almost one-third of new part-time jobs (Burleton, 2014: 14).

As with youth, seniors often experience nonstandard attachments to the labour market. For example, employed seniors are much more likely to be employed part-time than workers aged 25 to 54. By 2009, 58 per cent of employed women seniors were holding a part-time job along with almost one-third of their male counterparts (32 per cent) (Milan and Vezina, 2011: 18, 19; MacEwen, 2012). This possible[6] precarity in the labour market is also underscored by the fact that 40 per cent of senior (65+) workers were self-employed (MacEwen, 2012). In short, both older and younger Canadians are often experiencing precarious attachments to the labour market as paid work continues to be characterized by growing numbers of part-time, casual, contract, short-term, and self-employed positions. Predictably, as with young workers, the nonstandard positions occupied by seniors often translate into low (and insecure) wages. Fully one-third (33 per cent) of employed seniors 65+ are low wage earners (earning less than two-thirds of the median hourly wage, or less than $13.33 per hour in 2011). For example, 50 per cent of self-employed workers over age 65 earn less than $5,000/year (MacEwen, 2012).

Despite these vulnerabilities in the new economy, it appears likely that seniors will continue to increase their labour force participation. Given government policies intended to facilitate the labour market participation of older workers (such as the Targeted Initiative for Older Workers and the Third Quarter Initiative), the sheer size of the oncoming baby boomer and, as discussed below, growing concerns about retirement funding, reliance on senior workers appears poised to expand in coming years. As indicated in Table 10.1, it is the older cohorts (55+ and 65+) who are experiencing increases in their labour market engagement while younger workers (20 to 24 years old) have seen a decline in participation and employment rates at the same time as their unemployment rates have grown (Burleton et al., 2014). Even amongst older seniors—those aged 65 to 69—participation in the paid labour force has grown dramatically. Between 2000 and 2010, men aged 65 to 69 almost doubled their employment rate, and comparable women saw their rate skyrocket from 6.9 per cent in 2000 to 16.6 per cent in 2010, almost a three-fold increase (Carriere and Galarneau, 2011: 6).

Senior women stand out as a particularly important ingredient in the emerging labour force. They are actually increasing their workforce attachment faster than comparable males and "account for a disproportionate share of net employment gains" (Burleton et al., 2014: 14). By 2014, women aged 55 and older comprised 25 per cent of the permanent female labour force aged 25 and over; comparable men accounted for only 20 per cent of the permanent male labour force aged 25 and over (Statistics Canada, 2015b: Table 282-0080). As apparent in Table 10.2, over the past decade, increases in senior women's presence in the permanent, and especially the temporary, labour forces have outpaced senior men's. However, this pattern does not imply that senior women are "taking over" in the labour market. Women, even as seniors, continue to occupy a more marginal—in terms of income, status, and clout—position than their male counterparts. For example, when one examines those seniors (50 years of age and older) who are working long hours (50+) and most of whom are in managerial or professional occupations, they are overwhelmingly men (Cooke and Cooper, 2013).

Table 10.1 Labour Force Statistics by Age Cohort

Indicator	20 to 24 year olds		55+ year olds		65+ year olds	
Unemployment rate	2008*	8.8%	2008	5.7%	2008	3.7%
	2013**	10.9%	2013	6.5%	2013	4.7%
Participation rate	2008	78.6%	2008	34.5%	2008	10.4%
	2013	76.4%	2013	37.4%	2013	13.0%
Employment rate	2008	71.7%	2008	32.5%	2008	10.0%
	2013	68.1%	2013	35.0%	2013	12.4%

*September 2008 throughout
**August 2013 throughout
Source: Table derived from Table 4 in Burleton, Derek., Sonya Gulati, Connor McDonald, Sonny Scarfone. 2014. Jobs in Canada: Where, What and for Whom? TD Economics, p. 13

Table 10.2 Senior Men and Women in the Permanent and Temporary Labour Force

Gender/Job Permanency	2004 % of Labour Force Aged 25+	2014 % of Labour Force Aged 25+
Males 65+ permanent employees	1.2	3.0
Females 65+ permanent employees	1.0	3.2
Males 65+ temporary employees	4.0	6.8
Females 65+ temporary employees	2.0	5.0

Source: Derived from: Statistics Canada 2015, Table 281-0080

The growth in labour force age-diversity has important implications in the workplace. For example, recent research suggests older workers approach working from a different vantage point than their younger colleagues; in particular, they are more likely to connect job satisfaction to good collegial relationships. In contrast to younger workers, they put less emphasis on income, advancement opportunities, job security, and having an interesting job. However, significantly, these differences appear to be nation dependent and vary depending on cultural context (Drabe, Hauff, and Richter, 2015). Nonetheless, these findings support the notion that older employees are different from their younger counterparts and, as a result, their growing presence in the workforce is likely to impact labour force experiences.

Is the Workplace a Chilly Climate for Older Workers?

A variety of concerns have been raised about the aging profile in the Canadian labour market. In particular, analysts are suggesting there may be a squeezing out of young entrants to the labour market and, as a result, growing generational conflict as younger workers fear not only their entrance but also their advancement will be hobbled by the presence of so many older workers. Indeed, newspapers have explicitly suggested that the growing presence of older workers in the labour force comes at the expense of "debt-saddled graduates" who are being "forced" to both delay their careers and move back into their parents' homes (Goar, 2012). These notions of "greedy" senior workers are one strand contributing to a chilly workplace climate for older workers.

In addition, various ageist stereotypes continue to undermine employed seniors. These include beliefs that older Canadians are slower, not up-to-date, less physically fit, less physically attractive, asexual, forgetful, technologically challenged, and less skilled.[7] Such views set the stage for discriminatory and exclusionary practices (Cracium and Flick, 2014). Popular stereotypes—the Walmart greeter—encourage employers not to hire seniors, to marginalize them in poor quality work, or to push older employees into retirement; simultaneously, they encourage fellow employees to disrespect or exclude seniors (Biggs, Carr, and Haapala, 2015). For example, research suggests that older workers receive more negative performance ratings and fewer developmental opportunities from younger managers (Shore, Cleveland,

and Goldberg, 2003). A 2011 report from the **Canadian Association of Retired Persons** (CARP) found that about 50 per cent of seniors polled felt age discrimination in the workplace was common (MacEwen, 2012).

A 2013 study by CARP and Ceridian Canada Limited reported that employed seniors believe that employers assume older workers cannot keep up with advances and also cost more in terms of benefits. The net result is a tendency when faced with applicants with equal qualifications but distinguished by age to hire the younger worker (Smolkin, 2013: B1). Recent increases in age-discrimination lawsuits support this view that age-discrimination is a significant issue (Gray, 2014b) (see Box 10.1). As a result, CARP and other advocacy groups are vigorously lobbying to end work-place age discrimination.

Box 10.1 Everyday Work Experiences

The Workplace Bias against Older Workers

Workplace age discrimination may take a variety of forms. The kinds of legal cases which are gaining headlines include instances where older workers have been dismissed to make way for a "younger, less expensive worker." In some instances, these older workers may find themselves shoved out the door with minimal severance packages, despite years of employment. Older *contract* workers, despite decades of employment, may find that, with no explanation, their contracts are not renewed as they move into their late 60s. Once unemployed, re-entry may be difficult. For example, a 63-year-old CARP volunteer who was "let go" after working for 43 years at a multinational manufacturing company finally gave up on her career after two years of job search and eight interviews.

In a particularly well-publicized 2011 case, seven Oakville area women who were aged 62 to 78 had their hours as product demonstrators cut to zero. They were told that InStore Focus, Canada's largest consumer sampling company, for whom they were demonstrating products in various Metro stores in the Toronto area, had made it clear in a new contract that they wanted "soccer moms" (clearly, younger women) demonstrating their products (Pigg, 2012: B1). In response, the aggrieved seniors went to the media and filed an age discrimination case with the Ontario Human Rights Commission.

Seniors are responding to all forms of workplace discrimination by becoming activists (Goar, 2014; Sawchuk, 2009; Beard and Williamson, 2011), by demanding their human rights and by launching lawsuits. Significantly, the courts are responding strongly wherever age discrimination is found. An Ontario court awarded a 70-year-old machine operator who was judged to be the victim of age discrimination an additional 22-month ($69,000) severance package after 20 years work. Similarly, a 72-year-old civil servant was awarded her job back along with several years of back pay (Gray, 2014b). With these larger settlement packages, courts are recognizing that

continued

despite the positive attributes of many senior applicants—experience, maturity, fewer childcare responsibilities—older workers who are forced out of employment may find a difficult and long path back to paid employment (CARP, 2012).

Geoff Robins / for the Toronto Star

Pictured here are six of the seven women who filed an age discrimination complaint with the Ontario Human Rights Commission against InStore Focus and Metro stores. These women claimed that while their working hours as product demonstrators was reduced to zero, new product demonstrators, all of whom were 20 to 60 years younger, were hired.

However, it must be acknowledged that age discrimination does not simply target seniors. There are comparable biases against younger workers and youth in general who may be caricatured as unreliable, unskilled, immature, and disrespectful. The difficulties currently experienced by young workers (15 to 19) suggest many employees in service industries are taking the opportunity to hire older workers who are perceived as bringing with them more education, experience, and skills (Burleton et al., 2014: 14).

The financial consequences of age discrimination reveal similar contradictions. Wage growth over the past 30 years clearly suggests that youthfulness as well as older age are not inherently beneficial or detrimental in the new labour market. For example, between 1981 and 2011, average hourly wages increased by 17 per cent among men aged 45 to 54 but by only 1 per cent amongst men 25 to 34. Amongst women 45 to 54 years old hourly wages grew by 33 percent, more than twice the 14 per cent increase for young women (25 to 34). Much of this age gap emerged between 1981 and 1998 as youth unionization rates declined and youth found employment in less well-paid industries and occupations. However, between 1998 and 2011 these differences have tended to *reverse* themselves as unionization fell amongst older male workers (as manufacturing collapsed) and young workers found well-paid work in construction, mining, and oil and gas. During this same time period, the wages of younger women were similarly benefited by shifts in unionization patterns and by their improved educational qualifications (Morissette, Picot, and Lu, 2012). Most recently, the collapse of international oil markets in 2015 likely have undermined the wage position of young male workers. In short, while ageism in the workplace is clearly an important concern, the significance of age in labour market experiences must be understood as shifting rapidly in response to emerging economic realities.

Retirement Decisions: Constraints or Free Choices?

In many respects the landscape of employment shifted when the provincial and federal governments enacted laws ending mandatory retirement[8] at age 65. In December 2012, mandatory retirement of federally regulated employees was eliminated when Section 15(I)(C) of the *Canadian Human Rights Act*, which permitted mandatory retirement policies, was repealed by Bill C-13. While 65 may persist in the public imagination as a significant marker in decisions about retirement, the law no longer mandates age 65 retirement for the overwhelming majority of employees.

Tables 10.3, 10.4, and 10.5 provide an overview of the growing presence of workers aged 65+ in a variety of OECD nations and the particularly dramatic increase in women workers 65+.

As a result of new retirement laws around the globe, there has been a dramatic shift in the age and gender profiles of the labour force and, increasingly seniors must decide whether or not to remain in paid work and whether to accept or seek out alternative structures of employment such as part-time work or self-employment. This decision-making process includes not only whether or not to

Table 10.3 Total Number of Employed Persons Aged 65+, 2000, 2014 (persons, thousands)

	Time		
Country	**2000**	**2014**	**% Change over Time**
Canada	209	683	226
Denmark	20	74	279
Germany	362	965	167
Greece	92	57	–39
Italy	327	469	43
Sweden	76	177	133
United Kingdom	459	1,102	140
United States	4,179	7,972	91

Source: OECD (2015) Labour Market Statistics: Labour Force Statistics by age and sex, OCED Employment and labour market statistics (database).

Table 10.4 Total Number of Employed Women Aged 65+, 2000, 2014 (persons, thousands)

	Time		
Country	**2000**	**2014**	**% Change over Time**
Canada	65	261	301
Denmark	6	26	333
Germany	122	361	196
Greece	27	17	–37
Italy	87	114	31
Sweden	25	64	156
United Kingdom	171	456	167
United States	1,773	3,594	103

Source: OECD (2015) Labour Market Statistics: Labour Force Statistics by age and sex, OCED Employment and labour market statistics (database).

retire but also, if retiring—when to retire; how to retire (**phased-in retirement** or abrupt retirement); and how completely to retire (possibly, part-time or contract employment, self-employment, or leaving the labour force entirely).

Clearly, the "decision" to exit the paid labour market may, in fact, be **involuntary**. As discussed in more detail below, onerous care-giving responsibilities, plant closures and layoffs, injury or ill health, and high unemployment rates may all force a worker out of paid work. Currently, almost one in four fully retired Canadians retired due to ill health or disability, and another 7 per cent retired to provide care to a partner (Jackson, 2014). Since 2009, such **involuntary retirement** has resulted in almost a two-year reduction in expected working life for both men and women. Job losses due to economic reasons account for two-thirds of this pattern (affecting mostly male workers) and ill-health and family responsibilities for about one-third (affecting mostly female workers). Such involuntary retirement

Table 10.5 Total Number of Employed Men Aged 65+, 2000, 2014 (persons, thousands)

	Time		
Country	**2000**	**2014**	**% Change over Time**
Canada	145	422	191
Denmark	13	48	269
Germany	240	604	152
Greece	66	39	–41
Italy	240	355	48
Sweden	51	113	121
United Kingdom	288	646	124
United States	2,406	4,378	82

Source: OECD (2015) Labour Market Statistics: Labour Force Statistics by age and sex, OCED Employment and labour market statistics (database).

is clearly not randomly distributed through the labour market. As evident above, women are particularly implicated in terms of family care-giving responsibilities. Similarly, health and physical well-being may be particularly relevant in specific sectors of the labour market. Industrial workers, for example, may be especially likely to find that decades of employment have taken a significant physical toll (Algarni et al., 2015).

Within these specific patterns, there is, of course, a general connection between reduced health and well-being and increased age. Despite highly publicized examples of celebrities who appear to be "ageless" and cultural industries devoted to the denial of aging, few Canadians are as robust at 60 as they were at 30 (Leicht and Fitzgerald, 2014). Seniors in general are much more likely than other segments of the population to have chronic health conditions, and this proclivity increases with age. In 2009, 80 per cent of women and 75 per cent of men 65 to 74 had at least one chronic health condition (ranging from high blood pressure to cancer). By age 85 and older, 57 per cent of women and roughly 40 per cent of men had high blood pressure and/or arthritis. More than one in four women and almost one in four men in this age category were afflicted with heart disease. In addition, a significant proportion of seniors (with higher rates amongst women and amongst older seniors) reported "usually experiencing pain." Living with pain may result from not only illness but also previous injury or accident. One in three women and one in five men 65 to 74 reported such pain experiences (Milan and Vezina, 2011: 30). In the event of injuries, on or off the job, the older worker often takes longer to recover, reflecting age-related physical changes, and, interestingly, older (65+) workers are less likely to be offered vocational rehabilitation so that they are able to return to work (Algarni et al., 2015). A recent report noted that more than half of fully retired workers 55+ had three or more chronic health conditions, and one-quarter of fully retired workers 55+ listed poor health as their retirement rationale (MacEwen, 2012). In short, health problems may significantly affect any decision to continue to work, retire, and/or reduce employment, and this will continue to be the case in the absence of efforts to address such barriers to work (Smith et al., 2014).[9]

Some workplaces are moving toward more accessible and physically benign forms of employment as the emphasis grows on creating knowledge- and technology-based jobs. This pattern (for example, the use of robotics in manufacturing) may mean that coming generations of workers will be able to continue to work well into their 60s and 70s (Miller and Nyce, 2014). In this regard, future advances in science, medicine, and technology may mute the effects of injuries and health on seniors' paid employment but appear unlikely to negate them.

While physical concerns may push workers out of paid employment, financial issues may drive them back in. A recent (2008) Statistics Canada survey reported that only 30 per cent of older workers (55+) retired "because they were financially ready" (MacEwen, 2012). Since the 2008 recession it is likely that many more senior workers are concerned about their financial preparedness for retirement (CARP, 2014). Not only are there concerns about whether an individual has accrued adequate retirement savings to be able to "afford" retirement, the actual security of that pension may be unclear. In several high-profile instances, employers have revealed that pension funds are inadequately funded and some have introduced measures to manage their pension liabilities by reducing the pension incomes of existing retirees. For example, some private and, even public, employers, notably in cases of bankruptcy (Atlas Steel [Welland, Ontario], US Steel [Hamilton, Ontario], Nortel Canada, and the City of Detroit) have successfully managed to reduce their economic obligations and, therefore retirees' pension incomes by pleading financial distress. When Nortel, for example, filed for bankruptcy protection, it left 20,000 former employees with an underfunded pension plan (Barmak, 2011). US Steel, which has teetered on the brink of bankruptcy, has generated headlines suggesting the Hamiltonians who were US Steel pensioners could lose $4,354 per year (Rieti, 2015). General Motors revealed in 2010 that its pension plans were underfunded worldwide by $27 billion (*Toronto Star*, 2010). Such events contribute to a growing sense of insecurity regarding private and public retirement funding and weigh against retirement.

Increasing personal debt amongst seniors also undermines any inclination to withdraw from the labour market (Goar, 2013). Growing debt amongst seniors may be seen as a direct outcome of new societal realities: increased costs of higher education, high rates of youth unemployment, and increased numbers of young Canadians returning to their parental homes. Regardless of the impetus—a vacation of a lifetime or pressing family need, low interest rates and easily accessed lines of credit have indeed encouraged seniors to rack up debt three times faster than the average Canadian (Goddard, 2011; McDaniel, Gazso, and Um, 2013). In addition, stagnant "real" wage growth, exceptionally low interest rates and the dramatic growth of nonstandard employment likely also make important contributions to the increasing indebtedness of seniors (Roseman, 2014). Regardless of the direct and indirect causes, significant indebtedness does not set seniors up for retirement. As Kevin Leicht and Scott Fitzgerald (2014) point out the popular mantra that "60 is the new 30" may simply reflect the grim reality that Americans (and Canadians) simply cannot afford to be 60 (2014: 236).

Of course, the regional and national economic climates may also be significant factors in retirement. Whether there is appropriate work available, whether plants are closing or laying off employees, and whether government policies facilitate seniors' re-engagement with paid work all impact retirement decisions (Burleton et al., 2014: 13). Recent research documents the intersection of local unemployment rates with retirement age. Economic regions with higher unemployment rates had a persistently younger retirement age (62.7 years of age) than regions with lower rates and also had a significant impact on rates of retirement before age 62 (Galarneau et al., 2015).

In sum, retiring from the labour force is far from a simple one-time personal decision. Gender roles, racialized realities (including Aboriginal status), and immigrant status all intersect with financial well-being, social class, and actual employment opportunities in steering retirement decisions. For example, women typically assume responsibility for care work in the family. If a spouse, older parent, or in-law is in need of care the burden may fall more heavily on women and have direct consequences for her "choice" to retire. In the absence of adequate state-funded supports (such as in-home care for ailing/disabled seniors) women may find they simply cannot find the time and energy to continue to combine paid employment and their care-giving unpaid work and, hence, they *decide* to retire.

Women's retirement realities are also structured by their paid employment histories which, in turn, are typically framed by familial and caregiving roles.[10] Even for contemporary young women (born between 1980 and 1995), gender roles continue to leave a mark on their employment patterns (Finch, 2014; Marshall, 2011: 18). Caregiving—for children or other family members—directly impacts on women's experience of aging and is consistent with the tendency of married women to retire[11] sooner than their single counterparts and for full-time women workers to be more likely to exit employment (Galarneau et al., 2015: 4; Proulx and Le Bourdais, 2014).

However, while caregiving pressures may encourage withdrawal from the labour force, women's past strategies to accommodate family caregiving may interfere with retirement. After all, married/common-law women are more likely than men to have an interrupted work history (for example, maternity leaves) and to work part-time as they accommodate the requirements of childbirth and child-rearing. The net result of these typical employment patterns is that women often earn less than their male counterparts, and this difference in average income persists into the senior years and is reflected in reduced pension income (Hunsley, 2013a; Lee et al., 2015). In short, typical gendered employment patterns undermine women's ability to accrue their own pension benefits and adequately finance their retirement (Milan and Vezina, 2011).

Not surprisingly, between 1976 and 2008 women's retirement income (pension benefits, superannuation payments, or annuities generated by employer pension plans) have grown alongside women's increased labour force participation. From 1976 to 2008, retirement income as a portion of senior women's income expanded dramatically from only 15 to 54 per cent. Despite these dramatic gains, it is clear that many women, in the event of divorce or widowhood,[12] are likely to face higher rates of low income than comparable men (Milan and Vezina, 2011: 21, 23). In this gendered reality, withdrawal from paid work may simply not mesh with the realities of financial well-being.

A similar argument could be made about racialized minorities, including Aboriginal Canadians and immigrants. Recent immigrants (during the first 10 years of residence in Canada) are likely to experience lower employment incomes and higher rates of underemployment. Such patterns impact on both income levels as well as the accumulation of pension benefits. Similarly, Aboriginal Canadians are characterized by lower employment rates; in 2011 62.5 per cent of Aboriginal people (aged 25 to 64) were employed in contrast to 75.8 per cent of non-Aboriginals (Statistics Canada, 2015a: 22). Whenever Canadians are under-represented in the paid labour force, their decisions to retire are likely to be negatively impacted by the prospect of financial difficulties post-retirement.

Finally, these pressures for and against retirement must be contextualized by the government policies which determine pension benefits. One of the great success stories of government anti-poverty initiatives concerns Canada's seniors. Through the introduction of more generous **Old Age Security (OAS)** and **Guaranteed Income Supplements (GIS)** the federal government ensured that senior Canadians today are much less likely to live below the low-income cut-offs (although many live close to them). These policies have been particularly important for lifting senior women, the majority of seniors, out of impoverishment. As recently as the end of the 1970s, more than one-third of senior women lived with low income, and in 1980 more than half of senior women living alone were categorized as low income after taxes. Policies which provided more generous government transfer payments to seniors meant that by 2008 only 7.6 per cent were living with low income after tax. Senior men, who have always been better off than their female counterparts, saw their low income after tax rate drop to 3.6 per cent (Milan and Vezina, 2011: 24). The significance of increased government benefits is very clear. In 2008, government transfers accounted for more than half (53 per cent) of senior women's total income. In contrast, such transfers made up only 38 per cent of senior men's total income. Not surprisingly, as women have increased their life-long paid employment, their reliance in their senior years on government transfers has declined. Nonetheless, government benefits continue to make it financially feasible for many women to retire and future alterations to such policies would be game-changers. In early 2016, the Federal budget, under the newly elected Justin Trudeau government, restored Old Age Security eligibility to age 65 (from 67) (Stone 2016).

Indeed, the game does appear to be changing. In recent years, as governments have increasingly embraced neoliberal policies, there has been a pronounced tendency for government initiatives (and aging discourses in general) to shift responsibilities to individuals (Rudman, 2015). In this context, numerous governments and the OECD propose that the solution to the issues surrounding an aging population (for example, growing pressures on health care funding) simply cannot be managed through state interventions. After all, by 2011 the state pension obligations of France and Germany were three times the size of their economies (*Toronto Star*, 2012: B4). In Canada, concerns have been raised about the future viability of the **Canada/Quebec Pension Plan (CPP/QPP)**. Currently, analysts suggest that despite economic upheaval and an explosion in the numbers of seniors, the fund should remain sustainable. Nonetheless, increases in worker contributions as well as the creation of provincial pension plans continue to be debated (Marshman, 2013). In 2016 the Federal government decided to gradually boost CPP benefits from $13,110 a year to $17,478 and to correspondingly increase CPP benefits by 2016. As a result of this increase in benefits for retirees and improved stability for CPP funding, Ontario Premier Kathleen Wynne announced that previous plans to establish a separate Ontario Retirement Pension Plan would be retired (Benzie and Ferguson 2016).

One currently popular solution, adopted in Canada and internationally, is for governments to turn to workers themselves and propose policies to encourage seniors (65+) to remain in the paid labour force (Flavelle, 2014; Hofacker, 2015). While governments around the world have moved to dispense with mandatory retirement (improving the prospects for continued paid work after age 65), they have also moved to postpone public pension entitlements. Canadians, Americans, and Germans were, for example, eligible for old age pensions around age 65 until recent legislation either encouraged (with financial benefits) postponed applications or introduced gradual increases in the mandated age of eligibility (typically to 67) (Ormsby, 2012). Recently, analysts have proposed governments raise pension entitlement to age 70 (*The Economist*, 2011). In Canada, the federal government has postponed, starting in April 2023, the age of eligibility for Old Age Security (OAS) and Guaranteed Income Supplement (GIS) benefits from 65 to 67 (affecting those Canadians born on April 1, 1958 or later). Postponed access to OAS and GIS means some seniors would need to replace (at maximum) $14,000 per year per person and even the basic OAS benefit amounts to over $5,000—an amount that may be difficult to generate from low wage part-time and self-employed positions (MacEwen, 2012).

Meanwhile, employers have also been striving to reduce their pension liabilities and download responsibility for retirement finances onto individual employees. Of course, many employers do not offer pension benefits, particularly if their employees are part-time, contract, casual or, generally, nonstandard. Most Canadians do not have a workplace pension plan. As of 2012, 38.4 per cent of all employees were covered by a **registered pension plan (RPP)**. The slim majority of these employees enjoying registered pension plans worked in the public sector (51.4 per cent). Reflecting women's increased public sector employment (which typically includes pension coverage), in 2012 for the first time, women's membership in RPPs equalled men's (Statistics Canada, 2014f).

Not only do almost two-thirds of Canadian workers not have registered pension plans, the nature of pension entitlement for those who enjoy it is shifting significantly. In particular, there has been a dramatic move from **defined benefit plans**[13] (which entitled retirees to a specified *income* upon retirement) toward **defined contribution plans** (which specifies workers' *contributions* to a pension fund but provides no guarantees as to the eventual payout since the eventual value of contributions would depend on investment outcomes). By 2011, 39 per cent of Canadian pension plan sponsors (and close to 80 per cent of British and U.S. employers) had closed their defined benefit plans to new entrants and replaced them with defined contribution plans. From 2001 to 2011 the number of employees participating in registered pension plans and covered by defined benefit pension plans dropped from 84 per cent to 72 per cent (with such plan holders mostly in the public sector) while defined contribution[14] plans (mostly in the private sector) continued to grow in number (Statistics Canada, 2014f).

The majority of Canadian workers (almost two-thirds of employees in 2012) who have no formal employment-based pension plans are often unable afford to solve their retirement financing by making significant contributions to **Registered Retirement Savings Plans (RRSPs)** or **Tax-Free Savings Accounts (TFSAs)** (Statistics Canada,

2014f). The latest statistics (2012) indicate that only one in four Canadian tax filers contributed to an RRSP (Statistics Canada, 2014e). Those families covered by workplace pensions (RPPs) appear to be on the "good" side of a financial divide because they also tend to have significantly more wealth (such as real estate equity, investments, or RRSPs) than families not covered by such pensions. This suggests that many of those not covered by workplace pensions are not accumulating wealth in some other fashion and, as a result, they are more likely than their RRP-covered counterparts to face aging with limited financial support (Messacar and Morissette, 2015: 6).

As a result, many seniors have very real concerns about **longevity risk**—the concern that they will outlive their retirement savings (Mackenzie, 2015). Should they outlive RRSPs and other retirement investments, such as TFSAs, retirees may be forced to live on the limited and potentially very inadequate benefits provided by the CPP/QPP, even when supplemented by the GIS and the OAS. Currently, policy advocates are debating improvements to CPP/QPP along with the possibility of an **Ontario Retirement Pension Plan** (ORPP). In the absence of such policy action, the risk of under-funded retirements and pensions adequate only to ward off destitution remain significant issues (Schirle, 2013). According to noted Canadian economist Michael Wolfson, without an expansion of CCP/QPP or the development of provincial pension initiatives, a large portion of middle-income Canadians (as many as 50 per cent) will face a dramatic decline in their standard of living in retirement—"a drop of 25 per cent or more in net income replacement by age 70" (Wolfson, 2015: 6).

At present, hemmed in by these financial and cultural realities, it appears many Canadians are not even considering "early" retirement and, in fact, are delaying their exits from paid work. In the 1980s and early 1990s there was a marked trend toward early retirement amongst Canadians 55 and over, but in 1997 the downward trend in the employment rate amongst those 55 and older reversed, and the employment rate amongst this age group has since increased. Regardless of education level, Canadian workers are postponing retirement (Carriere and Galarneau, 2012). A 2015 survey found that nearly one-third of Canadians, up from 16 per cent in 2008, expect to work full-time at age 66, and more than one-third of working Canadians surveyed fear outliving their savings. In stark contrast, in 2008, 51 per cent expected to be retired at 66 (Yew, 2015). Similarly in the United States, the percentage of workers anticipating delayed retirement increased from 33 per cent in 2009 to 43 per cent in 2013, and most are planning a delay of three or more years. By 2013, 50 per cent of US workers planned to retire after age 65 and 31 per cent plan to retire on or after age 70 (Miller and Nyce, 2014: 2). As suggested by leading Canadian researchers, perhaps we are moving toward "retirement lost" (McDonald and Donohue, 2011).

Issues and Dilemmas of Retirement

Retirement, however, is not only a complicated decision impacted by a wide variety of social and personal factors, it is also often a "process." Workers may opt for partial or phased-in retirement where they make use of organizational options to reduce their workload (for example, to half-time) as they move toward retirement. They may create their own **phased-in retirement** by retiring from their paid work and returning to the labour market in a different full-time or part-time capacity or as a self-employed worker. This **bridge retirement** allows many workers to reduce their workload while still enjoying the benefits of their paid work, including social engagement and personal fulfilment (Mei, Eales, and Fast, 2013).

A recent study of older workers who left long-term jobs (12 years or more) found that 60 per cent of those 55 to 59 and 44 per cent of those 60 to 64 were re-employed, often quite soon, within the next 10 years. Men were more likely than women to be re-employed (Bonikowska and Schellenberg, 2014). Other researchers are drawing attention to the decision to "unretire." When retirees find themselves financially insecure and lacking positive retirement experiences or they miss elements of their former jobs, they may desire to return to the paid labour market (Schlosser, Zinni, and Armstrong-Stassen, 2012). Researchers are also exploring the ways in which psychological experiences of aging encourage or discourage retirees to "work after retirement" (Fasbender, Deller, Wang, and Wiernik, 2014). In short, evidence continues to grow that an exit from paid work may not imply permanent retirement or complete withdrawal from paid activities.

Retirement continues to stand as an individual and societal dilemma, and the solution to the aging population's relationship to productive labour remains unclear. Encouraging or mandating that older workers continue their employment offers only a limited, and potentially, faulty solution. For example, some women may be able to extend their paid work activities in order to make up for opportunity costs of caring for their families, but women who have a history of lengthy dis-attachment from the labour market due to caring responsibilities are actually less inclined to extend paid work, and they also (given their limited participation in the labour force) are entitled to fewer CPP/QPP benefits (Bazel and Mintz, 2014). In short, the senior female segment of the population, which is most likely to need paid work to shore up their financial resources in retirement (especially if they are living alone as a result of divorce or separation), is least likely to do so, and also will benefit little from proposed expansions to CPP/QPP (Finch, 2014).

In this regard, it is unsettling to see that although Canada remains below average in its senior (65+) income-poverty rates, its senior poverty rate rose between 2007 and 2010 at the same time as it fell in 20 other OECD countries. Particularly at risk are senior women in Canada who are divorced or separated (OECD, 2013). A similar relationship between women, pension policies, divorce, and impoverishment has been revealed in Belgium (Peeters and Wouter, 2015). Analysts fear a return to the "bad old days" when impoverished older women were commonplace.

Staying in the paid labour force, of course, may not "work" for many seniors or their employers, and some who are delaying retirement may be far from benefitting themselves or their workplace. For example, US research suggests that delayed retirement is becoming increasingly common amongst workers who are "disengaged, unhealthy and/or stressed" (Miller and Nyce, 2014: 8). A similar point could be made regarding the increasing numbers of aging Canadians who are delaying retirement but who find themselves in precarious, insecure work without the resources to save and plan for a secure retirement. Confronted by media campaigns underscoring the difficulties and importance of retirement planning, such individuals may simply withdraw into fear and anxiety (Cracium and Flick, 2014). They remain in paid employment but their low wages mean they cannot significantly benefit from individualized solutions such as TFSAs or RRSPs.

Of course, the decision to retire, the timing of retirement, and the nature of retirement are all impacted by larger changes in the workplace and in society. To the degree to which lobbying groups are able to effectively campaign against workplace age discrimination and underline the positive attributes of older workers, the balance between work and retirement may shift. In the process of ending the chilly climate for senior workers, employers, along with organized labour and employees themselves, have a key role to play in challenging myths and stereotypes surrounding these workers (Taylor, 2013). Similarly, much depends on how employers, including the public and private sectors, actively respond to the specific needs of older workers, for example, through the introduction of various flexible working arrangements and workplace accommodations such as phased-in or bridge retirement, permanent part-time work, reduced working weeks, and working from home options. What is needed is an approach by policy-makers and employers and by employees themselves which challenges ageism, including internalized ageism, and which pushes for a more imaginative and flexible approach to policy and practice. This means, importantly, recognizing the diversities amongst seniors and providing them "with both opportunities and support" (Martin et al., 2014: 1011–12). Whether or not employers, public agencies, and workers' groups ensure that organizational policies and practices provide physical and emotional support, retraining, and appropriate rewards and benefits all will impact on whether or not older workers are able to successfully stay in the labour force (Ng and Law, 2014).

Conclusion

At present, we remain far from such an enlightened and sympathetic approach to seniors. The social debate over population aging has intensified in terms of concerns about the "costs" of seniors and even images of "greedy" seniors who are prepared to live off younger generations. A recent newspaper headline declared "Canada spending heavily on its seniors" and the accompanying article suggests that younger Canadians—"Generation Squeezed"—are being short-changed since those 65 and older are receiving three times the social funding as those 45 or younger (Oved, 2015).

Knee-jerk reactions to such issues, such as encouraging seniors to continue to work or creating a social/economic context in which they have little choice but to continue in the paid labour force, are clearly not the solution to the economic woes of an aging population and societal concerns about the **dependency ratio**. After all, many seniors are simply not healthy enough to maintain paid employment (Milan and Vezina, 2011: 27). Furthermore, of course, such a productivist (employment) approach to population aging, which pushes seniors to stay in the labour market as a solution to economic problems, completely ignores alternative perspectives on aging that focus on the significance of family relations, personal development, and a meaningful long life (Biggs, Carr, and Haapala, 2015).

As discussed in Chapter 6, Canadians of all ages are experiencing an intensification of labour market engagement. More hours, days, and years dedicated to education, training, and retraining for work; locating work; commuting to work; and maintaining work are predictably reflected in increased stress for many workers. Recent research suggests that each generation of men, and increasingly women, are spending more hours over their lifetime in paid work (Hunsley, 2013b). The realities of retirement appear to be falling into line with these pervasive and constant demands by the labour market, even into old age. Although retirement may not be lost, certainly the ill, the poor, women caregivers and immigrants all may find themselves denied the "fantasy" retirement implied by **freedom 55** (McDonald and Donohue, 2011). Many social commentators are now decrying this future scenario where more and more Canadians work until they drop or are shuffled off to palliative care; they are demanding reconsideration of the quality of life we want for ourselves and others in their senior years.

Questions for Critical Thought

1. Why are diversities amongst seniors crucial to understanding the issues surrounding Canada's aging labour force?
2. What does the generalized loss of "freedom 55" say about changes in the labour market experiences in Canada?
3. Why is retirement best understood as a "process" rather than a "decision"?

Suggested Further Resources

Gifford, C.G. 1990. *Canada's Fighting Seniors*. Toronto: Lorimer. When Prime Minister Brian Mulroney proposed limiting pension benefits, Canadian seniors rose to the challenge and shook the public discourse about the political role of seniors. This landmark episode raises questions about the future potential for senior activism.

Lloyd-Sherlock, Peter. 2010. *Population Ageing and International Development.* Bristol: The Policy Press. Unlike so many contemporary discussions which focus exclusively on industrialized economies, here the authors examine aging and developing economies and focuses in particular on India, South Africa, and Argentina.

Suggested Websites

Canadian Association of Retired Persons

www.carp.ca

The Canadian Association of Retired Persons is a national, non-profit, non-partisan organization which advocates for financial security, health care access, and freedom from age discrimination for seniors in Canada.

International Federation of Ageing

www.ifa-fiv.org

For access to international information, research, policies and statistics concerning seniors, the International Federation of Ageing—an international, non-governmental organization (founded in 1973 with support from the American Federation of Retired Persons—AARP)—is an important source.

Notes

1. Throughout "senior" refers to those age 65 or older (65+) unless otherwise specified.
2. In 2031, women will comprise the majority (53.4 per cent) of Canadians 65 and older (Milan and Vezina, 2011: 6).
3. Women constitute the majority of seniors and this pattern intensifies with age. In 2010, 63 per cent of Canadians 80 and over were women (Milan and Vezina, 2011: 7).
4. Despite dramatic improvements in health care and medical interventions, aging does tend to impact negatively on physical and mental well-being. In 2011, for example, there were almost three-quarters of a million Canadians suffering with Alzheimer's disease and other dementias, and by 2031 this figure is project to reach 1.4 million (Government of Canada, 2014: 18).
5. There are, similarly, significant variations in the aging profile of census metropolitan areas. Some, such as Peterborough and St. Catharines-Niagara approach a 20 per cent rate while others, such as Saskatoon and Calgary, had 12 per cent or fewer seniors (Statistics Canada, 2012a).
6. Part-time employment is not by itself precarious. It may be permanent, benefited, unionized, and so on. However, it is also the case that much part-time work is insecure and poorly compensated.
7. Of course, given dramatic historical developments in technology and education, these stereotypes are not without some substance. A recent study of Canada, Norway, and the United States concludes that literacy skills decline with age. Literacy is defined in terms of a complex range of prose literacy, document literacy, and quantitative literacy—"the fundamental cognitive skills used in daily life" (Green and Riddell, 2013).
8. Some regulations around retirement do persist. For example, all judges in Canada are required to retire at 70 to 75, depending on the court. Federal senators cease to hold their positions at age 75.
9. However, it should be noted that advances in technology may reduce the physical burdens of some forms of employment, and advances in vocational rehabilitations may help neutralize the employment impact of injuries.

10. Once again, there are considerable diversities in women's experience of both employment and caregiving. Aboriginal Canadians, for example, may find there are significant barriers and challenges to caregiving for elders in First Nations Communities (Habjan, Prince, and Kelley, 2012).
11. However, it must be noted that increasing numbers of grandparents are raising their grandchildren, and this obligation may translate into postponed retirement, especially for the traditional major breadwinners—men (Bailey, Haynes, and Letiecq, 2013).
12. Being "in a couple" protects women (in particular) and men from low income status. In 2008 1.8 per cent of senior women and 1.5 per cent of senior men who were living in a couple were categorized as low income after tax. In contrast, 17.1 per cent of women and 12.1 per cent of men living alone were low income.
13. Not surprisingly, workers who are covered by a defined benefit plan tend to retire earlier (Miller and Nyce, 2014).
14. There are also various hybrid or composite pension plans which make up about 16 per cent of RPPs by 2012 (Statistics Canada, 2014f).

11 Unions, Industrial Relations, and Forms of Resistance

Learning Objectives

- To provide a profile of union membership in Canada
- To discuss the impact on working conditions and relevance of unions within the current economic climate
- To consider the role of unions in the new economy
- To question whether unions are effective vehicles of social change

Introduction

Canadians are passionate about the pros and cons of unions. Certainly, unions and the possibility of strikes are topics, like religion and politics, many wish to avoid at social gatherings. Those who champion the cause of unions point to the better wages, benefits, and working conditions within unionized workplaces, as well as to the heightened sense of security experienced by union members. For the naysayers, unions, at best, are annoying especially when they "shut down" services such as postal outlets, city buses, or waste collections; or prompt members to engage in work-to-rule campaigns as has been the case with teachers; or set up pickets, blocking entrances to businesses and services. The image of unions has often been tarnished by the media through their presentation of unions as disruptive organizations working on behalf of "greedy" workers at the public's expense. Ironically, many of the newsreaders, writers, and videographers presenting materials describing organized workers "disrupting" daily life are unionized themselves.[1]

Both the image and relevance of unions have recently been under attack. Some Canadians question the relevance of unions within the "new economy" which is dominated by services—fast food restaurants, retail outlets, movie theatres, and other entertainment establishments assumed often to be staffed by students or others desiring temporary or part-time jobs. Possible disruptions of services are regarded as inconvenient and union wages are targeted as contributing to skyrocketing prices of a range of consumer goods, from groceries to clothing and household goods. Others voice strong concerns about working in a de-unionized workplace and about the attacks on trade unions and workers' rights under neoliberalism.

This chapter starts with a profile of union membership in Canada and then considers the impact of unions and their contribution to positive work environments and equality. We then raise a number of questions regarding power and the "union advantage," while examining the role of unions within a service economy. Finally we consider cultural shifts toward individualism (individual responsibility and individual success), away from collective responsibility, and we question how unions might counteract this shift.

Unions Today: The New and Old Economy

In a landmark case in 2007, the *B.C. Health Services* decision, the Supreme Court ruled that collective bargaining is a fundamental right protected by the guarantee of freedom of association in Section 2(d) of the *Canadian Charter of Rights and Freedoms*. Unions' rights, however, are not without limits.[2] Employers are required to consider the union's demands in good faith, and Canadian labour laws impose the statutory duties to do so. However, it is not required that employers agree to any particular set of union demands nor is it even required that an agreement be reached. Collective bargaining is a complex process, with much legal wrangling involved.

In Canada, the majority of public sector workers, including teachers, nurses, and social service workers, along with private-sector workers in heavy industry and mining are more likely than others to be union members. Workers in retail, food services, tourism, banking, and finance are least likely to be union members. In 2014, 28.8 per cent of the Canadian labour force was unionized, down from 37.6 per cent in 1981 (Statistics Canada, 2015e). This included 71.3 per cent among workers in the public sector and 15.2 per cent of those in private-sector jobs (2014) (Statistics Canada, 2015e). The overall decline in the **unionization rate** or **union density** has been uneven, with greater declines experienced by men as compared with women, as indicated in Figure 11.1, and by younger workers, especially males. The declines in unionization rates may largely be explained by the economic shift from manufacturing and industries and occupations that traditionally enjoyed relatively high rates of unionization to the service sector, where rates are relatively low and unions have faced difficulties in organizing the workforces. The relatively high rates of unionization amongst women may be explained by their concentration in health care, social services, teaching, and public administration.

Permanent, full-time workers had the highest rates of unionization while those working part-time or, in temporary positions are least likely to be members of unions. As Figure 11.2 indicates, those working full-time, whether they are in permanent or temporary positions, are more likely to be unionized than workers in part-time positions. Again, this pattern relates to the type of occupation and the strength of union penetration in particular sectors or occupational groups.

The lag in union membership amongst part-time workers relates somewhat to union organizers' long-standing misconceptions regarding part-time workers'

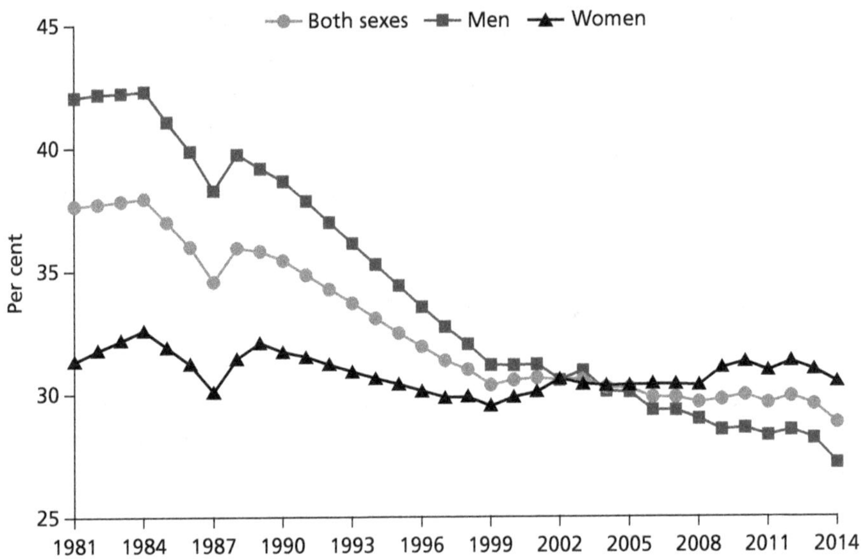

Figure 11.1 Unionization Rates of Employed Individuals Aged 17 to 64, 1981 to 2014
Source: http://www.statcan.gc.ca/pub/11-630-x/11-630-x2015005-eng.htm

relationship to work and job tenure. For many years union organizers were reluctant to organize part-time workers, viewing them as temporarily attached to their jobs. As indicated in Chapter 6, the majority of part-time workers are mothers who are assumed to be focusing primarily on balancing their home-based responsibilities and students who have their sights on full-time careers following graduation. Expectations of a low level of commitment to their jobs combined with a number of logistical factors have affected union organizing amongst part-time workers. Many organizers have argued that organizing campaigns are costly for unions and should be directed toward full-time labour forces where there has traditionally been

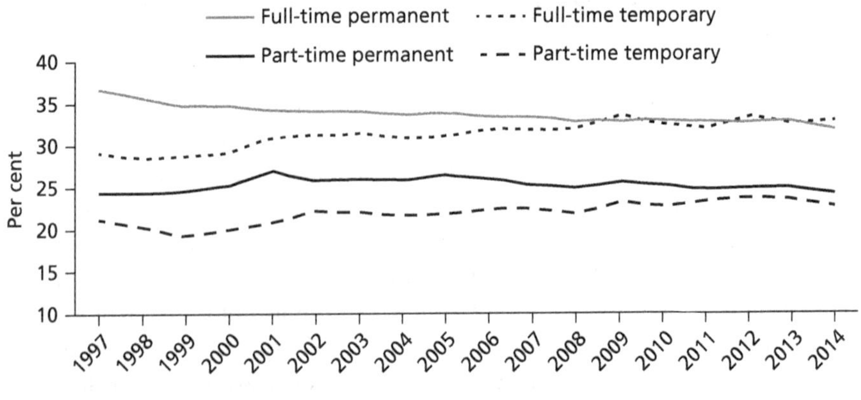

Figure 11.2 Unionization Rates by Type of Work and Job Permanency, Canada, 1997–2014
Source: Labour Force Survey (LFS), Custom Tabulation, CANSIM

greater success. Costs associated with organizing, along with assumptions about the "revolving door" within the part-time work force, weak workplace cultures, and disconnected work groups, have raised barriers to organizing, despite the proliferation of part-time employment, particularly in the service sector.

Keeping Balance: The Role of Unions

For decades on almost every picket line across the country, striking workers have sung: "Solidarity Forever, Solidarity Forever, Solidarity Forever, For the Union Makes Us Strong." These lyrics mark the labour movement. They ring out at rallies, Labour Day festivals, and May Day events, and provide a backdrop to site-specific slogans and chants on picket lines everywhere. Written by Ralph Chaplin in 1915, these lyrics,[3] (sung to the tune of "The Battle Hymn of the Republic") were a testament to the Industrial Workers of the World (IWW) and the "One Big Union" movement. In writing what has become the theme song of the labour movement, Chaplin captured the attention of labour activists everywhere by underscoring the importance of "strength in numbers" during a period of intense labour turbulence (Chaplin, 1968). As the lyrics suggest, unions represent the belief that workers can get a better deal at the workplace (better wages for their labour, benefits for themselves and their families, and protections against unscrupulous employers) by combining forces and confronting employers collectively.

As the agents representing workers, unions engage in **collective bargaining**, the process of negotiating the terms and conditions of work with an employer on behalf of the employees. The outcome of the bargaining process is the **collective agreement**, the legal document or contract that specifies the terms and conditions of work within the establishment. The collective agreement is the workers' book of rights. The specific outcomes of collective bargaining are meant to improve conditions of work, as well as to prevent the occurrence of injustices at work. The general outcomes of collective bargaining, however, are far-reaching, benefitting both unionized and non-unionized workers, as well as communities.

About 85 per cent of Canadians in the paid labour force are employees and about 15 per cent are self-employed (Statistics Canada, 2015f). As employees, workers are involved in an employment relationship that is fundamentally unbalanced with regard to power, decision-making, and advantage. Workers rely on their jobs as their source of support for themselves and their families, and often find themselves at crossroads having to choose between satisfying the whims of their employers, and tending to personal or familial matters. Balancing these two facets of life becomes increasingly difficult and not without considerable risk as "good" jobs disappear and as unemployment rates escalate. Some workers, including women, members of minority groups, recent immigrants, Aboriginal workers, workers with disabilities, and members of the LGBTQ communities may be further limited in their search for meaningful work or from accessing certain types of jobs. On the other side of the equation, employers have the upper hand, as they can easily replace most members of their labour forces. To individual workers, long lines of unemployed workers represent the competition, but to employers they represent choice. In the employer–employee relationship, the employer has the clear advantage while the employee is caught in a highly dependent and lopsided relationship. Although most workers may be easily replaced, especially in times of high unemployment, employers would be at a loss if they found themselves having to replace too many workers at once, as productivity levels may dip, institutional memory would be lost, and profits may decline. Employers rely on their regular, experienced, and skilled labour forces and this helps to tip the balance of power, at least slightly, in workers' favour. When workers act collectively, their power is enhanced. Working together they form an essential component of labour and production processes.

Unions: Compensation, Benefits, and Other Rewards

T.G.I.F.—thank goodness it's Friday—is a popular thought on the minds of many workers on Friday mornings. This slogan may be regarded as a testimony to unions' historical achievement in reducing work hours and guaranteeing workers time off. In addition to weekends, generations of hard-fought union struggles have brought Canadians the eight-hour day, paid lunch breaks, workplace health and safety legislation, employment standards (minimum wages, overtime pay, rest breaks), income supports for new parents, maternity leave, training for unemployed workers (labour market adjustment programs), public pensions, and equal pay for equal work. And the list goes on (Canadian Labour Congress, 2015).[4] Unions have helped to organize the extension of negotiated workplace-based achievements to the whole workforce by pressing for legislation to cover all workers. What this means is that not only union members have benefitted from unionization, but all workers and their communities have gained as well. Empirical evidence indicates that strong unions have a spillover effect on equality, social cohesion, and even environmental protection within the broader society. International evidence shows that where unions are strong, they reduce the pay gap between workers and management, men and women, racial minorities, and other workers. The ILO reports that, across 20 OECD nations, a 1 per cent increase in union density is associated with a 1.5 per cent reduction in the incidence of low-wage employment (ILO, 2015). All over the world unions are major forces in reducing inequality and poverty and broadening access to basic support for everyone.

Comparing the differences for workers in unionized and non-unionized environments, the advantages of unions are clear. The **union advantage** not only contributes to increased wages and more benefits, but it generally improves the workplace atmosphere and the quality of life of the workers (CLC, 2015). In Canada across the board, considering gender, age, employment status, hours of work, and industry, union members' wages outstrip those of non-unionized workers. For example, young workers who are unionized earn on average $3.16 an hour more than their non-unionized counterparts while unionized women earn, on average, $6.89 more than women who are not members of unions (CLC, 2015).

Table 11.1 compares union and non-union hourly wage rates by gender and age. The extra dollars contribute to communities by easing the way to home ownership and allowing union members to conduct business with local companies and service providers, including dentists, physiotherapists, naturopaths, and others whose fees may not be affordable on non-union incomes.

Within the OECD countries between 1980 and 2010, declining union density along with growing reliance on minimum wages has contributed considerably to increasing inequality within advanced economies, including Canada, (Jaumotte and Buitron, 2015a; Jaumotte and Buitron, 2015b; OECD, 2014a). A recent study found that the rising incomes of the top 10 per cent of earners was strongly associated with declining union density, and that higher union density was linked to greater income equality overall. This indicates that unions make a difference not only in redistributing income, but also in workers' bargaining power and their influence on corporate decisions, including the compensation of CEOs and other top earners (Jaumotte and Buitron, 2015a).

There is evidence that unions narrow the earnings gaps for visible minority workers. Hou and Coloumbe (2010) found that earnings of Canadian-born visible minority workers and whites were the same for similar jobs within the public sector, where union density is very high compared to the private sector. In the private sector, minority men earned considerably less than whites. Black men experience a large gap within the private sector, whereas Black women are paid considerably less in both the private and public sectors. Among Chinese and South Asians, small gaps exist for men only in the private sector. McInturff and Tulloch (2014) have found that in the public service, unions have been the mainstay

Table 11.1 Labour Force Survey Estimates (LFS), Average Hourly Wages of Employees (current dollars) by Union Coverage, Sex, and Age Group, 2008–2014

Union Coverage	Sex	Age Group	2008	2009	2010	2011	2012	2013	2014
Union coverage	Males	15 to 24 years	15.33	15.54	16.34	16.54	16.55	17.03	17.68
		25 to 54 years	26.19	27.02	27.79	28.2	28.77	29.58	29.98
		55 years and over	27.13	27.66	28.43	28.52	29.09	29.52	30.23
	Females	15 to 24 years	14.88	15.19	15.38	16.09	16.84	16.35	17.19
		25 to 54 years	24.38	25.24	25.97	26.52	27.21	27.8	28.49
		55 years and over	24.54	25.17	25.9	26.18	26.34	27.3	27.47
No union coverage	Males	15 to 24 years	12.59	13.05	13.11	13.5	13.82	14.22	14.43
		25 to 54 years	24.82	25.39	25.54	25.89	26.76	27.31	27.87
		55 years and over	24.33	24.56	25.24	25.65	26.55	27.09	27.32
	Females	15 to 24 years	11.14	11.58	11.83	12.15	12.46	12.76	13.01
		25 to 54 years	19.35	20.12	20.39	21.02	21.62	21.97	22.45
		55 years and over	18.47	18.86	19.67	20.04	20.47	21.35	21.55

Source: Statistics Canada. Table 282-0074 - Labour force survey estimates (LFS), wages of employees by union coverage, sex and age group, annual (current dollars unless otherwise noted), CANSIM (database). (accessed: 2015-07-14)

of support in strengthening workers' ability to fend off discrimination and employers' arbitrary actions. Comparing wages of workers in the public and private sectors, the researchers found that within the private sector, Aboriginal workers, visible minority workers, and women earned 30 to 44 per cent less than others with the same level of education (McInturff and Tullock, 2014: 5). Among those with a university education, Aboriginal workers still earn 44 per cent less than others while women earn 27 per cent less than men and visible minority workers earn 20 per cent less than their non-visible minority counterparts. In the public sector, where union density sits at 75 per cent, these gaps are significantly narrowed to 14 per cent for Aboriginals, 12 per cent for visible minority workers, and 18 per cent for women (2014: 6). While these gaps are still unacceptably large, it is clear that access to union representation is a significant factor in reducing inequalities, both in terms of earnings as well as in benefits and access to services won through collective bargaining.

What Do Unions Do?

Through collective bargaining, workers' representatives establish the terms and conditions of the employment relationship on behalf of workers[5] in a particular workplace, company, or industry. Once it is **certified**, the union is the legal **bargaining agent** for the **bargaining unit**, which defines the group of workers covered by the collective agreement. By forming unions and negotiating collectively for better wages, pensions, and benefits, and safer and more comfortable working conditions, workers aim to offset the power imbalance between the employer and each individual worker. Because it would be difficult for employers to replace their entire workforce at once, workers have much more clout dealing with their employer as a united group, rather than one at a time—especially when the workers are collectively willing to "flex their muscles" by imposing some costs on an employer through work stoppages, work-to-rule campaigns, or other collective actions in order to back up their bargaining goals. A union is simply the workers' representative that aims to establish fair parameters within which to counterbalance employers' power. Unions represent workers' historical attempts to share control over the conditions of their employment, and to protect themselves from competition, some pressures of the market, and employers' unfettered power.

Unions may be organized in many different ways. Unions may represent workers with a particular skill or profession. Some of the earliest unions in Canada, for example, were organized around particular *crafts* or trades; this model of unionization still applies in the construction industry, and in specialized professions (such as teachers' unions, medical associations, and nurses' unions). In Canada, bargaining mostly takes place at the local level, not at the industrial level. Some employers bargain with several unions. In other words, bargaining is decentralized. Some argue that this decentralized bargaining system tends to weaken the bargaining power of Canadian unions compared to unions in countries such as Germany and the Scandinavian countries where bargaining across whole industries is common.

Fragmented, decentralized bargaining reflects the reality of very different issues and economic circumstances in different workplaces and sectors of the economy, as well as in Canada's diverse regional economies.

Beginning in the 1930s, *industrial* unions were organized, representing most or all workers employed in a particular workplace, and thus uniting workers with different skills and job functions. In North America, the standard practice is to have a single union covering a specified group of workers within a workplace, or a group of workers with a particular skill or professional designation (e.g., carpenters, musicians, nurses). In some countries, it is possible for workers to choose among different unions, all operating in the same workplace, depending on their political or religious convictions. In a number of European countries and in Latin America, unions take on a broader function of political and/or community organizing, in addition to focusing on improving conditions within specific workplaces. The goal of this broader, more politicized trade unionism is to bring workers together to engage in campaigns for political and legislative change, economic and community development, and social justice.

Within any workplace, workers may decide that a union would best represent their collective interests by eliminating piecemeal arrangements made between individuals and management and by removing competitiveness, favouritism, and secrecy. In some cases, interested workers initiate contact with a union of their choice, whereas in others, organizers from a particular union may present themselves to the workers. Organizers will work with the group to explain the benefits of unionization while they attempt to gather signatures from a sufficient number of workers in order to take the list of sympathizers to the labour board for certification. After a union is certified to represent a group of workers, its central activity is to engage in collective bargaining with the employer in order to develop a collective agreement covering wages, benefits, and conditions of work. The collective agreement is in effect for a specified time period (usually two to three years). Once a collective agreement is in place, union representatives provide service to members by intervening in disputes with employers, carrying **grievances** forward, and educating members on their collective agreements, the labour movement, and workplace issues. Union representatives accompany a member through the grievance process when the worker feels that the employer has violated the terms of the collective agreement. If it is determined that the employer has violated the agreement, the employer is legally bound to change practice in accordance with the conditions specified in the agreement.

At any time, hundreds of collective agreements are active. In 2013, for example, 1,014 collective agreements were in effect, covering over 2.8 million Canadian workers (Government of Canada, Labour Program, 2014). For some Canadians, the idea of unions conjures up "trouble"—strikes, lockouts, or other disruptions to businesses and services. But strikes and other stoppages are fairly rare events and when they do occur, they are usually of short duration. Between 2004 and 2013, there were between 151 and 297 work stoppages per year, with a low of 151 in 2006 and 2013 and highs of 281 in 2012 and 297 in 2004 (Government of Canada, Labour Program, 2014). While some see strikes as an inconvenience, the right to strike is a cornerstone in Canada's labour relations system. For employers, the threat of a striking workforce and for the workers involved, the prospect of living on "**strike pay**" often leads the parties to settle quickly and reasonably. In Canada, unlike in the United States, it is illegal for employers to permanently replace workers who are on strike, and in both Quebec and British Columbia, employers cannot bring in replacements (offensively referred to as "scabs") during a legal strike. In Canada the Supreme Court has declared that the right to strike for unionized workers is protected by the Constitution. According to Judge Rosalie Abella, a strike is "an affirmation of the dignity and autonomy of employees in their working lives" (cited in Fine, 2015). Judge Abella's position is that the right to strike helps to even the playing field between employers and employees, distances itself from historical notions of striking workers as criminal conspirators, and is backed by modern labour law and international human rights agreements aiming to protect workers from difficulties they confronted in the past.

Protection and Security

While workers join unions primarily for economic reasons, they are also comforted by the knowledge that the union will work to ensure fairness at work. For individual workers, the collective agreement backed by the processes of grievance and **arbitration** symbolizes democracy at work. Most importantly, through their union, individual workers have a formal contract of employment that can be readily enforced. Members may grieve dismissal, disciplinary actions, and harassment by supervisors. Depending on the terms specified within the collective agreement, they may also grieve being passed over for promotion, favouritism by managers and supervisors, and unsolicited "changes in practice" to work assignments, hours of work, and work schedules. In non-union workplaces, workers must rely on informal means of settling issues. In some cases, this process opens the door to abuses and arbitrary decisions by management, and may result in termination for the worker. Although some large, non-union enterprises develop formal, written rules and procedures for their workforces, such methods do not offer workers the protection of a legally binding collective agreement. Without the backing of a union, workers must seek legal services privately, often resulting in exorbitant costs. For many workers, the risks of suing employers outweigh the possible award gained in a successful case.

In unionized shops, it is the backing of law that is most critical in safeguarding workers' rights at work. As we discussed in Chapter 5, minimum employment standards laws provide for minimum wages, maximum hours of work, and safe working conditions in all workplaces. Under the protection of Employment Standards alone, employees are left to their own devices to lodge a complaint against their employer. Not surprisingly, very few workers file complaints with their current employers for fear of reprisals (Mojtehedzadeh, 2015d). Often workers will lodge a complaint after dismissal but again they run into roadblocks as there is very weak enforcement of Employment Standards, employers are rarely penalized for infractions, and there are very few inspections of violating companies. Most commonly, workers file complaints for non-payment of wages, yet vulnerable workers are not provided with necessary backup to battle with their "Goliath."

Security and Satisfaction

With the backing of a union, workers are generally more satisfied not only with their jobs, but on a variety of levels as a result of the measure of security unions provide. In a study that examined union density and union membership involving 14 countries, including Canada, researchers found that life satisfaction was directly related to a country's level of union density and union membership (Flavin et al., 2010). Analyzing the responses of 14,000 surveys, researchers found that union members scored higher on the life satisfaction scale than non-members. Union membership raised life satisfaction more for workers earning below-average incomes, but less for those earning higher incomes. This difference may reflect the important work of unions in providing a level of security for lower-wage workers, many of whom may be caught in jobs for which they are overqualified or which provide few challenges. Workers with higher incomes may experience greater satisfaction with the intrinsic rewards and non-wage elements of their jobs. The study also noted that the most vulnerable workers are most positively affected by the security afforded with the higher levels of union density.

Some union naysayers assume that unionized workers are lazy, that they are protected by the union and therefore get away with minimal work. While a minority of workers in all work environments prefer to sit on the job, this is not the case for union members in particular. There is ample evidence that union members' productivity on average is higher than that of non-union workers. This in part may be due to the fact that they are happier at work. In general they report that their higher wages and the security they receive in their working environment contribute to a profound sense of pride and this makes them more willing to maintain high levels of productivity.

Despite the advantages unions clearly afford both to individuals as well as to their communities, even low-paid, precarious workers who would benefit greatly from union protection often express envy and bitterness toward workers who do enjoy the benefits of union protection. Their position implies that if the union members did not have the advantages afforded through unionization, then low-wage workers would be better off. "Blame-the-union," a sentiment voiced by some workers, ironically mimics the attitudes of corporate executives and conservative politicians who scapegoat organized labour for the economy's failings. In general, anti-union sentiment accelerates during economic downturns and fiscal crises, when unemployment rates are high and the public purse is opened to bail out business and industry while enduring the pressure to strengthen the social safety net. Under these circumstances, unions are portrayed as exclusionary, protecting only privileged workers and offering little to counterbalance economic woes. Yet, no country has ever achieved prosperity and created a large middle class without strong unions. The Everyday Work Experiences Box 11.1 examines the dilemma union members experience when they confront hostility within their community.

Box 11.1 Everyday Work Experiences

Dropping Down the Pay and Benefit Scale

Studying plant closures and interviewing men and women who have lost their jobs is heartbreaking. Most workers have not only lost their "work family" and source of economic security, but closures also signal dramatic changes in lifestyle. For unionized workers, the job loss comes with the loss of union protection, their link to the labour movement and connection to the union brotherhood and sisterhood. Some workers feel these losses immediately, expressing concern about working in a non-union shop and worrying about inconsistencies in pay scales, recognition of skills, and overall fairness. Some worry that they may be short-changed for no reason, just because the new boss may take a disliking to them, or "play favourites."

For unionized workers who have experienced a plant closure, finding a job to replace the job they lost is an uphill battle, not only because of the unrelentingly high rates of unemployment, and the long lines of job seekers at every opening, but because of the working conditions and expectations in non-union shops. In some cases, wages are half the rates they were earning in their unionized positions and there is forced overtime with no refusals allowed. There may be few, if any, benefits, and in some cases, working conditions are unsafe. These workers know that they cannot file a complaint and expect to keep their jobs.

At the same time, members of the public are not necessarily supportive. When Kellogg's announced the closure of its London, Ontario plant, an icon in the community for more than 100 years, many locals blamed the workers, declaring that they were losing their jobs because their (unionized) pay rates were too high and the company was assumed to be losing money. Considering profit and loss statements and the global reach of the corporation, this was clearly not the case. A few years prior to the closure announcement when Kellogg's locked the workers out in the middle of a bitterly cold winter, some passers-by who mistakenly thought the workers were on strike, rather than on lockout, jeered at those on the lines, calling the workers "greedy" and expressing no sympathy for their loss of work. Despicable behaviour? Yes. But, what is hardest to understand is why some people would prefer to see others (perhaps like themselves) working at or near the bottom, rather than raising the bar for all by struggling for decent wages that support families and enrich lives and communities.

The Fight for and the Case against Unions

The case against unions was made loudly in the United States in 2013, and again in 2014, when Hostess—makers of the iconic American snack Twinkies—announced that its plants would be closing, putting 18,500 workers on the street. Emotions ran high as consumers mourned the possible loss of the popular snack while the Bakery, Confectioners, Tobacconists, and Grain Millers (BCTGM) International Union bore the brunt of consumers' ire (Ferguson, 2012). The company announced its decision to close after engaging in a 10-month battle with its unions and a three-day strike by members of the Baker's union, prompted by a judge's decision to force the union to accept devastating concessions, including deep wage cuts and limits on the workers' pension plan (Feintzeig, 2012). Hostess sold its snack brands to private equity firms in 2013, a move that allowed a number of plants to remain open and the products to remain on stores' shelves, but a few days before the 84-year-old Schiller Park Plant in Chicago was to enter contract negotiations with the union, the closure of this location was announced, prompting a backlash against the union for the demise of the plant and the loss of 400 jobs (Bomkamp and Cancino, 2014).

Across the border in Canada, in December 2013, Kellogg's announced that it was closing its plant in London, Ontario. As in the Hostess case in the US, the workers at Kellogg's were organized by the BCTGM. The workers had always met all production targets and, unlike other Kellogg's plants, the London operation was highly adaptive, with the capability of producing corn, rice, wheat, and mixed grain cereals and all box sizes. The majority of workers were very satisfied with their jobs, including their wages and working conditions, and described the plant as their "second home" and their work group as their "Kellogg's family." But when the company moved the "wheat line" 350 kilometres down the road to Belleville, Ontario to a non-union facility a few years earlier, some workers, including a number who had previously experienced a plant closure, saw the "writing on the wall" and warned co-workers that a closure was possible.

Discussion surrounding unions and union rights has been at the boiling point for a few years, particularly in the US To understand the roots of the issue and the impact on Canada, we have to consider the establishment of free collective bargaining and union rights dating back to the years following the Great Depression. In the face of bitter opposition from the Republican Party, in 1935 the US Congress passed the *National Labor Relations Act*, also known as the Wagner Act, which guaranteed the basic rights of workers to organize and to engage in collective bargaining to establish better wages and working conditions for workers.

Meanwhile in Canada, workers had organized into unions or collectives since the early years of industrialization. Workers sought basic rights and protections akin to those provided in modern day employment standards. With solidarity building amongst workers, the federal government established the Department of Labour in 1900 in order to settle disputes between employers and workers, as well as to promote fairer policies and safe working conditions. Settling disputes between workers and

THE CANADIAN PRESS/Dave Chidley

Discarded work boots rest in front of the Kellogg's Canada sign at the Kellogg's plant in London, Ontario. The plant closed in December 2014 after a 107-year history of producing cereal, leaving 500 people out of work.

employers continued to be a thorny issue, one that would not be resolved easily. Major actions such as the Winnipeg General Strike and growing concerns over the Depression and the war prompted the government to find ways to dissipate labour activism. As a solution to the "labour problem," the government repressed militant unions such as the **International Workers of the World** (IWW) and the **One Big Union** and introduced the Wartime Labour Relations Regulations, known as Order in Council P.C. 1003 in 1944. P.C. 1003 introduced the provisions for collective bargaining as we know it today in Canada, outlawed unfair labour practices, and established a Labour Relations Board.

A few years later, in 1946, Supreme Court Justice Ivan Rand introduced the system of automatic dues check-off, known as the **Rand formula,** whereby the payment of union dues is automatically deducted from each employee's paycheque within unionized establishments, regardless of the workers' union status. The purpose of the Rand formula is to ensure that employees do not opt out of the union in order to avoid paying dues while reaping the benefits of union membership.[6] This does not mean that union membership is compulsory.[7] Under the Rand formula, individuals choose whether or not to join the union, but everyone pays dues. The system operates in a similar fashion to taxes. Citizens elect governments that levy taxes to pay for programs. If taxes were "voluntary" then there would be chaos with respect to paying for tax-supported systems such as health, education, and hospitals, along with other programs and services. In such a scenario, the social safety net would fray beyond repair and society would collapse. Those who oppose the Rand or similar dues check-off formulae are referred to as right-to-work advocates, and their stance is decidedly anti-union. In any case, unions are bound by the legal requirement of the "duty of fair representation" to represent all members of the bargaining unit whether or not they are members of the union.

In the United States, union security as provided through the Rand formula is not guaranteed. In 1947 the Taft-Hartley Act provided states with the authority to pass legislation disallowing automatic dues check-off, as in Canada, thereby granting individual workers the right to opt out of union membership despite reaping the benefits of the union within organized workplaces. This is known as Right-to-Work (RTW) legislation. The legislation entitles workers with all the benefits the union provides, including taking up their grievances, without their having to pay any of the costs (Gould and Kimball, 2015). The Right-to-Work movement has incurred real costs for workers. RTW legislation has worked to hinder unions in their attempts to bargain for better wages, benefits, and working conditions and, as a result, both union and non-union workers in RTW states have lower wages and fewer benefits compared with workers in other states (Gould and Kimball, 2015).

Currently there are 26 states that have RTW legislation. Gould and Shierholz (2011) have found that average hourly wages are 16 per cent higher in non-RTW states. RTW laws also limit the extent of employer-paid health care and pension benefits. With respect to workplace health and safety, researchers have found that the occupational fatality rate in the construction industry is 34 per cent higher in RTW states than in non-RTW states and that union density has a positive impact on workplace safety (Madland, Walter, and Eisenbrey, 2012). Clearly, RTW laws limit unionization (Moore, 1998). Limiting the collection of dues crushes union security, hampers the ability to service members fully, and dismantles unionization at its very core, as a collectivist organization (Stanford, 2012). In unionized workplaces, the union is required by law to bargain on behalf of all members of the bargaining unit. The RTW laws effectively limit unionization, placing individual entitlement ahead of collective well-being.

Proponents of RTW created a stir in 2009 when US President Obama sought to pass the *Employees Free Choice Act* (EFCA) aimed at moving US labour legislation closer to that of Canada. Right-wing pundits opposing the EFCA began to suggest that Canada's labour relations legislation contributed to limited choices for Canadian workers and that the Canadian system unfairly taxed employers and contributed to unemployment and job losses. Canadian labour scholars, however, have analyzed the arguments made by American right-wingers and concluded that their arguments are seriously flawed (Pupo, 2009; CRWS, 2009). Developments in the US, particularly the spread of right-to-work laws, especially in bordering states such as Indiana, and the suppression of collective bargaining rights in Wisconsin and elsewhere, clearly exert economic and political influence over developments in Canada. With the push for right-to-work laws in the US, conservative Canadian political parties (the Saskatchewan Party, the Wild Rose Alliance, and the Ontario Progressive Conservatives) introduced proposals mirroring those of the American right-to-work schemes (Stanford, 2012). Clearly, the post-war thinking that unionization was a reasonable means by which to manage income distribution and workplace relations has been swept aside.

A serious concern for Canada is whether US-based multinationals operating in Canada will repatriate their Canadian operations to RTW states to sidestep the considerably stronger labour laws. Caterpillar, for example, relocated its plant from London, Ontario to a RTW state (Cohn, 2012; Stanford, 2012) and Kellogg's moved most of the work from its London, Ontario to plants in the US while keeping its non-unionized operation in Belleville, Ontario open. In a study comparing union strength in Canada and the US, noted scholar Barry Eidlin (2015) demonstrates that the higher levels of union density in Canada have slowed the rate of the growing inequality as compared to the US and concludes that unions have played an important role in decreasing the class divide. In studying the growth of inequality in both Canada and the US between 1913 and 2012, Eidlin found that the pattern of growing inequality in both countries was similar until 1980. Since 1980, inequality continued to grow, but at a slower rate in Canada. Eidlin attributes this to the higher union density in Canada, noting that unions provide a measure of balance within the political process by defending working-class interests and contributing to more progressive labour laws. Countries with strong labour movements enjoy greater levels of equality because unions advocate for policies that benefit all workers. Unions challenge the power of employers in the workplace and generally within the economy. Clearly, strengthening the labour movement is the key to addressing growing levels of inequality, privilege, and power overall.

The Union Advantage: Preserving the Middle Class

Most Canadians understand the union's role in bargaining for higher wages. But unions also have a tremendous impact on lifestyle and life chances, prompting researchers to refer to union membership is "a ticket into middle-class stability" (Mackenzie and Shillington, 2015). Earnings amongst most union members are higher than average compared to those of non-unionized workers, and this has an impact on the quality and condition of life for individuals and their families as well as for the broader community. Among full-time workers earning "middle and upper middle class" wages, falling in the sixth to ninth deciles of income earners, about 47 per cent are union members, while only 8 per cent of Canada's lowest income earners belonged to a union (ibid.,: 12). Overall, between 1997 and 2011 the percentage of unionized workers remained stable at about 27 per cent. In the private sector, however, unionized jobs dropped from 21 to 14 per cent, resulting in plummeting wages that fell outside the "middle class." In Canada, as in the United Kingdom and the United States, a significant portion of full-time workers earn less than a middle-class wage (that is, at or below the fifth decile), and in real terms that means that these workers struggle to afford decent housing, to pay for their children's education, to engage in cultural events, to take part in recreational activities, and even to access some medical and dental services. According to the World Economic Forum (2013), one of the most serious global risks over the next decade is severe income disparity leading to financial collapse. Worldwide, the numbers of those in poverty are growing exponentially while wealth is becoming more concentrated in a global economy marked by risk and fragility (Lagarde, 2015).

While unions most familiarly fight for wages and benefits, or engage in what is known as **business unionism**, some unions adopt a much wider role by engaging in **social unionism**, becoming a voice working to preserve quality of life for all workers. They have joined forces, for example, with anti-poverty activists to promote the living wage (Jackson, 2012a), with social activists working on campaigns to promote social justice for migrant workers, and generally to support safety, security, and equality at work for members of the LGBTQ community. The labour movement continues to fight for expansion of public pensions, against privatization of public health care, for a public school system and accessible post-secondary education, for expanded childcare services, and for improvements to income support programs like employment insurance (EI) (CLC, 2015). The movement is concerned with access to work, fairness in community life, and promoting a collectivist outlook.

Ironically, businesses need unions too as they ultimately rely on the purchasing power of growing numbers within communities to thrive and expand. In communities that have experienced plant closures and accompanying de-unionization, small businesses feel the pinch—from coffee shops to retail outlets, and from personal services, such as hair and nail salons, to professional services, including dental hygiene and physiotherapy. Communities lose vibrancy, small communities are hollowed out, and the age range within some areas narrows as younger generations, who are more apt to spend on housing and consumer goods, move to find work. Even a rich country like the US is experiencing growing inequality, poverty, and hunger without a strong labour movement to improve on the distribution of wealth and income. In recent years, for example, corresponding to declining union density and the RTW movement, the US economy, one of the wealthiest in the world, has experienced growing rates of poverty that are among the highest levels of any developed country (US Census Bureau, 2013). In other words, union presence is one of the most important factors affecting equality. In Scandinavian countries where unionization rates are more than double the Canadian rates, the range of wages is narrow and the approach has been directed toward raising wages of lower income workers, rather than focusing on wage gains for union members (Krassa and Radcliff, 2014; Bergh, 2011).

Unions and Equality

Focusing on wages and benefits alone provides too narrow an understanding of the labour movement and its goals. While bread-and-butter issues do remain pivotal in collective bargaining, the labour movement aims to improve working conditions, access to work, and the general well-being of all workers. Where union density is high, there is a spill-over effect; that is, wages within a sector or region are similar whether or not the shop is unionized (Fang and Verma, 2002). As a further bonus, union wages within a community help workers who have traditionally been disadvantaged in the labour market, such as younger and less experienced workers and victims of discrimination including women, and immigrant and racialized workers (Walters and Mishel, 2003). With a more level playing field in terms of wage costs, employers compete on the basis of productivity and quality. In union shops, higher levels of productivity measured in terms of output per hours worked ultimately finance the union wage premium. Consumer goods produced by unionized workers may carry higher price tags in order to cover the higher wages, but this in turn boosts the economy as well. There are, indeed, hidden "costs" attached to the lower price of cheaply produced goods.

With regard to further contributing to equality and levelling the playing field, many unions engage in campaigns against discrimination, to promote social justice, and to stop violence against women. Many collective agreements include non-discrimination clauses beyond those mandated by law, and some establish pay and employment equity exercises that exceed legal requirements. Unionized workers can generally count on their union to ensure that their employers remain attentive to pay equity, employment equity, and other such measures and in fact are on record for having fought for their workers' rights in long, costly legal matters. For example, after a 10 year legal battle, the Communications, Energy & Paperworkers Union (CEP)[8] won a major pay equity settlement of $178 million in a landmark case against Bell Canada in 2002. The Canadian Human Rights Commission ruled that male and female operators had been paid differential rates and that 800 former female employees had suffered pay discrimination.

While unions have made some important equity gains, their work in ensuring an inclusive and fair labour force is far from complete. A recent study in Canada found that although union membership has generally risen for immigrants, visible minority immigrants experience greater difficulty accessing unionized jobs as well as promotions and career advancements compared with white immigrants and native-born Canadians (Verma, Reitz, and Banerjee, 2015; Keung, 2014). Unionization among visible minorities is lower than for the Canadian workforce as a whole, and this gap along with differences in earnings between native-born white Canadians, white immigrants, and visible minority immigrants persists. Some of these differences are related to the types of jobs visible minority workers hold, along with the systemic forms of discrimination they face. Although unions have little control over hiring decisions and practices, there might be greater emphasis on developing more inclusive hiring practices and employment equity procedures, as well as to negotiating around equity issues in collective bargaining.

Unions and the New Economy

Despite the benefits of unionization overall, it has been increasingly difficult to maintain a strong union presence within the "new economy." Union density has declined in Canada since the 1980s. The steady decline has contributed to a plummeting of the rate of union memberships amongst men and relates in part to losses in manufacturing and industries that have historically had a heavy union presence, including steel, auto, auto parts, heavy appliances, and resource industries. Since the late 1980s, the manufacturing share of employment has fallen from close to 20 per cent to just over 10 per cent in 2013, a low amongst OECD countries (Stanford, 2013). Along with this downward slide, the rate of unionization within manufacturing fell 4.1 percentage points between 1999 and 2012 from 31.1 to 27 per cent (Galarneau and Sohn, 2013). Losses in the auto sector, historically considered to be the premium private-sector workplace, have been devastating. The number of autoworkers in Canada dropped by 50,000 between 1980 and 2010, while productivity doubled and real wages increased only moderately (Gindin, 2012). New workers in the industry today are offered a starting wage rate that is 12 per cent lower (in adjusted figures) than it was in 1985. Further detracting from the appeal of what was once the most coveted job in industry is that 30 years ago it took a newly hired autoworker 18 months to earn the top hourly wage, whereas it now takes about 10 years (Gindin, 2012).

Changes in the goods-producing sector, together with growth in the service sector with its sizeable share of non-union establishments and anti-union employers, has translated into difficult times for the labour movement. Between 1981 and 2014, young workers experienced the greatest declines in unionization. This is not surprising since young workers' job opportunities lay primarily in retail and other service industries, where unionization rates are relatively low (Statistics Canada, 2015e). The dilemma is that the future of the labour movement hinges on attracting young workers to revitalize it, but young workers are not finding employment in traditional union strongholds at a pace that would offset unions' losses.

Competition within the global economy has prompted employers to bargain hard, insisting that unions accept major concessions during negotiations, setting workers back years with respect to gains they previously fought for and won. Although the neoliberal state has waged an attack on public sector unions for a number of years, the private sector unions have faced the biggest challenges. Private sector employers can readily and easily threaten to close domestic operations, to move overseas or to an RTW state, or to re-build as a non-union entity. This imbalance of power reduces the leverage of private sector unions not only to push for improvements in wages and working conditions, but also to accept losses in benefits, including coveted defined benefit pension plans, as noted in Chapter 10. In this scenario, private sector workers may question their unions' promises as they fall further behind their public sector counterparts who are viewed by some to be part of a labour elite. Divisions within the labour movement grow and detract from the important work of unions in building solidarity and equality and protecting workers' rights within the framework of democracy.

Unions, Power Relations, and Social Change

Unions have created a better world for workers by advancing their interests, improving their material conditions of work, questioning arbitrary and discriminatory decisions, and providing a measure of security. Unions, however, do not fundamentally change, nor do they challenge, the balance of power. Unions operate within the confines of capitalism, and although they are a valuable source of support and security for the working class, taking the lead in promoting equity and social justice in the broader community while protecting the rights of individuals at the point of production, they also operate to maintain industrial peace and leave the power structure intact. The union's job is to ensure that the terms of the collective agreement are met and that role involves ensuring that management upholds its part of the bargain, and that workers accept the parameters and conditions specified in the contract. The union is charged with disciplining the workers for attempting to change the conditions of employment while a collective agreement in effect. This includes engaging in **wildcat strikes** or other actions that interfere with conducting employers' business or lie outside the specified roles and performance expectations specified in the collective agreement.

The state also plays an important role in maintaining management's control over the workplace, by keeping workers at least minimally satisfied with a number of measures, including employment standards, health and safety legislation, and Employment Insurance, as discussed in Chapter 5. Historically, many of the state's policies and programs were aimed at calming labour unrest and maintaining the structure of power. This includes institutionalizing collective bargaining into a rigorous, bureaucratic, and legalistic process with a set of rules, contracts, and procedures overseen by the state through labour boards and other bodies. In this process, grievances may become long, drawn out affairs, usually settled away from the point at which they occurred and involving substantial amounts of time and resources to resolve. Under these conditions, workers are often alienated from the process of "settling differences." Unions and their members are legally bound to operate within the parameters set by labour law. This includes managing their memberships, even disciplining them, for engaging in actions such as work stoppages and slowdowns that contravene the collective agreement.

Conclusion

Unions matter. Unions make a difference in workers' lives by working to reverse and raise awareness about many blatant social injustices at workplaces and within the broader economy. Historically unions have won significant battles in setting forth a set of labour laws and policies that establish fairer and safer conditions at work. In the complicated configuration that has emerged between unions, employers, and the state, however, unions are limited agents of social change, operating within the prevailing structure of power relations. They raise questions about the framework of capitalist power, but they do not significantly alter it. Nevertheless, unions play important roles and engage in meaningful work altering the circumstances under which people earn their livelihoods and engage in community life.

Moving into the future, it is critical that unions remain engaged in addressing issues most relevant to young workers. This will require reforming their image as well as their organizing techniques and broadcasting their achievements. Older workers have witnessed and benefitted from the labour movement's successes in improving working conditions, in contributing to labour market policy (maternity/parental leave), and in fighting for equality measures (pay equity, racial equality, LGBTQ rights). Younger workers may have to be convinced of these achievements in order to move beyond the image of unions as protecting underperforming workers and as maintaining the seniority system at all costs. Young energetic workers may detest seniority rules that award senior workers first choice over shift selection and vacation time but at the same time understand first-hand the importance of the stability that accompanies a unionized labour market position.

Questions for Critical Thought

1. With new jobs in the Canadian labour market increasingly typified by precarious and nonstandard conditions, and with union density (unionization) in decline over the past three decades, what are the possible consequences of de-unionization for working people, both in the workplace and in their communities? What are the consequences for society at large?
2. In addition to negotiating collective agreements with private and public employers, what other roles do unions play in the day-to-day lives of Canadians?
3. How are *neoliberal* economic and social policies challenging and changing the role of unions in Canada?

Suggested Further Resources

Ross, Stephanie, Larry Savage, Errol Black, and Jim Silver. 2015. *Building a Better World: An Introduction to the Labour Movement in Canada*, 3rd edn. Halifax: Fernwood Press. This book provides a comprehensive introduction to the Canadian labour movement and trade unionism.

Stanford, Jim. 2008a. *Economics for Everyone: A Short Guide to the Economics of Capitalism*. Halifax and Winnipeg: Fernwood Publishing. This book provides an approachable "mini" course on how the capitalist economy works.

Suggested Websites

Canadian Labour Congress
http://canadianlabour.ca
The Canadian Labour Congress is the largest labour organization in Canada. It is an umbrella organization that brings together national and international unions, labour councils, and provincial and territorial labour federations, representing over 3.3 million Canadian workers.

The website provides information on current issues, research and campaigns. In addition, you may visit the websites of individual unions for their specific programs and campaigns.

The Progressive Economics Forum
www.progressive-economics.ca
The Progressive Economics Forum is an online discussion of progressive economists, academics, researchers, and activists on a wide range of labour market issues.

Notes

1. Target, the US mega-retailer, requires its employees to watch a video with a strong anti-union message. The video, "Think Hard Before You Sign," and a second version, "Think Hard: Protect Your Signature" are narrated by actors belonging to an actors' union.
2. In another landmark case in 2011, the Supreme Court refused to uphold the ruling of Ontario's Court of Appeal, referred to as the *Fraser* decision, that agricultural workers have the right to engage in a collective bargaining process that includes a statutory dispute-resolution process and legislative protection of a union's right to be the exclusive bargaining agent provided that there is majority support (Lancaster House Report, 2011).
3. While the chorus has remained unchanged over the years, the verses have been adapted. There is a Canadian version of the verses, and since the 1970s women have added their voices to the verses to reflect their "double day" of labour and their concerns as (paid) workers and union members.
4. A humorous look at what unions have contributed to Canadian workers may be found at http://www.ppwc.ca/what-have-unions-done-for-us/. This short YouTube video depicts a stern, anti-union company manager surrounded by a group of workers who list the union's contributions when he asks, "What have unions done for us?" See Public and Private Workers of Canada (PPWC, 2012).
5. All workers who are defined as employees in a particular bargaining unit would be included. Labour boards define the bargaining units, the employees that the union will represent. In defining the bargaining unit, the labour board takes into account whether there is a "community of interest" among the workers. For example, management, administration, and certain levels of supervisors are employees, but are excluded from the bargaining unit because they may be involved in hiring, firings, and other such activities where there is a clear demarcation of power between them and other members of the bargaining unit. In addition, the union may decide to represent only certain groups or categories of workers within a specific workplace.
6. Automatic dues check-off is required by the *Canada Labour Code* as well as by the majority of provincial labour relations regulations. Where the Rand formula is not mandatory, the issue of union dues is part of the collective agreement.
7. The exception is in closed shop arrangements, which occurs very infrequently.
8. CEP has since merged with the Canadian Autoworkers Union (CAW) to create UNIFOR (A Union For Everyone). The merger was finalized on 31 August 2013.

12 The Future of Work

Learning Objectives

- To examine the proverbial "race to the bottom" and assess where young workers today stand
- To consider the fields in which good jobs are booming
- To discuss directions for change by considering policy shifts and workers' actions

Introduction

For many workers today the future of work is grim. Young workers who are completing their education with hope of a long, fascinating career are confronted with the reality that they may have to spend more time at the part-time job they held during school years before settling into the career they trained for. The uncertainty they experience in the labour market affects personal decisions regarding home purchases, relocating, and family. In turn, the ambiguous futures of younger generations prevent communities from moving forward, and this consequently inhibits the growth of the labour market. In this age of insecurity, senior workers have also been short-changed by the loss of, or changes to, their pension plans, forced retirements, the dependency of adult children returning home, and inadequate savings to get them by in their golden years. In this scenario, many shudder to think of the prospects available for their grandchildren and future generations.

This chapter raises questions about the direction of change in the labour force and the labour market over the next few decades. Are workers caught in the proverbial "race to the bottom" with no exit in the foreseeable future? We will consider the prospects for "good" jobs to emerge within these volatile times. Finally, we will examine some of the possible directions for change and their impact on workers in the Canadian context.

Wastelands, Job Loss, and Declining Hope

During the last two decades, the Canadian landscape has been marked by brownfields. Rusty and decaying work sites, now quiet and still, surrounded by wire fences bearing "for sale" signs and real estate information have replaced the noise, hustle, and bustle of heavy machinery, forklifts at the loading docks, and transport trucks hauling Canadian-made products away. Lean times combined with free trade agreements and cheaper labour markets in the south and overseas have devastated Canadian industry. Between 2000 and 2012 about 20,000 factories closed across Canada, and manufacturing, now comprising only 11 per cent of Canada's GDP, has been overtaken by the retail sector as the largest source of employment (Freeman, 2015). In this scenario, the working class has lost the time-honoured tradition of a stable working life marked at retirement by the proverbial "gold watch" and a handshake for years of loyal service.

In painting the picture of post-war industrial Canada, however, we must be careful not to romanticize working conditions and life in Canada's working-class communities. Workers in both public and private sectors engaged in many long and difficult struggles in order to win raises in their wages, secure pension plans, guaranteed hours of work, maternity and parental leave provisions, seniority rights, and other measures that provided security and support in what was, for many workers, their lifetime labour market positions. But the victories have been bittersweet for some. Not only were some battles across bargaining tables very difficult, leaving workers out on the streets for months at a time and producing less than desirable results, but forms of racism and discrimination often kept women, Aboriginal workers, and minority members from the most coveted positions and with fewer possibilities for promotions and long-term employment.

Despite difficult conditions, bargaining issues, the neglect of health and safety precautions, and the environmental disasters, workers in the post-war years developed a sense of satisfaction, knowing that their jobs were marked by at least a degree of security. There was also a profound sense of pride experienced by members of the working class, who were involved in producing cars, washing machines, and other household products sold within their communities. Workers proudly participated in industrial sports leagues and wore their company's name emblazoned on their hockey jackets and baseball jerseys, sought sponsorship of little leagues, and consumed and championed their company's products. In many ways they realized that each day they spent on the production line contributed in a small but significant way to strengthen the backbone of the Canadian economy.

The Retail Shift

Today retail wastelands are replacing industrial wastelands. Vast parking lots and huge box-like structures now dot the landscape. These busy complexes often sit beside large expanses of tarmac tarnished by an occasional weed bursting through the asphalt and left idle by retail closures as the sector becomes more and more monopolized. The adjacent busy and idle lots stand as a reminder of the simultaneous boom in retail and the fragility of the market. Early in 2015 when Target announced that it was closing all of its 133 stores across Canada, after operating in

Canada for only 26 months, the fallout included 17,600 retail workers, three Canadian distribution centres, the Canadian corporate headquarters in Mississauga, Ontario (CTV News, 2015), and acres and acres of real estate and idle lands, with tremendous environmental impact. With Target, Future Shop, and a number of smaller retail chains, including Jacob, Mexx Canada, Sony, and Smart Set also shuttering their stores, and Sears standing on the brink of bankruptcy and actively laying off hundreds of workers (Canadian Press, 2015), opportunities even for casual employment within the sector are disappearing.

Retail work has been the so-called "go-to" work, relied upon by students, mothers with young children, and in recent years, seniors looking for a few dollars to supplement to their meagre pensions as well as for an outlet to socialize. Changes within the retail sector have not only affected the number of job openings, but they have also transformed the character of the jobs that are available. The big box format and the sheer size of many retail outlets make it difficult for some workers to get around and cover their areas, tidying piles of clothing and linens, pushing and lining up shopping carts, or keeping the shelves sufficiently stocked while answering shoppers' questions. Much of the work requires an element of physicality and it is tiring. The hours of operation have expanded in numerous types of outlets and in many regions. With many large outlets open 24 hours, or open late most evenings and weekends, extended seasonal hours, and even some holidays, many retail workers are finding that they are being asked to expand their windows of availability. Most understand that non-compliance may result in no work at all. When workers find themselves unable to work on the days they are scheduled, the onus is upon them to find their own replacements. Large, revolving staffs with limited assigned work hours prevent individuals from socializing with fellow workers or from becoming acquainted with other staff members, making it difficult to swap shifts when necessary. Relationships with immediate supervisors and regional and higher-ranking managers are less familiar, making the possibility of promotions or recognition even more elusive.

Similar to plant closures, retail bankruptcies and closures impact the wider community in addition to the workers immediately affected. Among those affected are maintenance personnel and numerous businesses that provided service to the outlets or benefitted from the additional traffic the retail establishments brought to the area. Once vacant, renovating and reusing the space is complicated and costly because of the sheer size, locations, and boxy structures. Even if the structures were partitioned into several smaller establishments, each unit would require retrofitting, involving an enormous waste of construction materials. The environmental footprint is massive, a testament to a bygone era of mass consumption and suburbanization.

With online sales accounting for almost 6 per cent of all retail spending in Canada (2013) (Shaw, 2013), warehouse or distribution centre workers are becoming the "new normal" amongst retail employees. In addition to Amazon and dedicated online retailers such as eBay, iTunes, and Well.ca, well-known major retailers covering the price spectrum from Walmart to Bloomingdale's and Macy's are casting for a greater share of Canadians' spending through their online divisions. The work behind online retail involves clerical skills (taking orders, billing), assembling orders, and shipping and handling. Through this process, the art of window decorating and retail design may be lost on the masses while still reserved for the well-to-do who may continue to rely on small niche markets providing personalized service. Serving customers in stores, salespersons are required to be well-groomed, patient, and sociable. To meet with customers' expectations and approval, gender and other characteristics are taken into account during the hiring process (Williams, 2006). In the warehouse, workers swap their high heels and business attire for work boots and safety equipment as they assemble packages for delivery. Work within distribution centres is heavy, requiring workers to drive forklifts, lift packages (up to specified weights), and engage in a continuous series of movements to assemble, wrap, and ship packages (Bonacich and Wilson, 2008). Large orders are palletized and driven by forklift into transport containers. These jobs may appeal to workers who prefer the "backstage" and the physical element, but at the same time they may block older workers and those with physical limitations from these "modern" retail experiences.

Spiralling Downward

Shuttered industries, idle retail outlets, and the success of discounters such as Walmart and Dollarama together indicate a bleak future for many young workers. In Ontario payday loan outlets outnumber McDonald's restaurants, a telling tale of workers who are forced to live paycheque to paycheque, especially given that more than half of the clients are repeatedly using the service, relying on it for recurring expenses (Hayes, 2015). Once workers start borrowing money to pay off credit cards and other bills, they get caught in a vicious circular trap. Their low wages coupled with the high cost of living do not provide the financial flexibility needed to end the downward spiral and they find themselves in a state of dependency on their partners, parents, loan companies, and possibly the state. Under these circumstances, many lose hope of achieving lifelong dreams—home ownership, marriage and family stability, security in later years, and a rewarding career. The race to the bottom may be more accurately regarded as a treadmill at the bottom.

While circumstances at the bottom of the income and occupational ladder are grim, a number of administrative and professional jobs have also been targeted by employers for cost savings and down-scaling. In the health care industry, university-trained nurses (RNs) have faced job cuts, and in some areas, difficulty finding work. Many of their duties have been assigned to Registered Practical Nurses (RPNs), two-year college graduates who are lower paid. RPNs are qualified to care for patients who are considered stable, including patients in long-term care, while RNs undertake crisis management and are involved with patients requiring critical care, such as in emergency departments and intensive care units (Armstrong and

Armstrong, 2010). While being called upon to care for the critically ill may pique the interest of RNs who enjoy the challenges and the ongoing learning experiences, the intensified working conditions they face may lead to burnout and exhaustion.

Much of the hands-on caring work in hospitals, long-term care facilities, and communities is now done by Personal Support Workers (PSWs), the lowest paid group amongst "nursing" staff within healthcare facilities and community care. Between 2007 and 2011, the number of PSWs has increased, and it is expected that there may be a shortage of those who work in support of health care (PSWHQ, 2015). Projections that there may be shortages of PSWs in the future are based on two factors: Canada's aging population and the changing employment practices within healthcare. As we see in the box below, some workers who have experienced first-hand the throes of job displacement are relying on the projected need for PSWs and workers in related in healthcare support services for a rosier future. Whether the projected shortages translate into job security for thousands of Canadians is uncertain. Cutbacks in health and the deployment of healthcare personnel are political matters, dependent on governments' priorities and their unrelenting adherence to an austerity regime.

Box 12.1 Everyday Work Experiences

Long-Term Care and Long-Term Security?

When talking to workers who were victims of plant closures, the topic of future work possibilities always came up. A number of workers, including those who had spent their working lives in factories, focused on health care as their number one choice. These workers who had lived through the heartache of having their jobs and lives collapse were turning to what they regarded as an industry that would provide them with a sound sense of security. They reasoned that healthcare industries were mainstays within their communities, the need for workers would continue to grow given the demographics of the population, and as healthcare workers they would be respected members of the labour force. Interestingly, there was a gendered dimension to these conversations.

Among the displaced workers redirecting themselves toward healthcare occupations were men whose identities were wrapped around the persona of the strong and virile industrial worker. They talked about their difficulties in reimaging themselves as caring personal support workers. Some were convinced that while healthcare was the right direction for them, given the security they felt that the industry would afford, they worried about the reception they would receive from prospective employers as well as from those they might care for. While these men focused on the gendered nature of care work as the biggest stumbling block for them as they prepared to dramatically change directions in their line of work, interestingly many of their female co-workers who, like them, had spent their working years in factories, struggled with similar issues in having to reimage themselves as caregivers. Both men and women, however, regarded their efforts as the price to pay for long-term security.

Similar to some of the trends within healthcare industries, workers within the educational sector have also been observing changes that may spark concerns about security, devaluation, and degradation of their jobs. Throughout the school systems, teachers are faced with growing class sizes along with pressures to "do more with less" with outdated library resources, shrinking budgets, and fewer out-of-class experiential learning opportunities. To help out in their classrooms, teachers rely on "volunteers," the unpaid work of parents who spend time accompanying classes on field trips, preparing materials for arts and crafts, coaching, and decorating classrooms.

In universities, dwindling public funds, stiff competition for fewer research dollars, larger classes, and more administrative responsibilities have all combined to place greater demands on faculty members' time. All of these activities have contributed to a fast-paced academic environment that leaves little time for mentoring promising students and for thoughtful "slow scholarship" that includes time to think, analyze, write, collaborate, and read (Mountz et al., 2015). Informally the university system is tiered, with many smaller universities focusing mainly on teaching and larger universities, with greater resources to attract research and development money through both public and private sources, focusing more heavily on research. Working conditions for faculty in these two contexts vary widely with respect to teaching course loads, research and publishing expectations, and contact with students.

Most universities today rely heavily on part-time or contract faculty, qualified teachers who are hired on a course-by-course basis and paid a fraction of the wages of full-time faculty. In Canada today, more than 50 per cent of undergraduate classes are taught by part-time faculty (Basen, 2014). Many contract faculty members teach large courses that require managing teaching assistants and attending to the myriad issues that occur in these circumstances (arranging make-up tests, dealing with complaints, etc.). Despite their efforts, however, these well-educated workers are highly insecure. They must reapply for their jobs each semester and they are not guaranteed work, despite their years of seniority at any one university.

Another threat to job security within higher education is the movement to online courses. Mounting online courses raises a number of concerns over intellectual property rights and the long-term security of those who teach in this format. At the same time that professors' administrative load has grown tremendously and now occupies a significant percentage of work time, universities have cut back deeply on the number of support staff, including administrative and secretarial staff within departments, technical assistants, and cleaners and maintenance workers.

Taking the High Road

The good jobs–bad jobs debate draws a distinction between the growing number of undesirable jobs and the shrinking number of good jobs that provide workers with decent working conditions, good salary and benefits, security, and other perks. Returning to this discussion, the debate speaks to the central tendencies within the labour market that are quite nuanced. The labour market is not simply bifurcated. There are employment fields that fall outside the good jobs–bad jobs continuum and are expected to provide first-rate opportunities in years to come.

Many of the new fields that will provide challenging employment are related to new technologies, robotization (mechtronics), software systems, and digital programming. Automobile development and manufacturing—once the domain of mechanical engineers and production workers who assembled, packed, painted, and packaged products—has undergone transformations that were once considered possible only in the far-flung future. Today the heart of the automobile development process is the software engineer who develops programs that simply run the car. Consider the components of the modern car with all its computer-assisted devices and sensors. Sophisticated electronics networks are now standard in most cars. The industry is now testing self-driving vehicles—technology that will impact truckers, bus drivers, cabbies, and others whose employment involves driving. Cars today are essentially a series of computers (embedded systems) on wheels. As we steer our cars, for example, we send a series of signals to embedded software systems that send us in the direction we intended. The labour process fuses what we have traditionally associated with the realm of manufacturing to the work structure identified with the business of white-collar work.

General Motors has recently reported that among the top 20 jobs it foresees for the future are electrical and software engineers (along with other engineers and technical positions). The company has more than quintupled the number of software engineers on staff since 2013 and has ended its practice of outsourcing to well-known Hewlett-Packard and other technology corporations (Norton, 2015). The impact of digitization is immense, and traditional manufacturing companies, including all major players in the auto sector, along with household names such as General Electric, are morphing into software companies (McKendrick, 2015). Opportunities abound for those who are highly educated in engineering and other mathematical and hard sciences.

Even within this good news story, however, there is an element of concern. While the newly abundant opportunities for software engineers provide hope for recent graduates, who will be the beneficiaries of these opportunities? What does this mean for women and labour market equality? Some analysts project that industries traditionally dominated by men, including engineering and architecture, will grow by leaps and bounds over the next decade, while administrative and office jobs traditionally occupied by women—in medical offices, the courts and legal system, and corporate and government offices—will disappear (Sagan, 2016). Recent data indicate that women are still underrepresented in natural sciences and engineering in university (NSERC, 2010). Women make up more than half of undergraduates in Canadian universities, but their numbers in engineering have not kept pace, and in fact, dropped from a high of 21 per cent in 2001 to about 18 per cent (Hango, 2013; Myers, 2010).

Various explanations have been put forth in discussing women's low level of involvement in engineering. In a recent study, Hunt (2016) dismissed earlier notions that women were disinterested in science and therefore do not excel in science and engineering occupations. Rather, she argued that women leave engineering because they are dissatisfied with the rewards (pay, opportunities to advance) offered to women. In other words, women's exit from engineering (or engineering's failure to retain women) is unrelated to the science, but rather is based on the culture and the employment prospects for women. Barnard et al. (2012) found that women identify engineering as a man's field and are concerned about the employment possibilities for women. Not only do their worries include the number of career opportunities that will be available to women, but they are also troubled by the "chilly climate" women may experience in the field. Demonstrating the ways in which women's experiences are gendered, Powell et al. (2012) argue that while women may construct an autonomous self-image, their decisions and choices, including career paths, are still shaped by gender. Women's discourse around career choices reveals deep challenges with regard to gender norms for achieving equality in fields traditionally identified as male domains, including engineering and technology. To overcome such profoundly embedded gendered constructions of self, it is important to develop new approaches for recruiting and retaining women in the field.

Along with the field of engineering, another area that may offer promising opportunities is ecology, sustainability, and the move toward "green" jobs. For those who are interested in the social impact of their jobs, the green movement may have appeal. In Canada today, the number of people employed in green energy outnumber those working in the oil sands; the sector grew by 37 per cent between 2009 and 2014 (Blackwell, 2014). The full potential for growth, however, has not yet been realized while governments, perhaps for political reasons, continue to fund the oil sands rather than committing more fully to sustainable energy and renewable resources. Environmental sustainability is a profit-making field, and until investors realize the potential, job growth in the area may be stalled. Developments in this area are highly politicized as environmental protection involves, for example, cutting into the profits of companies that produce elaborate (and wasteful) packaging for cosmetics and other items, while maintaining vigilance about banning the export of dangerous and environmentally unfriendly or hazardous production processes and waste from the Global North to the Global South.

Crises in Canadian Work: Looking Ahead

This book has raised a number of questions and hopefully, awareness, about crises in Canadian work. Throughout the chapters we employed a grounded approach by examining recent data, literature, and policies to explain the development and persistence of these crises. To do so, we adopted the framework of public sociology in order to examine structures and processes within work and workplaces that affect workers, communities, and the quality of life. This required us to look through the lens of real life, to examine the experiences of workers, and to expose the issues at play in workplaces across the country. Through this exposure, it is our hope that there may be indications of directions for positive change. This is not to say that this book provides solutions, but that there may be ways we can work to improve workers' everyday lives and circumstances in the near future.

Working Toward Political Solutions

Critical to advancing the lot of Canadian workers is the development of labour market policies that place workers in the driver's seat by identifying workers' need for decent wages, steady jobs, and a secure safety net to get through tough times. At minimum, pro-workers' policy development should include an overhaul of the *Employment Insurance Act* to re-establish the benefit as a fallback when workers, for whatever reason, become unemployed. As we read in Chapter 5, the system has been gutted, leaving only a minority of workers who should be able to draw upon the fund that they paid into through payroll deductions, to qualify. This includes migrant workers who are automatically eliminated due to their status as non-citizens, and those across Canada who do not meet the thresholds established in their region for the minimum number of hours worked in order to collect benefits.

Across Canada, sagging Employment Standards legislation also requires revision. Some of the principles embedded in labour market policies and practices relate to an earlier era when the economy was vibrant and the labour force approached full employment. In today's world of precarious employment with no guaranteed weekly hours of work, governments need to reconsider "best practices" and fully commit to promoting pro-worker (and therefore pro-economy and pro-productivity) policy development. Included in revised employment standards across the country should be the establishment of decent, liveable minimum wages. Economists have clearly established that raising minimums improves productivity and stimulates economies. Workers are happier, turnover declines, and families and communities benefit. In particular, decent living wages would ease the plight of young workers who are wedged between difficult poorly waged jobs and soaring student debt loads, and their desire to engage in family and community life independently. Higher wages would also improve conditions for racialized workers and recent immigrants who are caught between their need for employment and reliance on low-income jobs, and the barriers they face in having their foreign credentials recognized in Canada.

Finally, minimum standards have been declining, and many employers have been remiss with regard to paying wages on time, handing over vacation pay, offering benefits, and scheduling hours of work fairly. Many have also adopted harsh tactics in disciplining workers and have contributed to the culture of insecurity about work. In tough times it is important to cut workers some slack—allowing them to balance work and family responsibilities more easily and manage the multiple jobs they may have to hold to make ends meet. Employers should take into account workers' personal needs for accommodation, and should establish and practice fair equity principles regarding hiring, hours of work, promotions, pay increments, and supervisory practices. Legislation to ensure compliance should be enacted and enforced.

Ignoring the need to raise standards of employment leaves the labour movement with responsibility for ensuring best practices across the labour market. Having to spend time and resources to chase what should be rightly guaranteed to workers by law is a setback for labour. It prevents the movement from initiating and pursuing more progressive policies. Rather than relying on strong employment standards to establish a base on which unions might negotiate first and even subsequent contracts, some unions are finding themselves in the position of having to start in very basic positions in negotiations. In this scenario, employers become complacent, offering workers and their unions little more than what is already guaranteed by minimum standards. This leaves unions responsible for minimum standards rather than moving forward with more progressive forms of bargaining and giving rise to new directions in labour market policy development.

There are numerous ways to reorient Canadians' thinking about work and employment rights. One way is to take lessons from other societies, especially Scandinavian countries that have a rich legacy of supporting workers and families by establishing living wages, parental leaves, pensions, adequate vacation time, childcare support, and other benefits. Certainly these policies are costly, but what we would gain is a greater commitment to equality, without the growing gaps we currently observe between haves and have-nots. We would also develop capacity to capitalize on the unique set of skills, abilities, and talents each worker brings to the fore.

Establishing decent standards is only one aspect of developing respectful workplaces. In both the public and private sectors, it is important to work toward improved conditions, recognition of skills and experience, attention to flexibility to meet family and personal needs, and respectful and responsible managerial and supervisory practices. In the workplace there should be greater attention paid to equity issues in order to provide women, racialized workers, disabled workers, Aboriginals, and members of the LGBTQ communities a welcoming atmosphere and conditions and opportunities traditionally available to the white majority. To do this, we must commit resources to explore how workers might achieve gains around equity issues, especially in times of insecurity and precariousness when workers' primary concern is access to any work at all. We must seek to understand the possible avenues of change, whether it is greater access to education and training, decision-making bodies, or political office. Finally, we must strategize about new ways to implement equality rights within workplaces and settle on the consequences for non-compliance (Stinson, Warskett, and Bickerton, 2006). Finally, if we are to avoid or stop the race to the bottom, it is important to convince people that a "win" for some workers is a victory for all. Supporting workers on their picket lines and demonstrating a show of solidarity are significant ways to stand up for change. Achieving gains at the workplace is important to all. Those workers whose unions negotiate fair raises, decent pensions, and safe and clean working conditions are serving the entire community by setting standards above the minimum. Workers and unions must continue to strive for changes that will make a difference in the lives of so many and provide a dignified future for young workers by re-establishing vibrancy in their communities.

Activism: Workers Have Their Say

Declining standards and working conditions along with the loss of manufacturing and unionized positions makes workers' and local movements an important outlet and a way to educate publics about the state of affairs within workplaces and the vulnerability of different groups of workers. Workers' movements can make a real difference in the day-to-day experience of some workers. The movement to change conditions and raise wages at Walmart is an outstanding example.

In the United States, the pressure to raise the wages of Walmart workers was given a push by President Obama's initiative to raise the minimum wage across-the-board to $9.00 per hour in 2013[1] and to $10.10 in 2014. He and his administration argued that raising the minimum wage would help 28 million Americans pay their bills and lead at least a slightly more comfortable life (The White House, 2015). With the support of the United States federal government, Walmart workers sought change and early in 2015, Walmart announced that it was raising the pay of 500,000 full-time and part-time associates, 40 per cent of its US labour force of 1.3 million, to $9.00 per hour (O'Connor, 2015). Although US workers cannot live comfortably and easily on the $9 rate, certainly this move by the retail giant should be regarded as at least a limited victory. Despite the company's tactics of fear and intimidation, Walmart workers have engaged in numerous actions to improve their wages and working conditions, educating the public on the problems faced by Walmart workers who required food stamps to get by, who were passed over for promotion without explanation, and who were routinely asked to work "off the clock." Exposing such atrocities is vital, as these actions have tarnished the image of this self-proclaimed "pro-family" corporate giant worldwide.

For many in the US Canada, and elsewhere, making gains at Walmart is essential to the future of the working class, as this corporation has represented one of the toughest struggles anywhere for workers and their unions. Victories come against all odds, given that US labour laws favour employers who face few and weak disincentives for firing union activists, engaging in fierce anti-union campaigns, and committing numerous workplace atrocities such as locking workers in during overnight re-stocking shifts (Greenhouse, 2008).

Keeping a watch on Walmart is a critical aspect of the struggle for decent wages, fair practices, and the right to organize. Walmart is a global corporation with more than 10,000 stores worldwide, in 28 countries and on five continents (UNI Global Union, 2012). In Canada, the UFCW has led the way on the Walmart campaign, successfully organizing the store in Jonquière, Québec. Walmart fought back by engaging in a number of activities in an effort to crush the union. Walmart argued, for example, that supervisors should be included in the bargaining unit because they had little control over the workers under their charge (Adams, 2005). While the company lost that bid, they successfully avoided the union and negotiating the first contract with the Jonquière workers by declaring losses and closing the store. The union was unable to establish that Walmart's actions constituted unfair labour practices and has since been unable to organize Walmart stores on Canadian soil. The fight against Walmart is international and continues with the formation of UNI Global Union, an alliance of workers around the globe trying to make a difference. The effort has paid off. In Chile, Walmart workers in five banner stores achieved an historic collective agreement, and workers there are reporting that their benefits have improved with the union (Walmartworkerscanada, 2015). This achievement may raise the hope of tens of thousands of workers worldwide that their voices have been heard and that better working conditions are possible.

CP PHOTO/Jacques Boissinot

Pierre Martineau, left, and Patrice Bergeron, two of the Walmart workers who initiated the unionization, stand in front of their workplace in Jonquière, Quebec in 2004. Collective agreement could not be reached, and the store was closed in 2005, leaving almost 200 people out of work. In 2014, the Supreme Court of Canada sided with the union representing the former employees, and ruled that those who were terminated were entitled to compensation.

Conclusion

Many Canadian workers today spend their working hours in jobs that may be described as deskilled, devalued, degraded, dangerous, dirty, and difficult. Making ends meet by cobbling together enough hours of work from one or more precarious positions has become the preoccupation of thousands of Canadians. The primary message of this book is that work today is in crisis, and Canadians' insecurity and uneasiness about the future underscore the centrality of work in our lives. Unlike previous decades when workers' foremost concerns included the quality of work and work satisfaction, today, the primary discussion revolves around access to work, especially decent work. It is important that discourses around work are de-personalized and that workers readily understand that difficulties accessing and keeping secure, decent work do not fall in the realm of the individual. These are not, in C.W. Mills' terms, "personal troubles" but rather, are "social issues," and it will take concerted collective action and judicious political adjustments to address these problems. Hopefully Canadians will see beyond their own milieu and understand that the failings within the social, political, and economic structure underlie these issues.

The critical issue today is the pervasive sense of scarcity. Work, both paid and unpaid, is central to the lives of most people. Paid employment, in particular, is a significant connection to the community. With only poor work or no employment at all, the very foundations of our lifestyle and value system are challenged and workers' vulnerability is exacerbated. Access to reasonable work is essential as one's identity, self-expression, and overall satisfaction are linked to having a job.

As we look to the future it appears that work for many Canadians is in turmoil, and navigating the world of paid employment requires an understanding of the structures underlying employment realities today. It is important to urge policy-makers, politicians, labour leaders, and activists to consider the best possible courses of action to grant workers dignity and respect on the job, from publics, from employers, from governments, and from their communities.

Questions for Critical Thought

1. What are some of the factors leading to the downward spiral of job opportunities for young Canadians? Can this downward trend be reversed?
2. What are some of the equity issues and political questions that might be raised regarding the development of and access to good jobs?
3. What are some policy initiatives that may help to improve the lot of Canadian workers? What are some of the lessons about activism and change we may glean from campaigns waged against Walmart?

Suggested Further Resources

Ford, Martin. 2015. *Rise of the Robots: Technology and the Threat of a Jobless Future*. New York: Basic Books. Ford considers the future of work as technology and advanced robotics contribute to massive unemployment and inequality, as manufacturing and traditional forms of work continue to decline, and as work is increasingly deskilled.

Laird, Gordon. 2009. *The Price of a Bargain: The Quest for Cheap and the Death of Globalization*. Toronto: McClelland & Stewart. In this book, Laird argues that the "Walmartization" phenomenon—searching and expecting a plethora of cheaper and cheaper goods—is having an irreversible and detrimental impact on the global economy and workers' access to decent, safe, and clean environments.

Suggested Websites

Living Wage Canada

http://livingwagecanada.ca

Living Wage Canada is an important campaign developed to restore dignity and respect for workers by addressing the issue of poverty-level wages and the impact on Canadian workers, families, and communities. The campaign targets employers, governments, and communities to work together to establish living wages across Canada.

Justice for Janitors (J4J)

http://justiceforjanitors.ca

Justice for Janitors (J4J) is a workers' movement supported by political, labour, religious, and community leaders that is designed to establish better wages, benefits, and working conditions for those who clean luxurious, high-end buildings while earning poverty-level wages. The campaign developed through the Service Employees' International Union (SEIU) and now has 30 sites across Canada and the US.

Note

1. President Obama first called for a raise in the minimum wage to $9.00 per hour in his 2013 State of the Union Address, and subsequently in 2014 suggested a $10.10 per hour minimum. Soon after his call for the $9.00 minimum, 13 states made the adjustment.

Glossary

Ageism A term used to refer to systematic stereotyping and discrimination against individuals on the basis of their perceived age. While ageism may impute positive attributes, most attention focuses on the attribution of negative traits to seniors.

Aged seniors Social researchers and gerontologists have used a variety of categories to distinguish amongst populations of seniors. "Young seniors" is often used to reference individuals 55 and older. Aged seniors typically refer to those individuals who are 85 years of age or older.

Alienated emotional misbehaviour This kind of behaviour occurs whenever workers react to managerial directives by withdrawing their agency or otherwise disengaging their enthusiasm over the emotional scripts they have been taught.

Alienation Marx's term for separation of workers from the products of their labour as the result of being assigned to work repetitively on a small part of a product.

Arbitration A process through which an employer and a union settle a matter in dispute that they are not able to resolve through negotiation. Arbitration does not involve a work stoppage. A "neutral" third party, an **arbitrator**, jointly chosen by the union and the employer, makes a binding ruling on the matter.

Babbage principle By dividing work into different processes, each of which may be purchased according to the quantity of skill involved, costs of production are cheapened.

Baby boomers This term refers to those individuals born between 1946 and 1965. There was a dramatic upsurge in population growth after the end of World War II in 1945. As this population bubble works its way through the life course, it has a dramatic impact on every aspect of society.

Bargaining agent The specific union that is certified to represent a group of workers and negotiate on their behalf.

Bargaining unit A group of workers who are covered by a particular collective agreement. Members of the bargaining unit may be located in one or more worksites.

Bridge retirement This term refers to the popular practice of retiring from one's main employment in order to pursue an alternative position in the paid labour market (for example, as a part-time or self-employed worker).

Business unionism An approach to trade unionism in which unions focus solely on winning economic gains—wages and benefits—for their members through collective bargaining and avoid engaging in broader social and economic campaigns and activities.

Canada Pension Plan/Quebec Pension Plan (CPP/QPP) Introduced in 1966, these plans, indexed to inflation, are intended to protect workers from loss of income in retirement. Both plans provide similar benefits. This pension benefit is provided to individuals who have been employed in Canada and have made contributions to CPP and who are at least 60 years of age. Though eligible to receive reduced benefits from age 60, full benefits apply after reaching age 65 and increased benefits accrue if CPP is postponed after age 65. The benefit size will vary depend upon how long you have been making contributions to CPP. Individuals may request a child-rearing CPP provision if they had no or low earnings because they were a primary caregivers raising children.

Canadian Association of Retired Persons (CARP) This organization, mirrored after its American counterpart—the American Association of Retired Persons (AARP)—has emerged as an important advocate for seniors' issues, including lobbying the federal and provincial governments around issues of pension reform and age discrimination.

Casual/on call workers Nonstandard workers employed on the basis of being called upon whenever the employer needs help. Typically, there is no guarantee of employment beyond a few hours per week.

Centenarians This term refers to individuals who are 100 years old or older.

Certification The process through which a union organizes members and wins official, legal status and recognition from the employer and the labour board.

Child labour Children aged 5 to 17 years in working conditions that are physically or mentally harmful, socially or morally dangerous, interfere with schooling, or require children to attempt to combine school attendance with excessively long and heavy work.

Collective agreement The negotiated contract or legal document between the employer and the union specifying the wages and working conditions of a group of workers.

Collective bargaining The process through which a union and an employer meet to negotiate the terms and conditions of the collective agreement for members of the bargaining unit.

Commodification The process of transforming goods, services, ideas, etc. into a commercial or marketable entity.

Commodification of time Refers to the ways in which products and services available through the consumer market are sold as means to save time. In this way, time has been translated into time-saving commodities and services.

Commodity chain (or value chain) Refers to a chain of production or service provision that is spread across space, usually with a global footprint. Commodity or value chains are the result of the dispersal of a number of steps involved in creating a final product and include roles for intermediaries as well. These chains are characterized by centralized control over the processes.

Compartmentalization The separation of acts from feelings and attitudes. A skilled worker may put aside his/her pride, ideas, and interest in repetitious work to avoid inner conflict.

Competition ratio Refers to the competition over resources between younger (15 to 29 years) and older (30 to 64 years) cohorts (Cote and Allahar, 2006).

Compressed work week The workplace arrangement in which workers are permitted to compress their work week into a fewer number of longer days. For example, a 40-hour work week might be accommodated by 4 days of 10 hours a day.

Contingent work Refers to all employment that is dependent on employers' decisions. Casual, contract, and on-call work would, for example, fit into this category.

Contract workers Nonstandard workers employed in terms of an employment contract, typically written, which specifies the conditions of employment, most notably the length of time for which the employee is contracted to work. Contracts may be subject to renewal depending on the specified terms.

Credentialism or credential society The use of diplomas or degrees as a sorting and selecting mechanism to determine who is eligible for jobs, even though the diploma or degree may be irrelevant to the actual work.

Credentialism paradox The term denotes the disconnect between university level education and lower workplace skills (Cote and Allahar, 2006).

Critical sociology An approach to sociology that questions power, inequalities, and dominant practices with a view to exposing inconsistencies and injustices within societies.

Defined benefit pension plan Pension plans in which the employer and employee contributed to a pension fund and the employer guaranteed a specific pension benefit when the employee retired. Depending upon the workplace contract, the pension income might be adjusted to reflect changes in the cost of living. This is commonly referred to as the gold standard in pension benefits and is increasingly uncommon outside of public sector full-time permanent employment.

Defined contribution pension plan Pension plans premised on a specified contribution (typically a percentage of income to be matched by the employer) to a pension fund. The employer typically manages the investment of this fund. At retirement, the employee receives an income from this fund or a lump sum payment reflecting his/her contributions and the overall growth or decline of the fund during their employment. During periods of economic upheaval and recession, this pension scheme is problematic since pension funds may reflect declines in the stock market and the pay-out may be insufficient to meet the retiree's needs. Generally, with this plan there is unpredictability in retirement planning.

Degradation of labour The process by which jobs are cheapened, deskilled, and increasingly placed under management's control.

Deindustrialization The gradual loss of industry within a region or country, contributing to job loss, and social and economic change.

Dependency ratio This term refers to the relationship between the numbers of citizens who are currently or potentially active in the paid labour force (aged 15 to 65) and those who have retired from productive labour. Given changes in retirement as well as entry to paid employment, this is an imprecise measure of the ability of any nation to adequately provide for the needs of its "dependent" citizenry.

De-unionization The gradual loss of union coverage within a region or country, often as a result of deindustrialization.

Deskilling Occurs as the labour process is broken down and work becomes fragmented in such a way that individual workers have very limited skills. Each worker is assigned to a limited number of tasks, requiring less training. As a result, workers are easily replaced.

Detailed division of labour Refers to the subdivision of occupations and types of work in industrial societies. Under a detailed division of labour, craft is destroyed as workers are assigned only a couple of tasks within any production process and are unable to carry through any complete production process on their own.

Dual labour market Theory that argues that workers are split along gender, racial, ethnic, age, or other lines, resulting in a weakening of workers' bargaining power, to the benefit of employers.

Economic restructuring The reorganization of economic and state structures as new economic partnerships across national boundaries require revisions to trade agreements, foreign policy, and labour standards.

Emotional dissonance This occurs when the emotions employees display, as part of their job performance, do not match the emotions they actually feel.

Emotional labour The process by which either face-to-face or voice-to-voice interaction at work become commodified as wage labour.

Employment rate Represents the number of persons employed expressed as a percentage of the population aged 15 and over. The employment rate for a particular group such as women is the number employed in that group expressed as a percentage of the population of that group.

Export processing zones (EPZs) Special manufacturing enclaves, normally, though not always, isolated from the rest of the national economy. They are industrial zones offering cheap labour and special incentives to attract foreign investors. Imported materials often enter duty free and undergo some degree of processing before being re-exported.

Family-friendly work arrangements As mothers (and single parents) have played an increasingly prominent role in the labour force, strategies have been introduced to ease the conflict between workplace and family demands. See, for example, **flextime** and **flexplace**.

Family wage Refers to a worker's wages that are sufficient to support not only a spouse but also dependent children. During the Golden Age of Capitalism, many workers achieved a family wage through unionization.

Feminist political economy A theoretical approach focusing on the economic and political factors that produce inequalities. This approach emphasizes the importance of structural factors in explaining power and inequality under a capitalist economic framework.

Flexible working arrangements Efforts launched to make work arrangements more flexible and more compatible with family and other obligations. **Flextime**, including early starts and leaving late or **compressed** work weeks (where five days were compressed into four) are all examples of flextime arrangements. **Flexplace** refers to efforts to locate paid work in more convenient locations for workers, including working from home or working from a satellite office closer to home.

Flexibilization or flexibility Refers to initiatives undertaken by management to reduce labour costs by reducing the size of the permanent full-time labour force in favour of part-time, on-call, or casual workers. This initiative allows management to increase or decrease the size of its labour force corresponding to high demand/peak or low demand/slack periods.

Flextime Changes in the work day so that workers are able to start earlier or leave earlier while still completing a full (eight-hour) day at work. This practice typically benefits workers who wish to avoid traffic congestion and/or who seek to be home for children returning from school.

Fordism Refers to a form of production characterized by mass production, protected markets, and standardized work structures. It is named after Henry Ford, who promoted high efficiency and productivity through the use of the assembly line, while simultaneously increasing workers' wages in order to stimulate consumption, allowing workers who produced the autos to buy them as well.

Fragmentation The specialization and differentiation of activities, including work tasks and assignments.

Freedom 55 This term was popularized by a 1980s publicity campaign for a prominent Canadian bank, offering customers the prospect of retiring with financial security at age 55.

Full-time work This category covers a wide variety of schedules. In Canada it is usually identified with the 40-hour work week. Between 2000 and 2014, full-time workers in Canada averaged 40 hours per week (Statistics Canada 2015).

G8 countries Now known as the G20, the G8 refers to industrialized countries that meet regularly to discuss trade and other related issues. The G8 in 2011 included Japan,

Germany, Italy, France, United Kingdom, Canada, United States, and Russia. Since that time, more members have been added, resulting in the G20 designation.

Glass ceiling Often invisible, the ceiling that obstructs women's career progress. At a certain point in their careers, despite past successes, it appears that gender becomes an obstacle to further advances.

Global North Refers to more developed or industrialized countries that are primarily located in the northern hemisphere, notably in Europe, North America, and Asia. These economies enjoyed dramatic industrial growth and improvements in personal well-being through the nineteenth and twentieth centuries.

Global South Refers to less developed or industrializing countries that are primarily located in the southern hemisphere. These economies did not produce industrial growth and did not offer improvements in personal well-being through the nineteenth and twentieth centuries.

Globalization The global integration of national economies and the extensive movement of capital, goods, services, labour, investment, and ideas across the globe due to the expansion and intensification of capitalism.

Golden Age of Capitalism In the post-Second World War era (notably the 1950s and 1960s), labour was able to effectively mobilize and successfully demand improvements in wages, benefits, and work security. During this period, the economy boomed and working-class families tended to flourish.

Goods producing sector Also known as the secondary sector of the economy, it contains industries that produce a tangible product.

Grievance A formal complaint by a union member that the employer has violated one or more terms of the collective agreement.

Guaranteed income supplement (GIS) This non-taxable supplement is added to Old Age Security for those individuals who are deemed to be low income. Eligibility depends upon being a legal resident of Canada, being in receipt of OAS pension, and having an annual income (as an individual or as a member of a couple) that is lower than the specified "maximum annual income."

Interdependence A dynamic two-way process. For example, a growing number of goods producing industries are outsourcing service jobs that were previously performed in-house and are linked to what is produced. Furthermore, goods producing and service producing industries are creating information and communications technologies that are being applied more intensively in each other's sector (see Acharya, 2006).

Involuntary retirement This term refers to instances in which personal (health) or economic factors (plant closure) force retirement upon a worker.

Hidden curriculum The unwritten lessons of schools, such as obedience to authority, punctuality, and conformity to cultural norms.

Home working or working from home A form of work with various manifestations. Women who work from home may be telecommuting. However, they also may be engaged in highly skilled, well-remunerated self-employment (editors) or low skilled, poorly paid piecework (clothing/craft work).

Hours diversification Commencing in the 1970s, there has been a shift toward an increasing variety of time regimes in non-standard work. For example, part-time workers may work on a casual/on call, contract, or permanent basis with a resulting wide variety of actual hours worked in any time period.

Hours polarization A growing trend amongst workers for their working times to fall outside of the standard 40-hour week.

Household debt ratio The difference between household wealth and household indebtedness. The ratio is below 100 when the household has more wealth than debt and vice versa. Currently, the majority of Canadian families hold greater debt than assets.

International Labour Organization (ILO) An organization dedicated to promoting social justice and labour rights. Among the main objectives of the ILO is the promotion of decent work for all men and women.

International Workers of the World (IWW) Referred to as "wobblies," the IWW was formed in 1905 as a general union promoting workers' rights and protections, over and above their specific industrial union. The IWW promoted the concept of One Big Union.

Involuntary nonstandard employment (INE) A description of nonstandard employment drawing attention to its involuntary nature. As noted, nonstandard employment may be voluntary.

Involuntary part-time workers These are women and men who indicate they work part-time because of business conditions and/or their inability to find full-time work.

Job sharing This practice involves an arrangement where two workers share one full-time position as two part-time jobs. While workers are responsible themselves for negotiating task allocation and continuity of performance, they benefit from pro-rated benefits, enhanced job security, and other entitlements of full-time workers.

Job tenure This term refers to the amount of time, usually counted in months or years, a person holds her/his job and reflects broader patterns of stable and unstable employment.

Just-in-time A strategy for organizing production that minimizes inventory and storage at the production facility. Parts are produced or ordered from suppliers as they are needed.

Kaizen The notion of continuous improvement. Under lean production, techniques are regularly evaluated in order to improve efficiency.

Keynesianism Based on the ideas of John Maynard Keynes, this economic theory suggested that in order to sustain economic health and promote economic growth, it was essential to stimulate purchasing power along with production. This involved providing support to working classes through a strong welfare state, decent wages, and other forms of protection. These ideas departed abruptly from classical economic theories that relied on the market's ability to achieve equilibrium over time (Stanford, 2008: 55–7).

Labour force participation Refers to the number of individuals in the population aged 15 and older who are employed (includes self-employed, working on a family farm, business, or as a professional) or unemployed (limited to those looking for work or starting work shortly) (Statistics Canada, 2003).

Labour market Formal structures within the economy in which workers exchange their labour for wages.

Labour market marginalization Refers to the process in which specific segments of the labour force are pushed to the periphery in terms of workplace benefits—including wages, benefits, and security.

Labour market segmentation The tendency in the labour market for work to be divided along gender lines, with women occupying specific sectors and occupations—service/health services/nursing; while men tend to occupy others—resource extraction and manufacturing/factory work. This segmentation is then reflected in other differences in wage rates, unionization, occupational prestige, and so forth.

Labour process theory Explains the process of deskilling work and managerial strategies to maintain control over workers and work processes.

Lean production A strategy employed in industry whereby parts inventories are kept to the minimum needed at the time in order to reduce the need for warehouses for large quantities of parts and for large work stations. This system relies on a just-in-time process.

Lockout A work stoppage initiated by the employer that restricts the workers from entering the workplace. A lockout may occur when the collective agreement has expired and the union and employer are unable to reach a satisfactory collective agreement through collective bargaining.

Longevity risk The concern that retirees may outlive their pension savings and become reliant on the limited pension benefits provided through CPP/QPP, GIS, and **OAS**, and that they become a financial burden to their family and/or are financially unable to maintain their previous standard of retirement living.

Maquiladoras or Maquilas A group of manufacturing plants located in the border towns of northern Mexico that use cheap labour and tax incentives to import and assemble duty-free components for export.

Marriage bar The employment practice, popular through to the mid-1950s, that upon marriage women should be required to withdraw from paid employment.

McDonaldization A term coined by George Ritzer (*The McDonaldization of Society*) to refer to the increasing rationalization of tasks within everyday life.

McJob Refers to jobs characterized by low wages, few or no benefits, few opportunities for advancement, relatively low rates of unionization, and often part-time. These jobs are usually described as insecure and precarious.

Mommy wars The conflict popularized in the mass media in the early twenty-first century between various forms of mothering. Mothers who were full-time at home and prioritized their children's education and well-being were represented as pitted against mothers who worked full-time and relied on various childcare alternatives.

Multiple job holding Work patterns in which individuals combine employment of several part-time jobs or a full-time job along with one or several part-time jobs.

NEETs Not in Education, Employment, or Training. Refers to young people in Canada and European countries aged 15 to 29 who are vulnerable members of society, having few job prospects and little education or qualifications and womay be inclined to commit petty crimes.

Neoliberalism The set of policies that seek to reinforce free market, private property, and capitalist social relations through privatization, deregulation, flexibilization, free trade, de-unionization, and financialization. Neoliberalism embraces a conservative approach to state involvement, encouraging a reduction in the size of the state and its services. Citizens are encouraged, from this perspective, to rely on their own individual efforts in responding to personal or familial difficulties and crises.

New economy Refers to the continual development of new goods, technologies, and social relations under capitalism. Features of the new economy include flexibility in production systems and labour markets, technological innovation, global production networks, globalization, and neoliberal policies. The new economy tends to be characterized by increased labour market volatility, and increasingly powerful corporate conglomerates.

Nonstandard work Refers to work which is not standard; in other words, the wide variety of work that is not permanent, full-time work. It is not synonymous with precarious work.

Offshoring Refers to contracting out of business to a provider outside the nation.

Old Age Security (OAS) This policy was introduced in 1951 as a federal, universal flat-rate pension for citizens aged 70 and older. Today, it provides a monthly payment available to Canadian citizens aged 65 or older who have resided in Canada at least 10 years after 18 years of age. The amount of OAS is determined by length of residency in Canada after age 18. Employment history is not a factor since you can receive OAS if you have never worked or if you are still working. This is a taxable benefit and may be "taxed back" if your income is sufficiently high (Marshman, 2013).

On-site childcare Childcare facilities located in the workplace (on-site). Workers benefit from the ease with which they are able to to drop off, pick up, and monitor their children on their workd ays.

One Big Union An idea that was popular in the late nineteenth and early twentieth centuries to bring together the interests of all workers in order to find general solutions to the problems facing labour. This idea was associated with the Industrial Workers of the World (IWW) and was considered to be a radical concept.

Ontario Retirement Pension Plan This policy, which was proposed in 2014, would seek to establish an Ontario pension plan that would serve to improve the pension income of individuals working in Ontario.

Organization for Economic Co-operation and Development (OECD) This organization was founded in 1960 by 18 European countries, along with the United States and Canada. Currently, it has expanded to 34 countries, including both advanced and emerging economies. Its mission is to provide both data and analysis to help governments improve prosperity, address environmental issues, and fight social inequality.

Outsourcing A practice used by different companies to reduce costs by transferring portions of work to outside suppliers rather than completing it internally.

Part-time work The designation of part-time work varies internationally and even regionally. In Canada, part-time work is typically defined as fewer than 30 hours a week. However, part-time workers average between 18 and 19 hours per week (2000–2014) (Statistics Canada, 2015).

Participation rate Represents the number of working age persons expressed as a percentage of the population aged 15 and over who are either employed or unemployed but looking for a job. Typically, students, homemakers, and persons under 64 who are retired are not counted.

Phased-in retirement A policy that allows older workers to phase in to their ultimate retirement. During the phase-in period they typically reduce their workload over a period of years. In some instances, employers provide cash incentives to encourage workers to take up this option.

Precariat This term was popularized by Guy Standing (2014) and refers to the growing numbers of individuals, particularly youth, who are trapped in precarious (part-time, temporary, insecure) work around the globe. These people (often an intersection of young, immigrant, racialized, disabled persons) are trapped at the bottom of the class structure since they are chronically unemployed and underemployed.

Precarious (insecure) work This is not synonymous with nonstandard work. For example, permanent part-time work may be as secure and stable as permanent full-time employment. Precarious work is characterized by uncertainty, unpredictability, and riskiness. The employee does not know from day to day, week to week, month to month, or year to year whether or not and to what degree he/she will be employed (Kalleberg, 2009).

Primary sector This part of the economy is characterized by the extraction of raw materials.

Pro-immigration federal policies Canadian immigration policy is managed at the federal level. The federal government, over the past several decades, has encouraged immigration by setting relatively high levels of acceptance of new immigrants (approximately 250,000 per year), facilitating specific forms of immigration (family immigration) and creating new avenues for immigration (economic immigrants).

Public sociology Engages communities and opens communication between academics and publics in order to deepen our understanding of public issues. It diverges from professional or traditional sociology that employs a scientific framework to study theories and assumptions regarding social phenomena, drawing conclusions based on tested methodologies.

Racialization The process and practice of attributing biological and social differences to groups of people.

Rand formula Instituted by Justice Ivan Rand in 1946, the Rand formula requires all workers within a unionized workplace to have union dues automatically deducted from their paycheques. The underlying idea here is that all workers within a unionized workplace share the benefits of the collective agreement, regardless of whether they support or join the union.

Rationality The ethos of efficiency and the principle that rules and practical results are the keys to understanding and approaching human affairs.

Rationalization of society Refers to a widespread acceptance of rationality and forms of social organization largely built around this principle. This includes the process by which interactions are increasingly based on efficiency measures rather than on emotions, customs, or traditions.

Registered Pension Plans (RPPs) This term refers to formal pension plans, in either the public or private sector, which are provided by employers to their employees. Their actual forms vary from defined benefit to defined contribution to hybrid or composite plans.

Replacement levels When the birth of children is outnumbered by the death rate of a population, the population is considered to be below replacement levels. In the absence of other interventions, notably immigration, the size of the population will decline over time.

Registered Retirement Savings Plans (RRSPs) This policy was introduced in 1956 and allowed Canadians to set aside money in a fund which was only taxed when it was withdrawn—presumably in retirement and therefore at a lower tax rate.

Resistant emotional misbehaviour Forms of workplace behaviours whenever workers realize their interests are different from the managerial prerogatives of control and accumulation. Activities of resistance can take either individual or collective forms.

Reserve army of labour A portion of the labour force that is routinely not fully deployed—women, youth, children, the elderly, the disabled. In the event of crisis, as evidenced during the First and Second World Wars, this reserve army of labour is mobilized. The presence of this reserve army not only satisfies labour needs during crises, but it may undermine workers' efforts to control their labour. In the event of work stoppages, this reserve army may be mobilized.

Reshoring The process whereby a transnational corporation relocates part of its production or service back to its homeland from another country.

Restructuring Refers to the reorganization of both the economy and work, including production processes and management practices.

Right to request legislation This legislation, which has been enacted throughout much of Europe but is essentially absent in North America, guarantees employees the right to request, within limitations, alterations to their working-time arrangements.

Robotization Refers to automation or the process of a person adopting robot-like movements.

Sandwich generation With the increased longevity of seniors and the prolonged dependency of youth, many Canadian men and women find themselves providing care and support to both seniors and youth and, as a result, feel trapped in the middle of competing demands.

Satellite offices To accommodate workers who are employed from home, some organizations provide offices that function as satellites for their main offices/headquarters. These offices provide a more accessible location in which home-based workers may connect to other workers in their business. Those who work full-time in satellite offices benefit from a less arduous commute and great accessibility to their local community.

Secondary sector Part of the economy that is characterized by processing raw materials into manufactured goods.

Self-employment Refers to the practice of creating one's own employment through a self-run business. It may be a one-person business or may involve the employment of several other individuals. Self-employment is, by its nature, flexible but also potentially insecure. While some self-employed workers may have sufficient business to hire personnel for their enterprise, **own-account** self-employed workers have no employees and their business income relies completely on their personal efforts.

Service sector Otherwise known as the tertiary sector, this is today the largest and the most labour intensive portion of the economy, which includes both public institutions and private businesses.

Service workers For these workers, whose status ranks below the professional level, the key part of the labour process involves interaction with customers.

Short-term and limited term employment While job tenure may vary considerably from one workplace to another, analysts are concerned about the rapid increase in work which is either short-term (relative to other work) or strictly limited to a specific term.

Social division of labour The division of society by occupations and types of work.

Social unionism The idea that unions contribute broadly to social and political causes in order to advance the interests of their members and all members of the working class.

Sociological imagination A term coined by C. Wright Mills. It is a way of understanding individual experiences in larger social and historical contexts. It links the private troubles of the individual and the public problems and affairs of societies.

Standard Employment Relationship (SER) Typically refers to the permanent, 40-hour work week which is defined as full-time and which is often accompanied by benefits.

Sticky floor Refers to the fact that women may find it difficult to advance out of the bottom ranks of the labour force. They are often stuck at the bottom of their career ladder for longer periods than their male counterparts and may require great achievements in order to advance beyond the floor.

Strike A work stoppage in which union members collectively withdraw from work until a satisfactory agreement is attained through collective bargaining. Workers may vote in favour of a strike when their collective agreement has expired and the employer refuses to bargain or they remain at an impasse with the employer and cannot come to an agreement.

Strike pay Refers to payments made by the union to workers while they are on strike. Usually these payments are a small percentage of workers' regular earnings and they are meant simply to help workers "get by" while on strike. Unions have strike funds set aside for these payments.

Surplus value Refers to the labour power workers expend at their workplace over and above the time at work it would take them to produce enough to cover the cost of their wages. For example, a worker may be expected to produce 100 units per day. Once s/he produces 20 units, the amount that the capitalist will make on these 20 units will cover the costs of the worker's labour. For the rest of the time at work, making 80 more units, the worker is producing surplus value, or profits for the capitalist.

Tax-free savings account This policy, introduced in 2009, allows Canadians who are 18 and older who have a valid Social Insurance Number to place money in a tax-free account. These monies are not tax-deductible but these funds and any interest accrued are essentially tax free.

Telecommuting The practice whereby workers use telecommunications in order to work from home. Advances in technology and security have meant it is increasingly feasible for workers to accomplish all or part of their work from home and communicate these work results to their main office electronically.

Temporary workers All nonstandard workers who are employed on a non-permanent basis are considered temporary. The parameters of temporary employment are typically laid out in the employment agreement or contract. Full-time and part-time employees may both be hired on a temporary basis.

Term employment Refers to work that is for a designated period of time, either long or short.

Tertiary sector Part of the economy characterized by service sector employment.

Time crunch Term used to refer to the experiences of too much to do in too little time. Robinson and Godbey (2005) developed a time crunch index that seeks to quantify and distinguish the ways in which individuals experience time stress.

Transnational labour force Refers to the globalization of labour markets wherein workers are crossing national borders in search of work more frequently and in greater numbers.

Underemployed Graduates of universities and colleges who are working in low-paid, part-time jobs that do not require a degree but who are seeking full-time employment or are working in low-skilled, low-paying full-time jobs.

Underground economy Informal exchanges of goods, labour, and services that do not involve record keeping and therefore avoid taxation.

Unemployed youth Persons in Canada between the ages of 15 and 24 who during a reference period were without work, available for work, and actively seeking work.

Union advantage The benefits of union membership at work as well as in the quality of life.

Union density Union membership as a proportion of the labour force, including all waged and salaried workers.

Unionization rate The number of employed persons who are union members as a proportion of the total number of employed persons within the economy (or within a sector, industry, or other defined context).

Unpaid work The wide variety of work, which for various reasons, is not remunerated with money or some other form of financial compensation. The term was first extensively applied to describe women's (and men's) household work.

Wage gap Typically refers to the differences between average men's and women's wages. Controlling for occupation and labour sector, men earn on average higher wages than their female counterparts. While much of this difference has been eroded (in part through legislative initiatives), it continues to persist.

Wage penalty Refers to the fact that when women move into an occupation or profession and increasingly dominate it, the wages/salaries for that occupation or profession tend to decline.

Wildcat strike Refers to a work stoppage taken without the support or authorization of the union. It is an impromptu action taken by a group of workers while a collective agreement is in force, often to protest particular issues at work, such as unsafe conditions.

World systems global commodity chains (WSGCC) Refers to the spatial and hierarchical structure within a commodity chain, capturing the unequal distribution of rewards/surplus value.

Work restructuring Refers to a broad range of work and employment practices, including lean production, teleworking, flexibility initiatives, and new management and monitoring practices, as well as new contractual arrangements.

Work sharing Unlike job sharing, which is an individual work arrangement, work sharing refers to policies that seek to share whatever work is available amongst workers. The intent of such policies is to reduce un/underemployment.

Working time accounts This progressive employment benefit allows workers to "bank" their working times. In this way, they may accumulate hours to be used at a later date during periods of high workplace activity and also borrow hours when there are inadequate available hours in the workplace. This approach allows workers and employers flexibility while avoiding unemployment and layoffs.

Youth labour force All persons between the ages of 15 and 24 who were employed or unemployed over a specified time period.

Youth unemployment rate A percentage number whose formula includes the following variables.

$$\frac{\text{Number of Unemployed Young Persons} \times 100}{\text{Youth Labour Force}} =$$

Zero hours contract This contract implies no promise of paid work. The employee agrees to work for the employer with no guarantee of any hours of paid work. The employer benefits from maximum flexibility in terms of on-call workers and employees benefit from the promise of future work in an extremely tight labour market.

References

Acharya, Ram. 2006. "The services economy in Canada: An overview," in R. Lipsey and A. Nakamura, eds, pp. 77–130, *Services Industries and Knowledge-Based Economy*. Calgary: University of Calgary Press.

Ackroyd, Stephen, and Paul Thompson. 1999. *Organizational Misbehaviour*. London: Sage.

Adams, Roy J. 2005. "Organizing Wal-Mart: The Canadian campaign," *Just Labour* 6/7 (Autumn): 1–11.

Agarwala, T., et al. 2014. "Influence of managerial support on work–life conflict and organizational commitment: An international comparison for India, Peru and Spain," *International Journal of Human Resource Management* 25 (10): 1460–83.

Alba, D. 2014. "Apple and Facebook pay for female employees to freeze eggs," 14 October. http://www.wired.com/2014/10/apple-facebook-pay-female-employees-freeze-eggs/.

Albanese, Patrizia. 2011. "Addressing the interlocking complexity of paid work and care: Lessons from changing family policy in Quebec," in Catherine Krull and Justyna Sempruch, eds, pp. 130–43, *A Life in Balance? Reopening the Family–Work Debate*. Vancouver: UBC Press.

Albo, Gregory. 2010. "The 'new economy' and capitalism today," in N. Pupo and M. Thomas, eds, pp. 3–20, *Interrogating the New Economy: Restructuring Work in the 21st Century*. Toronto: University of Toronto Press.

Algarni, F.S., D.P. Gross, A. Senthilselvan, and M.C. Battie. 2015. "Ageing workers with work-related musculoskeletal injuries," *Occupational Medicine* 65: 229–37.

Alini, Erica. 2011. "The future of manufacturing in Canada," *Macleans* (September).

Allahar, Anton, and James E. Cote. 1998. *Richer and Poorer: The Structure of Inequality in Canada*. Toronto: James Lorimer.

Angus Reid Institute. 2015. "Canadians at work: Technology enables more flexibility, but longer hours too. Checking in is the new normal," *Canadian Public Opinion Poll*, 9 February.

Annan, Kofi. 2006. "The Secretary-General Address to the High-level Dialogue of the General Assembly on International Migration and Development," New York, 14 September. http://www.un.org/migration/sg-speech.html.

Appelbaum, R., and N. Lichtenstein. 2007. "A new world of retail supremacy: Supply chains and workers' chains in the age of Wal-Mart," *International Labor and Working-Class History* 70: 106–25.

Armstrong, Pat, and Hugh Armstrong. 2010. *Wasting Away: The Undermining of Canadian Health Care*. Toronto: Oxford University Press.

Arnett, J.J. 2000. "Emerging adulthood: A theory of development from the late teens through the twenties," *American Psychologist* 55: 469–80.

Arnett, J.J. 2004. *Emerging Adulthood: The Winding Road from Late Teens through the Twenties*. Oxford: Oxford University Press.

Arnett, J.J. 2006. "G. Stanley Hall's adolescence: Brilliance and nonsense," *History of Psychology* 9 (3): 186–97.

Arrighi, Giovanni, and J. Drangel. 1986. "The stratification of the world-economy," *Review* 10 (1): 9–74.

Association of Universities and Colleges of Canada (AUCC). 2007. "Enrolment," p. 31, *Trends in Higher Education*. AUCC: Ottawa.

Auger, Nathalie, Emilie Le Serbon, and Mikael Rostila. 2015. "Leaving Sweden behind: Gains in life expectancy in Canada," *Scandinavian Journal of Public Health*, 43: 340–7.

Bailey, S., D.C. Haynes, and B. Letiecq. 2013. "'How can you retire when you still got a kid in school?': Economics of raising grandchildren in rural areas," *Marriage and Family Relations* 49: 671–93.

Baily, Martin N., and Robert Z. Lawrence. 2001. "Do we have a new E-conomy?" *American Economic Review* 91 (2): 308–12.

Baker, Dean. 2012. "The bogus case against the minimum wage hike," *Real-World Economics Review Blog*, 5 January. https://rwer.wordpress.com/2012/01/05/the-bogus-case-against-the-minimum-wage-hike/.

Baker, M. 2011. "Maternal employment, childcare and public policy," in C. Krull and J. Sempruch, eds, pp. 47–63, *A Life in the Balance? Reopening the Family–Work Debate*. Vancouver: UBC Press.

Bakker, W., and L. Karsten. 2013. "Balancing paid work, care and leisure in post-separation households: A comparison of single parents with co-parents," *Acta Sociologica* 56 (2): 173–87.

Baldry C., P. Bain, and P. Taylor. 1998. "Bright, satanic offices: intensification, control and team Taylorism," in P. Thompson and C. Warhurst, eds, pp. 163–83, *Workplaces of the Future*. London: MacMillan.

Balzan, P., M. Dominguez, and M. Gonzalez. 2014. "Couple bargaining or socio-economic status? Why some parents spend more time with their children than others," *European Societies* 16 (1): 3–27.

Bangladesh Export Processing Zones Authority (BEPZA). 2015. "Year wise employment." http://epzbangladesh.org.bd/employments/employment_report/chittagong-export-processing-zone-2.

Baritz, Loren. 1960. *The Servants of Power: A History of the Use of Social Science in American Industry*. New York: John Wiley & Sons.

Barmak, S. 2011. "Where our pensions came from," *Toronto Star*, 24 April: A14.

Barnard, S., T. Hassan, B. Bagilhole, and A. Dainty. 2012. "'They're not girly girls': An exploration of quantitative and qualitative data on engineering and gender in higher education," *European Journal of Engineering Education* 37 (2): 193–204.

Basen, Ira. 2014. "Most university undergrads now taught by poorly paid part-timers," *CBC News*, 8 September. http://www.cbc.ca/news/canada/most-university-undergrads-now-taught-by-poorly-paid-part-timers.

Baskerville, Peter. 2015. "Reimagining the coffee supply chain." http://espressocoffee.quora.com/Reimagining-the-coffee-supply-chain.

Bauman, Zygmut. 2005. *Work, Consumerism and the New Poor*, 2nd edn. Maidenhead: McGraw-Hill International.

Baxter, J., S. Buchler, F. Perales, and M. Western. 2014. "A life-changing event: First births and men's and women's attitudes to mothering and gender divisions of labor," *Social Forces* 93 (3): 989–1014.

Bazel, P., and J. Mintz. 2014. "Income adequacy among Canadian seniors: Helping singles most," *The School of Public Policy SPP Research Papers* (University of Calgary) 7 (4): 1–17.

Beard, Renee L., and John B. Williamson. 2011. "Social policy and the internal dynamics of the senior rights movement," *Journal of Aging Studies* 25: 22–33.

Beaudry, Paul, Thomas Lemieux, and Daniel Parent. 2000. "What is happening in the youth labour market in Canada?" *Canadian Public Policy* 26 (Supplement): S59–S83.

Beaupré, P., P. Turcotte, and A. Milan. 2006. "When is junior moving out? Transitions from the parental home to independence," *Canadian Social Trends* Winter (82): 9–15.

Beland, Daniel, and John Myles. 2012. "Varieties of federalism, institutional legacies and social policy: Comparing Old-Age and Unemployment Insurance reform in Canada," *International Journal of Social Welfare* 21: 75–87.

Belt, Vicki, R. Richardson, and J. Webster. 2000. "Women's work in the information economy: The case of telephone call centres," *Information, Communication & Society* 3 (3): 366–85.

Bendit, René, and Ana Miranda. 2015. "Transitions to adulthood in contexts of economic crisis and post-recession: The case of Argentina," *Journal of Youth Studies* 18 (2): 183–96.

Benzie, Robert and R. Ferguson. 2016. "Wynne says CPP deal means no need for Ontario pension deal." http://www.thestar.com/news/queenspark/2016/06/21/wynne-says-cpp-deal-means-no-need-for-ontario-pension-plan.html

Berg, Peter, G. Bosch, and Jean Charest. 2014. "Working-time configurations: A framework for analyzing diversity across countries," *Industrial and Labor Relations Review* 67 (3): 805–37.

Bergh, Andreas. 2011. "The rise, fall and revival of a capitalist welfare state: What are the policy lessons from Sweden?" Stockholm: Research Institute of Industrial Economics. IFN Working Paper No. 873.

Bernard, A. 2013. "Unemployment dynamics among Canada's youth," *Economic Insights*. Statistics Canada Catalogue no. 11-626-X—No. 024.

Betcherman, G., and R. Morissette. 1994. "Recent youth labour market experiences in Canada," Analytic Studies Branch Research Paper Series Number 63. Ottawa: Statistics Canada.

Bhaskar, Ranjit. 2013. "New Canadians pushed to edges of the economy," *New Canadian Media*, 22 October. http://newcanadianmedia.ca/item/8924-new-candians-pushed-edges-of-the-economy.

Biggs, Simon, Ashley Carr, and Irja Haapala. 2015. "Work, aging, and risks to family life: The case of Australia," *Canadian Journal of Aging* 34 (3): 321–30.

Blackwell, Richard. 2014. "Green energy sector jobs surpass total oil sands employment,"

The Globe and Mail, 2 December. http://www.theglobeandmail.com/report-on-business/industry-news/energy-and-resources/green-energy-sector-jobs-surpass-oil-sand-employment-total/article21859169/.

Bloskie, C., and G. Gellatly. 2012. "Recent Developments in the Canadian Economy: Fall 2012." *Economic Insights*, No. 19. Statistics Canada Catalogue no. 11-626-X. Ottawa: Statistics Canada.

Bluestone, Barry, and Bennett Harrison. 1984. *The Deindustrialization of America: Plant Closings, Community Abandonment and the Dismantling of Basic Industry*. New York: Basic Books.

BMO Financial Group. 2015. "BMO annual Women's Day study: Fewer than half of Canadian women feel they've achieved work/life balance," *Yahoo.com*, 4 March. http://finance.yahoo.com/news/bmo-annual-womens-day-study-123000425.html.

Bolton, Sharon C. 2005. *Emotion Management in the Workplace*. Basingstoke: Palgrave Macmillan.

Bomkamp, Samantha, and Alejandra Cancino. 2014. "Hostess Twinkie plant in Schiller Park closes after 84 years," *Chicago Tribune*, 20 August. http://my.chicagotribune.com/#section/-1/article/p2p-81133137/.

Bonacich, Edna, and Jake Wilson. 2008. *Getting the Goods: Ports, Labor and the Logistics Revolution*. Ithaca: Cornell University Press.

Bonikowska, A., and G. Schellenberg. 2014. "Employment transitions among older workers leaving long-term jobs: Evidence from administrative data," Analytical Studies Branch Research Paper Series. Statistics Canada, Catalogue No. 11F0019M-No. 355. Ottawa: Minister of Industry.

Booth, Tamzin. 2013. "Here, there and everywhere," *The Economist*, 19 January.

Bosch, G., P. Dawkins, and F. Michon. 1993. *Times are Changing: Working Time in 14 Industrialised Countries*. Geneva: International Institute of Labour Studies.

Bosque, Melissa. 2013. "Thanks to NAFTA, conditions for Mexican factory workers like Rosa Moreno are getting worse," *ALTERNET*, 11 December. http://www.alternet.org/labor/after-20-years-nafta-thanks-nafta-what-happened-mexican-factory-workers-rosa-moreno.

Boyd, M., and D. Norris. 1999. "The crowded nest: Young adults at home," *Canadian Social Trends* Spring (52): 2–5.

Boyenge, Jean-Pierre. 2007. ILO database on export processing zones (Revised). Geneva: ILO.

Bracero History Archive. 2016. "About." http://braceroarchive.org/about.

Bracey, Leon. 2013. "Ringing up success? Call centres in Canada," *Business in Focus Magazine* April: 120–3. http://www.businessinfocusmagazine.com/2013/04/call-centres-in-canada/.

Braverman, Harry. 1975/2000. *Labor and Monopoly Capital: The Degradation of Work in the Twentieth Century*. New York: Monthly Review Press.

Broad, David. 2000. *Hollow Work, Hollow Society?: Globalization and the Casual Labour Problem*. Halifax: Fernwood Publishing.

Brook, Paul. 2009. "The alienated heart: Hochschild's 'emotional labour' thesis and the anticapitalist politics of alienation," *Capital and Class* 33 (2): 7–31.

Brotheridge, C. M., and A. A. Grandey. 2002. "Emotional labor and burn-out: Comparing two perspectives of people work," *Journal of Vocational Behavior* 60: 17–39.

Brough, P., et al. 2014. "Work–life balance: A longitudinal evaluation of a new measure across Australia and New Zealand workers," *International Journal of Human Resource Management* 25 (19): 2724–44.

Burawoy, Michael. 1979. *Manufacturing Consent: Changes in the Labor Process Under Monopoly Capitalism*. Chicago: University of Chicago Press.

Burawoy, Michael. 2005a. "For public sociology," *American Sociological Review* 70 (1): 4–28.

Burawoy, Michael. 2005b. "The critical turn to public sociology," *Critical Sociology* 31 (3): 313–26.

Burke, Jason. 2014. "Rana Plaza: One year from the Bangladesh factory disaster," *The Guardian*, 19 April. http://www.theguardian.com/world/2014/apr/19/rana-plaza-bangladesh-one-year-on.

Burleton, Derek, Sonya Gulati, Connor McDonald, and Sonny Scarfone. 2013. *Jobs in Canada: Where, What and For Whom?* Toronto: TD Economics.

Burleton, Derek, Sonya Gulati, Connor McDonald, and Sonny Scarfone. 2014. *Jobs in Canada: Where, What and for Whom?* Toronto: TD Economics. http://www.td.com/economics

Burris, Beverly H. 1989. "Technocratic organization and gender," *Women's Studies International Forum* 12 (4): 447–62.

Burton, Peter, and Shelley Phipps. 2010. "Families, time and well-being in Canada," *Luxembourg Income Study*. Working Paper No. 537. May. http://books.scholarsportal.info/viewdoc.html?id=381948.

Burton, Peter, and Shelley Phipps. 2011. "Families, time, and well-being in Canada," *Canadian Public Policy* 37 (3): 395–423.

Busby, Colin, and David Gray. 2011. "Mending Canada's Employment Insurance quilt: The case for restoring equality," *Policy Paper No. 144*. Toronto: C.D. Howe Institute.

Business News Network. 2014. "Quebec loses 625 jobs in 24 hours as two factories close," *BNN.ca*. http://www.bnn.ca/News/2014/7/9/Quebec-loses-625-jobs-in-24-hours-as-two-factories-close.aspx.

Bynner, John. 2005. "Rethinking the youth phase of the life-course: The case for emerging adulthood?" *Journal of Youth Studies* 8(4): 367–84.

Bynner, John, and Samantha Parsons. 2002. "Social exclusion and the transition from school to work: The case of young people not in education, employment, or training (NEET)," *Journal of Vocational Behavior* 60(2): 289–309.

Cady, K. 2013. "Flexible labor: A feminist response to late twentieth century capitalism?" *Feminist Media Studies* 13 (3): 395–414.

Callahan, Raymond E. 1962. *Education and the Cult of Efficiency*. Chicago: University of Chicago Press.

Campbell, C., and J. Pearlman. 2013. "Period effects, cohort effects, and the narrowing gender wage gap," *Social Science Research* 42: 1693–711.

Canadian Association of University Teachers (CAUT). 2013–2014. *CAUT Almanac of Post-Secondary Education in Canada*. Ottawa: CAUT.

Canadian Centre for Policy Alternatives (CCPA), and Jeff Fraser. 2014. *Tuition in Canada*. Ottawa: Canadian Centre for Policy Alternatives. http://apps.policyalternatives.ca/.

Canadian Federation of Students (CFS). n.d. "Student debt." http://cfs-fcee.ca/the-issues/student-debt/.

Canadian Labour Congress (CLC). 2015. "Why unions? Explore the union advantage." http://canadianlabour.ca/why-unions.

Canadian Press. 2015. "Canada's retail exodus: Here's who's closed stores in Canada," *Financial Post*, 15 January. http://business.financialpost.com/news/retail-marketing/canadas-retail-exodus-heres-whos-closed-up-shop-in-canada.

Cardwell, Mark. 2015. "Coffee consumption habits continue to shift in Canada," *Marketingmap.ca*. http://www.marketingmag.ca/consumer/coffee-consumption-habits-continue-to-shift-in-canada-139728.

CARP. 2012. "CARP Toronto chapter chair Adina Lebo and VP of advocacy Susan Eng talk workplace age-discrimination," *Carp.ca*. http://www.carp.ca/2012/06/12/carp-toronto-chapter-chair-adina-lebo-and-vp-of-advocacy-Susan-Eng.

CARP 2014. *CARP's Vision for Pension Reform*, October. http://www.carp.ca.

Carriere, Yves, and Diane Galarneau. 2011. "Delayed retirement: A new trend?" *Perspectives on Labour and Income*, 26 October: 3–16.

Carriere, Yves, and Diane Galarneau. 2012. "The impact of involuntary breaks in employment and level of education on the timing of retirement," *Labour Statistics Research Paper*. Statistics Canada Catalogue No. 75-004-M-No. 001. Ottawa: Minister of Industry.

Castells, M. 1996. *The Information Age: Economy, Society and Culture. Volume I: The Rise of the Network Society*. Malden, MA: Blackwell.

Castells, M. 2000. *The Rise of the Network Society: The Information Age, Economy, Society and Culture. Volume 1*. New York: Wiley.

Castles, Stephen, Hein de Haas, and Mark J. Miller. 2013. *The Age of Migration: International Population Movements in the Modern World*, 5th edn. London: Macmillan.

CBC News. 2014. "Canada's dismal wage growth still better than most of G20," *CBC .ca*, 5 December. http://www.cbc.ca/news/business/.

CBC News. 2015. "Minimum wage rises in 5 provinces today," *CBC.ca*, 1 October. http://www.cbc.ca/news/canada/minimum-wage-rises-in-5-provinces-today-1.3251126.

Cech, E., and M. Blair-Loy. 2014. "Consequences of flexibility stigma among academics, scientists and engineers," *Work and Occupations* 41 (1): 86–110.

Centre for Research on Work and Society (CRWS). 2009. *Just Labour*. Special Edition on the Employees Free Choice Act. Volume 15 (November).

Chandler, Alfred D. 1977. *The Visible Hand: The Managerial Revolution in American Business*. Cambridge: Harvard University Press.

Chaplin, Ralph. 1968. "Why I Wrote Solidarity Forever," reproduced in *IWW Industrial Archives*. http://www.iww.org/history/icons/solidarity_forever/1.

Charbonneau, Leo. 2013. "Sifting through the scant data on contingent faculty," *University Affairs*, 29 October. http://www.universityaffairs.ca/opinion/margin-notes/sifting-through-the-scant-data-on-contingent-faculty.

Charlesworth, Sara, and A. Heron. 2011. "New Australian working time minimum standards: Reproducing the same old gendered architecture?" *Journal of Industrial Relations* 54 (2): 164–81.

Chesley, Noelle. 2014. "Information and communication technology use, work intensification and employee strain and distress," *Work, Employment and Society* 28 (4): 589–610.

Chinoy, Ely. 1957/1992. *Automobile workers and the American Dream*, 2nd edn. Urbana: University of Illinois Press.

Chou, K., and K. Cheung. 2013. "Family-friendly policies in the workplace and their effect on the work–life conflicts in Hong Kong," *The International Journal of Human Resource Management* 24 (20): 3872–85.

Choudhary, Vikas, Jan van Hilten, and Roy Parizat. 2011. "Vietnam coffee supply chain risk assessment," *Vietnamica: Insights on Indochina's Economics*. http://www.vietnamica.net/vietnam-coffee-supply-chain-risk-assessment/.

Christofides, L., A. Polycarpou, and K. Vrachimis. 2013. "Gender wage gaps, 'sticky floors' and 'glass ceilings' in Europe," *Labour Economics* 21: 86–102.

Clawson, Dan. 1979. *Bureaucracy and the Labor Process: The Transformation of U.S. Industry, 1860–1920*. New York: Monthly Review Press.

Clawson, Dan, and Naomi Gerstel. 2014. "The time crunch: Will labor lead?" *New Labor Forum* 23 (3): 32–8.

Clement, Wallace. 1975. *The Canadian Corporate Elite: An Analysis of Economic Power*. Toronto: McClelland & Stewart.

Coffey, W.J., and J.J. McRae. 1989. *Service Industries in Regional Development*. Montreal: Institute for Research on Public Policy.

Cohn, Martin Regg. 2012. "Cohn: Tim Hudak's Tory vision for a low-union, low-wage Ontario," *The Toronto Star*, 30 June. http://www.thestar.com/news/canada/2012/06/30/cohn_tim_hudaks_tory_vision_for_a_lowunion_lowwage_ontario.html.

Colman, R. 2003. *A Profile of Women's Health Indicators in Canada*. Ottawa, ON: Health Canada, Women's Health Bureau.

Conrad, Margaret, Alvin Finkel, and Donald Fyson. 2015. *History of the Canadian Peoples: 1867 to the Present, Volume 2*. Toronto: Pearson Education.

Cooke, Gordon B., and T. Cooper. 2013. "50+ among the 50+: Who works long workweeks among older workers in Canada," *Community, Work and Family* 16 (1): 39–45.

Copley, F.B. 1923. *Frederick W. Taylor. Volumes I and II*. New York: Harper and Bros.

Cordova, E. 1986. "From full-time wage employment to atypical employment: A major shift in the evolution of labour relations?" *International Labour Review* 125 (6): 641–57.

Correll, S., E. Kelly, L. O'Connor, and J. Williams. 2014. "Redesigning, redefining work," *Work and Occupations* 41 (1): 3–17.

Coté, James E. 2014. "Towards a new political economy of youth," *Journal of Youth Studies* 17 (4): 527–43.

Coté, James E., and Anton Allahar. 1998. *Richer and Poorer: The Structure of Inequality in Canada*. Toronto: James Lorimer & Company.

Coté, James E., and Anton Allahar. 2001. "Youth: The disinherited generation," in Dan Glenday and Ann Duffy, eds, pp. 247–77, *Canadian Society: Meeting the Challenges of the Twenty First Century*. Toronto: Oxford University Press.

Coté, James E., and Anton Allahar. 2006. *Critical Youth Studies: A Canadian Focus*. Toronto: Prentice Hall.

Coté, James E., and Anton Allahar. 2007. *Ivory Tower Blues: A University System in Crisis*. Toronto: University of Toronto Press.

Coté, James E., and Anton Allahar. 2011. *Lowering Higher Education: The Rise of Corporate Universities and the Fall of the Liberal Arts*. Toronto: University of Toronto Press.

Coté, S., and L.M. Morgan. 2002. "A longitudinal analysis of the association between emotion regulation, job satisfaction, and intentions to quit," *Journal of Organizational Behavior* 23: 947–62.

Covert, B. 2014. "Freezing eggs: Privatizing the work/family class," *Toronto Star*, 19 October: A11.

Craciun, Catrinel, and Uwe Flick. 2014. "'I will never be the granny with rosy cheeks': Perceptions of aging in precarious and financially secure middle-aged Germans," *Journal of Aging Studies* 29: 78–87.

Craig, L., and Judith E. Brown. 2015. "Nonstandard employment and nonwork activities, time alone and with others: Can weekend workers make up lost time?" *Journal of Industrial Relations* 57 (1): 3–25.

Craig, L., and A. Powell. 2012. "Dual-earner parents' work–family time: The effects of atypical work patterns and non-parental childcare," *Journal of Popular Research* 29: 229–47.

Craig, L., A. Powell, and N. Cortis. 2012. "Self-employment, work–family time and the gender division of labour," *Work, Employment and Society* 26 (5): 716–34.

Cranford, Cynthia, and Leah Vosko with contributions from Katherine Laxer. 2008. "Gender and work database." http://www.genderwork.ca/gwd/?page_id=29.

Crettenden, A., A. Wright, and N. Skinner. 2014. "Mothers caring for children and young people with developmental disabilities: Intent to work, patterns of participation in paid employment and the experience of workplace flexibility," *Community, Work and Family* 17 (3): 244–67.

Crompton, Susan. 2011. "What's stressing the stressed? Main sources of stress among workers," *Canadian Social Trends* 92 (Winter): 42–51, Statistics Canada, Catalogue No. 11-008.

CTV News. 2015. "Target Canada closing, ending two-year foray," *CTV News.ca*, 12 April. http://www.ctvnews.ca/business/target-canada-closing-ending-2-year-foray-1.2323222.

Cuneo, Carl J. 1979. "State, class and reserve labour: The case of the 1941 Canadian Unemployment Insurance Act," *Canadian Review of Sociology and Anthropology* 16 (2): 147–70.

Cuneo, Carl J. 1980. "State Mediation of Class Contradictions in Canadian Unemployment Insurance, 1930–1935," *Studies in Political Economy* 3: 37–65.

Cwiek, Sarah. 2014. "The middle class took off 100 years ago ... thanks to Henry Ford?" National Public Radio. http://www.npr.org/2014/01/27/267145552/the-middle-class-took-off-100-years-ago-thanks-to-henry-ford.

Daguerre, Anne. 2014. "New corporate elites and the erosion of the Keynesian social compact," *Work, Employment and Society* 28 (2): 323–34.

Davies, A. R., and B.D. Frink. 2014. "The origins of the ideal worker: The separation of work and home in the United States from the market revolution to 1950," *Work and Occupations* 4 (1): 18–39.

Delawala, Imtiyaz. N.d. "What is Coltan?" *ABC News*. http://abcnews.go.com/Nightline/story?id=128631.

Dicum, Gregory, and Nina Luttinger. 2006. *The Coffee Book: Anatomy of an Industry from Crop to the Last Drop*. New York: New Press.

Douglas, S. 2005. *The Mommy Myth: The Idealization of Motherhood and How It Has Undermined All Women*. New York: The Free Press.

Drabe, David, Sven Hauff, and Nichole F. Richter. 2015. "Job satisfaction in aging workforces: An analysis of the USA, Japan and Germany," *The International Journal of Human Resource Management* 26 (6): 783–805.

Drache, Daniel, Anne LeMesurier, and Yanick Noiseux. 2014. *Non-Standard Work and Employment, The Jobs Crisis and Precarity: A Report on the Structural Transformation of the World of Work*. Toronto: PRACTA/GIREPS.

Duffy, A., and N. Pupo. 1992. *Part-time Paradox: Connecting Gender, Work & Family*. Toronto: McClelland Stewart.

Duffy, A., and N. Pupo. 2011. "Employment in the new economy and the impact on Canadian families," in C. Krull and J. Sempruch, eds, pp. 98–114, *A Life in the Balance? Reopening the Family–Work Debate*. Vancouver: UBC Press.

Dumont, Jean-Christophe, and Thomas Liebig. 2014. "Is migration good for the economy?" *Migration Policy Debates*. Paris: OECD.

Dunaway, Wilma. 2014. "Bringing commodity chain analysis back to its world systems roots: Rediscovering women's work and households," *Journal of World Systems Research* 20 (1): 64–81.

Durst, Douglas, and Michael MacLean, eds. 2010. *Diversity and Aging among Immigrant Seniors in Canada, Changing Faces and Greying Temples*. Calgary: Detselig Enterprises Ltd.

Duxbury, Linda, and Christopher Higgins. 2012. "Revisiting work–life issues in Canada: The 2012 National Study on Balancing Work and Caregiving in Canada," *Childcare Resource and Research Unit*. http://childcarecanada.org/documents/research-policy-practice/12/12/revisiting-work-life-issues-in-Canada.

Dwyer, P., and J. Wyn. 2001. *Youth, Education and Risk: Facing the Future*. London: Routledge/Palmer.

Eaton, S.C. 1996. "'The customer is always interesting': Unionized Harvard clericals negotiate work relationships," in C.I. MacDonald and C. Sirianni, eds, pp. 291–332, *Working in the Service Industry*. Philadelphia: Temple University Press.

Edwards, J.R. 2010. "The decline in work time and the increase in free time of manufacturing employees from 1890 to World War I," *The Journal of Private Enterprise* 26 (1): 47–59.

Edwards, Richard C. 1979. *Contested Terrain: The Transformation of the Workplace in the Twentieth Century*. New York: The Free Press.

EI Task Force. 2011. "Making EI work: Discussion paper." Toronto: Mowat Centre for Policy Innovation. http://www.mowateit askforce.ca/sites/default/files/EITF_discussionpaper.pdf.

Eidlin, Barry. 2015. "Class vs. special interest: Labor, power and politics in the United States and Canada in the twentieth century," *Politics and Society* 43 (2): 181–211.

E-importz.com. 2015. "Coffee statistics." http://www.e-importz.com/coffee-statistics.php.

Elliott, S., R. Powell, and J. Brenton. 2015. "Being a good mom: Low-income, black single mothers negotiate intensive mothering," *Journal of Family Issues* 36 (3): 351–70.

European Foundation for the Improvement of Living and Working Conditions (Eurofound). 2013. "Young people and 'NEETS'," *EMCC*. http://www.eurofound.europa.eu/emcc/labourmarket/youth.htm.

European Platform for Investing in Children (EPIC). 2014. "European Union–Sweden: Successful reconciliation of work and family." http://europa.eu/epic/countries/sweden/index_en.htm.

Evans-Pritchard, Ambrose. 2014. "Crisis stalks Europe again as deflation deepens, Germany stalls," *The Telegraph*, 13 August. http://www.telegraph.co.uk/finance/economics/11029679/Crisis-stalks-Europe-again-as-deflation-deepens-Germany-stalls.html.

Fang, Tony, and Anil Verma. 2002. "Union wage premium," *Perspectives on Labour and Income*, 3 (9). http://www.statcan.gc.ca/pub/75-001-x/00902/4168247-eng.html.

Faraday, Fay. 2012. *Made in Canada: How the Law Constructs Migrant Workers' Insecurity*. Toronto: Metcalf Foundation.

Farrell, Leslie, and Tara Fenwick, eds. 2007. *Educating the Global Workforce*. New York: Routledge.

Fasbender, U., J. Deller, M. Wang, and B. Wiernik. 2014. "Deciding whether to work after retirement: The role of the psychological experience of aging," *Journal of Vocational Behavior* 84: 215–24.

Fast, Janet, Judith Frederick, Nancy Zukewich, and Sandra Franke. 2001. "The time of our lives. . .," *Canadian Social Trends* Winter: 20–3.

Federation of International Employers. N.d. "History of working time." http://www.fedee.com/labour-relations/history-of-working-time/.

Feintzeig, Rachel. 2012. "Hostess closes plants as workers strike," *The Wall Street Journal*, 12 November. http://www.wsj.com/articles/SB100014241278873244398045781148622 62799942.

Ferguson, David. 2012. "Hostess closing plants and laying off 18,500 to avoid labor deal," *Rawstory*, 16 November. http://www.rawstory.com/2012/11/hostess-closing-all-plants-and-laying-off-18500-to-avoid-labor-deal/.

Fernandez-Kelly, M.P. 2007. "The global assembly line in the new millennium: A review essay," *Signs: Journal of Women in Culture and Society* 32 (2): 509–21.

Fernie, S., and D. Metcalf. 2000. "(Not) hanging on the telephone: Payment systems in the new sweatshops," in D. Lewin and B. Kaufman, eds, *Advances in Industrial and Labour Relations*. London: JAI Press.

Ferrao, V. 2010. "Paid work." *Women in Canada: A Gender-based Statistical Report*. Statistics Canada. Catalogue no. 89-503-X. Ottawa: Minister of Industry.

Fifarek, Brian J. 2007. "Globalization, offshoring and the location of innovation: A case study of rare earth technology," PhD thesis, unpublished. Carnegie Mellon University.

Fiksenbaum, L. 2014. "Supportive work–family environments: Implications for work–family conflict and well-being," *International Journal of Human Resource Management* 25 (5): 653–72.

Finch, Naomi. 2014. "Why are women more likely than men to extend paid work? The impact of work–family life history," *European Journal of Ageing* 11: 31–9.

Fine, Sean. 2015. "Canadian workers have fundamental right to strike, top court rules," *The Globe and Mail*, 30 January.

http://www.theglobeandmail.com/news/national/top-court-upholds-canadian-workers-right-to-strike/article22717100/.

Finnie, Ross. 2002. "Student loans: Borrowing and burden," *Education Quarterly Review* 8 (4): 28–42. Statistics Canada. Catalogue no. 81–003.

Fister, Emily. 2014. "What Makes Us Unequal? Being a Mom." The Tyee. September 6. http://thetyee.ca/News/2014/09/06/Being-A-Mom-Inequality/

Fitter, Robert, and Raphael Kaplinsky. N.d. "Who gains from product rents as the coffee market becomes more differentiated? A value chain analysis." *IDS Bulletin Paper.*

Flavelle, Dana. 2014. "Work longer, save more, OECD report recommends," *Toronto Star*, 9 December: S9.

Flavin, Patrick, Alexander C. Pacek, and Benjamin Radcliff. 2010. "Labour unions and life satisfaction: Evidence from new data," *Social Indicators Research* 98: 435–49.

Foremski, T. 2004. "Intel looks to Russia to build R&D," *The Financial Times.*

Foster, D., and X. Ren. 2015. "Work–family conflict and the commodification of women's employment in three Chinese airlines," *International Journal of Human Resource Management* 26 (12): 1568–85.

Foster, Karen. 2012. *Youth Employment and Un(der)employment in Canada. More Than a Temporary Problem?* Ottawa: Canadian Centre for Policy Alternatives.

Freeman, Sunny. 2015. "Manufacturers face new economic reality," *Toronto Star*, 15 August: B1, B4.

Frenette, Marc. 2007. *Why Are Youth from Lower-income Families Less Likely to Attend University? Evidence from Academic Abilities, Parental Influence, and Financial Constraints.* Ottawa: Ministry of Industry. Statistics Canada. Catalogue No. 11F0019, No. 295, February. http://www.statcan.gc.ca/pub/11f0019m/11f0019m2007295-eng.pdf.

Fudge, J. 2011. "Working-time regimes, flexibility, and work–life balance: Gender equality and families," in C. Krull and J. Sempruch, eds, pp. 170–93, *A Life in the Balance? Reopening the Family–Work Debate.* Vancouver: UBC Press.

Fudge, J., and Fiona MacPhail. 2009. "The Temporary Foreign Worker Program in Canada: Low-skilled workers as an extreme form of flexible labour," *Comparative Labour Law and Policy Journal* 31 (5): 5–45.

Fuller, Sylvia, and Natasha Stecy-Hildebrandt. 2014. "Lasting disadvantage? Comparing career trajectories of matched temporary and permanent workers in Canada," *Canadian Review of Sociology* 54 (1): 293–324.

Fullick, Melonie. 2015. "Past is prologue when it comes to contract faculty," *University Affairs*, 11 March. http://www.universityaffairs.ca/opinion/speculative-diction/past-is-prologue-when-it-comes-to-contract-faculty.

Gabriel, Y., and T. Lang. 2006. *The Unmanaged Consumer.* London: Sage.

Galarneau, D, R. Morissette, and J. Usalcas. 2013. "What has changed for young people in Canada?" *Insights on Canadian Society.* Statistics Canada. Catalogue no. 75-006-X. Ottawa: Minister of Industry, July.

Galarneau, Diane, and Thao Sohn. 2013. "Long-term trends in unionization," *Insights on Canadian Society.* Statistics Canada. Catalogue no. 75-006-X. Ottawa: Minister of Industry, November. http://www.statcan.gc.ca/pub/75-006-x/2013001/article/11878-eng.pdf.

Galarneau, Diane, M. Turcotte, Y. Carriere, and E. Fecteau. 2015. "The local unemployment rate and permanent retirement," *Insights on Canadian Society*, April. Statistics Canada Catalogue no. 75-006-X. Ottawa: Minister of Industry.

Galea, C., I. Houkes, and A. De Rijk. 2014. "An insider's point of view: How a system of flexible working hours helps employees to strike a proper balance between work and personal life," *International Journal of Human Resource Management* 25 (8): 1090–111.

Gallagher, K., and L. Zarsky. 2007. *The Enclave Economy: Foreign Investment and Sustainable Development in Mexico's Silicon Valley.* Cambridge, MA: The MIT Press.

Garside, Juliette. 2013. "Child labour uncovered in Apple's supply chain," *The Guardian*, 25 January. http://www.theguardian.com/technology/2013/jan/25/apple-child-labour-supply.

Garson, Barbara. 1989. *The Electronic Sweatshop: How Computers are Transforming the Office of the Future into the Factory of the Past.* New York: Penguin Books.

Gereffi, Gary, and Karina Fernandez-Stark. 2011. *Global Value Chain Analysis: A Primer.* Durham, NC: Center on Globalization, Governance and Competitiveness, Duke University. http://www.cggc.duke.edu/pdfs/2011-05-31_GVC_analysis_a_primer.pdf.

Gereffi, Gary, and M. Korzeniewicz, eds. 1994. *Commodity Chains and Global Capitalism*. Westport: Praeger.

Gereffi, Gary. 1994. "The organization of buyer-driven global commodity chains: How US retailers shape overseas production networks," in G. Gereffi and M. Korzeniewicz, eds, pp. 95–122, *Commodity Chains and Global Capitalism*. New York: Praeger Publishers.

Gereffi, Gary. 2014. "Global value chains in a post-Washington consensus world," *Review of International Political Economy* 21 (1): 9–37.

Gierveld, Jenny, Suzan Van der Pas, and Norah Keating. 2015. "Loneliness of older immigrant groups in Canada: Effects of ethnic-cultural background," *Journal of Cross-Cultural Gerontology* 30: 251–68.

Gilbert, Neil. 2004. *Transformation of the Welfare State: The Silent Surrender of Public Responsibility*. Toronto: Oxford University Press.

Gindin, Sam. 2012. "Culture of concessions has gutted organized labour," *Toronto Star*, 25 September. http://www.thestar.com/opinion/editorialopinion/2012/09/25/culture_of_concessions_has_gutted_organized_labour.html.

Glenday, Daniel. 1988. "Canada, the left, and free trade," *Queen's Quarterly* 95(2): 251–84.

Glenday, Daniel. 1989. "Rich but semiperipheral: Canada's ambiguous position in the world economy," *Review: Fernand Braudel Center* XII (2): 209–61.

Glenday, Daniel. 2011. "Power, compliance, resistance and creativity: Power and the differential experience of loose time in large organizations," *New Technology, Work and Employment* 26 (1): 29–38.

Globalexchange.org. N.d. "Coffee FAQ." http://www.globalexchange.org/fairtrade/coffee/faq.

Glomb, T.M., J.D. Kammeyer-Mueller, and M. Rotundo. 2004. "Emotional labor demands and compensating wage differentials," *Journal of Applied Psychology* 89 (4): 700–14.

Goar, Carol. 2012. "'Grey power' surprise in the labour market," *Toronto Star*, 29 February: A23.

Goar, Carol. 2013. "Canada's once-thrifty seniors load on debt," *Toronto Star*, 22 February: A19.

Goar, Carol. 2014a. "Senior citizens are mobilizing against ageism," *Toronto Star*, 10 December: A21.

Goar, Carol. 2014b. "Why Canada's job market hasn't recovered," *Toronto Star* 13 March. http://www.thestar.com/opinion/commentary/2014/03/13/why_canadas_job_market_hasnt_recovered_goar.html.

Goddard, J. 2011. "Seniors unafraid to take on debt," *Toronto Star*, 12 October: B1, B2.

Golden, Lonnie. 2009. "A brief history of long work time and the contemporary sources of overwork," *Journal of Business Ethics* 84: 217–27.

Gordon, J., and E. Rouse. 2013. "The relationship of job and elder caregiving involvement to work-caregiving conflict and work costs," *Research on Aging* 35 (1): 96–117.

Gordon, Michael E., and Lowell Turner, eds. 2000. *Transnational Cooperation Among Labour Unions*. Ithaca, NY: Cornell University Press.

Gotz, Irene. 2013. "Encountering Arlie Hochschild's concept of 'emotional labor' in gendered work cultures: Ethnographic approaches in the sociology of emotions and in European ethnology," in G. Koch and S. Everke Buchanan, eds, pp. 183–200, *Pathways to Empathy. New Studies on Commodification, Emotional Labor, and Time Binds*. University of Chicago Press.

Gould, Anthony M. 2010. "Time as a way of reconciling conflict and cooperation in the employment relationship: A view with a special application to new employment forms," *Just Labour: A Canadian Journal of Work and Society* 16 (Spring): 25–43.

Gould, Elise, and Will Kimball. 2015. "'Right to work' states still have lower wages," Economic Policy Institute, 22 April. http://www.epi.org/publication/right-to-work-states-have-lower-wages/.

Gould, Elise, and Heidi Shierholz. 2011. "The compensation penalty of 'right-to-work' laws," Economic Policy Institute, 17 February. http://www.epi.org/files/page/-/old/briefing-papers/BriefingPaper299.pdf.

Government of Canada. 1889. *Report of the Royal Commission on the Relations of Capital and Labour*. Ottawa.

Government of Canada. 2012. *Citizenship and Immigration: Trends in Economic Performance of Immigrants in Canada*. http://www.cic.gc.ca/english/resources/research/2012-migrant/sec05.asp#bftn22.

Government of Canada. 2013. *Labour Program: Standards and Equity: Federal Labour Standards: Hours of Work*. http://www.labour.gc.ca/eng/standards_equity/st/hours.shtml.

Government of Canada. 2014. *Action for Seniors—Canada's Economic Action Plan*. http://www12.hrsdc.gc.ca.

Government of Canada. 2015. *Facts and Figures 2014 Immigration Overview.* Department of Citizenship and Immigration. http://www.cic.gc.ca/english/resources/statistics/facts2014/permanent/01.asp.

Government of Canada. 2016. *Annual Labour Market Impact Assessment Statistics, 2007–2014.* http://www.esdc.gc.ca/en/reports/foreign_workers/2014/lmia_annual_statistics/province.page#s1.

Government of Canada. 2016a. *Federal Labour Standards.* http://www.esdc.gc.ca/eng/jobs/workplace/employment_standards/labour/index.page.

Government of Canada, Labour Program. 2014. "Overview of Collective Bargaining in Canada, 2013," 21 August. http://www.labour.gc.ca/eng/resources/info/publications/collective_bargaining/collective_bargaining.shtml.

Grandey, A.A., G.M. Fisk, and D.D. Steiner. 2005. "Must 'service with a smile' be stressful? The moderating role of personal control for U.S. and French employees," *Journal of Applied Psychology* 90: 893–904.

Grandey, Alicia. 2003. "When 'the show must go on': Surface acting and deep acting as determinants of emotional exhaustion and peer-rated service delivery," *Academy of Management Journal* 46 (1): 86–96.

Grant, Hugh, and James Townsend. 2010. "The incidence of poverty among Canada's elderly immigrants," in Douglas Durst and Michael MacLean, eds, pp. 125–47. *Diversity and Aging Among Immigrant Seniors in Canada: Changing Faces and Greying Temples.* Calgary, Alberta: Detselig Enterprises.

Grant, Tavia. 2012a. "The real youth jobs crisis: Underemployment," *Globe and Mail*, 30 October.

Grant, Tavia. 2012b. "Young leading job market exodus," *Globe and Mail*, 10 March: B8.

Grant, Tavia. 2013. "More Canadians turning to self-employment in shaky job market," *Globe and Mail*, 6 October.

Grant, Tavia. 2015. "Rise of the machines: Robots poised to transform global manufacturing,"*Globe and Mail*, 10 February. http://www.theglobeandmail.com/report-on-business/rise-of-the-machines-robots-poised-to-transform-global-manufacturing/article22884032/.

Grant, Tavia, Bill Curry, and David Kennedy. 2015. "The trouble behind Canada's job growth," *Globe and Mail*, 6 March: B1, B8.

Gray, Jeff. 2014a. "Billable milliseconds? Meet Ross, lawyer of the future," *Globe and Mail*, 12 December: B1, B4.

Gray, Jeff. 2014b. "The rise of the older worker—and age-discrimination lawsuits," *Globe and Mail*, 13 January. http://www.theglobeandmail.com/report-on-business/industry-news/the-law-page/the-rise.

Green, Anne E., and Ilias Livanos. 2015. "Involuntary non-standard employment and the economic crisis: Regional insights from the UK," *Regional Studies* 49 (7): 1223–35.

Green, David. 2015. "The case for increasing the minimum wage: What does the academic literature tell us?" *Canandian Centre for Policy Alternatives.* https://www.policyalternatives.ca/sites/default/files/uploads/publications/BC%20Office/2015/04/CCPA-BC-Case-for-Incr-Minimum-Wage_0.pdf.

Green, David A., and W. Craig Riddell. 2013. "Ageing and literacy skills: Evidence from Canada, Norway and the United States," *Labour Economics* 22: 16–29.

Green, Francis, Harvey Krahn, and Johnny Sung. 1993. "Non-standard work in Canada and the United Kingdom," *International Journal of Manpower* 14 (5): 70ff.

Greene, Jay. 2012. "Riots, suicides and other issues in Foxconn's iPhone factories," CNET *News*, 25 September. http://www.cnet.com/news/riots-suicides-and-other-issues-in-foxconns-iphone-factories/.

Greenhouse, Steven. 2008. *The Big Squeeze: Tough Times for the American Worker.* New York: Anchor Books.

Habjan, S., Holly Prince, and Mary Lou Kelley. 2012. "Caregiving for elders in First Nations communities: Social system perspective on barriers and challenges," *Canadian Journal on Aging* 31 (2): 209–22.

Haiven, Larry. 2010. "Regeneration among coal-mining communities in Canada and the UK: The role of culture," in N. Pupo and M. Thomas, eds, pp. 195–213, *Interrogating the New Economy: Restructuring Work in the 21st Century.* Toronto: UTP.

Hampson, Ian, and Anne Junor. 2005. "Putting the process back in: Rethinking service sector skill," *Work, Employment and Society* 24 (3): 526–45.

Hango, Darcy. 2013. "Gender differences in science, technology, engineering, mathematics and computer science (STEM) programs at university," Statistics Canada. Catalogue

No. 75-006-X. December. http://www.statcan.gc.ca/pub/75-006-x/2013001/article/11874-eng.pdf.

Hansen, Lawrence. 2003. "The origins of the Maquila industry in Mexico," *Comerico Exterior* 53 (11): 1–16.

Harms, John B., and Tim Knapp. 2003. "The new economy: What's new, what's not," *Review of Radical Political Economics* 35: 413–36.

Hayes, Molly. 2015. "Payday loan companies come under scrutiny: Anti-poverty activists call them 'predatory'," *Hamilton Spectator*, 29 July: A1, A6.

Healy, Joshua. 2015. "The Australian labour market in 2014: Still ill?" *Journal of Industrial Relations*, 57 (1): 348–65.

Henly, Julia, and Susan Lambert. 2014. "Unpredictable work timing in retail jobs: Implications for employee work–life conflict," *Industrial and Labor Relations Review* 67 (3): 986–1016.

Hennebry, Jenna L. 2008. "Bienvenidos a Canadå? Globalization and the migration industry surrounding temporary agricultural migration in Canada," *Canadian Population Studies* 35 (2): 339–56.

Hermann, Christoph. 2015. *Capitalism and the Political Economy of Work Time*. London: Routledge Taylor & Francis Group.

Heron, Craig. 2012. *The Canadian Labour Movement: A Short History*, 3rd edn. Toronto: James Lorimer & Company.

Herzog-Stein, Alexander, and Ines Zapf. 2014. "Navigating the Great Recession: The impact of working-time accounts in Germany," *Industrial and Labor Relations Review* 67 (3): 891–925.

Heuven, E., and A.B. Bakker. 2003. "Emotional dissonance and burnout among cabin attendants," *European Journal of Work and Organizational Psychology* 12: 81–100.

High, Steven, and David Lewis. 2007. *Corporate Wasteland: The Landscape and Memory of Deindustrialization*. Ithaca: ILR Press.

Hira-Friesen, Parvinder. 2014. "Precarious employment: Labour market insecurity among immigrants in Canada." PhD dissertation. Department of Sociology, University of Calgary. July.

Hochschild, Arlie. 1983/2003. *The Managed Heart: The Commercialization of Human Feeling*. Berkeley: California University Press.

Hofacker, Dirk. 2015. "In line or at odds with active ageing policies? Exploring patterns of retirement preferences in Europe," *Ageing and Society* 35: 1529–56.

Hofacker, Dirk, and Stefanie Konig. 2013. "Flexibility and work–life conflict in times of crisis: A gender perspective," *International Journal of Sociology and Social Policy* 33 (9/10): 613–35.

Holman, David. 2013. "An explanation of cross-national variation in call centre job quality using institutional theory," *Work, Employment and Society* 27 (1): pp. 21–38.

Holman, David, Rosemary Batt, and Ursula Holtgrewe. 2007. *The Global Call Center Report: International Perspectives on Management and Employment*. Cornell University ILR School.

Hopkins, Terrance, and Immanuel Wallerstein. 1977. "Patterns of development of the modern world-system," *Review* 12 (1): 1–145.

Hopkins, Terrance, and Immanuel Wallerstein. 1986. "Commodity chains in the world economy prior to 1800," *Review* 10 (1): 157–70.

Hoskins, Tansy. 2015. "After two years, the Rana Plaza fund finally reaches its $30m target," *The Guardian*, 10 June. http://www.theguardian.com/sustainable-business/2015/jun/10/rana-plaza-fund-reaches-target-compensate-victims.

Hou, Feng, and Simon Coulombe. 2010. "Earning gaps for Canadian-born visible minorities in the public and private sectors," *Canadian Public Policy* 36 (1): 29–43.

Huberman, Michael, and Chris Minns. 2007. "The times they are not changin': Days and hours of work in old and new worlds, 1870–2000," *Explorations in Economic History* 44: 538–67.

Human Rights and Business Country Guide. 2014. "Human rights in Bangladesh's export processing zones." http://hrbcountryguide.org/2014/05/human-rights-in-bangladeshs-export-processing-zones/#sthash.hKKzOOnw.dpuf.

Hunsley, Terrance. 2013a. "Work–life balance in an aging population," *Policy Horizons Canada*. http://www.horizons.gc.ca/eng/content/feature-article-%E2%80%93-work-life-balance-an-aging-population.

Hunsley, Terrance. 2013b. "Feature article—Work–life balance in an aging population," *Policy Research Initiative Government of Canada*. http://www.horizons.gc.ca/eng/book/export/html/1998.

Hunt, Jennifer. 2016. "Why do women leave science and engineering?" *ILR Review* 69 (1): 199–226.

Huppartz, Kate. 2009. "Reworking Bourdieu's capital: Feminine and female capitals in the field of paid caring work," *Sociology* 43 (1): 45–66.

Hurrell, S.A. 2010. "'I would and I can but I don't want to!': Skills withdrawal, the psychological contract and service organizations." Paper presented to the 28th International Labour Process Conference, Rutgers University, New Jersey, 15–17 March.

Hurst, Matt. 2008. "Who gets any sleep these days? Sleep patterns of Canadians," *Canadian Social Trends*, 22 April. http://www.statcan.gc.ca/pub/11-008-x/2008001/article/10553-eng.htm.

Huws, Ursula. 2003. *The Making of the Cybertariat: Virtual Work in a Real World*. New York: Monthly Review Press.

Huws, Ursula. 2013. "Working online, living offline: Labor in the Internet age," *Work Organization, Labour and Globalization* 7 (1): 1–11.

Huws, Ursula. 2014. *Labor in the Global Digital Economy*. New York: Monthly Review Press.

Indexmundi. 2016. "Green Coffee Imports by Country in 1000 60 KG bags." http://www.indexmundi.com/agriculture/?commodity=green-coffee&graph=imports

Industry Canada. 2013. *Key Small Business Statistics*. Catalogue No. Iu186-1/2013-1E-PDF, August. http://www.ic.gc.ca/eic/site/061.nsf/eng/02814.html.

Institute for Global Labour and Human Rights. N.d. "Factory collapse in Bangladesh." http://www.globallabourrights.org/campaigns/factory-collapse-in-bangladesh.

International Coffee Organization (ICO). 2014. "World coffee trade (1963–2013): A review of the markets, challenges and opportunities facing the sector." http://www.ico.org/news/icc-111-5-r1e-world-coffee-outlook.pdf.

International Labor Organization (ILO). 1996–2015. *Promoting Jobs, Protecting People*. http://www.ilo.org/global/lang-en/index.htm.

International Labor Organization (ILO). 1998. *Labor and Social Issues Relating to Export Processing Zones*. Geneva: International Labor Office.

International Labor Organization (ILO). 2011. Indicator 2: Youth unemployment rate. http://www.ilo.org/public/english/employment/yen/whatwedo/projects/indicators/2.htm.

International Labor Organization (ILO). 2015a. "Export Processing Zones (EPZS)." http://www.ilo.org/inform/online-information-resources/research-guides/export-processing-zones/lang--en/index.htm.

International Labor Organization (ILO). 2015b. "What is child labour?" http://www.ilo.org/ipec/facts/lang--en/index.htm.

International Labor Rights Forum (ILRF). N.d. "The chocolate industry has a century-long history of forced and child labor in the production of cocoa." http://www.laborrights.org/industries/cocoa.

International Monetary Fund (IMF). 2007. "The globalization of labor," in *World Economic Outlook: Spillovers and Cycles in the Global Economy*, pp. 161–92. Washington: International Monetary Fund.

Iseke, A. 2014. "The part-time job satisfaction puzzle: Different types of job discrepancies and the moderating effect of family importance," *British Journal of Industrial Relations* 52 (3): 445–69.

Ito, Takatoshi, and Frederic S. Mishkin. 2006. "Two decades of Japanese monetary policy and the deflation problem," *National Bureau of Economic Research*. Working Paper 10878. Volume 15.

Jaarsveld, Danielle, Ann Frost, and David Walker. 2007. "The Canadian contact centre industry: Strategy, work organization and human resource management," *Global Call Centre Industry Project*.

Jackson, Andrew. 2007. "The economics of the minimum wage," *The Progressive Economics Forum*, 27 January. http://www.progressive-economics.ca/2007/01/27/the-economics-of-the-minimum-wage-again/.

Jackson, Andrew. 2012a. "Why paying a living wage makes good business sense," *Globe and Mail*, 9 November. http://www.theglobeandmail.com/report-on-business/economy/economy-lab/why-paying-a-living-wage-makes-good-business-sense/article5152175/.

Jackson, Andrew. 2012b. "Canadian deindustrialization," *Behind the Numbers: A Blog from the CCPA*, 15 March. http://behindthenumbers.ca/2012/03/15/canadian-deindustrialization/.

Jackson, Andrew. 2014. "With more seniors working already, do we need to raise the retirement age?" *Globe and Mail*,

7 January. http://www.theglobeandmail.com/report-on-business/economy/economy-lab/with-more-seniors.

Jackson, Marla. 2008. "Employee health and well-being: Trends in the call centre sector," *Insights from The Shepell·fgi Research Group* 2 (1): 1–10.

Jacobs, Jerry A., and Kathleen Gerson. 2004. *The Time Divide: Work, Family and Gender Inequality.* New York: Harvard University Press.

Jaffee, Daniel. 2014. *Brewing Justice: Fair Trade Coffee, Sustainability, and Survival.* Oakland: University of California Press.

Jaumotte, Florence, and Carolina Osorio Buitron. 2015a. "Inequality and labour market institutions," International Monetary Fund Research Department, July. http://www.imf.org/external/pubs/ft/sdn/2015/sdn1514.pdf.

Jaumotte, Florence, and Carolina Osorio Buitron. 2015b. "Power from the people," *International Monetary Fund: Finance and Development* 52 (1). http://www.imf.org/external/pubs/ft/fandd/2015/03/jaumotte.htm.

Jenkins, Sarah, and Rick Delbridge. 2014. "In pursuit of happiness: A sociological examination of employee identifications amongst a 'happy' call-centre workforce," *Organization* 21 (6): 867–87.

Jones, Jacqui. 2013. *UK Service Industries: Definition, Classification and Evolution.* London: Office for National Statistics.

Kalleberg, Arne, and Kevin Hewison. 2013. "Precarious work and the challenge of Asia," *American Behavioral Scientist* 57 (3): 271–88.

Kalliath, P., and T. Kalliath. 2015. "Work–family conflict and its impact on job satisfaction of social workers," *British Journal of Social Work* 45: 241–59.

Kapsalis, Costa, and Pierre Tourigny. 2004. "Duration of non-standard employment," *Perspectives on Labour and Income* (December): 5–13.

Karman, Zeynep Erden, and Amr Elleithy. 2006. "Self-employed women's work–life imbalance an urgent need for policy response," *Status of Women Canada.* http://www.horizons.gc.ca/eng/book/export/html/2000.

Karnitschnig, Matthew, Anton Troianovski, and Jenny Gross. 2015. "Europe's anti-immigrant parties stand to gain ground in wake of Paris attacks," *Wall Street Journal*, 16 January. http://www.wsj.com/articles/europes-anti-immigrant-parties-stand-to-gain-ground-in-wake-of-paris-attacks-1421371307.

Kaufman, G., and E. Bernhardt. 2015. "Gender, work and childbearing: A couple analysis of work adjustments after the transition to parenthood," *Community, Work and Family* 18 (1): 1–18.

Kelly, K, L. Howatson-Leo, and W. Clark. 1997. "I feel overqualified for my job…," *Canadian Social Trends* 47 (Winter): 11–16.

Kembhavi, Rohan. 2012. "Canadian seniors: A demographic profile," *Elections Canada* (November). http://www.elections.ca/content.aspx?section=res&dir=rec/part/sen&document=index&lan=e.

Kenney, M., and R. Florida. 1993. *Beyond Mass Production.* New York: Oxford University Press.

Keung, Nicholas. 2014. "Wage gap for white/minority immigrants persists in union jobs," *Toronto Star*, 28 December. http://www.thestar.com/news/immigration/2014/12/28/wage_gap_for_whiteminority_immigrants_persists_in_union_jobs.html.

Kingston, Ann. 2015. "Why men should have it all/Why men can't have it all," *Maclean's Magazine*, 5 October: 49–52.

Kolm, Josh. 2013. "Why are so many of Canada's young people out of work? Generation Y's sense of entitlement is partly the result of empty career promises," *Globe and Mail*, 21 June. http://www.cbc.ca/news/canada/why-are-so-many-of-canada-s-young-people-out-of-work-1.1370260.

Korczynski, Marek. 2003. "Communities of coping: Collective emotional labour in service work," *Organization* 10 (1): 55–79.

Korczynski, Marek. 2009. "The mystery customer," *Sociology* 43 (5).

Korczynski, Marek, and Claire Evans. 2013. "Customer abuse to service workers: An analysis of its social creation within the service economy," *Work, Employment and Society* 27 (5): 768–84.

Korczynski, Marek, and University of Ottawa. 2004. "When production and consumption meet," *Journal of Management Studies* 41n (4): 575–99.

Korea Times. 2010. "YoungOne workers in Bangladesh clash with police, killing 4." http://www.koreatimes.co.kr/www/news/nation/2014/05/113_77916.html.

Krahn, Harvey. 1991. "Non-standard work arrangements," *Perspectives on Labour and Income* 3 (4): 35–45.

Krahn, Harvey. 1995. "Non-standard work on the rise," *Perspectives on Labour and Income* 7 (4): 35–42.

Krassa, Michael, and Benjamin Radcliff. 2014. "Evidence that higher minimum wages improve economic well-being: Research brief," *Scholars Strategy Network*, 12 November. http://journalistsresource.org/studies/economics/workers/evidence-that-higher-minimum-wages-improve-economic-well-being.

Lagarde, Christine. 2015. "Why 2015 is a make-or-break year for the economy," *World Economic Forum*, 24 January. https://agenda.weforum.org/2015/01/why-2015-is-a-make-or-break-year-for-the-economy/.

Lancaster House. 2011. Discussion of the Supreme Court's controversial decision in the Fraser case: *Collective Bargaining Rights Under the Charter.* 27 May. http://lancasterhouse.com/audioConferences/show/id/278.

LaRochelle-Cote, Sebastien. 2013. "Employment instability among younger workers," *Research Document.* Statistics Canada Catalogue no. 75-004-M—No. 002.

Law, John, and John Hassard, eds. 1999. *Actor Network Theory and After.* Oxford, UK: Blackwell.

Lee, Byron, Jing Wang, and Johanna Westar. 2015. "Work hour congruence: The effect on job satisfaction and absenteeism," *The International Journal of Human Resource Management* 36 (5): 657–75.

Lee, N., A. Zvonkovic, and D. Crawford. 2014. "The impact of work–family conflict and facilitation on women's perceptions of role balance," *Journal of Family Issues* 35 (9): 1252–74.

Leicht, K., and S. Fitzgerald. 2014. "The real reason 60 is the new 30: Consumer debt and income insecurity in late middle age," *The Sociological Quarterly* 55: 236–60.

Leidner, Robin. 1993. *Fast Food, Fast Talk: Service Work and the Routinization of Everyday Life.* Oakland: University of California Press.

Lewchuk, W. 2013. "Has there been a she-covery? The financial crisis of 2008 and its impact on the Ontario labour market," *Relations Industrielles* 61 (1): 25–45.

Lisenkova, Katerina, Marcel Merette, and Robin Wright. 2013. "Population ageing and the labour market: Modelling size and age-specific effects," *Economic Modelling* 35: 981–9.

Liu, X., and S. Dyer. 2014. "Revisiting radical feminism: Partnered dual-earner mothers' place still in the home?" *Women's Studies International Forum* 47: 1–10.

Livingstone, David W. 2010. "Job requirements and workers' learning: Formal gaps, informal closure, systemic limits," *Journal of Education and Work* 23 (3): 207–31.

Livingstone, David W., and Milosh Raykov. 2008. "Workers' power and intentional learning among non-managerial workers: A 2004 benchmark survey," *Relations Industrielles/Industrial Relations* 63 (1): 30–56.

Llena-Nozal, Ana. 2015. *Non-Standard Work and Inequality.* University of Luxembourg: OECD.

Lloyd, Anthony. 2012. "Working to live, not living to work: Work, leisure and youth identity among call centre workers in North East England," *Current Sociology* 60 (5): 619–35.

Longhurst, Andrew. 2014. "Precarious temp agency work requires public policy attention," *Canadian Centre for Policy Alternatives*, 3 July.

Lu, Vanessa. 2012. "Silver surge," *Toronto Star*, 24 February: B1, B2.

Lu, Yuqian, and René Morissette. 2010. "Women's participation and economic downturns," pp. 18–22, *Perspectives on Labour and Income.* Ottawa.

Lyon, Sarah. 2010. *Coffee and Community: Maya Farmers and Fair Trade Markets.* Boulder: University Press of Colorado.

Macdonald, C., and D. Merrill. 2009. "'It shouldn't have to be a trade'": Recognition and redistribution in care work advocacy," *Hypatia* 17 (2): 67–83.

Macdonald, David. 2011. *The Shadow Public Service: The Swelling Ranks of Federal Government Outsourced Workers.* Ottawa: Canadian Centre for Policy Alternatives.

Macdonald, David, and Erika Shaker. 2012. *Eduflation and the High Cost of Learning.* Ottawa: Canadian Centre for Policy Alternatives.

MacEwen, Angela. 2012. *Working after Age 65: What Is at Stake?* Canadian Centre for Policy Alternatives. http://www.policyalternatives.ca.

MacEwen, Angela. 2014. "Underemployment is Canada's real labour market challenge," Ottawa: CLC. http://canadianlabour.ca/issues-research/underemployment-canadas-real-labour-market-challenge.

Mackenzie, Hugh. 2015. "Fraser Institute report misses the mark on retirement security," *Behind the Numbers*, 30 July. http://behindthenumbers.ca/2015/07/30/fraser-institute-report-misses-the-mark-on-retirement-security.

Mackenzie, Hugh, and Richard Shillington. 2015. *The Union Card: A Ticket into Middle Class Stability*. Toronto: Canadian Centre for Policy Alternatives.

Madland, David, Karla Walter, and Ross Eisenbrey. 2012. "Right-to-work 101: Why these laws hurt our economy, our society and our democracy." Centre for American Progress Action Fund and Economic Policy Institute.

Mandel, H. 2013. "Up the down staircase: Women's upward mobility and the wage penalty for occupational feminization, 1970–2007," *Social Forces* 91 (4): 1183–1207.

Mangum, Catherine Lee. 2012. "Centrally planned innovation: A SWOT analysis of Russia's silicon valley." MA thesis. Unpublished. University of Washington.

Markoff, John. 2013. "Machine Grading Debated," *Hamilton Spectator*, 13 April: 1, 6.

Marr, G. 2015. "Canada household debt ratio hits new record of 163.3%," *Financial Post*, 12 March. http://www.financialpost.ca.

Marshall, K. 2010. "Employment patterns of postsecondary students," *Perspectives on Labour and Income* 11 (9): 5–17.

Marshall, K. 2011. "Generational change in paid and unpaid work," *Canadian Social Trends* 92 (Winter): 13–24.

Marshall, K. 2012. "Youth neither enrolled nor employed," *Perspectives on Labour and Income* (Summer): pp. 4–15.

Marshman, P. 2013. "Is CPP hit or myths for you?" *Toronto Star*, 7 February: B4.

Marston, Sallie A., and Paul L. Knox. 2006. *Places and Regions in Global Context*. Upper Saddle River, NJ: Pearson Prentice Hall.

Martin, G., D. Dymock, S. Billett, and G. Johnson. 2014. "In the name of meritocracy: managers' perceptions of policies and practices for training older workers," *Ageing & Society* 34: 992–1018.

Martinez, M. 2015. "Dads cherish Sweden's parental leave," *CNN News*, 5 April. http://www.cnn.com/2015/04/05/living/cnnphotos-swedish-dads-parental-leave/.

Marx, Karl. 1975. "Economic and philosophic manuscripts of 1844," in *Collected Works*, Volume 3. New York: International Publishers.

Maskin, Eric. 2014. "Theorist Eric Maskin: Globalization is increasing inequality," *The World Bank*, 23 June. http://www.worldbank.org/en/news/feature/2014/06/23/theorist-eric-maskin-globalization-is-increasing-inequality.

Matthews, Chris. 2014. "Wealth inequality in America: It's worse than you think," *Fortune*, 31 October. http://fortune.com/2014/10/31/inequality-wealth-income-us/.

McCloud, L., and R. Dwyer. 2011. "The fragile American: Hardship and financial troubles in the 21st century," *The Sociological Quarterly* 52: 13–35.

McCluskey, Martha, Thomas McGarity, Sidney Shapiro, and Matthew Shudtz. 2013. "At the company's mercy: Protecting contingent workers from unsafe working conditions." Center for Progressive Reform (CPR) White Paper #1301. January. http://www.progressivereform.org/articles/contingent_workers_1301.pdf.

McDaniel, S., A. Gaszo, and S. Um. 2013. "Generationing relations in challenging times: Americans and Canadians in mid-life in the Great Recession," *Current Sociology* 61 (3): 301–21.

McDonald, Lyn, and P. Donahue. 2011. "Retirement lost?" *Canadian Journal of Aging* 30 (3): 401–22.

McInturff, Kate, and Paul Tulloch. 2014. *The Difference that Public Sector Wages Make*. Toronto: Canadian Centre for Policy Alternatives. https://www.policyalternatives.ca/sites/default/files/uploads/publications/National%20Office/2014/10/Narrowing_the_Gap.pdf.

McKendrick, Joe. 2015. "GE and GM: Old companies become a new breed of software companies," *Forbes*, 22 June. http://www.forbes.com/sites/joemckendrick/2015/06/22/ge-and-gm-old-companies-become-a-new-breed-of-software-companies/.

McKenzie, D. 2014. "A long history of failure: Feeling the effects of Canada's childcare policy," *Canadian Journal of Law and Society* 29 (3): 397–412.

McKnight, Zoe. 2014. "Bell Canada ends controversial unpaid internship program," *Toronto Star*, 12 August: A2.

McMahon, T. 2013. "Million Dollar Babies," *Macleans* 126 (39): 46ff.

Mei, Zhaowen, Jacquie Eales, and Janet Fast. 2013. "Older Canadians in the paid labour force," Older Canadians—Burden or Benefit? Workshop, June. http://www.mysage.ca/public/download/documents/4057.

Mendelsohn, Matthew, and John Medow. 2010. "Help wanted: How well did the EI program respond during recent recessions?" Toronto: Mowat Centre for Policy Innovation.

Menzies, Heather. 1981. *Women and the Chip: Case Studies on the Employment Effects of Microtechnology.* Toronto: Institute for Research on Public Policy.

Messacar, D., and R. Morissette. 2015. "Employer pensions and the wealth of Canadian families," *Insights on Canadian Society,* 15 January. Statistics Canada, Catalogue No. 75-006-X. Ottawa: Minister of Industry.

Meyer, Stephen. 1981. *The Five Dollar Day: Labor Management and Control in the Ford Motor Company, 1908–1921.* Albany: SUNY Press.

Milan, Anne. 2015. "Families and living arrangements" in *Women in Canada: A Gender-based Statistical Report,* 7th edn, 10 November. Ottawa: Statistics Canada, Minister of Industry.

Milan, A., L. Keown, and C.R. Urquijo. 2011. "Families, living arrangements and unpaid work," *Women in Canada: A Gender-based Statistical Report.* Statistics Canada. Catalogue no. 89-503-X. Ottawa: Minister of Industry.

Milan, Anne, and Mireille Vezina. 2011. "Senior women," *Women in Canada: A Gender-based Statistical Report.* Statistics Canada Catalogue no. 89-503-X. Ottawa: Minister of Industry.

Miller, B., and S. Nyce. 2014. "Which workers are delaying retirement and why?" *Towers Watson Research Insider,* September. http://www.towerswatson.com.

Miller, C. 2014. "Paid leave encourages female employees to stay," *New York Times,* 28 July. http://www.nytimes.com/2014/07/29/upshot/how-paid-leave-helps-female-employees-stay-.html?_r=4&abt=00028&abg=1.

Miller, Daniel, and John Horn. 2014. "Lawsuit challenges a Hollywood pillar: Unpaid internships," *Los Angeles Times,* 6 April. http://articles.latimes.com/2014/apr/06/business/la-fi-ct-hollywood-interns-unpaid-internships.

Mills, C. Wright. 1959. *The Sociological Imagination.* New York: Oxford University Press.

Minnotte, K. 2012. "Family structure, gender, and the work–family interface: Work-to-family conflict among single and partnered parents," *Journal of Family Economic Issues* 33: 95–107.

Miranda, Ann. 2012. "Gender and transitions from school to work: Evidence of youth inequality in Argentina and consequences for youth policy," in M. Hans-Bleibtreu and M. Molgat, eds, pp. 263–75, *Youth Policy in a Changing World: From Theory to Practice.* Leverkusen (Germany): Verlag Barbara Budrich and Budrich UniPress.

Mirdha, Refayet Ullah. 2014. "EPZ investors worried over trade unions", *The Daily Star,* 31 August. http://www.thedailystar.net/epz-investors-worried-over-trade-union-39387.

Mojtehedzadeh, Sara. 2015a. "'Wild west' scheduling holds millions of Ontario workers hostage," *Toronto Star,* 3 May. http://www.thestar.com/news/gta/2015/05/03/outdated-employment-standards-act-holding-millions-of-Ontario-workers-hostage.

Mojtehedzadeh, Sara. 2015b. "Ontario employers cashing in on temporary workers," *Toronto Star,* 10 May. http://www.thestar.com/news/gta/2015/05/10/ontario-employers-cashing-in-on-temporary-workers.

Mojtehedzadeh, Sara. 2015c. "Metro deal sets new precedent for fair wages and schedules," *Toronto Star,* 17 July. http://www.thestar.com/news/gta/2015/07/17/metro-deal-sets-new-precedent-for-fair-wages.

Mojtehedzadeh, Sara. 2015d. "Complain and be fired or suffer in silence," *Toronto Star,* 25 May.

Mojtehedzadeh, Sara. 2015e. "Ontario employers get slap on wrist for mistreating employees," *Toronto Star,* 24 May http://www.thestar.com/news/gta/2015/05/24/ontario-employers-get-slap-on-wrist-for-mistreating-employees.html.

Montegue, Dena. 2002. "Stolen goods: Coltan and conflict in the Democratic Republic of Congo," *SAIS (School of Advanced International Studies, Johns Hopkins University) Review* 22 (1): 103–18.

Monthly Labor Review. 2015. "The relationship between access to benefits and weekly work hours," 1 June. Washington, DC: Bureau of Labor Statistics. http://stats.bls.gov/opub/mlr/2015/article/the-relationship-between-access-to-benefits-and-weekly-work-hours.htm.

Moore, W.J. 1998. "The determinants and effects of right-to-work laws: A review of the recent literature," *Journal of Labor Research* 19 (3): 449–69.

Morissette, Rene, Garnett Picot, and Yuqian Lu. 2012. "Wage growth over the past 30 years: Changing wages by age and education," *Economic Insights* (June). Statistics Canada. Catalogue no. 11-626-X. Ottawa: Minister of Industry.

Morris, J.A., and D.C. Feldman. 1997. "Managing emotions in the workplace," *Journal of Managerial Issues* 9: 257–74.

Mosoetsa, Sarah, and Michelle Williams, eds. 2012. *Labour in the Global South: Challenges and Alternatives for Workers*. Geneva: International Labour Office–Geneva, ILO.

Mountz, Alison, Anne Bonds, Becky Mansfield, Jenna Lloyd, Jennifer Hyndman, Margaret Walton-Roberts, Ranu Basu, Risa Whitson, Roberta Hawkins, Trina Hamilton, and Winifred Curran. 2015. "For slow scholarship: A feminist politics of resistance through collective action in the neoliberal university." *ACME: International e-Journal for Critical Geographies* 14: 3–24.

Munn, Andrew. N.d. "Computer industry impacts on the environment and society," University of Michigan. http://sitemaker.umich.edu/section002group3/coltan_mining_in_democratic_republic_of_the_congo.

Myers, Jennifer. 2010. "Why more women aren't becoming engineers," *Globe and Mail*, 9 November. http://www.theglobeandmail.com/report-on-business/careers/career-advice/why-more-women-arent-becoming-engineers/article1216432/.

Natural Sciences and Engineering Research Council of Canada (NSERC). 2010. "Women in science and engineering in Canada." November. Ottawa: NSERC Corporate Planning and Policy Directorate.

Negrey, Cynthia L. 2012. *Work Time: Conflict, Control and Change*. London: Polity.

New York Times. 1914. "[Ford] gives $10,000,000 to 26,000 employees," *New York Times*, 5 January. http://www.nytimes.com/learning/general/onthisday/big/0105.html#article.

Ng, Eddy, and Alan Law. 2014. "Keeping up! Older workers' adaptation in the workplace after age 55," *Canadian Journal of Aging* 33 (1): 1–14.

Noah, Timothy. 2013. "Labor of love: The enforced happiness of Pret A Manger," *New Republic*. https://newrepublic.com/article/112204/pret-manger-when-corporations-enforce-happiness.

Nordt, Carlos, Ingeborg Warnke, Erich Seifritz, and Wolfram Kawohl. 2015. "Modelling suicide and unemployment: A longitudinal analysis covering 63 countries, 2000–2011," *The Lancet Psychiatry* 2 (3): 239–45.

Norland, J.A. 1994. *Profile of Canada's Seniors*. Ottawa: Minister of Industry and Prentice Hall Canada.

Norton, Steven. 2015. "GM finds edge in software development," *The Wall Street Journal*, 18 February. http://blogs.wsj.com/cio/2015/02/18/video-gm-finds-edge-in-software-development/.

O'Connor, Clare. 2014. "These retailers involved in Bangladesh factory disaster have yet to compensate victims," *Forbes*, 26 April. http://www.forbes.com/sites/clareoconnor/2014/04/26/these-retailers-involved-in-bangladesh-factory-disaster-have-yet-to-compensate-victims/.

O'Connor, Clare. 2015. "Walmart to give 40% of workers pay raise to $9 per hour," *Forbes*, 19 January. http://www.forbes.com/sites/clareoconnor/2015/02/19/walmart-to-give-40-of-workers-pay-rise-to-9-per-hour/.

O'Connor, James. 1973. *The Fiscal Crisis of the State*. New York: St. Martin's Press.

OECD. 2004. "Trends in international migration." Annual Report. Paris: OECD.

OECD. 2007. "OECD employment outlook 2007." Paris: OECD.

OECD. 2012. "Indicators of immigrant integration 2012: Settling in." Paris: OECD http://www.oecd.org/migration/integration-indicators-2012/keyindicatorsbycountry/name,219003,en.htm.

OECD. 2013. "Pensions at a glance 2013." Paris: OECD. http://www.oecd.org/pensions/pensionsataglance.htm.

OECD. 2014a. "Does income inequality hurt economic growth?" *Focus on Inequality and Growth*, 9 December. http://www.oecd.org/els/soc/Focus-Inequality-and-Growth-2014.pdf.

OECD. 2014b. *Special Focus: Mobilizing Migrants' Skills for Economic Success*. Paris: OECD.

OECD. 2015a. Dataset– LFS–Average Annual Hours Worked. https://stats.oecd.org/.

OECD. 2015b. Labour Market Statistics: Labour Force Statistics by age and sex, OECD Employment and labour market statistics (database).

Olah, L., and M. Gahler. 2014. "Gender equality perceptions, division of paid and unpaid work, and partnership dissolution in Sweden," *Social Forces* 93 (2): 571–94.

Ontario Ministry of Education. 2015. "News release: Ontario building 30 new schools, over 2,000 licensed child care spaces." https://news.ontario.ca/educ/en/2015/11/ontario-building-30-new-schools-over-2000-licensed-child-care-spaces/, accessed 6 April 2016.

Ormsby, Mary. 2012. "Freedom 67 a global trend," *Toronto Star*, 4 February: IN1.

Ortiz, Fiona, and Feliciano Tisera. 2011. "A lost generation stuck in junk jobs," *Toronto Star*, 23 October: A15.

Osberg, Lars. 2009. *Canada's Declining Social Safety Net: The Case for EI Reform*. Ottawa: Canadian Centre for Policy Alternatives. https://www.policyalternatives.ca/sites/default/files/uploads/publications/National_Office_Pubs/2009/Canadas_Declining_Safety_Net.pdf

Oved, Marco C. 2014. "Dismissed unpaid employees back at work at the Walrus—with pay," *Toronto Star*, 4 May: A4.

Oved, Marco C. 2015. "Canada spending heavily on its seniors," *Toronto Star*, 11 February: S9.

Palmer, Bryan. 1983. *Working-Class Experience: The Rise and Reconstruction of Canadian Labour, 1800–1980*. Toronto: Butterworth & Co.

Palmer, Bryan. 2003. "What's Law Got To Do With It? Historical Considerations on Class Struggle, Boundaries of Constraint, and Capitalist Authority," *Osgoode Hall Law Journal* 41(2): 465–490.

Parizeau, Jacques. 2009. "The school mess," *Inroads: The Canadian Journal of Opinion* 25 (Summer/Fall): 74–7.

Parr, N. 2012. "Trends in differentials in workplace participation of mothers with young children in Australia 2002–2008," *Journal of Popular Research* 29: 203–27.

Parsons, Jeff. 2014. "Apple targeted by BBC Panorama over working conditions in China," *Mirror*, 19 December. http://www.mirror.co.uk/news/technology-science/technology/apple-targeted-bbc-panorama-over-4838616.

Pasamar, S., and R. Valle. 2015. "Antecedents of work–life involvement in work–life issues: Institutional pressures, efficiency gains or both," *The International Journal of Human Resource Management* 26 (8): 1130–51.

Patton, Mike. 2013. "Detroit files for bankruptcy protection: The facts, the figures, the fallout," *Forbes*, 22 July. http://www.forbes.com/sites/mikepatton/2013/07/22/detroit-files-for-bankruptcy-protection-the-facts-the-figures-and-the-fallout/.

Payson Center for International Development and Technology Transfer. 2011. "Oversight of public and private initiatives to eliminate worst forms of child labor in the cocoa sector in Côte d'Ivoire and Ghana," *Tulane University*, 31 March. http://issuu.com/stevebutton/docs/tulane_final_report?e=1162575/3403846#search.

Peck, J., and A. Tickell. 2002. "Neoliberalizing space," *Antipode* 34 (3): 380–404.

Peeters, H., and D. Wouter. 2015. "Lifecourses, pensions and poverty among elderly women in Belgium: Interactions between family history, work history and pension regulations," *Ageing and Society* 35: 1171–199.

PEPSO (Poverty and Employment Precarity in Southern Ontario). 2013. *It's More than Poverty: Employment Precarity and Household Well-being*. Hamilton: McMaster University Social Sciences/Toronto: United Way.

Perlin, Ross. 2011. "Down and out in the Magic Kingdom," *Guernica*, 1 May. https://www.guernicamag.com/features/perlin_5_1_11/.

Perlin, Ross. 2012a. *Intern Nation: How to Earn Nothing and Learn Little in the Brave New Economy*. London: Verso.

Perlin, Ross. 2012b. "Indentures are a sign of universities' decline into a factory system," *CAUT Bulletin*, October: A2.

Personal Support Worker HQ (PSWHQ). 2015. "Personal support workers in Ontario." http://personalsupportworkerhq.com/.

Peskowitz, M. 2005. *The Truth Behind the Mommy Wars: Who Decides What Makes a Good Mother?* New York: Seal Press.

Phillips, P., and E. Phillips. 1993. *Women & Work: Inequality in the Canadian Labour Market*. Toronto: James Lorimer & Company.

Pierson, R. 1986. *'They're Still Women after All': The Second World War and Canadian Womanhood*. Toronto: McClelland and Stewart.

Pigg, Susan. 2012. "Ageism complaint inspires job offer," *Toronto Star*, 22 August: B1, B2.

Ponte, S. 2002. "The 'Latte Revolution?' Regulation, markets and consumption in the global coffee chain," *World Development* 30 (7): 1099–122.

Porter, Ann. 2003. *Gendered States: Women, Unemployment Insurance and the Political Economy of the Welfare State in Canada, 1945–1997*. Toronto: University of Toronto Press.

Porter, John. 1965. *The Vertical Mosaic: An Analysis of Social Class and Power in Canada*. Toronto: University of Toronto Press.

Porzecanski, Katia. 2014. "Escaping default from Argentina to Venezuela proves tough," *Bloomberg News*, 11 September. http://www.bloomberg.com/news/2014-09-11/escaping-default-from-argentina-to-venezuela-proves-tough.html.

Preston, Alison, and Serena Yu. 2015. "Is there a part-time/full-time pay differential in Australia?" *Journal of Industrial Relations* 57 (1): 24–47.

Preston, Richard. 2012. "Smiley culture: Pret A Manger's secret ingredients: Service is always with a smile at Pret A Manger. So what keeps its staff buzzing?" *The Telegraph*, 9 March. http://www.telegraph.co.uk/foodanddrink/9129410/Smiley-culture-Pret-A-Mangers-secret-ingredients.html?Mangers-secret-ingredients.

Proulx, Christine, and Celine Le Bourdais. 2014. "Impact of providing care on the risk of leaving employment in Canada," *Canadian Journal of Aging* 33 (4): 488–503.

Public and Private Workers of Canada. 2012. "What have unions done for us?" 15 February. http://www.ppwc.ca/what-have-unions-done-for-us/.

Pugh, Douglas, Markus Groth, and Thorsten Hennig-Thurau. 2011. "Willing and able to fake emotions: A closer examination of the link between emotional dissonance and employee well-being," *Journal of Applied Psychology* 96 (2): 377–90.

Pupo, Norene. 1984. "Educational promises and efficiency ideals: The development of management education in Ontario, 1900–1960." Unpublished PhD dissertation, McMaster University.

Pupo, Norene, ed. 2009 Special Edition of *Just Labour*, Volume 15: *The U.S. Employees Free Choice Act* Fall: 1–146.

Pupo, Norene. 2011. "Walmartization and the McJob: The jobs that boomed in the new economy," in N. Pupo, D. Glenday, and A. Duffy, eds, pp. 66–81, *The Shifting Landscape of Work*. Toronto: Nelson Education.

Pupo, Norene, and Ann Duffy. 2003. "Caught in the net: The impact of changes to Canadian employment insurance legislation on part-time workers," *Social Policy and Society* 2 (1): 1–11.

Pupo, Norene, and Ann Duffy. 2011. "Unpaid work, capital and coercion," *Work Organization, Labour and Globalization* 6 (2): 27–47.

Pupo, Norene, and Andrea Noack. 2010. "Dialing for service: Transforming the public sector workplace in Canada," in N. Pupo and M. Thomas, eds, pp. 111–34, *Interrogating the New Economy: Restructuring Work in the 21st Century*. Toronto: UTP.

Pupo, Norene, and Mark Thomas, eds. 2010. *Interrogating the New Economy: Restructuring Work in the 21st Century*. Toronto: UTP.

Quintini, Glenda, and Sébastien Martin. 2006. "Starting well or losing their way? The position of youth in the labour market in OECD countries." OECD Social, Employment and Migration Working Papers, No. 39. OECD Publishing.

Rajotte, James, Chair. 2014. *Youth Employment in Canada: Challenges and Potential Solutions*. Report of the Standing Committee on Finance, Ottawa, House of Commons.

Retail Council of Canada. 2015. "Minimum wage by province." http://www.retailcouncil.org/quickfacts/minimum-wage.

Rieti, J. 2015. "U.S. steel pensioners could lose $4,354 per year: City," *CBC News*, 28 January. http://www.cbc.ca/news/canada/hamilton/news/u-s-steel-pensioners-could-lose-4-354-per-year.

Rinehart, James W. 2006. *The Tyranny of Work: Alienation and the Labour Process*, 5th edn. Toronto: Nelson.

Rinehart, James W., Christopher Huxley, and David Robertson. 1997. *Just Another Car Factory: Lean Production and Its Discontents*. Ithaca, NY: Cornell University Press.

Ritzer, George. 2011. *The McDonaldization of Society*, 6th edn. Thousand Oaks, CA: Sage Publications.

Roeters, A., and L. Craig. 2014. "Part-time work, women's work-life conflict, and job satisfaction: A cross-national comparison of Australia, the Netherlands, Germany, Sweden, and the United Kingdom," *International Journal of Comparative Sociology* 55 (3): 185–203.

Roseman, Ellen. 2014. "Seniors burdened by rising debt," *Toronto Star*, 9 June: B1, B2.

Rosen, R. 2014. "America's workers: Stressed out, overwhelmed, totally exhausted," *The Atlantic*, March. http://www.theatlantic.com/business/archive/2014/03/americas-workers-stressed-out-overwhelmed-totally-exhausted/284615.

Roy, Donald F. 1959. "Banana time: job satisfaction and informal interaction," *Human Organization* 18 (4): 158–68.

Russell, Bob. 2009. *Smiling Down the Line: Info-Service Work in the Global Economy*. Toronto: University of Toronto Press.

Saberi, Roxana. 2015. "Long hours, meager wages: Child labor continues in Myanmar," *Aljazeera.com*. http://america.aljazeera.com/articles/2015/4/14/child-labor-continues-in-myanmar.html

Sagan, Aleksandra. 2016. "Jobs dominated by women quickly disappearing," *Hamilton Spectator*, 6 February: A17.

Sargent, John, and Linda Matthews. 2009. "China versus Mexico in the global EPZ industry: Maquiladoras, FDI quality, and plant mortality," *World Development* 37 (6): 1009–82.

Satzewich, Victor. 1991. *Racism and the Incorporation of Foreign Labour: Farm Labour Migration to Canada since 1945*. London: Routledge.

Sawchuk, D. 2009. "The raging grannies: Defying stereotypes and embracing aging through activism," *Journal of Women and Aging* 21: 171–85.

Schaef, Anne Wilson, and Diane Fassel. 1988. *The Addictive Organization*. New York: Harper and Row.

Schawbel, Dan. 2014. "Why millennials should get used to work–life imbalance," *New York Times*, 29 October. http://time.com/money/3545722/millennials-work-life-balance/.

Schieman, S., and A. Narisada. 2014. "In control or fatalistically ruled? The sense of mastery among working Canadians," *Canadian Review of Sociology* 51 (4): 343–74.

Schirle, Tammy. 2013. "Senior poverty in Canada: A decomposition analysis," *Canadian Public Policy* 34 (4): 517–40.

Schlosser, E. 2002. *Fast Food Nation: The Dark Side of the All-American Meal*. New York: Perennial Books.

Schlosser, F., D. Zinni, and M. Armstrong-Stassen. 2012. "Intention to retire," *Career Development International* 17 (2): 149–67.

Schmitt, John. 2012. "Low-wage lessons." Washington, DC: Center for Economic and Policy Research. http://www.cepr.net/documents/publications/low-wage-2012-01.pdf.

Schofield, Hugh. 2014. "La belle epoque: Paris 1914," *BBC News Magazine*, January. http://www.bbc.com/news/magazine-25619822.

Schor, Juliet B. 1992. *The Overworked American: The Unexpected Decline of Leisure*. New York: Basic Books.

Schulte, Brigid. 2014. *Overwhelmed: Work, Love and Play When No One Has the Time*. Toronto: Harper Collins.

Scott-Dixon, Krista. 2004. *Doing IT: Women Working in Information Technology*. Toronto: Canadian Scholars' Press.

Shaiken, Harley. 1985. *Work Transformed: Automation and Labor in the Computer Age*. New York: Holt, Rinehart & Winston.

Shalla, Vivian. 1997. "Technology and the deskilling of work: The case of passenger agents at Air Canada," in A. Duffy, D. Glenday, and N. Pupo, eds, pp. 76–96, *Good Jobs, Bad Jobs, No Jobs: The Transformation of Work in the 21st Century*. Toronto: Harcourt Brace.

Shaw, Hollie. 2013. "On-Line retail sales to hit $34 billion in Canada by 2018," *National Post*, 23 July. http://business.financialpost.com/news/retail-marketing/online-retail-sales-to-hit-40-billion-in-canada-by-2018.

Shipley, L., S. Ouellette, and F. Cartwright. 2003. "Planning and preparation: First results of approaches to educational planning (SAEP)," *Education, Skills and Learning Research Paper No. 10*. Statistics Canada, Catalogue no. 81-595.

Shore, L., J. Cleveland, and C. Goldberg. 2003. "Work attitudes and decisions as a function of manager age and employee age," *Journal of Applied Psychology* 88 (3): 529–37.

Shorris, Earl. 2006. *The Life and Times of Mexico*. New York: W.W. Norton and Company.

Silcoff, Sean. 2012. "Canadian call centres ring up new growth," *Globe and Mail*, 6 September. http://www.theglobeandmail.com/report-on-business/economy/jobs/canadian-call-centres-ring-up-new-job-growth/article533634/.

Silver, Cynthia. 2000. "Being there: The time dual-earner couples spend with their children," *Canadian Social Trends*, (Summer): 26–9.

Skinner, N., and R. Ichii. 2015. "Exploring a family, work, and community model of work-family gains and strains," *Community, Work & Family* 18 (1): 79–99.

Smith, Joanna, and Laurie Monsebraaten. 2016. "Liberals deliver on Canada Child Benefit," *Toronto Star*, 22 March. http://www.thestar.com/news/canada/2016/03/22/liberals-deliver-on-canada-child-benefit/

Smith, Neil. 1996. *The New Urban Frontier: Gentrification and the Revanchist City*. New York, NY: Routledge.

Smith, Sabrina Joy. 2013. "The conflict mineral: Coltan mining in DR Congo and Australia," Australian Strategic Policy Institute, 22 July. http://www.aspistrategist.org.au/the-conflict-mineral-coltan-mining-in-dr-congo-and-australia/.

Smolkin, Sheryl. 2013. "Abilities, not age, are what must count in hiring," *Toronto Star*, 23 September: B1.

Standing, Guy. 2010. *The Precariat: The New Dangerous Class*. London: Bloombury Press.

Stanford, Jim. 2008a. *Economics for Everyone: A Short Guide to the Economics of Capitalism*. Halifax: Fernwood Publishing.

Stanford, Jim. 2008b. "Staples, deindustrialization, and foreign investment: Canada's economic journey back to the future," Journal of Political Economy 82: 7–34.

Stanford, Jim. 2012. "Wisconsin's disease crosses the border," *Globe and Mail*, 3 July.

http://www.theglobeandmail.com/globe-debate/wisconsins-disease-crosses-the-border/article4381590/.

Stanford, Jim. 2013. "Industrial policy, manufacturing employment and the loonie," *The Progressive Economics Forum*, 21 June. http://www.progressive-economics.ca/2013/06/21/industrial-policy-manufacturing-employment-and-the-loonie/.

Stanford, Jim, and Leah F. Vosko, eds. 2004. *Challenging the Market: The Struggle to Regulate Work and Income.* Kingston, ON: McGill-Queen's University Press.

Stanfors, M. 2014. "Women in a changing economy: The misleading tale of participation rates in historical perspective," *The History of the Family* 19 (4): 513–36.

Stanislavsky, K. 1961. *Creating a Role.* New York: Theatre Arts Books.

Statistics Canada. 1999. "General Social Survey: Time use," *The Daily.* http://www.statcan.ca/Daily/English/991109/d991109a.htm.

Statistics Canada. 2006a. *Women in Canada: A Gender-based Statistical Report.* Ottawa, ON: Statistics Canada.

Statistics Canada. 2006b. "University tuition fees," *The Daily*, 1 September.

Statistics Canada. 2012a. *The Canadian Population in 2011: Age and Sex.* Catalogue no.98-311-X2011001. Ottawa: Minister of Industry.

Statistics Canada. 2012b. *Generations in Canada: Age and Sex, 2011 Census.* Catalogue no. 98-311-X2011003. Ottawa: Minister of Industry.

Statistics Canada. 2012c. "Life expectancy at birth, by sex, by province." Table 102-0512. Catalogue no. 84-537-XIE. Ottawa: Minister of Industry.

Statistics Canada. 2012d. "Life expectancy, at birth and at age 65, by sex and by province and territory." Table 201-0512. Ottawa: Minister of Industry.

Statistics Canada. 2012e. "Centenarians in Canada: Age and sex, 2011 Census." Catalogue no. 98-311-X2011003.

Statistics Canada. 2012f. *Work Absence Rates 2011.* Catalogue No. 71-211-X. Ottawa: Minister of Industry. http://www.statcan.ca.

Statistics Canada. 2012g. *Portrait of Families and Living Arrangements in Canada: Families, Households and Marital Status, 2011 Census of Population.* Catalogue no. 98-312-X2011001. Ottawa: Minister of Industry.

Statistics Canada. 2012h. North American Industry Classification Index (NAICS) 2012 Catalogue no. 12-501-X

Statistics Canada. 2013a. Labour Force Survey, 1976 to 2011.

Statistics Canada. 2013b. Key Small Business Statistics—August 2013.

Statistics Canada. 2014a. "Percentage of persons by economic family types living in low income." Table 202 0804. Ottawa: Minister of Industry. http://www.statcan.ca.

Statistics Canada. 2014b. "Perceived life stress, 2013." Catalogue no. 82-625-X. Ottawa: Minister of Industry. http://www.statcan.gc.ca/pub/82-625-x/2014001/article/14023-eng.htm.

Statistics Canada. 2014c. "Life expectancy in Canada increased steadily throughout the 20th century." http://www.statcan.gc.ca/pub/91-003-x/2014001/section02/18-eng.htm.

Statistics Canada. 2014d. "Indicators of well-being, learning, educational attainment." http://well-being.esdc.gc.ca/misme-iowb/.3ndic.1t.4r@-eng.jsp?iid=29.

Statistics Canada. 2014e. "Registered retirement savings plan contributions, 2012," *The Daily*, 25 March. Statistics Canada catalogue no. 11-001-X. Ottawa: Minister of Industry.

Statistics Canada. 2014f. "Pension plans in Canada, as of January 1, 2013," *The Daily*, 28 August. Statistics Canada catalogue no. 11-001-X. Ottawa: Minister of Industry.

Statistics Canada. 2014g. Labour force estimates (LFS) by North American Industry Classification System (NAICS), sex and age group, annual Table 282-0008.

Statistics Canada. 2014h. Survey of Employment, Payrolls and Hours (SEPH), average weekly earnings by type of employee, overtime status and detailed North American Industry Classification System (NAICS), annual. Table 281-0027.

Statistics Canada. 2015a. *Aboriginal Statistics at a Glance*, 2nd edn. Catalogue No. 89-645-x2015001. Ottawa: Ministry of Industry.

Statistics Canada. 2015b. "Labour force survey estimates (LFS) employees by job permanency, North American Industry Classification System (NAICS), sex and age group," Cansim Table 282-0080. Ottawa: Minister of Industry. http://www5.statcan.gc.ca/cansim/a21.

Statistics Canada. 2015c. Demography Division. Table 051-0001—Estimate of population, by age group and sex (2014). http://www.statcan.gc.ca/tables-tableaux/sum-som/l01/cst01/demo31a-eng.htm.

Statistics Canada. 2015d. "Labour Force survey estimates (LFS), by sex and detailed age group, unadjusted for seasonality," CANSIM (database), Table 282-0001. http://www.statcan.gc.ca/cansim/a26.

Statistics Canada. 2015e. "Unionization rates falling," *The Daily*, 13 July. http://www.statcan.gc.ca/pub/11-630-x/11-630-x2015005-eng.htm.

Statistics Canada. 2015f. "Labour Force Survey estimates (LFS), employment by class of worker, North American Industry Classification System (NAICS) and sex," CANSIM Table 282-0012. http://www5.statcan.gc.ca/cansim/a26?lang=eng&retrLang=eng&id=2820012&paSer=&pattern=&stByVal=1&p1=1&p2=37&tabMode=dataTable&csid=.

Statistics Canada. 2015g. "Reasons for part-time work by sex and age group 2014," Table 282-0014 and 282-0001.

Statistics Canada. 2015h. "Labour force survey estimates (LFS), wages of employees by union coverage, sex and age group, annual (current dollars unless otherwise noted)," CANSIM (database) Table 282-0074.

Statistics Canada. 2015i. "Labour force survey estimates (LFS), multiple jobholders by usual hours worked at main and all jobs," CANSIM Table 282-0036. http://www5.statcan.gc.ca/cansim/a47.

Statistics Canada. 2015j. *Summary Tables: Reasons for part-time work by sex and age group*. http://www.statcan.gc.ca/tables-tableaux/sum-som/101/cst01/labor63c-eng.htm.

Status of Women Canada, Government of Canada. 2015. "Fact sheet: Economic security." http://www.swc-cfc.gc.ca/initiatives/wesp-sepf/fs-fi/es-se-eng.html.

Stavrou, E., W. Casper, and C. Ierofiakonou. 2015. "Support for part-time as a channel for female employment: The moderating effects of national gender empowerment and labour market conditions," *International Journal of Human Resource Management* 26 (6): 688–706.

Steiner, L. 2007. *The Mommy Wars: Stay-at-Home and Career Moms Face Off on Their Choices, Their Lives, Their Families*. New York: Random House.

Stewart, Heather. 2015. "Temporary and part-time jobs surge promotes inequality, says OECD: In the UK, non-standard work including zero-hours contracts accounted for all net jobs growth since 1995," *The Guardian*, 21 May.

Stinson, Jane, Rosemary Warskett, and Geoff Bickerton. 2006. "Advancing the equity agenda inside unions and at the bargaining table," Special Section, *Just Labour* 8 (Spring).

Stock, R., E. Bauer, and G. Bieling. 2014. "How do top executives handle their work and family life? A taxonomy of top executives' work–family balance," *The International Journal of Human Resource Management* 25 (13): 1815–40.

Stone, Katherine V. 2004. *From Widgets to Digits: Employment Regulation for the Changing Workplace*. Cambridge: Cambridge University Press.

Stone, Laura. 2016. "Federal budget to restore Old Age Security eligibility to 65." *Globe and Mail*. March 21. http://www.theglobeandmail.com

Stone, Pamela. 2007. *Opting Out? Why Women Really Quit Careers and Head Home*. Berkeley: University of California Press.

Strauss, Kendra. 2014. "Temporary Foreign Worker Program changes—Who do they help?" *Policy Note*, 10 July. Vancouver: Canadian Centre for Policy Alternatives. http://www.policynote.ca/temporary-foreign-worker-program-changes-who-do-they-help/.

Supplychainquarterly.com. 2010. "From bean to cup: How Starbucks transformed its supply chain." http://www.supplychainquarterly.com/topics/Procurement/scq201004starbucks/.

Swanberg, Jennifer E., E. Watson, and M. Eastman. 2014. "Scheduling challenges among workers in low-wage hourly jobs: Similarities and differences among workers in standard- and non-standard-hour jobs," *Community, Work & Family* 17 (4): 409–35.

Swedish Social Insurance Agency. 2014. "Parental benefits." http://www.forsakringskassan.se.

Sweet, S., et al. 2014. "Do options for job flexibility diminish in times of economic uncertainty?" *Work, Employment and Society* 28 (6): 881–903.

Sweet, Stephen, M. Pitt-Catsouphes, E. Besen, and L. Golden. 2014. "Explaining organization variation in flexible work arrangements: Why the pattern and scale of availability matter," *Community, Work & Family* 17 (2): 115–41.

Tamburri, R. 2014. "How call centre workers get back at abusive customers," *The Globe and Mail*, 6 March. http://www.theglobeandmail.com/report-on-business/careers/business-education/how-call-centre-workers-get-back-at-abusive-customers/article17357463.

Taylor, Frederick W. 1967. *The Principles of Scientific Management*. New York: W.W. Norton and Company.

Taylor, P., and Bain, P. 1999. "'An assembly line in the head': Work and employee relations in the call centre," *Industrial Relations Journal* 30 (2): 101–17.

Taylor, Philip, ed. 2013. *Older Workings in an Ageing Society: Critical Topics in Research and Policy.* Northampton, MD: Edward Elgar.

Taylor, Steve, and Melissa Taylor. 2000. "Emotional labour and sexual difference in the airline industry," *Work, Employment and Society* 14 (1): 77–95.

Teelucksingh, Cheryl. 2014. "Population, urbanization and the environment," in L. Tepperman, P. Albanese, and B. Curtis, eds, pp. 318–40, *Principles of Sociology: Canadian Perspectives*, 3rd edn. Toronto: Oxford University Press.

Tencer, Daniel. 2015. "Canadian employees burning out as businesses grow without hiring: Report," *The Huffington Post Canada*. http://www.huffingtonpost.ca/2015/01/06/hiring-canada-employee-burnout-hays_n_6424.

The Economist. 2011. "70 or bust! Current plans to raise the retirement age are not bold enough," *The Economist*, 7 April.http://www.economist.com/node/18529505?story_id=18529505.

The Economist. 2013. "Mexico's maquiladoras: Big Maq attack," *The Economist*, 26 October. http://www.economist.com/news/business/21588370-50-year-old-export-industry-provides-millions-jobs-has-reinvent-itself-quickly.

Thomas, Mark. 2009. *Regulating Flexibility: The Political Economy of Employment Standards.* Montreal & Kingston: McGill-Queen's University Press.

Thomas, Mark. 2011. "Regulating labour standards in the global economy: Emerging forms of global governance," in G. Teeple and S. McBride, eds, pp. 95–117, *Relations of Global Power: Neoliberal Order and Disorder.* Toronto: University of Toronto Press.

Thompson, P. 2003. "Disconnected capitalism: Or why employers can't keep their side of the bargain," *Work, Employment & Society* 17 (2): 359–78.

Thompson, P., Callaghan, G., and Van den Broek, D. 2004. "Teams without teamwork? Explaining the call centre paradox," *Economic and Industrial Democracy* 25 (2): 197–218.

Thompson, Paul. 1989. *The Nature of Work: An Introduction to Debates on the Labour Process*, 2nd edn. London: Macmillan.

Tobio, C., and J. Cordon. 2013. "A social policy model for the reconciliation of employment and family life from a gender equality perspective," *International Review of Sociology* 23 (2): 379–400.

Toneguzzi, M. 2015. "More women have become self-employed since the recession, but are still underrepresented among entrepreneurs," *Calgary Herald*, 18 January. http://calgary-held.com/business/growing-number-of-women-entrepreneurs?_ISa=bbbd.

Toronto Star. 2010. "General Motors adds $4 billion to underfunded pension plans," *Toronto Star*, 3 December: B3.

Toronto Star. 2012. "Fears grow over EU 'pension bomb'," *Toronto Star*, 12 January: B4.

Turcotte, M. 2010. "Working at home: An update," *Canadian Social Trends*, December: 3–11. http://www.statcan.gc.ca/pub/11-008-x/2011001/article/11366-eng.pdf.

Turcotte, M. 2011. "Women and education," *Women in Canada: A Gender-based Statistical Report*. Statistics Canada Catalogue No. 89-503-X. Ottawa: Minister of Industry.

Turcotte, M. 2013. "Family caregiving: What are the consequences?" *Insights on Canadian Society*. Statistics Canada Catalogue No. 75-006-X. Ottawa: Minister of Industry.

Turcotte, Martin. 2007. "Time spent with family during a typical workday, 1986 to 2005," *Canadian Social Trends*, 19 June: 2–11.

Turcotte, Martin, and Stephanie Gaudet. 2013. "Social participation of full-time workers," *Research Document*, Statistics Canada Catalogue No. 75-004-M—No. 003. Ottawa: Minister of Industry.

Ulmer, Darcy. 2004. "What the world needs now? More hours in a day," IpsosGlobal Survey. http://www.ipsos-na.com/news/pressrelease.cfm?id=2352.

UNI Global Union. 2012. "Walmart's global strategy: Undercutting workers' rights," October. http://www.ufcw.ca/templates/ufcwcanada/images/directions12/october/1274/uni_wmt_wtpaper9-27-12.pdf.

United Food and Commercial Workers (UFCW). 2014. "Call centre workers at Answernet Telepartners join the union—UFCW 206," UFCW Canada: Canada's private sector union, Toronto, 11 August.

Uppal, S. and S. LaRochelle-Cote. 2014. "Changes in the occupational profile of young men and women in Canada," *Insights on Canadian Society*. April. Statistics Canada Catalogue no. 75-006-X. Ottawa: Ministry of Industry.

US Census Bureau. 2013. "Poverty Facts," *Income and Poverty in the United States: 2013.*

http://www.povertyusa.org/the-state-of-poverty/poverty-facts/.

Verma, Anil, Jeffrey Reitz, and Rupa Banerjee. 2015. "Unionization and income growth of racial minority immigrants in Canada: A longitudinal study," *International Migration Review*, April: 1–32.

Villalobos, J. Rene, et al. 2004. "Inbound for Mexico," *Industrial Engineer* 36 (4): 38–61.

Vincent, Carole. 2013. "Why do women earn less than men? A synthesis of findings from Canadian microdata," *CRDCN Synthesis Series*, September.

Vincent, Richard, and Larry McKeown. 2008. "Trends in the telephone call centre industry," Statistics Canada Service Industries Division, Catalogue No. 63F0002XIE, No. 053. February. http://www.statcan.gc.ca/pub/63f0002x/63f0002x2008053-eng.pdf.

Vincent, Steven. 2013. "The emotional labour process: An essay on the economy of feeling," *Human Relations* 64 (1): 1369–92.

Viscusi, Gregory. 2014. "Europe sacrifices a generation with 17-year unemployment impasse," *Forbes*, 7 October. http://www.bloomberg.com/news/2014-10-07/europe-sacrifices-a-generation-with-17-year-unemployment-impasse.html.

Voice of America. 2010. "Ivory Coast arrests 3 journalists over cocoa story," *Voice of America*, 16 July. http://www.voanews.com/content/ivory-coast-arrests-3-journalists-over-cocoa-story-98661144/161593.html.

Vosko, Leah. 2007. "Precarious part-time work in Australia and in transnational labour regulation: The gendered limits of SER-centrism," *Labour and Industry* 17 (3): 45–70.

Vosko, Leah. 2011. *Managing the Margins: Gender, Citizenship and the International Regulation of Precarious Employment*. New York: Oxford University Press.

Vosko, Leah, and Mark Thomas. 2014. "Confronting the employment standards enforcement gap: Exploring the potential for union engagement with employment law in Ontario, Canada," *Journal of Industrial Relations* 56 (5): 631–52.

Vujinovic, N. 2014. "'...There's no substituting actual time with your child': Understanding first-time mothers' readiness to return to work," *Journal of Industrial Relations* 56 (4): 488–507.

Wacquant, Loic. 2009. *Punishing the Poor: The Neoliberal Government of Social Insecurity*. Durham, NC: Duke University Press.

Wada, M., C. Backman, and S. Forwell. 2015. "Men's discursive constructions of balance in everyday life," *Community, Work & Family* 18 (1): 117–33.

Wall, G. 2013. "'Putting family first': Shifting discourses of motherhood and childhood in representations of mothers' employment and childcare," *Women's Studies International Forum* 40: 162–71.

Wallerstein, Immanuel. 1983. *Historical Capitalism*. New York: Verso.

Wallerstein, Immanuel. 2014. "Antisystemic movements, yesterday and today,"*American Sociological Association* 20 (2): 158–72.

Walmartworkers Canada. 2015. "Walmart workers in Chile achieve historic agreement." http://www.walmartworkerscanada.ca/index.php?option=com_content&view=article&id=71:walmart-workers-in-chile-achieve-historic agreement&catid=8&Itemid=119&lang=en.

Walters, Matthew, and Lawrence Mishel. 2003. "How unions help all workers," Economic Policy Institute, 26 August. http://www.epi.org/publication/briefingpapers_bp143/.

Watkins, M. (Chair). 1967. *Foreign Ownership and the Structure of Canadian Industry: Report of the Task Force on the Structure of Canadian Industry.*

Wattis, L., K. Standing, and M. Yerkes. 2013. "Mothers and work–life balance: Exploring the contradictions and complexities involved in work–family negotiation," *Community, Work & Family* 16 (1): 1–19.

Weber, M. 1958. *The Protestant Ethic and the Spirit of Capitalism*. New York: Scribner's.

Weber, M. 1969. *Economy and Society*. Totawa, NJ: Bedminster Press.

Weinshenker, M. 2015. "The effect of fatherhood on employment hours: Variation by birth timing, marriage and co-residence," *Journal of Family Issues* 36 (1): 3–30.

Wharton, Amy S. 1993. "The affective consequences of service work managing emotions on the job," *Work and Occupations* 20 (2): 205–32.

White, J.M., T.F. Martin, and S.K. Bartolic. 2013. *Families Across the Life Course*. Toronto: Pearson. The White House. 2015. *Raise the Wage*. https://www.whitehouse.gov/raise-the-wage.

Whitrow, G.J. 1988. *Time in History: Views of Time from Prehistory to the Present Day*. Oxford: Oxford University Press.

Wilkins, Roger. 2006. "The consequences of underemployment for the underemployed," *Journal of Industrial Relations* 49 (2): 247–75.

Williams, C. 2010. "Economic well-being," *Women in Canada: A Gender-based Statistical*

Report. Statistics Canada Catalogue no. 89-503-X. Ottawa: Minister of Industry.
Williams, Cara. 2002. "Time or money? How high or low income Canadians spend their time," *Canadian Social Trends*, Summer: 7–11.
Williams, Christine L. 2006. *Inside Toyland: Working, Shopping and Social Inequality.* Berkeley and Los Angeles: University of California Press.
Wolfson, Michael. 2015. "What, me worry? Income risks for retiring Canadians," *Canadian Centre for Policy Alternatives,* July. http://www.policyalternatives.ca.
Woodman, Dan. 2013. "Researching 'ordinary' young people in a changing world: The sociology of generations and the 'missing middle' in youth research," *Sociological Research Online* 18 (1). http://www.socresonline.org.uk/18/1/7.html.
Woodman, Dan, and J. Wyn. 2013. "Youth policy and generations: Why youth policy needs to 'rethink,' youth," *Social Policy and Society* 12 (2): 265–75.
World Cocoa Foundation. 2014. "Cocoa market update," 1 April. http://worldcocoafoundation.org/wp-content/uploads/Cocoa-Market-Update-as-of-4-1-2014.pdf.
World Economic Forum. 2013. *The Global Risks Report 2013.* Geneva: World Economic Forum.
World Economic Forum. 2014. *The Global Gender Gap Report—Insight Report.* Geneva: World Economic Forum.
Worstall, Tim. 2012. "The story of Henry Ford's $5 a day wages: It's not what you think," *Forbes*, 3 April. http://www.forbes.com/sites/timworstall/2012/03/04/the-story-of-henry-fords-5-a-day-wages-its-not-what-you-think/.
Wylie, I. 1997. "Human answering machines," *Guardian*, 26 July: 23.
Wyn, J., and L. Andres. 2011. "Navigating complex lives: A longitudinal, comparative perspective on young people's trajectories," *Early Intervention in Psychiatry* 5 (1): 17–21.
Wyn, J., and Dan Woodman. 2006. "Generation, youth and social change in Australia," *Journal of Youth Studies* 9 (5): 495–514.
Yalnizyan, Armine. 2009. *Exposed: Revealing Truths About Canada's Recession.* Ottawa: Canadian Centre for Policy Alternatives.
Yalnizyan, Armine. 2013. "Boost the minimum wage, boost the economy," *The Progressive Economics Forum*, 27 February. http://www.progressive-economics.ca/2013/02/27/boost-the-minimum-wage-boost-the-economy/.
Yardley, Jim. 2013. "Report on deadly factory collapse in Bangladesh finds widespread blame," *The New York Times*, 23 May. http://www.nytimes.com/2013/05/23/world/asia/report-on-bangladesh-building-collapse-finds-widespread-blame.html?_r=0.
Yates, S., and M. Payne. 2006. "Not so NEET: A critique of the use of 'NEET' in setting targets for interventions with young people," *Journal of Youth Studies* 9 (3): 329–44.
Yew, M. Acharya-Tom. 2015. "A third of us don't plan to retire by 66," *Toronto Star,* 18 February: B3.
Young, M. 2015. "Work–family conflict in context: The impact of structural and perceived neighborhood disadvantage on work–family conflict," *Social Science Research* 50: 311–27.
Zeytinoglu, I. and Gordon Cooke. 2000. "Gender, race and class dimensions of nonstandard work." *Industrial Relations.* Volume 55, Issue 1, 133-168.
Zeytinoglu, I., and Gordon Cooke. 2008. "Non-standard employment and promotions: A within genders analysis," *Journal of Industrial Relations* 50 (2): 319–37.
Zornick, George. 2012. "Large, profitable companies employ most minimum-wage earners," *The Nation*, 19 July. http://www.thenation.com/blog/168969/large-profitable-companies-employ-most-minimum-wage-earners#.
Zuberi, D. 2011. "Contracting out hospital support jobs: The effects of poverty wages, excessive workload, and job insecurity on work and family life," *American Behavioral Scientist* 55 (7): 920–40.
Zuboff, Shoshana. 1988. In the Age of the Smart Machine: *The Future of Work and Power.* New York: Basic Books.
Zuzanek, J., and B. Smale. 2015. "More work—less leisure? Changing allocations of time in Canada, 1981 to 1992," *Society and Leisure* 20 (1): 73–105.

Index